When the State Meets the Street

When the State Meets the Street

Public Service and Moral Agency

Bernardo Zacka

The Belknap Press of
Harvard University Press

CAMBRIDGE, MASSACHUSETTS
LONDON, ENGLAND
2017

Interior design by Dean Bornstein

Library of Congress Cataloging-in-Publication Data
Names: Zacka, Bernardo, 1983– author.
Title: When the state meets the street : public service and moral agency /
    Bernardo Zacka.
Description: Cambridge, Massachusetts : The Belknap Press of Harvard
    University Press, 2017. | Includes bibliographical references and index.
Identifiers: LCCN 2017005846 | ISBN 9780674545540 (alk. paper)
Subjects: LCSH: Civil service—Moral and ethical aspects—Northeastern States. |
    Municipal officials and employees—Northeastern States. | Local government—
    Moral and ethical aspects—Northeastern States. | Northeastern States—
    Officials and employees.
Classification: LCC JF1601 .Z34 2017 | DDC 172/.2—dc23
LC record available at https://lccn.loc.gov/2017005846

For Marc and Yolande

Contents

Preface

I first encountered the state at checkpoints. Lebanon in the 1990s had no shortage of agencies to staff them. The occupying Syrian Army, the Lebanese Armed Forces, and the country's often-competing security agencies—the Internal Security Forces, the General Security, and the State Security—all had outposts on the street.

When crossing a checkpoint, you come face-to-face with an armed officer who remains largely inscrutable. The encounter is not conducive to conversation. It is also riddled with uncertainty. From your seat in the car, you can never know for sure what the officer—almost always a *he*—is on the lookout for, nor what exactly the scope of his prerogatives are. And the very last thing you want to do is appear to question his authority by trying to find out.

The experience begins with a well-rehearsed sequence of movements: you slow the car down, turn on the dome light, lower the volume on the radio, and put on an earnest face. What happens next is a highly discretionary and personal interaction: eyes meet, a searching look is thrown at the vehicle, a question or two is sometimes asked, and a judgment is made regarding who passes and who doesn't. The outcome is variable and hinges, or so it seems, on contingent circumstances: on how the encounter unfolds, and on who happens to be stationed there that day.

This way of experiencing the state, through a personal encounter with a low-ranking official endowed with discretionary power, is not limited to the realm of security, nor is it exclusive to Lebanon. It is a daily reality, in developing countries as well as in advanced liberal democracies, for the millions of people who depend on public services, and for those who— often through no fault of their own—regularly come into contact with law enforcement.

Years later when I began my graduate studies in political theory these personal encounters with frontline officials were, to my surprise, nowhere to be found. Although they loomed large in my imagination of the state, they seemed to have disappeared behind layers of abstraction. The modern state, I learned, was impersonal, its agents (in principle, if not in practice) interchangeable, their actions constrained by administrative procedures and a voluminous body of law. Democratic theory appeared primarily concerned with the legitimacy of these laws and their substantive merits, as well as with the principles according to which our institutions should be designed. Amid this emphasis on procedures, laws, and institutional design, something about our everyday, tangible experience of the state seemed to have been lost. This was a picture of democratic institutions that was strangely devoid of the people who infuse life into them.

I started wondering what it would mean to put our encounters with frontline officials—personal, contingent, and discretionary as they often are—at the center of our account of the democratic state. I presumed that a theory of the state would remain incomplete, both descriptively and normatively, if it did not account for such encounters—if it did not tell us something about how the state interacts with its citizens at the point of service provision and law enforcement, and how it ought to do so. Perhaps starting from the bottom up would also provide us with a different entry point into normative reflection. Instead of working our way down from abstract ideals to constitutional norms and laws and only then considering the question of implementation, perhaps we could make progress by starting from the opposite end, with the moment of service provision, and working our way back to questions of policymaking and institutional design.

These are the questions that first got me interested in street-level bureaucracy, and that eventually led me to conduct participant observation alongside frontline public service workers in an urban antipoverty agency. As a client of the state, I soon realized that I had only a limited window into the everyday challenges of service provision and law enforcement. From my seat in the car, I could not distinguish discretionary decision-making from punctilious rule-following, courteous restraint from utter indifference. If I wanted to understand why bureaucrats appeared and acted the way they did, I had to cross over to the other side and try to find out what the encounter looked like from behind the desk, window, or counter. What was it like for someone to *be* the everyday face of the state? What did the job consist in? What challenges, pressures, joys, and anxieties did it involve?

Like most of those who interact with the state as clients, I began my fieldwork with a rather unflattering view of bureaucracy, and an even more damning impression of street-level bureaucrats. I emerged from it, like many of those who study street-level bureaucracy, with a far more nuanced appreciation for the complex moral and psychological terrain that frontline workers must navigate, and with no small amount of admiration for those of them who manage to retain sensitive and balanced moral dispositions in an environment that often conspires against them.

The result, I hope, is a book that is critical, but sympathetic—one that aims to bring street-level bureaucrats into the fold of democratic theory, and that aspires to offer at once a theory of their behavior and a framework for morally assessing it.

When the State Meets the Street

Introduction

It is not a compliment to be called a bureaucrat. The word evokes rigidity, narrow-mindedness, insensitivity, coldness, lack of initiative, and, above all, rule-worship. These attributes are so ingrained in our collective imagination that they have become definitional. According to *The New Oxford Dictionary of English,* a bureaucrat is not just "an official in a government department" but, more specifically, "one perceived as being concerned with procedural correctness at the expense of people's needs."[1] Webster's tells us that the word is often used to designate a "government official confirmed in a narrow rigid formal routine."[2] Dictionary.com makes a further leap, this time into the cognitive realm: "an official who works by fixed routine without exercising intelligent judgment."[3]

To the extent that bureaucrats have these unflattering characteristics, they inherit them, in large part, from the organizations to which they belong. David Foster Wallace takes himself to be speaking for "most ordinary Americans" when he writes of bureaucracies: "I hated and feared them . . . and basically regarded them as large, grinding, impersonal machines—that is, they seemed rigidly literal and rule-bound the same way machines are, and just about as dumb."[4] He goes on to describe the individuals who work in such bureaucracies, and who acquire, as if by osmosis, the characteristic traits of the organization: "My primary association with the word *bureaucracy* was an image of someone expressionless behind a counter, not listening to any of my questions or explanations of circumstance or misunderstanding but merely referring to some manual of impersonal regulations as he stamped my form with a number that meant I was in for some further kind of tedious, frustrating hassle or expense."

There is a sketch by Sergei Eisenstein, the Russian film director, that could serve as a perfect visual companion to Wallace's quote (Figure 1).[5] It is titled, aptly enough, *The Bureaucrat.* The sketch depicts a broad-shouldered, balding man, with a mustache and without a neck, looking down from behind tinted glasses and holding up his hand as if to say "No." It is drawn on a printed page that has the graphic markers of officialdom—one filled with words so small and densely packed that they morph into an almost

FIGURE 1. *The Bureaucrat,* by Sergei Eisenstein. Sergei Eisenstein, "The Bureaucrat," fund 1923, list 2, file 1555, page 2, the Russian State Archive of Literature and Arts, Moscow.

uniform background. The bureaucrat's body claims the page and frames the text: he appears to be consubstantial with the script—an imposing, inscrutable, and unapproachable wall of words.

Eisenstein thought of his sketches as minimalist caricatures of sorts; they were meant to capture, with a few simple strokes, the "nuclei of expressiveness" behind a variety of social figures. In this drawing, the bureaucrat appears both as an outgrowth of bureaucracy and its tendency to ceaselessly produce paperwork, and as a personification of such an organization in all its forbidding and intimidating character.[6] Bureaucracies and bureaucrats: a match so perfect that it has fascinated novelists as diverse as

Georges Courteline, Nikolai Gogol, Franz Kafka, George Orwell, Naguib Mahfouz, Upamanyu Chatterjee, and Ismail Kadare; a pairing so dreadful and grotesque that it is, alternatively, the stuff of nightmares and that of satire.

The mixture of hostility and incomprehension toward bureaucracy that Wallace and Eisenstein record, almost a century apart, is widely echoed across the social sciences. Economists have denounced bureaucracy for its lack of adaptability, its inefficient allocation of resources, and its tendency to expand past its optimal size.[7] Political scientists, sociologists, and anthropologists have criticized its bias in favor of elites, its resistance to change, its capacity to usurp the powers of elected officials, and its tendency to be captured by special interests.[8] They have also deplored the extent to which it can disregard, alienate, or even degrade its own workers as well as the citizens whom it is meant to serve.[9] More pointedly, scholars have shown that the bureaucratic encounter itself—the moment at which ordinary people come into contact with public agencies—can be demeaning, disempowering, and paternalistic; that it can contribute to reinforcing status distinctions; and that it can discourage citizens from being active participants in political life.[10] As Charles Goodsell puts it, "Bureaucracy, institutionally, is said to sap the economy, endanger democracy, suppress the individual and be capable of embodying evil. It is denounced on the right by market champions and public-choice theorists and on the left by Marxists, critical theorists, and postmodernists."[11]

Even those who have a more nuanced appreciation of bureaucracy feel compelled to begin their studies, as I have, by acknowledging the disrepute into which public agencies have fallen—if only to explain why, or to challenge the correctness of the popular verdict. Peter Blau opens his classic work *Bureaucracy in Modern Society* with the invective "That stupid bureaucrat!" He goes on to solicit the reader's sympathy: "Who has not felt this way at one time or another? When we are sent from one official to the next without getting the information we want; when lengthy forms we had to fill out in sextuplicate are returned to us because we forgot to cross a 't' or dot an 'i'; when our applications are refused on some technicality—that is when we think of bureaucracy."[12]

What brings together most critics of bureaucracy, besides the indignation that they voice, is the standpoint from which they write: that of clients who, as Wallace puts it, are invariably in for some further kind of hassle. What these critics typically leave out, however, is the other side of the story—the viewpoint of the bureaucrats around whom the drama also unfolds. We know that clients frequently experience bureaucracies as slow, unresponsive, demeaning, and arbitrary—but what do such bureaucracies look like from within, from the standpoint of those who stand behind the expressionless masks and who are so often reduced to lifeless caricatures? We know how citizens see the state. But how does the state see its citizens?

This question takes us into the world of street-level bureaucrats—the social service workers, police officers, counselors, and educators who are responsible for delivering public services and enforcing the law and who, as such, effectively serve as the face of the state for ordinary citizens.[13] These bureaucrats are caught in a predicament. The proper implementation of public policy depends on their capacity to act as sensible moral agents who can, among other things, interpret vague directives, strike compromises between competing values, and prioritize the allocation of scarce resources. And yet, they must operate in a working environment that is particularly challenging and that tends, over time, to erode and truncate their moral sensibilities. While public service agencies depend on the moral agency of street-level bureaucrats, they proceed, at the same time, to undermine that very agency.

This book explores the factors that lead to this predicament and the remedies that can be offered to it. It pays close attention to how street-level bureaucrats experience their everyday work; to how their understanding of their role and responsibilities is shaped by the environment in which they evolve; and to how well their behavior and self-understanding stack up against the normative values that we would expect a democratic state to uphold when interacting with those who are subject to its authority.

The following pages draw extensively on empirical work by political scientists, sociologists, and anthropologists as well as on eight months of ethnographic fieldwork I conducted as a receptionist at the Norville Community Development Initiative, an antipoverty agency in a large city in the northeastern United States (I have altered the name of the agency and of the city in which it is located, and I use pseudonyms to protect the confidentiality of staff members). What will become apparent, as I begin to draw on this material, is that it offers a portrait of bureaucratic life that is much more fluid, flexible, and open to contingency than one might expect when looking at such organizations from without. The structure of rules and regulations with which bureaucrats must comply is not as tight as it may appear to outsiders, and it leaves significant room for discretion. This discretion, in turn, allows bureaucrats to develop different styles of work and to give expression to them.

Take the rule-bound, mechanistic simile that Wallace offers—that of bureaucracy as an orderly collection of moving parts that operate in a cold, repetitive, and unthinking fashion—and contrast it with the impression that emerges from the following account, which draws on my first set of field notes.

It was my first day on the job, and the task I had been given sounded simple. I was to assist the main receptionist, DeShawn, by acting as a greeter of sorts. The instructions DeShawn gave me were brief. "Say 'Good morning, welcome to the Norville Service Center, do you have an appointment?' If they do, check with whom; ask them to fill an intake form; and escort them inside, to the other waiting room. Then, walk over to the cubicle area, and inform the case manager that his or her clients have arrived. If they do not have an appointment yet, have them speak to me and I'll schedule something for them." This, he told me, would be a good way to familiarize myself with the office and the clients.

The reception area, with which I would become intimately acquainted over the following eight months, was located on the first floor of a three-story building, in a low-income and predominantly African American neighborhood of Norville. It consisted of seven rows of neatly arranged plastic chairs facing the receptionist's desk. The room was spacious, tidy and clean. It opened onto a small corridor that led to another waiting room and to the case managers' offices. The walls were pastel green, and the lighting fluorescent.

The Center, one of Norville's largest antipoverty agencies, assisted low-income clients in applying for food stamps, public housing, fuel assistance, earned income tax credit, head start programs, and citizenship. It served as a non-profit contractor for the state, and received most of its funding through federal grants—a type of arrangement that has become increasingly common since the 1980s.

I had come freshly prepared for the day, around 8:30 AM, wearing formal business attire, as requested by the Director of the Center ("we must project a good image," he had told me over the phone). I felt uncomfortable in my outfit—a relic from two years spent working as a management consultant in Manhattan after college—and I recall thinking that my skinny tie may betray me and ruin my attempt to pass as a regular volunteer.

At 9 AM, the first clients started walking in. I rehearsed my routine, and everything went well. I thought I was in control. But the first glitch occurred soon enough: an old African American woman came in with a question. I realized, half-amused, half-panicked, that nothing, in the brief instructions I was given, had prepared me for such a possibility. I attempted to direct her to DeShawn, but he was on the phone with someone else. Before I could decide what to do, two other clients had entered the office and were trying to make eye contact with me. One of them handed me a letter, and said "John told me to come back with this, it's urgent; I need to speak to him." The other asked to use the Center's photocopying machine—"they always let me do that," he said, pointing to DeShawn, who was still on the phone. Before I knew it, I found myself pacing back and forth between the reception area, the case managers' offices, and the photocopying machine.

All this time, new clients kept arriving. Several clients at a time; clients with children who refused to acknowledge the invisible boundary between the reception area and the back-office; clients who spoke so loudly on their cell phones that they had to be asked to lower their voice; clients who wanted to use the fax machine; clients who wanted to use the rest-rooms—all of them, or so I recall, speaking to me at once. Even my co-workers started turning to me: DeShawn asked me to make photocopies and to answer the phone while he was away from his desk, others wanted me to deliver documents to various offices in the building. Somewhere along the line, as I was moving back and forth between the various clients, the phone, the fax machine, and my co-workers, trying to improvise as best as I could to fill any gaps in DeShawn's instructions, I noticed that I had dropped my smile.

It was around then, too, that I came to understand the significance of a piece of information the Director had mentioned earlier that day. This was the start of "fuel assistance" season, one of the busiest times of the year, and the office had, as of that morning, stopped accepting walk-ins because case managers were already operating at full capacity. Most clients were unaware of this change, and came in without appointments, expecting to get their paperwork done. For many of them, I would later find out, this involved taking time off from work. This was the kind of day where one did not want to be a greeter.

One after another, I had to break the news to them: "I'm sorry but we can't help you today, we're no longer taking walk-ins. Would you like to schedule an appointment for some other day?" As my words sank in, I could see a mixture of deception and contained anger spread across their faces—torn as they were, I imagined, between the urge to vent their frustration, and the thought that, since I stood between them and the fuel they needed to make it through the cold northeastern winter, it might be better not to risk alienating me. One client—a middle-aged white man, with loose jeans covered in paint marks, an oversized jacket, and a scarred face, dragging two screaming children, one in each hand—could not contain himself. He lashed out at me, at the top of his lungs "ARE YOU SERIOUS? YOU'VE GOTTA BE FUCKIN' KIDDIN' ME!" I became acutely aware of the physical proximity at which he was standing, and of the absence of any protective boundary between the two of us. And I thought back, once again, to my skinny tie and to how ridiculous I must have looked.

I felt gripped at the time by three competing impulses. The first was a movement of sympathy. I could understand the client's frustration and thought for a moment of setting other tasks aside so as to focus entirely on his case. But I did not know how to help. And what about all the others who were able to remain composed? Should their needs be ignored simply because they did not raise their voice? My second impulse was exactly opposed to the first. I felt the need to re-establish my authority, and to regain control over the situation. There were several clients in the room, and I could not let our interactions degenerate into a screaming match. Perhaps I should find a way to put the client back in his place? But I rapidly corrected myself. Surely, I thought, my job was not to discipline people. I remembered being told, during my first phone interview, that the Center was supposed to be a place where clients could come for help when everyone else had turned them down.

So I gave in to the third impulse. I convinced myself that there was nothing personal in the client's anger, and that I should continue working as if nothing had happened. It probably was a numbers game: I couldn't help him, but if I pressed forward, and did my job as diligently as possible, I would be able to help many others. So I stared at him blankly, and said, "I'm sorry, but I'm just doing my job," and moved on to the next task. I remember being shocked at hearing these words roll from my mouth, barely three hours into the job. I consoled myself by thinking that there really was nothing else I could have done.

But this certainty about my powerlessness, and the psychological relief it provided, vanished in the early afternoon. One of the case managers, Paulina, came to see me in the reception area and informed me that one of her clients had not showed up ("It happens all the time," she explained). She told me that I should feel free to come see her if someone was here without an appointment, and if I thought they needed to meet with a case manager. Maybe she could take care of them.

"If I thought they needed to meet with a case manager"? And so with this conditional, I was on my way from being a mere operator to being a gatekeeper endowed with circumscribed but very real discretionary power. And I quickly discovered that I could also disguise the boundaries of my discretion by claiming, as I had done earlier in the day, that I was "just doing my job."

Over the course of the eight months I spent volunteering at the Norville Service Center, I became more knowledgeable about the job and more comfortable interacting with clients. The standards I was expected to use in making discretionary decisions also became clearer through informal conversations with colleagues, and as I became steeped in the culture of the organization. But the vagueness did not disappear entirely, and the advice I received from my colleagues varied considerably. As I soon found out, they had different working styles, and it was up to me to choose whom I wanted to listen to.

The fundamental test I experienced on the first day—how to adapt myself to the demands of the role in an ethically responsible yet psychologically sustainable way—stayed with me throughout the job. I knew, and was reminded by my manager and colleagues, that I had to treat clients fairly; that I had to be as responsive as possible to their needs; that I had to behave toward them with respect and consideration; and that I had to process their cases as efficiently as I could. But how could I do all of these things at once? How could I remain attentive to all of them without succumbing to the three temptations I experienced—that of being overly sympathetic, harsh, or disengaged? What follows is a foray into this question—a question that pressed itself on me from my very first day on the job, and one to which hundreds of thousands of street-level bureaucrats provide an answer every day.

Moral Agency in Adverse Institutional Conditions

By virtue of their position at the interface of state and society, street-level bureaucrats are required to take decisions that are highly consequential for ordinary citizens.[14] On any given day, they must determine, within the ambit of the law, who will have access to public services and how much of these services they will be entitled to. They are responsible for conferring administrative status, and hence official recognition, to people's personal problems. Their demeanor also contributes to shaping how the encounter with the state will be experienced—whether it will "feel" welcoming or transactional, considerate or inquisitive, respectful or demeaning. The bureaucratic encounter is not simply a moment in which goods are distributed; it is also a moment of citizenship, in which status and standing are assigned. *How* one is treated is just as crucial as *what* one gets.

While any particular encounter with bureaucracy is charged with significance for the specific individual whose case is at stake, the cumulative effect of these encounters matters at a societal level too. It is, in part, through our encounters with street-level bureaucrats that our perception of the legitimacy and trustworthiness of our political institutions is shaped.[15] Some studies have even shown that *how* policies are implemented can have a greater impact on people's perception of legitimacy than *what* those policies are.[16]

This book is an attempt to bring our personal encounters with street-level bureaucrats to the center of our thinking about the democratic state. I will have more to say momentarily about who street-level bureaucrats are and about the distinctive characteristics of street-level work. Before I do so, however, I want to explain what is at stake theoretically in focusing on this category of actors. When political theorists write about the state, they generally concentrate on the characteristic features of democratic institutions, on the complex processes through which the views of citizens are translated into a body of laws and policies, and on the merits of these laws and policies. The approach I adopt here starts at the other end of the political process: it begins not with the policies that the state pursues or the principles according to which it is structured, but with the ways in which it intervenes in the lives of ordinary citizens at the moment of service provision and law enforcement.[17] With this comes a shift in imaginative standpoint. We are no longer in the seat of voters, legislators, or participants in a hypothetical social contract but instead find ourselves in the midst of ordinary interactions with frontline officials in waiting rooms, classrooms, or welfare offices.

By adopting this different starting point, I aim to provide an account of how the democratic state ought to interact with those who fall under its legitimate authority. By this, I do not mean *what* policies such a state should pursue, but *how* it ought to pursue them.[18] As I will try to show throughout the book, such an account is, in large part, an account of how street-level bureaucrats ought to inhabit their role—an account, that is, of the kind of moral sensibilities, affective dispositions, and role conceptions that we would want and need them to have as they go about implementing public policy.

There are several ways of occupying the role well and, depending on our moral views and political convictions, we may reasonably disagree on which of these is best. But while we may not be able to reach consensus on a positive characterization, I believe that there are ways of performing the role that most of us would recognize as undesirable or unbefitting. I therefore proceed indirectly. I focus on the pathologies and try to offer, in contradistinction, a sense of the moral dispositions that we would deem appropriate. My aim, however, is not just to sketch a profile of the kind of moral agents we would want at the front lines of the state. It is also to investigate how we might be able to orchestrate an institutional environment that can support them in being such agents.

We have reason to be concerned with how street-level bureaucrats inhabit their role because, contrary to popular representations of bureaucracy where they often appear as rigid automata, they are in fact vested with a considerable margin of discretion. They must give content to hierarchical directives that are often vague, ambiguous, and conflicting. As agents of the democratic state, they are also exposed to a plurality of normative demands that frequently point in competing directions: they must be efficient in the use of public resources, fair in dealing with clients, responsive toward their needs, and respectful when interacting with them. The proper implementation of public policy depends on their capacity to remain sensitive to these plural demands and to balance them appropriately in light of specific situations.

These tasks would be difficult to discharge in any context, but street-level bureaucrats must perform them in an environment that is particularly challenging—one that forces them to contend not only with drastic limitations in resources and a chronic shortage of staff but also with incompatible objectives, unrealistic targets, arcane rules, and an endless stream of emotionally trying encounters with clients. As frontline workers in the public services, they are condemned to being front-row witnesses to some of society's most pressing problems without being equipped with the resources or authority necessary to tackle these problems in any definitive way. They must navigate a terrain mined by conflicting expectations that cannot all be satisfied at once, while knowing that they are likely to be held personally responsible, by clients and superiors alike, for any shortcomings in service provision. We will see in the following pages that when experienced day in, day out, the psychological pressures fomented by such an environment tend to erode the moral sensibilities of bureaucrats and to truncate their understanding of their role and responsibilities.

This leaves us with a predicament: while public agencies rely, for their proper functioning, on the moral agency of street-level bureaucrats, they place these bureaucrats in a working environment that tends to undermine that very agency. This book explores how this predicament comes about and how we might respond to it. It seeks to address two questions: How do the pressures of everyday work gradually truncate the moral dispositions of street-level bureaucrats? And how can we equip such bureaucrats to respond to these pressures while remaining sensitive and balanced moral agents?[19]

In brief, I argue that the challenges that street-level bureaucrats face in implementing public policy come to view only when we step back from the moment of ethical decision-making so as to consider more broadly the moral dispositions they adopt on the job. By moral disposition, I mean to refer to how they tend to perceive and interpret situations and cases, to how their moral sentiments are mobilized, and to how they understand their role and responsibilities. These dispositions act as filters that regulate how bureaucrats make use of their discretionary power.

The shift from the study of decisions to that of dispositions can help us capture how the pressures of everyday work slowly truncate the moral outlooks of street-level bureaucrats. The problem is not that bureaucrats lose their capacity for sound moral reasoning, but that the moral perception and role conception that feed into such reasoning become overly narrow and specialized. This brings into focus a family of dispositions—indifference, enforcement, and caregiving—that are troubling because they are reductive takes on the role that street-level bureaucrats are meant to play. Those who settle for such dispositions lose touch with the plurality of demands they must attend to and focus instead on a single dimension of the role. These "pathological" dispositions, which I will discuss at greater length in Chapter 2, are more insidious than the well-known problems of corruption, abuse of discretion, or incompetence, because bureaucrats can fall into them even as they remain wholeheartedly dedicated to their mission, within the scope of their prerogatives, and in full mastery of the technical skills necessary to fulfill their role.

Bureaucrats tend to gravitate toward such reductive dispositions because they provide some measure of relief from the psychological pressures of everyday work. These pressures are occasioned, in large part, by the conflicting demands inherent to the job, and by the gap that exists between the lofty aims that such bureaucrats must pursue and the far more modest resources they are given in practice. Since bureaucrats do not have the capabilities to live up to the demands of the role, they narrow their understanding of these demands to bring them in line with the capabilities they can marshal in practice.

Resisting the drift toward such reductive dispositions is a complex affair. It calls for keeping a certain pluralism alive within the organization— both in the minds of bureaucrats and in the environment in which they operate. This, I hope to show, is not something that can be achieved through formal institutional design alone. It is a three-tiered effort that requires a combination of practices at the individual, group, and managerial levels.

As individuals, street-level bureaucrats must learn to cope with the psychological strain endemic to street-level work. They must find creative ways to regulate and control the intensity of the pressure to which they are exposed so as to better mitigate its transformative effects. I show, in Chapter 3, that they can do so by deploying a regime of everyday practices of the self.

While street-level bureaucrats must exert themselves, as individuals, to resist the pull toward moral dispositions that are overly narrow, I show in Chapter 4 that they must strive, as a group, to retain a range of dispositions that are sufficiently diverse. If the danger at the individual level is the pull toward moral specialization, the danger at the group level is the pull toward conformism and uniformity. The existence of a diverse array of moral dispositions within bureaucratic agencies serves as an institutional irritant that stimulates the moral perception of bureaucrats, and that forces them to remain attentive to a plurality of normative considerations.

The task for managers is to tread a path between these two pitfalls: that of excessive specialization and that of uniformity. It is to create an environment in which street-level bureaucrats can develop and maintain a diverse range of balanced dispositions. To do so, managers must carefully orchestrate an array of signals, formal and informal, which pull in competing directions. It is the lack of alignment between these signals that provides bureaucrats with the space and resources necessary to craft their own moral dispositions, and it is their relative strength that delimits the range of moral dispositions that are sustainable in the long run. As I show in Chapter 5, the failure to properly orchestrate such signals can lead to the creation of impossible situations—situations in which bureaucrats are pulled in directions that are so antithetical that they can no longer operate as integrated moral agents.

If the implementation of public policy is to respond to a plurality of normative standards, as I believe it should do in a democracy, it must be enacted by bureaucrats who are themselves sensitive to such standards. For this to happen, the desired pluralism must be reflected within the organizational environment in which such bureaucrats evolve. The proper implementation of public policy depends, as such, on the friction between a plurality of normative worlds within public agencies. The pathologies of street-level work arise either when bureaucrats do not respond well to such pluralism or when the pluralism itself disappears because one of the worlds takes systematic precedence over the others and comes to eclipse them. When this happens, bureaucrats are led toward reductive moral dispositions— dispositions that entice them to focus exclusively on a subset of the normative considerations to which they ought to remain attuned.

From Decisions to Dispositions

To take an interest in the moral dispositions of street-level bureaucrats, as I do throughout this study, is to be concerned with a range of questions that lie upstream from the moment of ethical decision-making: how they think of themselves, how they understand their role, how they value different courses of action, how they perceive incoming clients, and how they interpret events. It is to take seriously, as well, the fact that their sense of self can be profoundly transformed by the role that they occupy, and can enlarge to encompass the organization to which they belong. It is to be concerned, finally, not so much with offering prescriptive advice on how to perform any given task as with enabling street-level bureaucrats to develop the kind of moral dispositions that will allow them to answer such questions well for themselves.

By examining how we can enable bureaucrats to retain adequate moral dispositions, I depart from three other ways in which one might be inclined to respond to the pervasiveness of discretion at the front lines of the state: by thinking about how to constrain it; by reducing it to an exercise in moral reasoning and providing principles to guide it; or by focusing on the virtues of those who must wield it.

Discretion at the front lines of the state makes us uneasy, and rightly so. It raises the specter of arbitrary treatment, personal domination, bias, and corruption. It is especially unsettling when wielded by unelected officials. Political theorists and institutional architects have long argued that one can alleviate the worries related to discretionary power by placing both preconditions on discretionary action (ex-ante) and penalties for improper action (ex-post).[20] They have stressed the importance of administrative rule-making; emphasized the need for due process, transparency, and strict measures of accountability; and recommended the adoption of systems of checks and balances that prevent the concentration of power in a single actor.[21]

But while these precautionary measures are all necessary to constrain and structure the use of discretion, they are far from sufficient to guide it. So long as the directives that street-level bureaucrats inherit are not fully determinate, they cannot fulfill their duties simply by knowing what *not* to do. They must also engage in a positive moral exercise—they must determine which course of action or style of work, among the many that are open to them, would be best to follow.

There is another way to approach the topic of discretionary power that stems from such a recognition. It involves thinking of public officials as ethical problem-solvers who confront successive moral puzzles. The key is to help them make the right decisions. This may involve thinking about the various principles of moral reasoning that such officials should use, or about the professional codes of conduct that could give them adequate guidance. It may also involve working with psychologists and behavioral economists to identify the sources of decisional bias or "irrationality" that cloud their decision-making, and to devise ways to correct them.[22]

The problem with such an approach, and its focus on the moment of ethical decision-making, is that it presents an overly narrow account of the obstacles that public officials face in making sound use of their discretion. It fails to account, in particular, for the fact that ethical questions do not come with a label but need to be perceived as such before they can be addressed. The way in which bureaucrats come to recognize moral problems, however, depends heavily on their moral disposition: on the interpretive lens they adopt, on their normative and affective sensibilities, and on the way in which they understand their role and responsibilities. These factors both precede and inform the decisions they ultimately take.

Instead of thinking about how to constrain the discretion of street-level bureaucrats or how to prepare them to be better ethical decision-makers, I will examine how we can enable them to develop and sustain the kind of moral dispositions that will allow them to perform their role well. In this respect, my approach bears a close affinity to the work of virtue ethicists and their insistence on the importance of character. But while I am sympathetic to virtue ethics, I depart from it in at least two ways, which I elaborate at greater length in Chapter 3. Depending on the conception of virtue that one holds, these divergences could be seen either as a friendly amendment or as a critique of some of virtue ethics' central tenets.

While virtue ethicists often seek to identify stable character traits that befit a particular social role, I try to show in what follows that no such traits are unmitigated blessings when it comes to frontline officials. Street-level work calls, rather, for the capacity to move flexibly between a variety of attitudes and stances in response to ever-changing situations and challenges. My account diverges from virtue ethics in a second way. Whereas virtue ethicists tend to stress the importance of environment and habituation for the *acquisition* of character traits that individuals can then carry with them across contexts, I underscore the extent to which individuals depend on their environment and on situationally specific practices for the *maintenance* of adequate moral dispositions. I hope to show, accordingly, that when we think about moral agency and moral dispositions, we must look not just at individual character but at the ongoing practices through which individuals relate to the environment in which they are situated.

Toward a Political Theory of Implementation

In his preface to *Street-Level Bureaucracy,* Michael Lipsky observed that public policy remains an abstraction until it is carried out. In an important respect, public policy just *is* the sum total of the actions taken by street-level bureaucrats. As scholars in the field of implementation studies have long argued, we cannot know what the state does simply by looking at the text of the law because policies undergo important transformations in the process of implementation.[23] If we are to detect these transformations, understand their causes, and assess their merits, we need to look at what public officials actually do and why they do it. This is one of the rationales for studying the state from the bottom up.

For all their importance as mediators between state and society, however, street-level bureaucrats have received surprisingly little attention from political theorists. This neglect is not merely accidental. As a discipline, political theory has had a lot to say about the general rules and standards that make up the law and the protections they should afford to individuals, but comparatively little about how the state ought to enact or enforce such law.

It has had much to say about *policymaking* but relatively little about *policy implementation.*

But the normative difficulties that we face, as a polity, do not end once we have agreed on a legitimate set of institutions and on a range of policies to enact. These policies still need to be implemented, and this is where the world of bureaucracy comes into play. As we will see throughout this study, the process of policy implementation opens up a host of distinctive normative challenges—challenges that are not merely derivative from, or subsidiary to, the ones that arise in the course of policymaking. As such, it merits our attention in its own right.

Take any law that is just or legitimate, and its implementation will have to respond to a further set of normative demands. It will have to be enacted in a way that is efficient, fair, responsive to the needs of individual citizens, and respectful of them. How to interpret these various considerations, how to resolve conflicts that arise between them, and how to apply them to specific cases are normative challenges that are intrinsic to implementation. A normative theory of the democratic state that did not engage seriously with such challenges would remain incomplete.

But there is more. The normative questions that arise in the course of policy implementation—how to interpret demands such as "respect," how to weigh competing considerations, and how to bring them to bear on specific cases—are of a distinctive kind. These questions cannot be settled at a high level of generality and call for contextual judgment. We can sometimes encode answers to such questions in rules and procedures, but there is a limit to how much we can do so in advance of being confronted with specific cases and situations, lest we blindly prejudge them. This is why we often delegate the interpreting, weighing, and balancing of these plural considerations to street-level bureaucrats who are closest to individual cases and best acquainted with their specificities. An account of how the state ought to interact with its citizens, then, is in large part an account of how these bureaucrats ought to inhabit their role and of how our institutions can support them in doing so. A political theory of implementation has, at its heart, a political ethics for street-level bureaucrats.

I believe that the normative significance of policy implementation has been obscured to date by a range of reductive views as to what implementation entails. On one such view, policy implementation consists merely in executing directives, and striving to attain objectives, that have already been spelled out in legislative statutes. Bureaucracies are understood to be mere instruments for the execution of the political will or, in other words, morally inert tools for the execution of decisions taken from without. The tasks they have to perform may be complex and may require technical proficiency, but the normative questions—the questions about which ends to pursue, and which values to prioritize—will already have been settled by legislators.

As we will see in Chapter 1, this "morally inert" view of policy implementation has been widely challenged since the birth of the field of public administration. Political scientists have observed that legislative statutes are often both vague and ambiguous and tend to leave much to the discretion of bureaucrats. They have shown, as well, that bureaucrats are frequently solicited as partners in the drafting of legislation; that the decisions they have to take about how to implement a particular policy can be political questions in their own right; and that the process of implementation typically uncovers a variety of normative issues that could not have been foreseen. In short, the worlds of politics and administration are intertwined and cannot be easily separated. Besides the empirical inaccuracies that plague the "morally inert" view of policy implementation, one could also argue that the strict division of labor it envisions between politics and administration is undesirable, and I will try to make such a case in Chapter 1. To put it simply, such a view overestimates our capacity, as well as our readiness, to formalize our normative commitments, and does not sufficiently appreciate the costs at which such formalization would come.

Political theorists have long recognized, of course, that the separation between politics and administration does not obtain in practice, even though some may continue to hold on to such a separation as an attractive ideal. But to the extent that they are willing to grant that public agencies are involved in making normative decisions, they appear to presume, by and large, that such decisions are concentrated in the upper echelons of the bureaucratic hierarchy, and that the place of moral and political judgment diminishes substantially further down the ranks. This would explain why political ethics—which has traditionally, since Machiavelli, focused on political leaders—has had something to say about senior bureaucrats (such as ministers, regulators, or "technocrats") but has remained largely silent about the rank and file.[24]

The presumption that senior bureaucrats matter more from a normative standpoint than lower-ranking ones finds support in two of the dominant models of bureaucracy: as hierarchies driven by rules, and as chains of principal–agent relationships. According to the first model, bureaucracies are vertical organizations in which superiors control the actions of their subordinates through detailed rules of conduct. While senior officials may inherit vague legislative mandates, they are responsible for translating such mandates into precise standard operating procedures. The lower one goes in the hierarchy, the more specific the directives to follow and the narrower the objectives to attain. In this model, top-level bureaucrats are solicited as moral and political agents who are entrusted with the value-laden task of giving specific content to vague legal directives, whereas frontline workers are enlisted as technical operators who are expected to follow procedures and attain objectives that have been specified on their behalf. The only moral question left for these workers to answer is that of compliance or disobedience: whether to obey the directives they receive or not.[25] This question becomes especially salient when the policies that street-level bureaucrats must implement are unjust, illegitimate, or morally repugnant.

As an alternative to the rule-bound model, it is possible to look at bureaucracy as a chain of principal–agent relationships.[26] This model starts from the premise that bureaucrats have an informational advantage over their principals and that the organization as a whole would gain from giving them the discretion to make use of it. The challenge, however, is that the preferences of bureaucrats are not necessarily aligned with those of their principals, and that monitoring and enforcement are both costly. In such conditions, managers must design an incentive system such that the interests of their subordinates are aligned with their own.[27] If designed properly, such a system should harmonize the pursuit of bureaucrats' preferences with the advancement of the organization's overall mission. From a normative standpoint, this model brings into relief two threats: that of distortion—when bureaucrats go rogue and advance their own (principled) preferences of what the organization ought to do over those of their principals—and that of corruption, when bureaucrats fail to realize that there are limits to how far they can pursue their own (narrow) self-interest while holding claim to their role as agents of the state.

Despite their differences, these two models of bureaucracy—the "rule-bound" model and the "principal–agent" model—have two characteristics in common. Both locate the center of normative decision-making among senior officials who are responsible for orchestrating the formal structure of the organization (What rules to put in place? What system of incentives to adopt?). Both models assume, as well, that it is possible to avoid relying on the moral agency of lower-ranking bureaucrats, save for the question of compliance, since they are merely responsible for following rules diligently or for acting in line with their self-interest.

The problem with these two models of organizational behavior is that they mask the everyday moral choices that frontline workers must make in the conditions that most frequently obtain: namely, when their interests are reasonably well aligned with those of their principals, and when the political institutions that they serve are sufficiently just and legitimate not to warrant shirking or outright disobedience. These two models overstate, respectively, the extent to which rules can provide determinate guidance and the extent to which the preferences of principals are well determined. They also presume that the ambiguity or vagueness that is characteristic of legislative statutes will resolve itself within bureaucracies as various layers of superiors try to control the behavior of their subordinates.

But this is not always the case. As we will see in Chapter 1, not all normative ambiguities can or should be resolved before they reach the street. Frontline bureaucrats will frequently inherit normative guidelines that lend themselves to various interpretations, and whose meaning varies greatly depending on context and culture. They will have to find creative ways to adapt and refine administrative categories to fit a complex world that often eludes them; they will be forced, as well, to contend with questions of prioritization that arise because of limited resources. In all these ways street-level work gives rise to its own normative questions.

But that is not all. Policy implementation at the street level also brings into play its own distinctive set of normative considerations. We can begin to think of those if we accept, as Joseph Heath succinctly puts it, that public administration has a "'job to do,' one that can be specified independently of the particular wishes of the government of the day."[28] Once public administration is assigned the task of providing a particular service, it acquires direct obligations to the public. In particular, it takes it upon itself to provide this service in a way that is—among other things—efficient, fair, responsive, and respectful.

The criterion of *efficiency* embodies the technocratic ideal of good management. Simply put, public administrators are entrusted with a limited amount of public resources, and we, as citizens, expect them to make these resources go as far as possible. This means being economical, speedy, and effective in the course of everyday work. We can measure the importance of efficiency, as a standard of evaluation, by the stridency of the criticisms that public administration draws when it fails to live up to it. The various waves of reform that have profoundly transformed the administrative state since the 1980s derive much of their support from the perception of public service agencies as slow, wasteful, and ineffective.

But the standard of efficiency, on its own, does not capture what is distinctive about public service agencies. What sets these agencies apart from other types of organizations is that they interact with people in their capacity as citizens and provide them with services to which they are entitled as a matter of right. This distinguishes services provided by the state from services provided by charities or services that can be purchased on the market. In a democracy, moreover, citizens are meant to be political equals and have a claim to being treated by their state with equal concern and respect. Public administrators, then, have a duty of *fairness* or impartiality. They must treat clients on the basis of principles that such clients could reasonably be expected to endorse. On this count, public administration derives its legitimacy less from its capacity to "get things done" than from its capacity to stand, in some way, "above politics," and to remain, like the law, at equal distance from all. Here again, the importance of the criterion can be measured by how seriously we take its violation—when officials are accused, for instance, of favoritism, bias, or discrimination.

The third normative standard—of *responsiveness*—captures the thought that no two cases are exactly alike. If public administration is to be legitimate, it is not enough for it to be impartial and to treat people equally; it must also be attentive to the specificities of their needs, demands, and circumstances. In *Democratic Legitimacy,* Pierre Rosanvallon argues that the importance accorded to responsiveness to particularity is a relatively recent transformation within democracy—one that resonates with elements from the politics of recognition and the ethics of care and that signals the move toward a "legitimacy of proximity." Democratic citizens, he notes, are no longer willing to accept a one-size-fits-all model of treatment on the part of their state. They expect officials to listen to them and to be able to respond with some level of flexibility to the specificities of their case. This desideratum is the counterpart to a range of familiar criticisms targeted at public service agencies: that they are distant, unconcerned, immured in red tape, and less responsive to the particularities of clients' situations than their counterparts in the private sector.

When making discretionary decisions, street-level bureaucrats ought to remain sensitive to these plural considerations—of *efficiency, fairness,* and *responsiveness,* as well as to that of *respect,* which, we will see in Chapter 2, intersects in complex ways with them—and must contend with the fact that they often pull in competing directions. Making the most efficient use of limited public resources may involve allocating them in a way that is not fair; adhering strictly to standards of fairness may curtail the flexibility that is necessary to be responsive to people's individual needs; responsiveness, finally, may detract from fairness, and may slow down the pace of work and thus stand in the way of efficiency. As Lipsky and others have observed, much of the routine of street-level work involves negotiating difficult compromises between these normative desiderata.[29]

To sum up, then, policy implementation is not just a seamless continuation of policymaking. It gives rise to its own breed of normative questions and brings into play its own normative standards. Lipsky's dictum that street-level bureaucrats effectively "make policy" does not simply mean that they are the channels through which public policy is enacted. It also means that public policy is still underdetermined by the time it reaches them, and that it takes shape as they carry it out.[30] As they resolve its ambiguities, address its oversights, and assign priority to its various components, public policy takes one of several instantiations it could have taken. To the extent that we, as members of the public, are exposed to the discretionary power of street-level bureaucrats, and to the extent that such bureaucrats are partially responsible for giving countenance to public policy, we have good reason to be concerned with their moral dispositions, and with their capacity to remain sound and balanced moral agents despite the pressures of everyday work.

Street-Level Bureaucrats

The label "street-level bureaucrat" designates a broad category of frontline workers in public service. It encompasses welfare workers, social workers, counselors, police officers, and educators. To use a distinction made famous by Pierre Bourdieu, these bureaucrats belong to both the "Left hand" of the state, the one that delivers social services, and to the "Right hand," the one that enforces order and economic discipline.[31]

There are important differences among street-level bureaucrats pertaining, for instance, to the nature of the decisions they take, to the populations they interact with, and to the kind of encounters they have with clients. Unlike teachers, police officers carry guns and sometimes make life-or-death decisions; unlike welfare workers, these officers interact not just with individuals seeking services but with the population at large; and unlike social workers, who have repeated encounters with clients through which a personal relationship can develop, our encounters with police officers are often episodic and happen on a one-time basis (although this is of course more true for the highway patrol than for officers stationed on a beat).

While I try to do justice to the important differences that exist between the various professions that street-level bureaucrats occupy, I focus primarily in this book on what they have in common. Since the field of inquiry is already vast, I restrict my attention to the workings of street-level bureaucracy in the United States, drawing occasionally on examples from other "advanced liberal democracies" such as France and the United Kingdom, countries that espouse broadly democratic values and have guarantees of due process, a commitment to the rule of law, and a modern administrative apparatus.[32]

Scholars have found it useful to speak of street-level bureaucrats as a single category—notwithstanding differences among professions—because of similarities in the structure of everyday work at the front lines of public service across agencies.[33] Three commonalities are particularly noteworthy: street-level bureaucrats are at the bottom of organizational hierarchies; they interact with clients directly; and they are vested with a meaningful margin of discretion. The label can arguably be stretched to include 911 call operators, who do not see their clients in person but whose "voice-to-voice contact imposes the emotional demands of more typical face-to-face encounters," but it leaves out line agents, such as IRS data transcribers, who do not have direct contact with clients, and those, such as toll collectors, whose discretion is so constrained that they effectively can be—and often have been—replaced by automated systems.[34]

As mediators between state and society, street-level bureaucrats have a foot in two worlds that are often out of tune with one another. Street-level work is traversed by the tensions that arise between these two worlds and by the need for street-level bureaucrats to navigate between the "two bodies" they occupy in each.[35] These bureaucrats are at once powerful and powerless, personal and impersonal, creative and rule-bound, de facto experts and low-ranking subordinates.

As frontline workers, street-level bureaucrats occupy some of the lowest and least influential ranks of the various agencies to which they belong. Such workers have been described as those "rewarded the least, valued the least, and considered the most expendable and replaceable."[36] And yet, street-level bureaucrats are also responsible for personifying their agencies—and with them, the state—to citizens. As employees, their influence is largely circumscribed (unless they are unionized); as representatives of the state, they are powerful gatekeepers. This asymmetry, between how they are perceived from within their own organizations and how they are perceived from without, colors their everyday work.

Another distinctive characteristic of street-level work, which sets it apart from the activities of legislators or senior bureaucrats, is that it does not involve making decisions about policy. Frontline workers are expected, rather, to apply existing policies to specific cases—a task that relies heavily on practical judgment. But street-level bureaucrats do not make such judgments at a distance, by looking at files from the comfort of an office. Their job involves direct face-to-face encounters with clients. They come to know the individuals and the personal stories that are attached to each case. This proximity with clients makes their role particularly interesting from an ethical and psychological standpoint: they are at once representatives of an impersonal legal order and participants in encounters that can be very personal and intimate.

As intermediaries between citizens and the state, street-level bureaucrats must also act as translators between the complex and nuanced realities of everyday life and the more regimented world of public administration. They are responsible for translating the personal stories they hear from their clients into an administrative "case," a task that often involves some measure of creative redescription and force-fitting. But street-level bureaucrats must also translate in the opposite direction: they are expected to explain the bureaucratic process, with its labyrinthine rules and procedures, to clients who are as foreign to bureaucracy as they are dependent upon it. It is, at least in part, on the basis of the reasons that bureaucrats provide for their actions that citizens come to form an opinion about their state— about how much they trust it, how legitimate it is, and what standing they have in its eyes.[37]

A central feature of street-level work, finally, is that it involves—amid all the rules and standard operating procedures that we rightly associate with bureaucracy—a considerable degree of discretion and independence. Street-level bureaucrats often work alone and are hard to monitor. Given that they occupy the lowest ranks of the bureaucratic hierarchy, they also find themselves forced to resolve any ambiguity, vagueness, or conflict that exists in public policy—for they cannot delegate it any further. And yet, despite the discretion they have in practice and the tacit knowledge they accumulate on the job, such bureaucrats typically lack the social recognition and technocratic markers of expertise that usually come with discretionary power and that serve to legitimize it to the greater public. (By contrast, think of judges or scientific experts.)

One of the challenges in studying street-level bureaucracy today is that it is changing before our very eyes. When Lipsky first coined the term thirty-five years ago, the great majority of street-level bureaucrats were government employees. This is no longer the case. Since the 1980s, and under the impetus of a body of ideas known as "New Public Management" or "Reinventing Government," public agencies have increasingly contracted out the provision of public services to private nonprofit and for-profit organizations.[38] As we will see in the following pages, this increasing reliance on contracting has been accompanied by the adoption of managerial practices drawn from the private sector—such as performance-based management—which have altered the organizational environment in which street-level bureaucrats work on both sides of the public / private divide.

While the transition from "public agencies" to "public service agencies" raises a host of important questions about accountability, authority, and mission incompatibility, the original findings of the literature on street-level bureaucracy have, by and large, held up remarkably well in the realm of non-profit service provision.[39] In a new concluding chapter written in 2010 for an updated edition of *Street-Level Bureaucracy,* Lipsky suggests that this might be because "the controls, performance measures, and agency review procedures imposed on private [nonprofit] agencies by public authorities have become increasingly rigorous, tending to drive out whatever differences in the treatment of clients attributable to private or public status that might at one time have prevailed."[40] This convergence may be especially tight for nonprofits, like the one in which I conducted my fieldwork, which have relied on government funding to such an extent and for so long that any sense of independent mission and special priorities they might once have had are by now long gone.

By contrast, for-profit agencies, which remain beyond the scope of this book, depart more substantially from the standard street-level bureaucracy profile.[41] This is, in part, because their employees are often differently motivated, and their organizational culture not always well aligned with the public service ethos. But it is also because their managers inherit, on top of the responsibilities associated with the provision of social services and sometimes competing with them, an obligation to advance the interests of shareholders, usually taken to mean maximizing profit or return on investment.[42]

In addition to the changes brought about by contracting, street-level bureaucracy is also being transformed by technology. Many of the interactions that people used to have with bureaucrats, especially to solicit information, can now be done online or over the phone. In some domains, the use of information systems has also contributed to displacing the locus of bureaucratic discretion. Some scholars have gone so far as to herald the gradual replacement of street-level bureaucracy (where officials have a significant amount of discretion over individual cases) by screen-level bureaucracy (where officials enter forms into a computer program that makes decisions for them), and possibly even by system-level bureaucracy (where officials are no longer involved in handling individual cases but spend their time developing the relevant algorithms).[43]

While such prognostics must be taken seriously, we must be careful not to overstate the speed, reach, and inevitability of technological change. As we will see in the following pages, street-level bureaucrats still make plenty of significant decisions in the course of face-to-face encounters, and in some agencies the scope of their discretion has actually increased with recent waves of administrative reform.[44] We must be careful, as well, not to treat technological change as a *fait accompli*. The fact that we now have the technology required to replace people with screens and algorithms does not mean that it is always a good idea to do so. By shedding light on how the bureaucratic encounter takes place in more traditional, face-to-face settings, the following pages will help us think more clearly about the proper role of technology in public service delivery. Understanding how personal encounters between bureaucrats and clients play out, and what significance they have for the parties involved, can give us a yardstick to assess what we stand to gain and to lose by moving to a different model of service provision. It is precisely because the state is changing so much that it is incumbent upon us to look closely at what it is, or what it was until recently, so that we can critically assess what it is becoming and help shape what it might become.

Methodology and Fieldwork

This book draws on an eclectic array of sources. It engages with political theory in the Anglo-American and Continental traditions, with contemporary moral philosophy, and with social theory. But it also situates normative questions in a richly textured account of bureaucratic life that remains sensitive to institutional context and lived experience. This account builds on empirical research in anthropology, sociology, political science, and psychology; on literary representations of bureaucracy; and on eight months of participant observation I conducted in an antipoverty agency.

This eclecticism is called for by the subject matter at hand. To be interested in the conditions of possibility of moral agency is to be interested in questions of moral psychology that are open to experimental inquiry. It is to be concerned with how individuals are influenced by their environment and how they adapt themselves to it—questions of interest to sociologists and political scientists. It is to be attentive, finally, to the everyday experience of social actors—how they perceive their surroundings, how they think of themselves, and how they attribute meaning to events—questions that are evoked suggestively in literature, that are of direct concern to anthropologists, and that lend themselves to exploration through participant observation.

On a methodological front, I hope that this study will attest to the potential for cross-pollination between political theory and ethnographic modes of inquiry. The window that ethnography opens onto individual experience, and the attention it devotes to context, can prompt us to think more carefully about how moral and political questions actually present themselves to ordinary agents in the thick of everyday life. It can also help us gain a more nuanced appreciation for the various ways in which moral agents interact with, and depend upon, the environment in which they are situated. In turn, I hope to show that political theory has something important to contribute to an anthropology of morals, because it can provide us with an interpretive lens to grasp the moral and political valence of everyday practices that would otherwise appear devoid of significance.

For quite some time now, a number of political theorists have been dissatisfied with the level of abstraction at which much of contemporary normative political theory proceeds. Political realists and proponents of non-ideal theory have, each in their own way, decried the extent to which normative theory has become detached from the realities of politics.[45] They have enjoined us, instead, to start the process of normative reflection from the here and now, thinking about what might be required of us in our present circumstances and trying to understand the practices of politics and morality as they actually exist. I take these criticisms seriously and will attempt in the course of this study to practice a more grounded kind of political theory—one that is informed by an ethnographic sensibility. Rather than open with a methodological preamble about what it might mean to engage in such a form of political theory and why we might want to do so, I will try to make my case by exemplifying it. Save for a few necessary remarks along the way, I will leave my reflections on methodology for the book's conclusion, by which point the reader will have had a chance to see it at work.

As a contribution to a more realistic theory of the state, I begin by taking street-level bureaucracies, street-level bureaucrats, and public policy largely as I, and others, have found them, and attempt to examine the challenges of street-level work in these conditions. I use the experience of street-level bureaucrats, in turn, as a starting point to critically assess existing institutional arrangements, managerial practices, and policies. The organizations we will encounter in the following pages are, for the most part, understaffed and underfunded. The bureaucrats we will meet are, by and large, well intentioned and motivated to do their job well, although their understanding of what this means and their level of dedication to the ideal public service vary considerably. Petty corruption, while not absent, is not as prevalent or pressing a concern as it is in some developing countries. The policies that street-level bureaucrats are asked to implement, finally, are for the most part legitimate enough or just enough ("just-ish") not to warrant shirking or outright disobedience, even though they may be far from ideal.

These conditions are in some ways better, and in others worse, than they conceivably could be—but they are currently ours. Some of the tensions I describe in the following pages would be alleviated if public agencies were funded far more generously. And while unjust laws, corruption, and improper motivation could be more rampant, we will see that street-level work is ethically fraught and challenging even in the absence of such familiar problems.

The organization in which I conducted my fieldwork, and to which I will refer from now on as the Norville Community Development Initiative (NCDI), is in many ways representative of the new face of public service provision. The NCDI was founded in the early 1960s as a private nonprofit organization dedicated to addressing the "human side" of urban renewal projects. With the passage of the Economic Opportunity Act under Lyndon B. Johnson in 1964 and the beginning of the War on Poverty, it was designated as Norville's official antipoverty agency. While the NCDI started with a militant community empowerment agenda, it gradually morphed into a human services organization that both administers and helps clients apply for a wide range of governmental programs.

Low-income families visit the NCDI to apply for Head Start programs, fuel assistance for winter heating, food stamps, and the Earned Income Tax Credit. The NCDI also runs job assistance programs, financial counseling sessions, and an after-school program. It provides housing assistance to families in need; assists seniors by providing Medicare counseling sessions; helps families access child care through referral and voucher programs; provides recommendations for public housing; and assists clients in applying for citizenship.

The agency is responsible for reaching out to potential clients; for determining which services they are eligible for; for helping them apply for such services; and when necessary, for sending their completed applications to governmental offices for approval. It is also responsible for verifying the accuracy of the documents that clients provide; for assessing the veracity and consistency of their claims; and for monitoring compliance with program requirements. The NCDI thus combines service and regulatory functions and, given the volume of clients who pass through it, it is also effectively a "people-processing" organization—one whose primary function is not to change the behavior of clients but to confer "public statuses" on them.[46]

By the time I joined the organization, it operated a network of sixteen neighborhood sites scattered throughout the city and served close to 100,000 families annually. Its yearly budget was close to 150 million dollars, practically all of which came from governmental grants at the federal (~70 percent), state (~10 percent), and local (~15 percent) levels. The NCDI was granted a quasi-monopoly over the services it provided, and its performance was reviewed cyclically by federal, state, and local officials.

The neighborhood site to which I was assigned as a receptionist—hereafter referred to as the Norville Service Center (NSC)—was one of the largest in the city. It served a predominantly African American neighborhood (~65 percent) with large Asian and Hispanic communities. The NSC was housed in a large three-story townhouse at the intersection of a quiet residential street and a medium-sized road, across the street from a public school. It shared its location with the Norville Hispanic Center (NHC), a branch of NCDI that specialized in providing services to Hispanic clients, which had a dedicated Spanish-speaking staff. The NHC had its own entrance, reception desk, and director. It could be accessed directly through the parking lot of the NSC. Over the course of the eight-month period I spent at the NCDI, I had the opportunity to work as receptionist both at the Norville Service Center and at the Norville Hispanic Center. This made for an ideal comparative setup: it allowed me to be exposed to two different organizational cultures and managerial styles, as well as to two different groups of clients within the context of a single institutional framework (the NCDI).

The Norville Service Center employed five to seven case managers; the Norville Hispanic Center employed three. Both centers also relied heavily on the help of interns and volunteers like me, many of whom stayed with the organization for several years. Most of the staff members and interns had close connections with the neighborhood, and their demographics broadly reflected those of the client population, which was predominantly African American and Hispanic and about three-quarters female. Full-time staff members had a variety of professional backgrounds; most had prior training in "human services" or exposure to social work, but many did not and were recruited by the organization after serving as volunteers for a long period of time.

As a receptionist, my primary responsibilities involved greeting clients in person and on the phone, answering their questions, informing them of the status of their appointments, and updating their administrative records ahead of their meetings with case managers. I also had to perform miscellaneous administrative tasks, sometimes away from the front desk, in a cubicle adjacent to those of case managers. When there was a shortage of staff or experienced interns, I would be asked to meet with clients individually to help them apply for specific services. Given my physical proximity to the offices and cubicles of case managers and the open-door culture of the organization, I could overhear the conversations that staff members were having with one another and would frequently be invited to sit in on their meetings with clients for the purposes of training.

Outline of the Book

I begin, in Chapter 1, by examining the reasons for which street-level bureaucrats have discretion and the normative grounds on which such discretion can be justified. In Chapter 2, I proceed to examine how street-level bureaucrats inhabit their spaces of discretion. I argue that we can best understand the ethical challenges that such bureaucrats face by focusing not on the individual decisions they must take but on the broader moral dispositions they develop on the job. I give analytic content to the notion of a "moral disposition" and show that such dispositions shape how bureaucrats make use of their discretionary power. With the aid of this conceptual groundwork, I proceed to identify three dispositions that frequently appear among street-level workers—indifference, caregiving, and enforcement—and show that they are, each in its own way, pathological.

The following three chapters draw on my ethnographic fieldwork at the NCDI to examine why the pressures of everyday work drive street-level bureaucrats toward such dispositions, and what can be done to counteract such a drift. Chapter 3 takes up these questions from the standpoint of individual bureaucrats, Chapter 4 from the standpoint of peer-level dynamics, and Chapter 5 from the perspective of managerial practices and public policy. Each of these chapters puts the accent on a distinct failure of moral agency—a failure of role conception (Chapter 3), a failure of moral perception (Chapter 4), and a failure of moral integrity (Chapter 5).

I conclude with some reflections on the nature of administrative rationality, on the need for a bottom-up normative theory of the state, and on the potential for synergy between political theory and ethnography.

CHAPTER ONE

Street-Level Discretion

Most citizens come to experience the state and its policies through their encounters with street-level bureaucrats.[1] It is no secret to anyone familiar with waiting rooms, border crossings, or police stops that such bureaucrats wield a certain margin of discretion. But just how extensive is this discretion, and what is its nature? What reasons, if any, can we offer to explain and justify its existence? More importantly, perhaps, is this discretion merely a feature of our present institutions, with their existing defects and lacunae, or would it remain necessary or desirable even if such institutions could be reformed?

The answer to these questions depends, in part, on an empirically informed understanding of how bureaucracies operate and of what bureaucrats *do*—of the kinds of judgments, decisions, and choices that they are required to make when they aim to fulfill their role in good faith. Bureaucrats are expected to *apply* and *implement* policy decisions. What does this entail? Getting a better sense of the requirements of the job will allow us to formulate a more accurate description of the moral responsibilities that come with it. This will take us back to one of the perennial debates in the ethics of public administration—one that opposed Carl Friedrich to Herman Finer in the 1940s.[2] Does bureaucratic responsibility consist primarily in obedience to orders and procedures, or does it call for a more creative form of discretion that involves and discloses the moral character and professional identity of the bureaucrat?

According to the *Merriam-Webster's Dictionary of Law*, discretion is "the power of a public official or employee to act and make decisions based on his or her own judgment or conscience within the bounds of reason and the law."[3] A few features of this definition are worth noting before we proceed further. First, discretion involves the power to exert choice among a range of alternatives between which the law does not discriminate. Discretion is not simply what an official can "get away with"—it presupposes a legitimate, or authorized, exercise of power. Second, discretion is not coextensive with morally justified choice. In some cases, an official may be morally required to disobey the law. We would not describe this, however, as an exercise of discretion.

Third, the definition indicates that the use of discretion is typically constrained both externally (by the law) and internally (by a standard of reasonableness). Discretion is not "doing as one pleases" within the bounds of the law. The official must be able to explain on what grounds he or she selected a particular alternative among the many that were available. Discretionary decisions can be reviewed, and they often are; there are good and bad uses of discretion, and when the standard of reasonableness is not met, we speak of an "abuse of discretion."

It is important to note, finally, that there is a difference between the formal discretion to which officials are entitled "on paper" and the real discretion they actually wield on the ground.[4] Real discretion can be both wider and narrower than formal discretion. The police rookie who accompanies an experienced sergeant on patrol will soon learn that certain official rules are effectively arcane and should be applied selectively, and that other nonofficial norms must be followed religiously, even though they do not appear on the books. Discretion is constrained not only by formal means (such as sanctions or rules) but also by informal norms, which are typically enforced by peers.[5] In this chapter, I will be concerned exclusively with formal discretion, but I will return to the question of real discretion and informal controls later on in Chapter 4.[6]

In what follows, I will argue that even though rules contribute to constraining the discretion of bureaucrats, and even though they sometimes provide principles that can guide positive acts of judgment, they often fall significantly short of singling out a particular course of action. Rules and procedures exclude many alternatives, but leave open a range of options that frontline workers must choose from.[7] The world of street-level bureaucrats is one of bounded discretion.

But there is more: the nature of discretion at the street level is not simply technical or instrumental. Like judges, before whom the law can fall silent, street-level bureaucrats are often compelled by the very nature of administrative procedures to make *normative judgments:* they are forced to "make policy," much as judges are forced to "make law."[8] They are responsible not only for assessing facts and selecting appropriate procedures; they must also weigh competing values and goals against one another and give countenance to objectives that are often vague. As such, the proper functioning of our bureaucracies *as they exist today* necessarily rests on street-level bureaucrats' capacity to exert sound and independent moral judgment. These conclusions, which are in line with those that Friedrich reached for senior bureaucrats, emerge when we move away from a rule-saturated model of bureaucracy to one that gives proper consideration to the ubiquitous presence of uncertainty and ambiguity in the life of organizations.

My primary concern in the following chapters will be to examine how street-level bureaucrats inhabit these spaces of discretion, how they negotiate compromises among the plurality of goals and values they must remain sensitive to, and how they find the resources to do so in an environment that often makes good moral judgment remarkably difficult.

As political theorists may point out, however, there is some danger in developing a normative model of the responsibilities of street-level bureaucrats by looking at what their job requires them to do *given how bureaucracies operate today.* The danger is that we may be conceding too much to the imperfect state of our current institutions. It is one thing to explain why street-level bureaucrats *do* have discretion and how they should deal with it; it is another to explain whether they *should* have discretion in the first place. I will try to argue, therefore, that discretion is not simply a fact we must contend with but often (though certainly not always) a necessary and desirable feature of our institutions.

While these claims are modest, they may meet with some resistance. The idea that street-level bureaucrats should be routinely entitled to make value judgments is bound to raise a familiar range of concerns on liberal, democratic, and republican grounds.[9] Liberals might worry that such discretion would violate the rule of law—that it would expose citizens to the unpredictable, biased, and moralizing judgment of low-ranking officials. Democrats might be reluctant to entrust discretionary power to officials who have a weak democratic pedigree and who are not subject to direct mechanisms of democratic accountability. Republicans, finally, might find the prospect of discretion at the point of service provision particularly unsa-vory because it elicits the threat of personal domination—it makes vulner-able citizens depend upon the potentially arbitrary judgment of a particular other.[10]

The idea that discretion over questions of value might be justified at the street level also runs against a deeply ingrained normative ideal of bureau-cracy as a neutral conduit for policy implementation. This ideal—which I will call following Evelyn Brodkin the "compliance model" of bureaucratic responsibility—holds that bureaucrats should be concerned only with de-vising ways to attain the policy goals chosen by elected representatives.[11] They bring "technical competence" to the realization of the democratic will, but under no circumstance should they be in the business of making normative (i.e. moral or political) judgments themselves. This ideal is at-tractive, in part, because it alleviates some of the worries we might have about discretion by tightly constraining its nature and scope.

In its most radical variant, which I will tackle in this chapter, the com-pliance model maintains that all important normative questions (per-taining to tradeoffs and prioritization between goals, or to the weighing of various ethical considerations) should be answered by the organization on behalf of its frontline staff. The answers may be inscribed in procedures, in a carefully calibrated system of rewards and incentives, or in an impercep-tible pattern of information flow. The point, however, remains the same: if organizations are properly designed, they should only have to rely on the moral responsibility of frontline operators in the minimal sense of elic-iting compliance. We should not be looking for morality "inside" indi-vidual bureaucrats, but in the formal structure of the organization of which they are part—morality, according to this view, ought to be *exteriorized*. The compliance model is not hard to debunk as a descriptive account of how bureaucracies work, but it is more tenacious as a normative ideal for how they should work.

As a response to the compliance model, I will seek to establish the fol-lowing three claims:

(1) Spaces of discretion at the street level are not simply "aberrations" that result from poor management (and that could, as such, be easily curtailed);

(2) Such spaces of discretion necessarily involve *normative* judgment—by which I mean judgment that implicates questions of value—and not merely technical or "expert" rationality;

(3) While spaces of discretion at the street level must be tightly controlled, we will often (though not always) have good reasons to preserve them.

Taken together, these three claims form a challenge to the compliance model of bureaucratic responsibility, both as a "measuring stick" (i.e., as a standard against which to assess the performance of bureaucratic agents given the current state of our bureaucracies) and as a normative ideal in its own right (i.e., as depicting an intrinsically desirable state of affairs that our bureaucracies should aspire to).

The chapter proceeds as follows. In the first section, I describe the compliance model of bureaucratic responsibility and the "rational" theories of organization that underpin it. In the second section, I begin to address the shortcomings of the compliance model by sketching the case that can be made for normative discretion at the upper echelons of the bureaucratic hierarchy. I then explain why the reasons that can be offered in favor of such discretion do not transfer well down the ranks. In the third section, I lay out the sources of discretion at the street level and the grounds on which such discretion can be justified. I conclude by stating the case against the compliance model and by arguing that we need a broader conception of bureaucratic responsibility.

The Compliance Model and "Rational" Theories of Organization

There was a time, according to Dennis Thompson, when political theorists "understood the role of bureaucrats much as Hobbes had explained the role of public ministers: they resemble 'the nerves and tendons that move the several limbs of a body natural.' Because nerves and tendons of the body politic do not initiate anything on their own, political theory could safely ignore them."[12]

According to this view, which I have called the "compliance model" of bureaucratic responsibility, bureaucracies are a neutral conduit for the implementation of directives issued by legislators. There is a clear division of labor between politicians, who make policy decisions, and administrators, who execute them. Woodrow Wilson and Frank Goodnow were early proponents of such a view. Wilson claimed, in a seminal article, that administration is "removed from the hurry and strife of politics . . . . It is a part of political life . . . only as machinery is part of the manufactured product."[13] Goodnow wrote in a similar spirit:

> There are, then, in all governmental systems two primary or ultimate functions of government, viz. the expression of the will of the state and the execution of that will. There are also in all states separate organs, each of which is mainly busied with the discharge of one of these functions. These functions are, respectively, Politics and Administration.[14]

This normative view of the proper relationship between politics and administration found support in a family of theories of organization—most notably, those of Frederick Taylor, Max Weber, and Herbert Simon. These theories share a tendency to look at organizations as "rational systems."[15] Seen from this perspective, organizations are instruments designed to faithfully implement a set of goals that have been specified from the outside. They are rational inasmuch as they seek to attain these goals as efficiently as possible.[16] In the case of bureaucracies, the goals are specified by elected representatives through legislation. Since bureaucracies, according to this perspective, are simply *instruments* for the execution of the political will, they do not raise any distinctive normative questions of their own.[17]

In the context of my broader argument in this chapter, the rational systems perspective will work as a countermodel. I present it here because it serves as the organizational basis for the compliance model of bureaucratic responsibility. I will try to show, starting in the next section, that this perspective significantly downplays the extent and the nature of bureaucratic discretion. Once the scope of this discretion is clarified, it will become apparent, I hope, that "compliance" with directives accounts for only a subset of the tasks that bureaucrats must regularly perform.

According to the rational systems perspective, two characteristics of organizations are largely responsible for their instrumental effectiveness: goal specificity and formal structure.[18] Organizations take complex objectives and break them down into more manageable tasks. Lower-level bureaucrats do not work directly with the text of the law, which is often ambiguous and open to interpretation. They are expected to comply, rather, with rules and standard operating procedures that have been rendered ever more precise by layer upon layer of "principals" eager to control and optimize the actions of their "agents."

It is not enough, however, for individual bureaucrats to pursue specific goals independently. They must also be able to work together so as to achieve the high-level objectives of the organization. Their activities have to be coordinated and synchronized. This is where formal structure comes into play.[19] *Hierarchy* ensures that proximate goals pursued by various actors at each sublevel ultimately add up to the goals of the organization. *Discipline and control* guarantee compliance with directives received from above.[20] *Fixed jurisdictional boundaries* encourage specialization and rein in the use of discretion. *Impersonal rules and procedures,* finally, make the behavior of individual agents predictable and regular—they reduce friction and "transaction costs" due to uncertainty and disseminate "best practices" in the form of standard operating procedures (SOPs).[21] The organization, in short, takes it upon itself to specify both the goals that bureaucratic operators ought to achieve and the procedures they ought to follow so as to achieve them.

According to Weber, the formal attributes of bureaucracy give it a "rational-legal" character, which distinguishes it from patrimonial forms of organization and enables it to display the regularity, reliability, and (possibly) the efficiency of a machine.[22] In order to be perfectly integrated into the bureaucratic calculus and its precise choreography of moving parts, individual bureaucrats are, in the words of Weber, "de-humanized"[23] and relegated to the status of "cogs,"[24] whose performance ought to be controllable and predictable.

But this mechanistic simile must be taken with a grain of salt. The rational systems perspective does not necessarily reduce bureaucrats to automata. On the contrary, the rational-legal structure of a bureaucracy may allow individual bureaucrats to exert a comparatively greater degree of discretion than in more traditional forms of organization.[25] Since the principles and procedures in place are stable and clearly formulated, and since they do not depend on the capricious "whims" of a superior, they can serve as a reliable guide for independent action and can, accordingly, reduce the need for close and direct hierarchical supervision. Bureaucracies may be efficient, then, not because they eliminate discretion (like a machine) but because they provide an environment in which such discretion can flourish and be adequately channeled.

It is important to note, however, that according to the rational systems perspective, bureaucracies are hospitable only to a specific *kind* of discretion. Herbert Simon addresses this question directly. Drawing on the fact/value distinction, he argues that we must distinguish judgments regarding *states of the world* (that have a high factual component) from judgments of *value* (that are normative in that they specify the ends we ought to pursue).[26] As we go down the hierarchical ladder, the "factual" component of judgments increases and the "value" component decreases. Low-ranking bureaucrats do not set their own ends, but have some flexibility in choosing the most effective means to attain the ends they are instructed to pursue, based on their factual knowledge of "what works." This is what it means to say that bureaucrats exert *technical* discretion.

"Technical discretion" involves three distinct components: (1) an interpretive judgment as to the meaning of the rules that must be implemented, (2) a "subsumptive" judgment relating observable features of the world to the categories picked out by the rules, and (3) an "expert" judgment as to which of the actions or procedures available are most apt to attain the desired ends.

(1) Rules and instructions do not apply themselves and in some sense, as Wittgenstein has shown, they *could not.* Rules presume a shared background understanding and an agent capable of drawing reasonably well on such a background.[27] Bureaucrats do not simply execute; they must first understand and interpret what they are asked to do. A patrol officer may be instructed to arrest cars that are "weaving within a single lane" on suspicion of driving under the influence (DUI).[28] The officer must first know what it means to "weave within a single lane," and how it differs from "switching lanes," "attempting to switch lanes and swerving back on track," "avoiding a pothole," and so forth.

(2) The officer must then determine whether any specific case is an instance of the cases that the policy aims to pick out.[29] He or she must understand not only what weaving within a single lane means but also

whether *this* (this driver, with this level of traffic, at this time of the day, under these weather conditions) is a particular instance of it.

(3) Given the wide range of situations that bureaucrats encounter, organizations cannot offer tailored procedures to cover each and every case. Public officials are, accordingly, given some latitude to select the procedures or means that are most likely to advance organizational goals. A vocational rehabilitation counselor may be asked to help a client reenter the workforce. This could be done by enlisting them in a training program, by scheduling counseling sessions, by providing medical assistance, or simply by trying to boost their damaged self-esteem over the course of repeated face-to-face interactions. Which strategy is most appropriate will depend on the particularities of the case.

Technical discretion can be quite demanding, and the aforementioned judgments difficult to make. The rational systems perspective rests on the belief that organizations may be able to simplify such judgments to a considerable extent by providing bureaucrats with a set of "objective" criteria on which to base their decisions. Fire safety inspectors, for instance, are not simply instructed to determine whether a building is "safe" or not. They are typically given precise guidelines as to what makes a building safe. This comes in the form of a checklist of several items, such as: "There must be at least 1 fire extinguisher for every 6 workers."[30] Such a rule will address most routine cases and will leave room for discretion only in borderline situations (Is a broken fire extinguisher a fire extinguisher? What about an extinguisher that works but is hard to reach on the wall?).[31]

It is important to note at this stage that "technical discretion," along the three dimensions sketched above, accounts for many—perhaps even most—of the tasks that bureaucrats perform on a daily basis. In this respect, the rational systems perspective captures an essential aspect of bureaucratic life—even though, as we will soon see, it leaves out what may well be the most interesting part. It also presents an ideal of bureaucracy that is normatively attractive precisely because it limits the scope of individual discretion to technical matters and because it demands, in everything else, compliance with well-specified organizational directives. This allows the rational systems perspective to reconcile features dear to democrats, liberals, and republicans. I mention these features here not so much to vaunt the merits of the rational systems perspective as to highlight the risks we may incur by moving away from it. Three such features deserve to be singled out.

First, the bureaucracies described by the rational systems perspective are practically immune, by design, to a loss of democratic legitimacy. They are organized along a strong principle of hierarchy, which makes bureaucrats responsive to the will of elected representatives through a chain of "commands" issued by the legislature and relayed downward through the bureaucratic echelons. Since bureaucrats do not have discretion over the choice of "ends," and since the goals they must achieve are specific and well defined, they cannot distort the democratic will (unless they make a *mistake*, for which they can be reprimanded).

Second, the limitation of discretion to technical questions alleviates a host of worries regarding arbitrary treatment, partiality, or personal dependence and diminishes the fear that the personal values of bureaucrats may interfere with how they conduct official business. If bureaucrats are expected to settle only matters of "fact" rather than questions of "value," chances are higher that they will indeed act impartially and impersonally. The rules and policies they are asked to follow could, of course, be morally wrong or arbitrary, but this would be a *political,* not an administrative, problem.

Third, the rational systems perspective sets the stage for an attractive and parsimonious model of accountability. Since bureaucrats are entitled to only technical discretion, their performance can be assessed by resorting to managerial criteria of efficiency and effectiveness. If a normative problem were to arise, it should be possible to trace it either to individual bureaucrats who overstepped their prerogatives or to the directives that these bureaucrats were instructed to follow. In either case, it should be relatively easy, in principle, to find the culprits (the disobedient bureaucrats or, going up the ranks, those who designed the procedures and gave orders to follow them) and to hold them personally responsible.[32] This model of accountability is attractive not only for citizens, who can in theory find someone to blame for bureaucratic errors, but also for bureaucrats: it absolves them of personal responsibility for the content of their actions so long as they are in line with the rules in place. In the division of moral labor, it accords them a rather modest role.

Discretion up the Ranks

The compliance model of bureaucratic responsibility, and the rational theories of organization on which it relies, have come under criticism for offering an account of the relationship between politics and administration that is both empirically inaccurate and normatively undesirable. Most critics have focused on the limitations of the compliance model for thinking about the responsibilities of senior bureaucrats—officials who are in a position to steer their agencies either by developing administrative procedures or by participating in political decision-making. In what follows, I review some of the arguments that have been offered to that effect and show that while they are convincing at the top level of the bureaucratic hierarchy, they do not travel well as we move down the ranks. Street-level discretion is a matter that needs to be examined on its own.

In the preceding section, I ran together two somewhat distinct characterizations of the split between "politics" and "administration." The first, which appeared in the quotes by Wilson and Goodnow, emphasized the distinction between policymaking and policy execution. The second, which appeared in reference to Herbert Simon, stressed the distinction between normative questions (i.e., questions of value or of interest that pertain to what we ought to do) and technical questions. Given how bureaucracies operate today, neither of these characterizations is accurate.

The distinction between policymaking and policy execution fails to capture the split between politics and administration on multiple fronts. It does not reflect the extent to which top-level bureaucrats are involved in the drafting of legislative statutes as key providers of information, topical expertise, and practical know-how. It also fails to acknowledge that many bureaucratic agencies have been able to wrest a considerable degree of independent policymaking power away from the legislature. As Daniel Carpenter has shown, they have acquired such autonomy less by fiat than by leverage: by building their reputation and forging coalitions that support the services they provide, thereby inducing politicians to grant them free rein in advancing their favored policies.[33]

The distinction is oblivious, finally, to the fact that policymaking continues *within agencies* even after a statute has been drafted. One reason for this is that the writing of detailed provisions would demand a costly investment of time and resources from legislators.[34] Another is that legislators lack the expertise and information required to develop effective rules of conduct and normally prefer to delegate such tasks to the executive. As a consequence, agencies tend to inherit policy statutes that are abstract and incomplete, and that lend themselves to being operationalized in a variety of ways. It is understood that these statutes would only come to acquire clear and precise meaning *within* bureaucratic agencies.

If the distinction between "policymaking" and "policy execution" fails to capture the split between politics and administration, the distinction between "values and interests" on the one hand and "facts and expertise" on the other does not fare better. Bureaucrats are meant to contribute information to the policy process. Yet the very facts they have at hand are often tainted by political interests. Public agencies are involved in close working relationships with a variety of private and public actors assembled around complex "issue networks."[35] Senior bureaucrats are indebted to their partners in these networks for data, expertise, and manpower. But many of these partners, of course, have a vested interest in the outcome of the policymaking process. The information that senior bureaucrats garner is often colored by the selective research emphases of corporations, think tanks, and lobbyists and framed in a way that is congenial to their interests. More importantly, perhaps, senior bureaucrats are expected to consult such actors before taking major decisions.[36] The technical terrain on which these consultations take place does not change the fact that they are essentially a form of interest aggregation and adjudication—that is, a kind of politics in disguise.

The language of "technical discretion" can also be deceptive. Senior bureaucrats have jurisdiction over the choice of "means" to attain a given goal. They are well placed to know, however, that any choice of process will affect stakeholders differently. The nature of the "technical" solution can be a political question in its own right.

Finally, and perhaps most importantly, the characterization of top-level bureaucrats as fact-driven experts who are excluded from the realm of normative judgment presupposes, if it is to be achievable, a background of definitive, determinate, and well-specified goals issued by the legislature. Scholars of delegation, however, have found that policy statutes are often vague, ambiguous, and conflict ridden.[37] Importantly, such ambiguity reaches far beyond the scope of technical matters—which legislators would understandably prefer to leave to the discretion of bureaucratic experts—to encompass the *goals* that policies are meant to achieve.

The reasons for this ambiguity in goals are multiple. Some are related to the dynamics of policymaking in pluralist societies. Vagueness is often the byproduct of the protracted process of compromise that is required to secure a legislative majority. Others are more strategic in nature. Politicians are typically averse to the possibility of alienating a fraction of their electorate by taking a stance on controversial issues when they can avoid doing so. They may prefer to settle for ambiguous statutes.[38] Ambiguity may also allow them to shift responsibility for making tough choices among competing goals to the realm of bureaucracy, and to limit themselves to intervening on behalf of aggrieved constituents—a kind of intervention for which they can reap political rewards.[39] For all these reasons, some laudable, others less so, senior bureaucrats often inherit vague goals and broad mandates.[40] They come to acquire a significant amount of discretion in deciding what to pursue and what to prioritize. Clearly, these questions are not just "technical."

These empirical observations do not of course tell us what we should *make* of the participation of top-level bureaucrats in policymaking. The inadequacy of the clear separation between politics and administration as a *descriptive* account does not necessarily call into question its standing as a *normative ideal*. It is clear, at any rate, that inviting top-level bureaucrats into the process of policymaking comes at a cost, both in terms of democratic legitimacy (since they are unelected), and in terms of responsiveness to the public interest (since they risk being captured by special interests).[41]

While these worries remain alive in democratic theory, there are at least five arguments one could offer in favor of a more permeable boundary between politics and administration at the top level of the bureaucratic apparatus. One could point to the advantages that derive from including the informed and expert opinion of top-level bureaucrats in the policymaking process ("expertise"). One could argue that career civil servants with life tenure are more insulated from outside pressure than politicians and therefore less likely to be captured by special interests ("independence"). One could insist on the lack of a viable alternative: short of forcing legislators to spend their precious time writing excruciatingly precise statutes and short of hiring an army of staff members with the required expertise to do so, bureaucratic discretion at the upper echelons of bureaucracy is inevitable ("inevitability").

One could also claim that ambiguity and conflict in policy statutes play a desirable role in encouraging a rich and multifaceted conception of bureaucratic responsibility ("responsibilization").[42] When organizations are given a clear objective, especially one that can be translated into observable and measurable outcomes, they have the deplorable tendency to pursue it single-handedly at the expense of other, less tangible aspects of their mission ("What you measure is what you get"). Some amount of ambiguity and conflict in policy statutes can help keep this tendency in check. Finally, one could seek to allay fears about discretion by pointing out that senior bureaucrats often have a long record of commitment to public service and by arguing that, while they are not subject to electoral accountability, they are nevertheless held directly accountable by interest groups and by the prospect of judicial review ("mitigation").

The first four families of arguments—those from "expertise," "independence," "inevitability," and "responsibilization"—serve as pro tanto reasons in favor of granting senior bureaucrats discretion, while the fifth, "mitigation," serves to alleviate our worries about the exercise of such discretion. But these arguments do not transfer well down the ranks.

While senior bureaucrats can often lay claim to being experts in their respective fields, frontline officials often lack the educational credentials and social standing to be recognized as such. While valuable, the practical know-how they acquire on the job cannot easily be formalized. It is often seen, accordingly, as insufficiently credible and reliable to ground a claim to technocratic expertise. From an informational standpoint, street-level bureaucrats also lack the panoramic view that senior officials can acquire by virtue of their position in the organization. The latter have access to information that has been aggregated across various field sites and hundreds, if not thousands, of clients. Street-level bureaucrats, on the other hand, stand much closer to particular cases. While their knowledge of these cases is unrivaled, one might be worried that this very proximity might cloud or bias their judgment and prevent them from having enough perspective to make substantively correct decisions.

The argument from "independence" does not fare much better. Unlike their more senior counterparts, many street-level bureaucrats, especially those who work in organizations contracted by the state, do not have life tenure but precarious jobs. They are concerned not just with advancing the public interest, but also with making ends meet. Their claim to independence is further compromised by the nature of their encounters with clients, which can be personal and emotionally charged.

The argument from "inevitability" also seems unsubstantiated. One might readily grant that the role of a judge, prosecutor, or scientist cannot be precisely codified, but it is not immediately clear why that of a frontline worker could not. From a distance, the tasks that such workers are called upon to perform might seem rather straightforward. Indeed, with the growth of e-government, machines appear to have already taken over some of the functions that were once performed by street-level bureaucrats, much like ATMs, a couple of decades earlier, reduced the need for bank tellers.[43]

We will see in the next section that the argument from "responsibilization" carries somewhat better to the street level, but it is not obvious why it would. Issuing a multiplicity of potentially conflicting goals may be a sound management strategy for Congress, given that Congress cannot get into the operational details of an agency. Yet isn't such operationalization precisely what top-level bureaucrats are responsible for? Why, then, would we still need to preserve ambiguous goals, and the wide conception of responsibility that comes with them, at the street level?

Even the argument from "mitigation" appears questionable. For one, frontline bureaucrats are often junior employees who lack a long history of commitment to public service and who may not yet have a distinguished track record of performance. Their clients, moreover, are hardly in a position to hold them accountable. Unlike interest groups, clients of public service agencies tend to be vulnerable and are not well equipped to press for their rights.[44]

In sum, then, the case for discretion at the street level cannot be easily derived from the case for discretion at the top level of the bureaucratic apparatus. In fact, some of the arguments offered to support the discretion of senior officials actually work *against* street-level bureaucrats. While our discussion so far has shown that the compliance model of bureaucratic responsibility may be inadequate up the ranks, it has, if anything, reinforced our presumption that it should be upheld at the bottom. The aim of the next section is to challenge this presumption by explaining why discretion exists at the street level and on what grounds it can be justified.

Discretion at the Street Level

The compliance model of bureaucratic responsibility rests on a series of assumptions it inherits from the rational systems perspective on organizations. It presupposes that bureaucracies are able to provide their operators with specific goals; to limit the exercise of discretion to technical questions; to channel discretionary judgment by providing "objective" criteria; and to enforce proper behavior through hierarchical oversight, or through a well-calibrated system of incentives. It is because of these assumptions that rational theories of organization can sometimes compare low-level bureaucrats to "cogs" or "information processors" who reliably and consistently implement policy directives.

We have seen that these assumptions are tenuous at the senior levels of public administration. In this section, I argue that they do not fare better at the street level. I discuss several factors—goal ambiguity, conflicting goals, limited resources, fuzzy boundaries, uncertainty, soft evidence, unpredictability, entangled ends, and information asymmetry—that are pervasive at the front lines of public service and that explain why street-level bureaucrats retain a wider scope of discretion than the compliance model of bureaucratic responsibility can account for.

But my aim is not simply explanatory: I try to show, where possible, that there are good, normative reasons to preserve street-level discretion. This normative argument is distinct from the explanatory one, and since I will be pursuing them together, I should take a moment to distinguish them here. To make an argument for why we *ought* to preserve a margin of discretion at the front lines of public service, it is not enough to list the sources of discretion as they exist today. If these sources of discretion are of our own making, we need to provide an argument for why we should maintain them (the fact of "goal ambiguity" can explain *why* street-level bureaucrats have discretion but not whether they *should*; to make the latter point, we need to explain why goal ambiguity ought to be preserved). If the sources of discretion are not of our own making but features of the external world, we need to provide an argument to explain why our response to such fea-

Sources of Discretion

tures of the world ought to include discretion (discretio: directly from the fact of "uncertainty" but from our choic uncertainty, and this choice needs to be justified).

The alternative to giving street-level bureaucrats discre them to follow detailed rules that reduce the need for ir ment. Relying on such rules would allow us—as a democratic polity—to secure greater direct control over the actions of such officials.[45] It would alleviate fears of arbitrary and inconsistent treatment at the hands of the state. But direct control is not all that we, as a democratic public, aspire to. We also expect frontline workers in the public services to be effective (i.e., to deliver on the goals we have set for them, without distorting them) and efficient (economical in their use of resources). We expect them to treat citizens in a way that is fair and respectful; we insist, as well, that they be as responsive as possible to the special circumstances and needs of individual clients.

The normative case for the existence of discretion at the front lines of public service rests on this plurality of desiderata and on the tensions that arise between them. While strict rules may yield democratic control, they sometimes get in the way of the other normative standards against which we also measure the performance of public service agencies—standards such as effectiveness, efficiency, fairness, respect, and responsiveness. My argument in the following pages underscores this point. The price for direct control through rules is one that we will often be unwilling to pay because it would involve sacrificing some of our other, equally well-ingrained, normative commitments.

Let me now turn to the various sources of discretion at the street level with a view to showing both how they lead frontline officials to confront questions of normative character, and why preserving such discretion might be desirable. I will then bring the argument of this chapter to a close by explaining why we need a richer conception of bureaucratic responsibility than that provided by the compliance model.

Ambiguous Goals

One of the main sources of discretion at the street level comes from the ambiguity of the goals that frontline workers inherit from their superiors. In practice, goal ambiguity means that street-level bureaucrats have some

49 ·

eeway in giving countenance to the ends they pursue—a morally charged task obscured by the rational systems perspective on organizations. Police officers, for instance, are required to "maintain order"—an objective that is crucial to their mission, yet one that remains notoriously elusive.[46] What counts as a disturbance of order? According to whom, and under what conditions? Unlike law enforcement, which involves well-specified criminal acts, order maintenance refers to a "condition" (order) that "can never be defined unambiguously because what constitutes order is a matter of opinion and convention."[47] Courts and precedents can help clarify the meaning of "order" over time but cannot entirely remove the ambiguity that is central to the term, and the variety of meanings it takes across beats and neighborhoods.

It is possible, of course, to reduce such ambiguity by compelling officers to follow clear metrics and procedures. For much of the twentieth century, American police departments sought to do just that. Yet for all its benefits, this increased regimentation of police work came at a cost. The drive for goal clarification led officers "to emphasize those aspects of their job that were most easily standardized and recorded" and to neglect other, equally important tasks, such as "managing family or barroom quarrels and handling rowdy street youths."[48] According to James Q. Wilson, "one part of the police job, order maintenance, was sacrificed to another part, law enforcement."[49] The rebirth of community policing in the late 1970s and early 1980s can be seen as an attempt to redress the balance by bringing back the ambiguous terrain of "order maintenance" to the center of police activities.[50]

The example of the police suggests that while goals must be clarified when they are needlessly vague, there is a significant cost to overclarification. "The dilemma for accountability," Michael Lipsky writes, "is to know when goal clarification is desirable because continued ambivalence and contradiction are unproductive, and when it will result in a reduction in the scope and mission of public services."[51] So long as goals remain ambiguous, street-level bureaucrats will retain a margin of discretion in shaping them. The choices they make in doing so are not merely technical but value-laden. Discretion here is desirable insofar as it allows street-level bureaucrats to pursue policy goals whose meaning varies depending upon context, and which would be impoverished if they were to be further clarified.[52]

Conflicting Goals and Values

The goals that street-level bureaucrats inherit are not only ambiguous but sometimes also conflicting. As I indicated earlier, some of these conflicts result from the strategic dynamics of policymaking and would disappear in a more responsible political culture. But others are here to stay. As Isaiah Berlin and proponents of value pluralism have long argued, we are committed to a range of values that are incommensurable and that often stand in tension with one another.[53] Some of these tensions can be resolved abstractly ex-ante, in legislation, and passed down to public agencies in the form of precise directives. But others are best addressed on a case-by-case basis, in light of the particular context at hand.

Street-level bureaucrats occupy a demanding role in this regard because they are at the outmost, client-facing, nodes of the bureaucratic apparatus—where conflicts, however distressing, must be resolved. Police officers are expected to enforce the law *and* to foster good community ties; intake workers must attend to the special needs of applicants *and* process as many of them as possible. Street-level bureaucrats are expected to strike reasonable compromises between such competing objectives in light of the concrete situation at hand. This calls for an exercise in moral or political judgment.

Street-level bureaucrats are also expected to attend to a host of "process values" that are not necessarily "goals" in themselves but that constrain how an agency should go about achieving its goals.[54] Even well defined objectives (e.g., to process incoming claims as efficiently as possible) are not to be achieved at any cost. Considerations of transparency, courtesy, and respect also come into play and help protect the self-respect of clients. It is important to remember, in this regard, that as the "face of the state," street-level bureaucrats are responsible not only for taking decisions but also for explaining and justifying these decisions to clients. When doing so, they must be thorough, patient, and considerate. But any concession to such "process values" consumes time and resources that could be spent differently—for instance, on processing clients faster or serving a greater number of them. How much is enough on each of these dimensions of value? When should one compromise one for the other? Discretion is desirable insofar as it gives bureaucrats the flexibility to answer these questions in light of the particularities of individual cases and circumstances.

Limited Resources

The tension between competing goals and process values is accentuated, in the public service sector, by a chronic limitation in administrative resources—a problem on which the rational systems perspective remains conspicuously silent. It is because time, money, attention, and empathy are limited that street-level bureaucrats have discretion over where and when to apply them. The problem is familiar: police officers cannot arrest everyone who commits an infraction—they exert discretion in deciding which offenses to pursue and which to ignore. But it extends far beyond the realm of law enforcement. Intake workers at a welfare agency, for instance, cannot spend as much time as they ideally would with each applicant. They must decide whom to assist in filling out paperwork and whom to ask to step aside and come back with a completed application. Social workers have a limited supply of genuine empathy before they burn out. They must decide which stories to lend a compassionate ear to and which ones to cut short.

The need to make such difficult choices, when resources are limited, reflects our conviction that to treat people equally is not always to treat them the same. Given that the capacity to properly fill out forms, for example, is a key condition for getting state assistance, and given that this capacity is unevenly distributed among applicants, it is only fair that street-level bureaucrats would get some latitude in trying to even out the playing field. An applicant who has difficulty speaking English will require more assistance than a native speaker. Since street-level bureaucrats are closest to the applicants, and since they are best positioned to know who may require more resources, it is sensible that we would, within reasonable bounds, rely on them to make such decisions.

Scholars have suggested that the problem of limited resources in public service agencies would not be easily eliminated by adding more staff or increasing budget.[55] The demand for public services is elastic and will typically rise until it exceeds the supply. It is the anticipated length of the waiting line that in part regulates how many people show up.

The problem posed by the allocation of limited resources is of course not exclusive to public service agencies. It has attracted considerable attention, for instance, in the realm of healthcare provision.[56] Some have suggested that the norms of the medical profession, which encourage doctors to be fully devoted to their individual patients, are ill adapted to answering questions of prioritization and resource allocation. They have claimed, accordingly, that the question of scarce resource allocation should not be left entirely to the discretion of doctors but should be regulated by hospital managers and inscribed in institutional principles and procedures. This could help usher in a healthy division of moral labor between doctors and managers.[57]

This argument carries to street-level bureaucracy. While the exercise of judgment is, in the last resort, unavoidable, the development of institutional principles can facilitate and guide such judgment and provide common standards for accountability and consistency. This may be particularly important for some of the most difficult and recurring questions (e.g., how should one weigh small benefits for a large number of people versus large benefits for one?). So long as sufficiently granular answers to these questions cannot be articulated in the abstract, however, institutional principles will have to coexist with a significant margin of frontline discretion.

Fuzzy Boundaries

When implementing existing policies, street-level bureaucrats are responsible for sorting clients and their actions into categories defined by law. The rules they inherit are typically of the form "If person x belongs to category A, then do y," or "If a person commits an act x, which is of the category B, then do y." An important source of discretion comes from the fact that the categories (A, B) often have ill-defined boundaries. Street-level bureaucrats are, accordingly, entrusted with the power to "draw the line" where they see fit. This is not just a technical question but one that implicates a value judgment.

While it is true that fuzzy boundaries can sometimes be clarified, they are hard to avoid entirely. Vagueness often reflects the distress of policymakers at having to disentangle precise categories of people (suffering from a difficulty "A") from a social reality that is much more complex (in which problem "A" is bound up with other problems "B" and "C" through intricate

53 ·

causal linkages). Take the example of the Social Security Administration (SSA) disability program. Congress has expressly specified that "persons are disabled if *unable* to work by reason of their *medical* condition."[58] This definition establishes a distinction between "persons who have medical problems and who cannot find work on that account" and the subcategory of "persons who have medical problems and on that account are neither substantially gainfully employed nor indeed able to work."[59] The disability program covers only the latter. Workers who are able to work despite their health problems will not count as "disabled," even if their condition is severe enough that employers will systematically prefer to hire other candidates. As Jerry Mashaw points out, this stems from a desire to distinguish the disability program from other government programs that are meant to address the problem of unemployment.

The definition adopted by Congress has the benefit of being clear, but it rests on a questionable assumption, namely, that someone's ability to do a job has an intrinsic meaning distinct from its economic implications. Mashaw asks, "Can it really be sensible to say that although a person is, because of medical impairments, too far back in the labor queue ever to be employed, yet that same person is not disabled because of these same medical impairments?"[60]

When such difficulties became apparent, Congress reversed course and clarified its mandate: the Social Services Administration "should avoid turning disability into unemployment, but . . . should be 'realistic' about it." Congress also instructed the SSA to take into consideration two factors—age and educational levels—that have no relation to a person's "medical disability" but that may have considerable influence over their likelihood to find gainful employment. The purpose of these measures was to blur the boundaries of a category that had been defined too clearly. The vagueness that resulted effectively gave low-ranking adjudicators the leeway to handle a range of cases (people who are able to work but who cannot find work because of their medical condition) that would otherwise have fallen through the cracks. Discretion here is desirable insofar as it allows frontline officials to do justice to the particularities of cases that would otherwise be arbitrarily distinguished by hard boundaries.

If fuzzy boundaries can be necessary to allow street-level bureaucrats to respond adequately to the needs of individual clients, they can also emerge out of a concern for fairness, as lawmakers try to expand the contours of a benefit program to cover all those who have a legitimate claim to being covered. We subscribe to the belief that cases that are alike in all *relevant respects* should be treated alike. The specification of what those "relevant respects" are is a task for policymakers. The latter face a difficult tradeoff between instituting clear cutoff lines, which would promote transparency and consistency across street-level bureaucrats, and acknowledging that similarity must be assessed along many dimensions, some of which may be less measurable and more "subjective" than others.

Consider, for instance, the American with Disabilities Act's (ADA) definition of disability that inspectors from the Equal Employment Opportunity Commission (EEOC) must use. The definition specifies that with respect to an individual, the term "disability" means:

(A) a physical or mental impairment that substantially limits one or more of the major life activities of such individual;

(B) a record of such an impairment; or

(C) being regarded as having such an impairment.[61]

The boundaries demarcated by clauses A and B are relatively clear: the medical record should, in most cases, be able to speak directly for itself. Clause C, however, is more elusive. It requires the inspector to assess whether potential employers *perceive* the job candidate as disabled. This assessment is, of course, not based merely on an impressionistic judgment. It calls for a close investigation of the reasons employers offer for not hiring the candidate. But the explanations offered, especially in the context of an investigation, are not always reliable, and the facts required to assess them not always forthcoming. A hiring decision, after all, does not turn only on clearly observable metrics (such as test scores) but also involves a host of other factors that are hard to pin down.

The application of clause C is therefore likely to be more discretionary, and harder to review, than the first two. And yet, lawmakers seem to have decided that it would be unfair to scrap the clause. Individuals who are *regarded* as disabled effectively suffer the consequences of disability in finding employment, even if they lack the medical condition. In an important respect, they are "similar" to the individuals covered under clauses A and B.

This example goes to show that even when we could institute clean cutoff lines, we sometimes prefer not to. There are conditions in which we are willing to tolerate the risk of a certain kind of arbitrariness (inconsistency at the hands of street-level bureaucrats) if the alternative involves the rigid institutionalization of another kind of arbitrariness (an arbitrary cutoff point).

Uncertainty

In addition to dealing with fuzzy boundaries, street-level bureaucrats must also make judgments under conditions of uncertainty. When deciding how to interact with clients, they must typically assess a series of "factual premises." How long has the applicant been unemployed? Is the applicant disabled? The answer to these questions will, in turn, guide the bureaucrat toward the choice of an appropriate procedure. While some factual premises can be gathered easily and unequivocally, the facts may, at times, be uncertain. Uncertainty is an unavoidable feature of the world we live in, and one that will keep plaguing the implementation of public policy. The question is not whether we should accommodate such uncertainty (decisions will ultimately *have to be taken*), but how we should handle it and to whom we should entrust its handling.

Since decisions under uncertainty are frequent and since they must often be taken rapidly, street-level bureaucrats typically develop rules of thumb ("If in doubt, do x"). These rules of thumb actually express values or preferences. Adjudicators who decide that under doubt they will err on the side of recognizing a claimant as "disabled," or officers who decide to treat cases where the suspect may be armed as if the suspect were indeed armed, are expressing preferences, respectively, regarding who should count as "disabled," or regarding the level of risk that an officer should be expected to tolerate.

Since responses to uncertainty exhibit some regularity, one may wonder why they should be delegated to street-level bureaucrats at the point of application. The question hinges, in part, on how much regularity rules of thumb actually provide (how rule-like are they?). In some cases, it may be possible to replace them with formal procedures, and this may be advisable since heuristics often serve as a refuge for implicit biases and idiosyncratic preferences.

To the extent that discretion over the handling of uncertainty remains at the street level, however, it is because we presume, quite reasonably, that the people who are most apt to make such rules of thumb, and to know when the rules ought to be suspended, are those who are closest to the case at hand, both because they possess unrivaled knowledge of the specifics of the case and because they can draw on an accumulated reservoir of tacit knowledge.

Soft Evidence

Another factor that contributes to expanding the scope of street-level discretion is that frontline workers are routinely asked to pay attention to considerations that are hard to measure and assess—that is, to "soft evidence," which is often qualitative and experiential.

It may be difficult to determine, for instance, whether a person should count as "disabled" under any sensible administrative definition of the term.[62] The difficulty in collecting the required factual premises may be due to a lack of evidence (the medical record could be fragmentary) or to uncertainty in the evidence (it may be unclear whether the medical condition is likely to maintain itself over time). But the difficulty could also be due to the fact that some of the evidence that is deemed pertinent does not lend itself well to being measured objectively: To what degree is the person's functioning impaired by the disability? How well do they "deal with it"?

The difficulty in assessing such soft evidence is compounded by the fact that many of the judgments that street-level bureaucrats must make are about people.[63] A child protective services worker who finds bruises on a child's hands must decide whether or not the explanation that the parents provide is convincing.[64] A police officer must decide, similarly, whether or not to give a ticket to someone for a minor speed infraction. In the absence of hard data (Did the parents abuse the child? Did the driver intend to break the speed limit, and will they do it again?), street-level bureaucrats are forced to rely on a combination of "hard facts" and a host of somewhat more subjective cues. The child protective services worker will pay close attention to the nature of the bruises and to the parents' previous record but will also stay attuned to the logical flow of the story, to the parents' tone of voice, to their hesitations, their demeanor, and to how they address the child. The police officer will look at the driver's record but will also take note of his tone, attitude, expression of remorse, and other signs that may indicate whether or not he has "learned his lesson." Street-level bureaucrats do not simply assess observable facts—they are forced, by the nature of their work, to gauge people.

The difficulty in assessing soft evidence is further exacerbated by the frequent absence of independent criteria to assess, in retrospect, whether the ultimate decision (for instance, disabled or not) was correct. One cannot look at the claimant's life pattern after the decision for confirmation or indictment. A claimant who has been categorized as "disabled," and who is thus entitled to benefits, will be more likely to remain unemployed; a claimant who has not will be more likely to take up a physically demanding job. The decisions of bureaucrats are in part self-fulfilling prophecies. The potential for a gradual calibration of judgment over time is thereby limited.

While the use of soft evidence opens the possibility of inconsistent treatment, there are at least two reasons why we should be reluctant to disregard such information altogether. First, soft evidence may combine a host of considerations that cannot be precisely disentangled or measured but that can nevertheless be pertinent. There are various factors that go into explaining why a policeman finds a situation "threatening," or whether a border protection officer has "reasonable suspicion" to search someone's baggage. It would be extremely difficult to parse out precisely what goes into such judgments, which have been cultivated by years of training and experience. Preserving a space for discretion along these lines amounts to a recognition of epistemic humility: we may not be able to offer a programmatic recipe that performs better.

Second, soft evidence often tracks features of the world that we think are important, even though we cannot properly measure them. We tend to think, for instance, that it matters *how well* someone is able to function with a disability, and that the level of assistance they receive should take this into consideration. Taking into account the lived experience of individuals is part of what it means to treat them with respect. Ignoring such information—on the grounds that it is soft and that it therefore opens the way for bureaucratic discretion—would be tantamount to disregarding our own normative convictions.

Unpredictability

The rational systems perspective does not pay much attention to how organizations relate to their surrounding environment. As organization theorists have pointed out, however, characteristics of the environment can have serious implications for the internal structure of organizations. If the tasks that an organization has to perform are well defined, and if they have to be performed in a stable environment, then rules and standard operating procedures can be developed and followed ad infinitum (one can think, for instance, of a controlled factory setting). If an organization is more sensitive to its environment, however, and if this environment is unpredictable, then the organization may have to reduce its reliance on rigid rules and procedures and grant its operators the discretion to respond with more flexibility to unforeseen situations.[65]

By virtue of their position at the outward-facing nodes of the bureaucratic apparatus, street-level bureaucrats are exposed, first and foremost, to the unpredictability and volatility of the surrounding environment.[66] Policemen do not know, and cannot anticipate, the full range of situations they will likely confront, much less the particular response that will be appropriate. Social workers cannot foresee the specific combination of unfortunate events that may affect a particular claimant. We give street-level bureaucrats discretion because we know that factors can add up in unexpected ways and because we want them to have enough flexibility to be able to respond to such situations adequately.

It would be possible, of course, to curtail this discretion by spelling out, in advance, how bureaucrats ought to respond to future cases on the basis of how we think they ought to respond to cases we are already familiar with. H. L. A. Hart warns us, however, that to do this would be "to secure a measure of certainty or predictability at the cost of blindly prejudging what is to be done in a range of future cases, about whose composition we are ignorant. We shall thus indeed succeed in settling in advance, but also in the dark, issues which can only reasonably be settled when they arise and are identified."[67]

(It is worth noting that in addition to being a feature of the external environment, unpredictability can also be a strategy that organizations intentionally adopt to prevent clients from outmaneuvering them. This is perhaps clearest in the example of the checkpoint I mentioned in the preface. If those crossing knew exactly what officers were on the lookout for they would adapt in advance and the checkpoint would cease being effective.[68] But the same is true when it comes to the tax code, unemployment benefits, and a whole range of governmental programs: strict rules invite gamesmanship. Discretion can serve to discourage it.)

Entangled Ends

The rational systems perspective distinguishes discretion as to the choice of "means" (discretion over process) from discretion as to the choice of "ends" (discretion over outcome). Under the rubric of "technical discretion," bureaucrats are expected to exert only the former. In practice, however, the choice of means can be hard to disentangle from the choice of ends. I made this point earlier in relation to senior bureaucrats. It also holds at the street level.

Consider the following example, which brings together several of the forms of discretion discussed so far. Upon noticing a group of loud customers assembled outside a bar, a police officer has to decide whether to disperse them or look the other way. The choice, here, is one of ends: the officer has to decide whether maintaining order is, in this specific case, more important than cultivating an amicable rapport with the local community that could be "cashed in" in more serious situations. Should the officer decide to intervene, however, various means are available. Depending on the neighborhood, on the bar, on the age of the people involved, on what is being said, on whether the officer is alone on patrol or with a colleague, and so forth, the officer will have to decide whether to approach the group with a friendly demeanor or a severe one, whether to ask them politely to go back home or to demand to see identification, whether to wave the threat of an arrest or not. The strategy most conducive to maintaining order is highly context dependent.

But this way of presenting the decision process—as a two-step choice involving first ends, then means—can be misleading. The officer may know, for instance, that an aggressive approach might be most effective at dispersing the gathering but may also suspect that it might lead to an escalation and to a potential arrest. The prospect of such an outcome may lead him to revisit his choice of "ends" (after all, it may be a better idea to maintain peaceable ties with the community) or to radicalize the nature of the end he had initially selected (this will no longer be about "maintaining order," but about enforcing the law and "showing presence"). Such a process of calibration between means and ends, or process and outcome, is as much an exercise in moral judgment as it is an exercise in technical discretion. When means and ends are so entangled, it may be impossible to give street-level bureaucrats the technical discretion we think they ought to have without also effectively giving them normative discretion.

Information Asymmetry and Moral Hazard

I have tried to explain, so far, why street-level bureaucrats have a significant margin of discretion, why this discretion ranges over questions of normative character, and on what grounds it can be justified. It is important to note, however, that the question of discretion is not entirely in our hands. Our capacity to constrain it, should we choose to do so, is limited.

The rational systems perspective rests on the assumption that it is possible for supervisors to control the performance of their subordinates. This may be feasible in organizational environments where principals can observe the actions of their agents ("the output") and where they can assess the quality of such "output" by determining how well it actually advances the goals of the organization ("the outcome").

But the work of street-level bureaucrats does not always lend itself to this kind of control. Frontline workers are often required to work alone and outside, and some of the tasks they perform require privacy with clients. This makes their actions hard to observe. More importantly, perhaps, many of the tasks they must perform do not yield an outcome that can easily be tracked and appraised. It may be possible to keep track of *what* street-level bureaucrats do (How many tickets did they give? How many cases did they close?), but it is hard to assess *how well* they do it when one is not present with them at the decision point (Did they give tickets to the right people? Did they pay proper attention to the client's case before closing it?).

From a principal–agent standpoint, street-level bureaucracy gives rise to an acute problem of moral hazard. Much of what principals know about what street-level bureaucrats do, and how well they do it, is conveyed by street-level bureaucrats themselves. And the latter, of course, have an incentive to dissimulate poor performance and to focus exclusively on observable metrics. In such circumstances, there is no guarantee that organizational goals will be pursed in good faith, or that rules and procedures would be followed even if they existed.

This sobering observation can lead managers down a different path. Since they cannot adequately appraise the actions of their subordinates, they find themselves forced to rely, at least partially, on their subordinates' own sense of responsibility. Such a sense of responsibility, however, is not cultivated by adding more rules or by developing more granular performance metrics, but by promoting bureaucrats' self-regard, by creating a culture based on trust, and by resorting to a range of "soft" managerial tools that shape the "ethos" of the organization and the internal values of its operators. Interestingly, it is the very recognition that hierarchical control has limited reach that may drive managers to expand the scope of their subordinates' discretion in an effort to change the organizational culture of the workplace.[69]

Such an approach has at least two advantages. First, relying on internal values, rather than on external monitoring, can lower transaction costs, and therefore make the organization more efficient.[70] Second, accepting the reality of discretion and making room for it can motivate workers to invest themselves more fully in their role. John Patty and Sean Gailmard have argued, in this vein, that one of the reasons why principals might want to endow their agents with discretion and autonomy is to incentivize them to develop the expertise and knowledge required to perform their job well. The thought is that agents are more likely to invest themselves at work if they are given space to express their own preferences and values. Patty and Gailmard suggest that the benefits of granting discretion may sometimes outweigh the costs, even if the agents' values and preferences diverge somewhat from those of their principals.

Conclusion

The various factors I have just discussed—ambiguous goals, conflicting goals, limited resources, fuzzy boundaries, uncertainty, soft evidence, unpredictability, entangled ends, and information asymmetry—all contribute to expanding the scope of street-level discretion far beyond the "technical discretion" allowed in the compliance model of bureaucratic responsibility, and in the rational systems perspective on organizations that undergirds it. Recall that "technical discretion," as I presented it in the first section, involves three types of judgment: (1) an interpretive judgment as to the meaning of the rules or the nature of the objective to be pursued, (2) a subsumptive judgment relating a state of the world to administrative categories, and (3) an expert judgment as to which means are most conducive to attaining the desired goal.

We have seen, however, that street-level bureaucrats are forced to go beyond the *interpretive* exercise described in (1), because the goals they inherit are often too vague, ambiguous, and conflicting to yield determinate guidance. In the absence of the goal specificity promised by the rational systems perspective, street-level bureaucrats have no choice but to set their own ends, within the scope of reasonable construals. This takes them outside the realm of technical discretion proper and forces them to engage in the moral and political task of assessing, weighing, and resolving questions of value.

We have seen, as well, that the subsumptive judgments described in (2) can be rather intricate because they must be made under uncertainty, because they involve subjective factors, and because the administrative categories themselves often have vague boundaries. We are a far cry from the "objective criteria" promised by the rational systems perspective. Street-level bureaucrats must provide answers to questions such as: Where should the line be drawn? Which way should one lean when the facts are unclear? What criteria, or reference scale, should one use when gauging subjective assessments? These are questions that cannot be settled on purely technical grounds and through which value judgments will inevitably transpire.

We have observed, moreover, that the expert judgments made in (3) are not exclusively technical either. Such judgments can impinge upon the choice of ends and can reveal new values or objectives that must then be evaluated, appraised, and weighed against others. Even here, at the "heart" of technical discretion, the moral faculties of street-level bureaucrats are solicited.

We have noted, finally, that because of limited resources, street-level bureaucrats are required to make judgments about resource allocation: *whom* to apply resources to, and *how much*. These are not technical questions: they involve assessing the needs of various people, comparing the urgency of their problems, and striking difficult compromises between values such as efficiency, responsiveness, and fairness.

I have tried to suggest, in parallel, that while street-level discretion ranges over questions of value, and while it is sometimes excessive and in need of being curtailed, it would be a mistake to seek to eliminate it altogether. There are several reasons why discretion is desirable at the front lines of the state. Such discretion allows bureaucrats to effectively pursue policy goals that cannot be precisely codified because their meaning varies depending upon context and situation ("Ambiguous Goals"). It enables them to attend to conflicts between goals and process values and to tackle difficult questions of resource allocation in a way that is sensitive to context and responsive to the particularities of citizens' circumstances and needs ("Conflicting Goals and Values," "Limited Resources"). It allows bureaucrats to mobilize their local knowledge to decide how to best handle cases that fall on fuzzy boundaries and that involve uncertain or soft evidence that it would be unfair or disrespectful to ignore ("Fuzzy Boundaries," "Uncertainty," "Soft Evidence"). It gives bureaucrats flexibility to adapt to unanticipated cases and situations without blindly prejudging them ("Unpredictability"). It can also encourage bureaucrats to invest themselves more fully in their work ("Information Asymmetry and Moral Hazard"). Discretion over questions of value may, finally, prove impossible to disentangle from desirable forms of technical discretion ("Entangled Ends"). These considerations will not always outweigh the risks that discretion poses, but they often will.

We are now in a position to revisit the two challenges to the compliance model that I promised in the Introduction:

(1) *Given how our bureaucracies operate today,* it would be a mistake to use the compliance model of bureaucratic responsibility to assess the performance of street-level bureaucrats across the board. Such a model rests on an overly narrow characterization of what bureaucrats are called upon to do, and relying on it would have several unwelcome consequences. It would direct our attention disproportionately to procedural compliance and divert it from the substantive judgments that frontline bureaucrats make.[71] It would deprive us of the means to

hold such bureaucrats accountable for their judgments.[72] It would also encourage bureaucrats to disguise their substantive judgments under the guise of rule-following, which would make them harder to detect.

(2) *Even if it were possible to engage in institutional reform,* we would still have good reason to preserve a substantial margin of discretion at the front lines of the state. Most importantly, perhaps, such discretion is necessary in contexts where the policy goals and values (e.g., efficiency, fairness, responsiveness, respect) of the democratic state are ambiguous or pull in competing directions. Reducing the scope of discretion, in such conditions, would make agents of the state less able to attend to the particularities of citizens' circumstances and needs in ways that can do justice to these goals and values.

The following chapters start from the premise that street-level discretion is here to stay, and examine how the moral dispositions of bureaucrats inform its exercise.

CHAPTER TWO

Three Pathologies
The Indifferent, the Enforcer, and the Caregiver

We have seen that although street-level bureaucrats occupy the lowest ranks of the administrative state, they nevertheless retain a significant margin of discretion in performing their role. This discretion, moreover, is not merely technical, but also ranges over questions of value: frontline workers are expected to balance normative considerations that do not always go together and must give practical content to hierarchical directives that are frequently vague, ambiguous, and conflicting. The existence of such discretion makes it possible for street-level bureaucrats to inhabit their role in a variety of ways.

The purpose of this chapter is threefold: to provide a framework for thinking about how street-level bureaucrats inhabit their role; to describe three common yet pathological ways in which they do so; and to suggest, in contradistinction, the outlines of a seemingly modest ethic for street-level bureaucrats—one that I will develop further in Chapter 3. I argue that if we want to understand how street-level bureaucrats make use of their discretion in ethically charged situations, we cannot restrict our attention, as organizational theorists and moral philosophers often do, to the moment of ethical decision-making alone and to the process of moral reasoning that precedes it.[1] We need to look, more broadly, at the moral dispositions that street-level bureaucrats develop while on the job, because these dispositions are antecedent to, and in part determinative of, the decisions they take.[2] Moral dispositions shape how bureaucrats perceive and frame the cases they encounter and what considerations they are inclined to prioritize when responding to them.

Shifting our attention from the study of decisions to that of dispositions brings into focus a host of ethical tasks that lie upstream from the moment of moral decision-making. It allows us to shed light, as well, on a range of pathological dispositions—indifference, caregiving, and enforcement—that are distinct from the more familiar problems of corruption, rule breaking, and abuse of discretion. These dispositions are troubling not because they incite bureaucrats to transgress the boundaries of their role but because they involve reductive, or overly specialized, takes on the role. They are, moreover, insidious; those who fall prey to them can fail to live up to their responsibilities even as they remain well intentioned, civic-minded, and within the scope of their prerogatives.

The chapter begins, in the first and second sections, with an extended commentary on two stories in which street-level bureaucrats recount prior interactions with clients. I rely on these stories, which were collected by Steven Maynard-Moody and Michael Musheno, to identify some of the characteristic features of the bureaucratic encounter and to shed light on how bureaucrats experience such encounters.[3] By drawing on empirical material gathered by other scholars, I hope to show that there is value in re-analyzing qualitative data, as is more common with quantitative data. It is important to keep in mind, as I present these stories, that they are *retellings*: they are not just faithful descriptions of the bureaucratic encounter but also attempts to rationalize, justify, and legitimize one's behavior before an audience. This makes the stories more, rather than less, interesting for the purposes of my argument, and I will try to explain why as I unpack them.

For the sake of comparability, the two stories I have chosen are told by vocational rehabilitation counselors working in a broadly similar organizational environment. The stories themselves are not meant to be outlandish—they will have an air of *déjà vu* to those familiar with street-level bureaucracy—but they are not ordinary either, and this is what makes them "good" stories worth telling.[4] I have picked these stories not because they are representative of the average bureaucratic encounter (whatever that might be) but because in them we see street-level bureaucrats adopt a range of dispositions that are common at the front lines of public service—dispositions that I and others have observed while conducting fieldwork. To be sure, these dispositions are not the only ones available to street-level bureaucrats (one cannot pretend to offer a general descriptive account on the basis of only two stories), but they capture bureaucrats' stances toward three of the core demands of street-level work: people processing, service provision, and regulation.

In the third and fourth sections, I make use of three concepts—local dispositions ("modes of appraisal"), enduring dispositions ("moral dispositions"), and "role conceptions"—to extract from the two stories a framework that can be useful more broadly. I show that dispositions vary along two primary dimensions that track, respectively, the level of the bureaucrat's personal involvement in the case at hand and the nature of such involvement. In the fourth and fifth sections, I focus on the dispositions that occupy the three extreme poles along these two dimensions—indifference, enforcement, and caregiving—and examine them from the standpoint of normative political theory. I argue that these dispositions are, each in its own way, pathological because they involve a reductive commitment to one dimension of the role at the expense of others.

The Counselor and the "Pussycat"

A vocational rehabilitation counselor recounts one of her encounters with a client:

> I had a male client who came in for service. He had a physical problem. He was an upholsterer—this was his profession. He had a back injury, and he was having a lot of trouble because he had to lift furniture and do a lot of pulling with his hands and arms. I think he probably got a worker's comp settlement out of it, but he wanted to go back into that type of work. He wanted to know what could be done for him so he could go back.
>
> I sent him "work hardening," where they teach you how to lift properly and do exercises to strengthen your muscles. He went through it successfully and he was able to go back to work in his profession.[5]

The story so far describes a "routine case handled routinely."[6] The counselor receives a client who has a well-defined need (to go back to work after a back injury); the need falls squarely within the counselor's jurisdiction (vocational rehabilitation). The counselor draws on her expertise to identify an appropriate solution (work hardening), which successfully resolves the problem.

As in most routine cases, the interaction takes place on a technical register and remains highly impersonal. We learn little about the client. The only details mentioned are those directly relevant to the administrative case (his professional history and his current difficulties). And we learn virtually nothing about the counselor. Her subjective features—her state of mind, her appreciation of the client, her own personal history—are effaced.

Notice that the encounter is traversed, through and through, by a subtle asymmetry of power. The client enters the stage as a "claimant" who comes to ask for services and who has much at stake in the outcome of the interaction. The counselor, on the other hand, is effectively a "gatekeeper" who has little at stake personally and can decide whether to grant access to services or not. The language itself is telling. The client is uncertain—he does not know what treatment he should ask for nor whether he is entitled to it ("he wanted to know"); the counselor can respond to these doubts with authoritative answers and concrete practical guidance ("I sent him"). The asymmetry also manifests itself in what the narrative overlooks. From the perspective of the counselor, the encounter starts when the client enters her office. From the perspective of the client, however, the face-to-face meeting is only one part of the bureaucratic experience, and typically not the longest. The counselor's story leaves out the time he had to spend in the waiting room and the relative status that such time assigns to the two parties even before their encounter takes place.[7]

The passage provides us with an example of what organizational theorists typically describe as an instance of "decision-making." The counselor emits an "output" (the resolution to send the client work hardening) on the basis of informational "input" that she gathers through the exchange. There is, of course, some truth to this characterization. But notice that there is no indication in the passage that the counselor effectively experienced the process *as a decision*—that is, as a mental exercise that requires stepping back from the case at hand, reflecting upon it, and resolving to pick one alternative over others. Here again, the choice of words is important. The counselor does not say that she "decided" to send the client to physical training; she simply says that she sent him there, as if that followed immediately from the description of the client's situation. This raises the possibility that the counselor may have simply "known" what to do without having to pass through the mediating processes (of "formal reasoning" and "forming a resolution") that are typically involved in making a decision. Upon hearing the client's story, she simply responded as she had to—*she just sent him there.*

With street-level bureaucrats, as with most workers engaged in repetitive tasks, knowledge is not stored far away, only to be accessed by a cognitive exercise; it is rather embodied and embedded in quasi-automatic modes of response. We are typically in the realm of tacit knowledge.[8] It is interesting to note, in this respect, that when street-level bureaucrats are asked to describe how they go about handling cases, they often resort to the language of "instinct."[9] They reserve the language of "decision-making" for those nonroutine cases in which regular ways of doing (*manières de faire*) must be suspended.

Since the word "decision" is a useful shorthand to describe the resolutions that bureaucrats arrive at, I will continue to use it in what follows. It should be understood, however, that unless otherwise stated, I remain agnostic as to whether these resolutions are experienced, or arrived at, *as decisions.*

But let us return to the story and see how it unfolds. If it had ended here, it would have been a textbook case of vocational rehabilitation. As is so often the case, however, things get more complicated.

> But in the middle of all this [the training], he [the upholsterer] was . . . always getting himself into trouble. He had a live-in who had children. This man had never been married. He was in his early thirties. She was an older woman. She had two or three kids.
>
> He was a very interesting person. Looked real tough. Dressed in black—black jeans; big black motorcycle boots; long, long hair, down to his waist, pulls it back in a ponytail; wears dark glasses; wears muscle shirts, looking real mean and tough. But he is a pussycat.
>
> He is a rescuer. He is a rescuer, he feels sorry for people. This woman didn't have a place to live, and she had a story of woe and problems, and he took her into his home with her kids. They got romantically involved. There were constant problems.

> She got involved with some other guy while she was living with [the client]. He was going through emotional problems and grieving. He came in and was telling me all these things, and he was very agitated and crying.
>
> So I said, "I think you could benefit from some individual therapy so you can deal with all the problems you are having. I can take you over to the mental health center. I'll call ahead. I'll take you over there and get you set up."
>
> He said, "Okay."[10]

The story takes an interesting turn. We learn that the client, who had allegedly been successful reintegrating into his profession, is in a state of psychological distress and needs further assistance.

Several aspects of this passage are worth highlighting. First, and perhaps most obviously, the interaction goes beyond the routine. The provisional solution that had been offered at first (work hardening) turns out to be insufficient, and the client comes back to seek additional help. The nature of the new difficulty, which is no longer physical but psychological, calls for another kind of rapport, and for a different solution. But while this case is not standard, it is far from extraordinary. Deviations from the "textbook case"—due to errors and complications, or to the insufficient granularity of administrative rules and categories (see Chapter 1)—are frequent. This story is an example of what we could call the "ordinary nonroutine": cases that cannot be handled promptly but that fall within the range of situations that street-level bureaucrats are familiar with. Routine and "ordinary nonroutine" form the bulk of street-level work. We can contrast them with the "extraordinary nonroutine"—that is, with cases that are unexpected and that public officials are potentially ill prepared to handle (e.g., emergencies).

We also learn from this passage that the interaction between the worker and the counselor was not a one-off event, but that it took place over a period of time and that it may have involved several interactions ("he *was always getting* himself into trouble"). Such protracted relationships are more common for some street-level bureaucrats (counselors, teachers) than for others (reception agents), but they occur across the board. There are at least two reasons for this. First, a relatively small stratum of the population consume a disproportionate share of public services, and this inevitably makes for "repeat clients." Second, clients who receive public services are asked to check in regularly with governmental agencies as a way of monitoring progress, of tracking changes in status, and of dissuading potential fraud—repeat encounters serve as a tool of governance. It is not unusual, therefore, for counselors, welfare workers, and reception agents, much like police officers stationed on a beat, to become well acquainted with their clients over time. It is because these encounters with clients are multiple and because they take place face-to-face that the counselor is able to provide a detailed description of the client's clothing style (motorcycle boots, long hair, muscle shirts), personal life (he had a live-in, they got romantically involved), and character traits (he is a pussycat and a rescuer).

The face-to-face nature of street-level work has another important consequence: it invites clients to present their own life stories, often at considerable length. Needless to say, such stories do not come with administrative labels, but with an abundance of information that must be sorted out and interpreted before it can be utilized. It is up to the bureaucrat to "translate" these stories into actionable administrative categories. The client who is betrayed by the woman to whom he has kindly opened his home is suffering from "emotional problems." He is in need of "individual therapy," which can be delivered by a "mental health center." As any real exercise in translation, this process calls for a certain margin of creative re-description and force-fitting.[11]

Let me now turn to what is perhaps the most striking difference between the first and second part of the story: the transformation in the nature of the description of the client. Recall that in the first passage, the client was practically reduced to the features of his case (an upholsterer with a back injury). This bare sketch gives way in the second passage to a rich and multifaceted portrait that ranges over physical attributes, personal history, and character traits. The client acquires individuating features and comes to life as a full-fledged person. It is as if the counselor had taken off her bureaucratic spectacles and had finally acknowledged the man behind the "case."

It is important to note that while the description starts out being neutral (he had a live-in, he had never been married) or ambivalent (getting into trouble, interesting person), it quickly acquires a positive undertone. Despite the client's toughness, we learn that, deep inside, he is a "pussycat" and a "rescuer." These terms are key because they are descriptive and valuational at once (to use a phrase coined by Bernard Williams, they are "thick ethical concepts"[12]). They describe the client, but one cannot help but discern in their use a hint of sympathy or acquiescence. The client becomes endearing—and how could he not? A rough man with a heart of gold, who breaks down in tears over a woman, in full biker gear. . . .

We can almost picture the scene. And the fact that it seems a bit too perfect—a Hollywood cutout with gendered overtones—is telling. The counselor is not merely recording the features of the client "as they truly are." She is, in part, constructing an identity for him, building up his personality as a coherent whole on the basis of selective cues.[13] It is hard to tell where description ends and construction starts. We can hazard to guess, however, that some of the counselor's own observations did not readily fit the portrait presented here, and that these observations were discounted— as they typically are—when the overall picture was drawn up (in the counselor's mind) and put in story form (for the consumption of others).

Notice that the changing nature of the description goes hand in hand with an implicit transformation in the disposition of the counselor. In this passage, she no longer engages with the client as a distant bureaucrat routinely handling a case. She has become involved as a *sympathetic listener* or, perhaps even further, as a *confidante*, patiently hearing the stories of the client and witnessing his emotional distress. The counselor has been "pulled out," so to speak, of her bureaucratic indifference, and is now involved in the interaction *as a person*. Her perceptual and affective faculties are stirred and mobilized by the client's story. We are a far cry from Weber's ideal of an impersonal and dehumanized bureaucrat.

With this kind of buildup, it is not surprising that the counselor would be willing, by the end of the passage, to go out of her way to help the client receive therapy. If the outcome of the encounter—the determination to go and help—comes as an anticlimactic *dénouement*, it is because the counselor's inclinations have already been built into the description of the situation. The case, or justification, for helping the client is embedded in the sympathetic tone of the narrative and in the use of normatively laden descriptors like "pussycat" and "rescuer." This should serve as a reminder that "war stories" are not just descriptions or explanations of the factors that motivated workers to act the way they did but also attempts at rationalizing their behavior and justifying it to others. This makes these stories particularly interesting because they help us capture variations in the repertoires of normative justification that street-level bureaucrats utilize. (As we will see in Chapter 5, such variations exist not just between agencies, but even among colleagues in the same workplace.)

It is interesting to observe, in this regard, the considerations on the basis of which the counselor comes to the conclusion that she ought to help the client. There is no indication, in the story, that she may have actively considered, and ultimately dismissed, the many reasons (moral and practical) that could be marshaled in favor of *not* helping the upholsterer. Wouldn't the counselor's time be better spent with other clients? Wouldn't the decision to help set an unsustainable precedent? Wouldn't she run the risk of being reprimanded by her superiors? Instead of offering a detailed evaluation of the pros and cons of helping the client, the counselor seems to have been intent, rather, on assessing his *deservingness.* Once the upholsterer was found to be trustworthy, endearing, and in need, the decision to help followed.

But the story is not over yet. It takes another turn, as the counselor and the client encounter an unresponsive intake worker.

> I drive him over there [the mental health center]. He wants me to go in with him because he has never had to deal with anything like this before. I go in. There's an intake worker. She's not the warmest, friendliest person. I talked with her a while. She sends us to the business office.
>
> "How are you going to pay for this? It's fifty dollars an hour."
>
> And [the upholsterer] says, "I can't do this. I can't pay for this."
>
> "Well, then you are going to have to write something about your financial situation to see if we can reduce your costs."
>
> We go back to the intake worker and talk to her a while. "Well, I can schedule you for an appointment in two weeks."[14]

The setting of the story has now changed from the counselor's office to the mental health center. We learn that the counselor drove the client there and that she has agreed to accompany him inside. We hear her present the client's case first to an unresponsive intake worker, then to a business representative. When that procedure fails to yield the desired result, we see her engage with the intake worker again so as to negotiate a reasonable price and schedule an appointment. The counselor does all of this on behalf of the client, while he remains mostly silent and fades into the background.

The transition that was announced at the end of the last passage has, so it seems, now come to full fruition: the counselor is no longer a sympathetic listener—she has effectively become an *advocate* on behalf of the client. This transformation in the disposition of the counselor comes hand in hand with a reconfiguration of her relationship to the bureaucratic apparatus. Recall that, in the first part of the story, the counselor appeared firmly encrusted in her administrative environment. She received the client in her office, and we can presume that she addressed him, both literally and figuratively, from across the desk. At no moment did she dissociate herself from the institution that she was representing. Up to that point, the counselor formed an integral part of what clients often refer to, disparagingly, as "the system."

But the counselor has now landed on the other side of the counter. She stands side by side with the client, trying in vain to induce an unresponsive intake worker into taking action. It is the intake worker who has now come to personify the coldness and rigidity of the bureaucratic system ("she's not the warmest, friendliest person"). The intake worker's response is, of course, the one we most commonly associate with bureaucracy—a kind of obstinate indifference.

Note that there are several reasons that could account for the intake worker's lack of responsiveness. Some may be practical. She may be worried about "getting into trouble" for making an exception or may simply be reluctant to go the "extra mile" ("Why bother? The day is almost over"). But the worker's impassivity could also betray a moral stance. She may have come to believe, for instance, that the upholsterer's case is not particularly urgent and that it would be unfair, accordingly, to schedule him ahead of other patients. She may also have become suspicious because of the presence of the counselor. "Surely," she could be thinking, "this client should not be entitled to receive preferential treatment simply because he happened to enlist the help of an articulate advocate."

If the counselor was "pulled out" of her bureaucratic impassivity through her encounter with the client, the intake worker has, on the contrary, withdrawn deeper under the bureaucratic cloak. As we will see later, this does not necessarily mean that the worker is unconcerned, but only that she has developed one of the attitudes that can best be expressed via the appearance of bureaucratic rigidity. Punctilious adherence to rules can be a manifestation of indifference, but it can also be a way of punishing "undeserving clients." We will see an example of this in the second story.

For now, notice that the counselor voices no sympathy for the intake worker and for the questions or dilemmas that the worker might be facing. This is so despite (or perhaps because of) the similarity between the intake worker's position and the one that the counselor was occupying earlier in her office. Now that the counselor has become involved as an *advocate,* the intake worker is no longer the bearer of a different breed of normative considerations (from the standpoint of which coldness and rigidity could well be virtues) but simply an obstacle to overcome on her way to advancing the interests of her client.

It is important to note, finally, that even though the counselor now engages with the bureaucratic apparatus from the standpoint of the client, she is far from being an ordinary client herself. The fact that she is an insider gives her an edge in navigating the inscrutable and alienating world of bureaucracy. Street-level bureaucrats acquire, over time, a deep knowledge of how the bureaucratic process works. They form networks that range across agencies. They know whom to call and how to frame a case so as to maximize chances of success. Even at the mental health center, the counselor has more power and influence than the upholsterer, who is forced to rely on her as a providential guide. This informal know-how is one of the most precious resources that street-level bureaucrats can distribute to their clients. And yet, unlike the official resources they have at their disposal (goods, services, time), the allocation of "tips," "advice," and "suggestions" is an informal affair that remains largely closed off to hierarchical scrutiny.

Despite her efforts, however, the counselor fails to secure an early appointment for the client. The story goes on:

[The upholsterer] is getting very angry and agitated. I kept saying, "It's okay, it's okay. Take it easy."

He said, "This isn't going to work. I'm not going to do this." He was getting very agitated.

So I said to the intake worker, "We need to leave now because he needs to talk to someone right now."

We went out to my car at the mental health center parking lot, and I sat there approximately two hours doing crisis counseling because he needed it right then. He couldn't be put off; he was angry and agitated. He was in such an emotional state that I said to myself, "Okay, I'll do it." I knew that I was going to have to do it because he needed it right then, and there wasn't anyone else who was going to provide that service to him. . . .

Eventually, I closed his case because he went back to work, but I hear back from him every six months. He gets himself into trouble, and he'll come back. We'll go through the crisis counseling, and he's fine until next time.[15]

After the failure of routine treatment and advocacy, the counselor finds herself in a challenging position. The client with whom she has, by this stage, been extensively involved, is worked up and the situation, she feels, is about to spin out of control. "Very angry and agitated," "very agitated," "right now," "right then," "couldn't be put off," "angry and agitated," "such an emotional state"—all make an appearance within the space of six sentences. Since the intake worker was unwilling to recognize the urgency of the case, the counselor finds that she has no other choice but to take matters in her own hands. She proceeds, accordingly, to administer a two-hour-long session of crisis counseling in her car. In this passage, the counselor is no longer merely an *advocate* for the client—she has effectively turned into a *caregiver.*

This fourth (and last) change in disposition is perceptible in the implicit justification that the counselor provides for offering treatment. She does not initiate crisis counseling because the client "deserves" it, because the pros and cons have added up this way, or because her official role requires her to do so, but simply because the client *needs* it. This reference to the client's need as a determining consideration is a staple of the caring professions. As a *caregiver,* the counselor does not pause to wonder whether she has already spent enough time with the upholsterer; she does not bother to estimate how many other cases she could have addressed in two hours. In the context of a caring relationship, these considerations are beside the point.

But is the counselor justified in caring for the upholsterer to such an extent? The gap between her initial standing as an office-bound administrator of the state's resources and her current conduct as a provider of individualized therapy in a parking lot is so wide that one can legitimately wonder whether she has not, in fact, overstepped the boundaries of her official role. I do not wish to settle this question here but simply to point out that if this were indeed the case, the counselor would have overstepped her prerogatives gradually, without crossing any clearly demarcated boundary. Departures from one's role are often the imperceptible result of a seemingly contiguous series of decisions and transformations rather than the outcome of a singular act of dissent or disobedience. ~·Decisions

It is important to note, as well, that the counselor concludes the story on a positive tone. She seems untroubled by her ongoing relationship with the upholsterer, who regularly comes back for help even though his case has long been closed. She puts a favorable spin on the story: each counseling session is good for *a full* six months. But one could, of course, present the same fact in a more somber light: despite the counselor's help, the client *still* breaks down every six months. Depending on one's interpretation of that fact, the ongoing relationship could appear to be benign and supportive, or it could take the allure of a protracted, and potentially perverse, form of personal dependence. It matters a great deal, of course, which way the counselor comes to see things. The bureaucratic encounter does not end with a decision or with the provision of a service. It ends, rather, with a retrospective assessment and evaluation of the interaction and with a set of lessons drawn for future use (Was it a good idea to act as an advocate for the client? Did crisis counseling work? Was crisis counseling a one-off, extraordinary service or should its provision be routinized?).[16]

The counselor's story provides us with a good glimpse into the world of street-level bureaucrats. For all its richness, however, the story leaves out three important features of street-level work. I mention them here briefly and will take them up at greater length subsequently. First, the story makes no mention of the counselor's peers. We know, however, that interpersonal relationships between workers and small-group dynamics play a considerable part in shaping the responses of street-level bureaucrats to individual situations and their approaches to the role more generally.[17] Peers provide support, exert pressure, and act as relays for informal norms. They also serve as thinking partners when a difficult situation comes up. Cases that do not readily fit into standard operating procedures are often decided on the basis of secondary norms of adjudication, which are developed informally among colleagues (I discuss such norms in Chapter 4).[18]

The story also makes no mention of the counselor's personal background. There is a vast literature in public administration that discusses how factors such as class, race, and gender affect the way in which bureaucrats perceive clients and construct identities for them.[19] I will have little to add to existing scholarship on this front. I will have much more to say, however, another characteristic of street-level bureaucrats that is partly explained by the factors just mentioned: the way they come to conceive of their role.

The story of the counselor shows that street-level bureaucrats can move back and forth between various ways of engaging with clients *in the course of a single encounter* (in this case, from being an *indifferent bureaucrat* to being a *sympathetic listener,* an *advocate,* and, finally, a *caregiver*). I call these transient ways of inhabiting the role "local dispositions" or "modes of appraisal." But bureaucrats also develop more enduring styles of work ("moral dispositions") and conceptions of what their role is about *in general* ("role conceptions"), and these lead to systematic regularities *across encounters.* Moral dispositions and role conceptions do not determine a bureaucrat's behavior in any given case but correspond to a propensity to handle cases according to a particular mode of appraisal (e.g., an inclination toward responding as an indifferent, as an enforcer, or as a caregiver). I will return to this in the third and fourth sections.

The third major absence is, oddly enough, the client. In this story, the upholsterer appears to play a passive role. He is there awaiting to be "constructed" and guided by the counselor. But appearances can be deceptive. Clients bring their own strategies and techniques of "presentation of self" to the encounter.[20] People familiar with waiting rooms are keenly aware of the margin of discretion that individual bureaucrats have and are eager to turn it to their advantage. The Internet is replete with advice on how to make an impersonal bureaucrat see you as a person. The tricks involve being respectful, adopting a submissive attitude, treating them as an expert, empathizing with their workload, and so on.[21] This should serve to remind us that if the upholsterer came across as a sympathetic roughneck, as opposed to an irresponsible crybaby or a brute, it is as much *his* doing as it is that of the counselor.

The Undeserving Quadriplegic

The story of the counselor's encounter with the "pussycat" is one of increasing personal involvement. As the story develops, the counselor steps away from being an *indifferent bureaucrat*, routinely processing a "case," and becomes invested on the side of the client. Yet personal involvement in a case does not always take the form of compassion and sympathy; it can, just as often, take the form of suspicion and hostility. I want to present, somewhat more rapidly, a story that is in many respects the mirror image of the one we have just examined. It is told by another vocational rehabilitation counselor and relates to the case of a quadriplegic client, John:

> I have known this guy, [John], for probably five years now. He's a quad. He was one of those wild kids who thought the world was his, and if you drink enough and take enough [drugs]—well, he got really loaded and tried to fly his car over some trees, and it didn't quite make it, so now he is a quad. The catch is, he still thinks if he wants it, he should get it—and he does. . . . An example is attendant care.
>
> John is always going to need attendant care. Period. But John pushes the wire, you know. If you give him two hours, he wants ten. So John gets what I think we can allow: twenty hours a week for attendants.[22]

Here again, the story starts out as a "routine case handled routinely." We learn that John has lost mobility in all four limbs as a result of a driving accident. This makes him utterly dependent on attendant care for everyday activities. John is dissatisfied with the level of assistance he currently receives and asks for more. The counselor turns down the request by appealing to his understanding of the rules ("John gets what I think we can allow").

Up to this point in the story, the counselor is still largely disengaged from the case. Even though the nature of John's disability calls for some measure of sympathy, the counselor voices none. If anything, we can detect a nascent sense of suspicion toward John, one that will acquire considerable proportions later on. The counselor insists on telling us *why* John got into the accident—due to substance abuse. He also makes it a point to stress John's brash or aggressive character—it is this character that got John into the accident and that still manifests itself in his interactions with the bureaucracy. Still, the counselor's tone is fairly restrained.

But as the story moves along, the client becomes even more insistent:

> Attendant care is supposed to be for bodily type things, you know, dressing, bathing, bowel, bladder, that kind of thing.
>
> Well, John's idea of an attendant is to do those things and go get him a newspaper and cigarettes and light a cigarette, stick it in [John's] mouth, and stand there and turn the pages. Go to class [for John] and take notes. Drive him here and there. You know, we are talking darn near personal slaves, minimum-wage slaves.
>
> So, John insists he has to have at least ten hours a day. Well, that is more than twenty hours a week, and the counselor says, "This is all that is allowed, period."[23]

In constantly pushing for more services, John unsettles an unspoken arrangement that governs the interaction between street-level bureaucrats and their clients. The latter are expected to remain somewhat quiescent and deferential—even though they are, properly speaking, not asking for "help" but for services they are legally entitled to. The counselor, who was already wary of John because of his lifestyle before the crash, becomes even more vigilant.

We learn that John may be taking advantage of the system by asking his attendants to perform services he is not entitled to receive. Interestingly, the counselor does not treat John's misuse of state resources as a mere administrative matter; he voices his *personal indignation*. He does so by inverting the relationship of the quadriplegic to his attendants—it is no longer John who is dependent on his attendants for help; it is they who are enslaved to him.

In other circumstances, the counselor may have erred on the side of leniency. Not here. Since the counselor suspects John of trying to game the system, he responds by upholding his commitment to the rules in place. The rules, which were practically absent from the first story, now reappear in full force; it is through them that the "system" can be protected from clients like John. We see here that while rules often act as a constraint on behavior, they can also serve as a "tool" that can be mobilized selectively to separate the deserving from the undeserving.[24]

The counselor's categorical refusal ("this is all that is allowed, period") would have been enough to silence most clients. But John turns out to be uncharacteristically tenacious. He tries to circumvent the counselor—and he succeeds.

> Well, since that was not good enough, he promptly called [his U.S. senator]. So the next thing we know we are getting a call: the [state welfare] commissioner is calling the rehab commissioner who is calling the supervisor who is calling my old supervisor who is calling me, and now John has got all the hours he wants.
>
> So what happens is, I can sit here and say, "This lady has got to have a car to get a job. She's got the job, everything is set, but she needs $1,000."
>
> "No, that is not something we do. We don't buy cars, period."
>
> But [the decision to give ten hours a day of attendant care] comes down from top down. So what happens is if you yell enough at the right people, and you know the system, then they don't like that, so they will fix the problem just to shut [the complainer] up.
>
> So on this particular guy, we have spent a fortune. . . .
>
> The squeaky wheel is the one that won't shut up. So the poor little nice guy who is just kind of sitting there, they get whatever crumbs or whatever happens to come along that we can do.[25]

Instead of accepting the decision of the counselor, John contacts his representative, who puts downward pressure on the agency. The counselor is forced to reverse his decision in view of his superiors.

This goes to show that clients too have both formal and nonformal resources at their disposal. The intervention of an elected representative or of a powerful advocate is, by all means, a rare occurrence, but it is always a lingering possibility and one that street-level bureaucrats are keen to avoid. Should such an intervention occur, however, it does not necessarily resolve the matter once and for all in favor of the client. The relationships between street-level bureaucrats and their clients are often protracted (the coun-selor claims that he has known John for over five years), and this opens many opportunities to soften or bend hierarchical directives.

After being publicly rebuked, the counselor is no longer merely suspi-cious; he feels betrayed. His authority has been questioned and, most im-portantly, an undeserving client has received benefits to which he should not have been entitled. It is important to note the language in which, and the grounds on which, this frustration is vented. The initial focus of the counselor's complaints—the "undeservingness" of the client—is supplanted by two other considerations: fairness and efficiency. What the counselor finds most revolting about John's story is that he was able to "bend the rules" while other clients, whose needs are far more modest and sensible, are treated "by the book" simply because they happen to be less aggressive and vocal. The problem is not just that a client of questionable moral worth gets expensive services, but that he gets *preferential* treatment on the basis of a criterion (his aggressiveness) that should make no difference. This is *unfair* to all the "poor little nice guys" out there. But there is a second consideration at play that is proper to vocational rehabilitation: the idea that counselors should exert some discretion in allocating funds on the basis of a client's propensity to reenter the workforce. The counselor draws a contrast be-tween the case of a lady who has a job ready at hand and only needs a car (a guaranteed success if only the funds were available) and the case of John, who will continue depleting the agency's resources while rehabilitation is practically impossible.

Both of these considerations, pertaining to fairness and to the effi-cient allocation of resources, require stepping back from the case at hand and treating it comparatively, as part of a broader ensemble of cases. What would be fair to John *given what others can expect to get?* How likely is he to reenter the workforce *compared to other clients?* This is precisely the kind of mental exercise—an exercise in distanciation, contextualization, and comparison—that the counselor in the first story did not engage in. As she became more sympathetic to the case of the upholsterer, that particular client's needs came to occupy her attention exclusively. Other clients, and the considerations pertaining to them, dropped from the picture.

The opposite has taken place here. The counselor has become increasingly more guarded and ill disposed toward the case. John is no longer a quadriplegic worthy of sympathy; he is a "crook" who is taking advantage of the system and depriving others of services to which they should be entitled. Since the counselor refuses to let himself be drawn into John's world via sympathy, other clients remain very much within his field of awareness and, with them, considerations of fairness and efficiency. The counselor's perspective is not that of a *caregiver* nor that of an *impassive bureaucrat,* but that of a *watchful fiduciary* of the state's resources.

The story, however, does not end here. Once the counselor has split the world between "poor little nice guys" and bad guys like John, a sense of purpose looms on the horizon: the counselor is tempted to step in to defend those who are taken advantage of. From being involved as a *watchful fiduciary* of the state's resources, it is a small step to getting involved as an *enforcer* of sorts. Much like his peer in the previous story, the counselor resolves to take matters into his own hands. But there is little he can do while John is "protected" by the hierarchy. The counselor has to wait for John to make a false step. In the meanwhile, he continues to monitor the case closely.

During this period of scrutiny, any new piece of information is interpreted as a confirmation of John's moral decrepitude. The counselor's opinion has, by now, become so solidly anchored that it is practically unfalsifiable. We learn, for instance, that John is forced to make frequent visits to the hospital because he keeps having "sores on his butt." Far from seeing these wounds as the unfortunate consequence of John's dependence on attendant care for hygiene or perhaps as a sign that he needs additional help, the counselor sees them, rather, as yet another manifestation of John's poor character. John keeps having sores because "he doesn't take care of himself."[26]

It is one of these visits to the hospital that finally gives the counselor an opening to intervene under the aegis of the rules.

> I just had no idea John was in the hospital. He had been billing me with his attendant hours while he was in the hospital.

And I called him and said, "What the heck are you doing? I can't pay for attendants in the hospital, for God's sake. They are supposed to be providing those things while you are in the hospital."

He says, "Well, no, they don't, so I have to have my person. They can brush my teeth better."

And, it's like, "Oh, for God's sake, John."

"Well, the hospital people won't get me cigarettes."

"You don't need cigarettes. You are in the hospital. Grow up."

He had a fit because I would not pay for his attendants.

He said, "Well, they have to go to class for me to take notes."

I said, "No, they don't. Attendants don't go to class and take notes. You need a note taker, and we will get you a note taker. That is not an attendant.[27]

John has finally broken a rule. This is the chance the counselor had been waiting for. He stops the payments and replaces the attendants by new note takers who will be less likely to satisfy John's special wishes. The counselor has succeeded in rectifying what he had seen, all along, as an injustice.

Modes of Appraisal

In commenting on the previous two stories, I relied on the notion of a "disposition" to describe gradual transformations in how bureaucrats approached their clients. The concept needs to be fleshed out. A disposition, as I have used the term, refers to three interconnected elements. It is at once:

(1) A way of perceiving or interpreting a situation—that is, a *hermeneutic grid;*
(2) A mode of *affective attunement;*
(3) A *normative sensibility*—a particular way of "weighing" factors, which gives salience to some considerations over others.

I alluded to several such dispositions in the stories above. Let me take three by way of illustration. When I said at the beginning of the first story that the counselor responded to the client as an *indifferent,* this meant, along the three dimensions sketched above:

(1) That she listened to the client's story with a view to extracting the bits of information that were administratively relevant (hermeneutic grid);

(2) That she remained unmoved by the story—that is, neither hostile nor well disposed toward it (affective attunement);

(3) That she was concerned with handling the case as rapidly and efficiently as possible (normative sensibility).

When I said that the same counselor had later become involved as a *caregiver,* this served to indicate:

(1) That she was now on the lookout for signs of strain and distress;

(2) That she was moved by the upholsterer's story and that she felt sympathetic toward him;

(3) That she was concerned with meeting this particular client's needs rather than with allocating her services most efficiently or most equitably.

When I suggested, at the end of the second story, that the counselor had responded as an *enforcer,* this meant:

(1) That he approached the case with the expectation that the client would try to take advantage of the system;

(2) That he remained guarded and suspicious;

(3) That he was preoccupied with preventing and punishing abuse.

Notice that the three elements constitutive of a disposition (hermeneutic grid, mode of affective attunement, and normative sensibility) form harmonious psychological ensembles: they involve orientations toward clients that are consonant with one another. It would be odd for a bureaucrat to be wholeheartedly devoted to meeting a client's needs while remaining, at the same time, guarded and suspicious.

As evidenced in the two stories, dispositions can and do change within the course of a single encounter as the interaction proceeds and new information surfaces. I propose to call such transient, situation-dependent dispositions "local dispositions" or "modes of appraisal" (in reference to how bureaucrats appraise their clients). It is important to keep in mind that the notion of a mode of appraisal is an interpretive tool that I have brought to bear on the stories above. Bureaucrats are not necessarily aware of the modes of appraisal they adopt at any given moment. I have inferred their existence, and tried to suggest their usefulness as interpretive devices, by detecting subtle changes in the behavior of bureaucrats and in their use of language.

We must distinguish such "modes of appraisal" from the more enduring professional identities or "moral dispositions" to which bureaucrats are committed across encounters. "Moral dispositions" revolve around a more explicit understanding of one's role and responsibilities—a "role conception," which is largely situation-independent. I will have more to say about moral dispositions and role conceptions shortly.

By describing the stories above in terms of dispositions, both local and enduring, I depart from the tendency, prevalent in both organization theory and moral philosophy, to focus on the standalone decisions that individuals take and on the process of moral reasoning that allegedly determines these decisions.[28] This shift is necessary for two reasons. First, as we were able to witness from the stories themselves, the interaction between street-level bureaucrats and clients involves far more than decisions. It involves manners of speech, body language, and the expression or concealment of emotions. These qualitative facets of the encounter are normatively significant (they are essential, for instance, to providing respectful or considerate treatment) and should not be eclipsed by the decision taken at the end. The concept of a disposition is helpful, in part, because it conveys something about the "style," or manner of conduct, of the bureaucrat.

The second reason to focus on dispositions is because they are, to a large extent, antecedent to, and in part determinative of, the decisions that are ultimately taken. Such decisions are informed by what street-level bureaucrats see or hear (hermeneutic grid), by how they feel (affective disposition), and by what they prioritize (normative sensibility). Dispositions contribute to shaping what bureaucrats will find salient in any particular case or situation.[29] Dispositions, then, give us a holistic perspective on what street-level bureaucrats bring to the encounter at any given moment—both in terms of style and in terms of propensity to reach a certain decision.

The stories I presented above illustrate two different successions of local dispositions or modes of appraisal. In both, the counselors were pulled from their standpoint as *indifferent* or *disinterested* bureaucrats and became

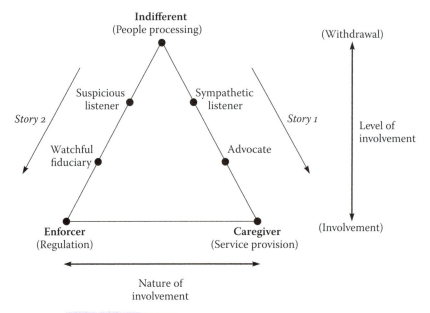

FIGURE 2. Three dispositional orientations.

more involved in the case at hand. In the first story, the counselor gradually opened up to the client: she became involved as a *sympathetic listener*
and thereafter as an *advocate* and *caregiver*. In the second story, the counselor grew increasingly more guarded: he became involved as a *suspicious
listener* and thereafter as a *watchful fiduciary* and *enforcer*. These two
transitions correspond to a specialization and radicalization of sorts: a
specialization, because in veering toward caregiving and enforcement, the
counselors' hermeneutic grid, affective disposition, and normative sensibility became increasingly more targeted, which led them to focus on some
aspects of the case and rendered them impervious to others; a radicalization, because the counselors were increasingly willing to go out of their
way, and to spare no effort, to respond adequately to the demands of the
case as they saw them.

The diagram in Figure 2 visualizes these two series of transitions. The
dispositions we have encountered can be distinguished along two dimensions that track, respectively, the level of the bureaucrat's involvement in the
case at hand and the nature of such involvement. A frontline worker can
remain disengaged and withdrawn or can get personally involved. What

accounts for the diagram's triangular shape is that to get involved is to get involved for *something*—either to offer more tailored service or to subject the client to greater scrutiny.

Going forward, I will be primarily concerned with the dispositions that correspond to the three vertices of the diagram: indifference, caregiving, and enforcement. Taken as ideal types, these dispositions mark out three poles, or orientations, toward which street-level bureaucrats tend to gravitate. I suspect that these dispositions recur with some frequency because they delimit the range of attitudes that one can develop toward three core demands of street-level work. Indifference, caregiving, and enforcement involve a commitment, respectively, to people processing (which calls for rapidly sorting clients into predefined categories), service provision (which requires more tailored attention to their specific needs), and regulation (which demands stricter scrutiny with regard to eligibility criteria and compliance with program requirements). These three types of demands coexist somewhat uneasily with one another, but all three appear, albeit in different mixes, in most public service agencies.[30] I will have more to say in the next chapters on *why* it is that street-level bureaucrats are frequently drawn, or pulled, toward these dispositional poles. For now, though, it is worth noting that indifference, enforcement, and caregiving were common among my colleagues at the NCDI, and that other scholars too have witnessed them in their own research sites.[31]

Between the poles of indifference, caregiving, and enforcement, the level and nature of bureaucrats' involvement are a matter of degree and gradation. The intermediary dispositions we encountered—*suspicious listener, watchful fiduciary, sympathetic listener,* and *advocate*—are meant to be suggestive. There are certainly others, and the differences between them could be drawn with a finer brush.

As we saw in the two stories, modes of appraisal evolve in response to new information. Transitions between them can occur depending on what surfaces in the course of an encounter. In the two stories I presented, the transitions that occurred were unidirectional (they pointed toward more involvement) and proceeded along a single branch of the diagram (toward caregiving or enforcement). But this is not necessarily the case. A bureaucrat can get involved and then revert to a state of indifference; or start out being well disposed toward a client and then, on the basis of new information, end up being guarded and suspicious.

While modes of appraisal evolve in response to new information, it is important to keep in mind that they also contribute to shaping and constraining how bureaucrats perceive new information. They serve as filters and, as such, exhibit a certain amount of inertia, or resistance to change. This is, in part, because they come with a particular hermeneutic outlook: a way of making sense of new information. Incoming data that is in line with this outlook comes into sharp focus, while data that is hard to reconcile with it is discounted.[32] A counselor on the lookout for suspicious behavior is more likely to observe such behavior than to notice acts of good faith. Modes of appraisal also come with a mode of affective attunement: cues that resonate with it are experienced vividly, while others are toned down. A counselor who is guarded and hostile is more likely to be outraged by an inadvertent word than to be moved by a sign of distress. The more targeted a mode of appraisal is—the more specialized its hermeneutic outlook, mode of affective attunement, and normative sensibility—the more it constrains what a bureaucrat can see and the more resistant to change it accordingly is.

Moral Dispositions and Role Conceptions

The discussion so far has centered on the interactions that street-level bureaucrats have with clients in the course of a single encounter. Yet frontline workers handle dozens, if not hundreds, of cases per week and do not approach each of those as if it were their first. They develop, over time, a style of their own—a professional identity or moral disposition—that colors their approach to new cases. Intuitively, the distinction between local, situation-dependent dispositions ("modes of appraisal") and enduring, situation-independent dispositions ("moral dispositions") captures the thought that while we may adopt different selves at different moments, we also tend to exhibit durable patterns of psychological continuity over time.[33]

While modes of appraisal can and do change within the course of a single encounter, moral dispositions are forged over time and tend to change at a slower pace over a comparatively large number of encounters. They revolve around a more explicit core of beliefs as to what it means to perform one's role well (a role conception). Moral dispositions inform bureaucrats' behavior in specific interactions by channeling them preferentially toward some modes of appraisal and away from others. One way to think about this is that moral dispositions come with a default mode of appraisal that must then be dislodged by situation-specific information.

One could then speak as such: someone who *is* an enforcer (who is committed to that moral disposition) is someone who has the propensity to appraise cases *as* an enforcer (according to that mode of appraisal). This leaves open the possibility that an enforcer may, at times, act "out of character" and appraise cases *as* an indifferent or *as* a caregiver depending on what transpires in any particular encounter. If we knew the moral dispositions of the counselors in the two opening stories, we would have been able to tell whether they were responding to clients "in character" or "out of character." Were they indifferent bureaucrats who happened to be drawn to caregiving and enforcement in those particular encounters? Or were they, respectively, a caregiver and an enforcer who were inclined all along to respond to clients as they eventually did?

While modes of appraisal tell us something about the manner of conduct of bureaucrats and their decision-making inclinations at any given moment, moral dispositions capture something about how bureaucrats tend to comport themselves and how they tend to make decisions in general, across a range of encounters. The reason for concerning ourselves with moral dispositions and modes of appraisal is the same—namely, that they play a part in shaping how bureaucrats are likely to behave and to make use of their discretionary power.

(We will see in Chapter 3 that the relationship between modes of appraisal and moral dispositions is actually bidirectional. By adopting modes of appraisal that are systematically out of step with their moral dispositions, street-level bureaucrats can voluntarily take themselves "out of character" as part of a project of self-reform and gradually transform their enduring dispositions.)

Unlike modes of appraisal, which have to be teased out from how bureaucrats act and from what they say during a particular encounter, the role conceptions that serve to anchor bureaucrats' moral dispositions can be obtained more readily in the form of first-person accounts gathered through interviews. Role conceptions give workers a sense of continuity and identity, a personal narrative that ties together what they do on a day-to-day basis and that serves to justify and rationalize their behavior. If modes of appraisal act as selective screens that shape what bureaucrats perceive when they interact with a particular client, role conceptions perform a similar function, but with regard to the bureaucrat's understanding of his or her role: they serve to prioritize certain aspects of the role over others and to restrict the bureaucrat's attention to them.

Let me offer, for the sake of illustration, three examples of role conceptions that correspond to the dispositions of indifference, caregiving, and enforcement. I have taken the liberty to draw these role conceptions from a variety of sources—a French immigration agent, a midwestern vocational rehabilitation counselor, and a police officer from the Bay Area—because they are particularly articulate and succinct.[34]

We begin with a French immigration agent who puts people processing at the center of her understanding of the role:

> As for myself, I don't bother going out my way; if the paperwork is incomplete, or if the application is incorrectly filled, I dismiss the person from my counter; I only speak French, so I'm not supposed to understand what they tell me; and it's simple: when you dismiss one of them who acts as if he didn't understand French, he is typically pushed away by the one who was behind him, and who now wants to take his turn. . . . I aspire to meet my target, and nothing more. I am not like those other agents who try to come to terms with foreigners, and who therefore fail to get much work done and end up delaying the rest of us.[35]

The agent explains, in these few lines, that she feels responsible only for "doing her job." Her understanding of what this entails is narrow but betrays a pragmatic attitude: she has been given a target (a certain number of cases to close), and she will do her best to reach it. This involves accepting applications that are complete and rejecting applications that are incomplete—there is nothing more to it than that. She will not "waste" time speaking to applicants or justifying her decisions. Not only would this be counterproductive; it would, in some sense, go against the spirit of the role as she understands it.

Her relation to clients is one of indifference. She remains distant and refrains from giving them individuating features. They are designated as a group ("one of them," "foreigners") and seem to be interchangeable (another one will take his place). To the extent that some hostility is discernible, it remains moderate. The agent is not indignant at the fact that the "foreigners" do not speak French or that they pretend not to do so; she simply points it out and explains how she uses it as a strategy to facilitate meeting her target. Notice that the agent implicitly presupposes a distinction between her own self and the role that she has been asked to play. In playing the role, she has agreed to set aside her personal inclinations, passions, sense of purpose, and values. Her job, as she understands it, consists in acting in accordance with the incentive structure that has been put in place by her hierarchy.

Compare the agent's "pragmatic indifference" to the role conception of a midwestern rehabilitation counselor who thinks of himself primarily as a service provider or caregiver:

> I had a counselor who told me one time, he said, "Well, I have talked to so many people this month, so I am going to cut it off because I have got my quota." I said, "Well, what about these other people?" And he said, "Well, what is in it for me?" I think, "Well, there are more people that need the service, so that is what is in it for you."
>
> I think that we do that here in that I work for the citizens, particularly those with a disability. The agency for whom I work is really just a conduit for my paycheck, which enables me to provide services, so I have loyalty to [the agency] so long as it is accomplishing its mission, but I am not primarily an employee of [state social services agency]. . . . At any point that it ceases to fulfill its mission, it is my responsibility to change it. In other words, the system is here for the consumer and not vice versa.[36]

The counselor voices his commitment to serving the needs of his clients in no uncertain terms. He insists that his allegiance to the agency is conditional on its capacity to live up to such an ideal of service. He is neither disengaged nor indifferent: he conceives of his job, rather, as a mission. To be a good counselor *is* to go out of one's way. The role is not extrinsic to his own values or sense of purpose—it is a conduit for them. Here, the relevant line of demarcation is no longer between "us" as agents of the state and "them" as "foreigners" or "applicants." It is between the two parties who are engaged in a service or caring relationship and the institutions or actors that get in the way of such a relationship.

Contrast both of these role conceptions, finally, to that of a police officer in Oakland, who places the enforcement of social and legal norms at the center of his role conception:

When I was in the air force . . . a chaplain came up to me and said I should remember three questions. . . . Where did you come from? What are you going to do here? Where are you going after? So I kept asking myself that question about my work. And the answer I finally came to was, I was down here to protect life and property from the animals, the strong-arm thugs. I was here to protect the pensioners and the old women, and the young servicemen from the thugs, the prostitutes who'd entice a guy into a room and when she got him there, she'd say, "Pardon me, let me see if my husband is around," and she'd open the door and in would walk two dudes who'd look real mean and send that serviceman running, feeling lucky he got away with his pants. I figured the old people really needed help; they really had to get shielded. So I began to feel I was really doing a job that needed to be done.[37]

Much like the counselor above, the police officer expresses a strong sense of personal commitment to his role. It is not "just a job"; it is a job that needs to be done, a vocation. To be a good police officer, however, is not to provide customized services to those in need—it is, rather, to get involved in a fight on behalf of those who are weak, and against those who seek to take advantage of them ("the animals"). The officer's language bears resemblance to that of a self-proclaimed vigilante: in a world that is divided into two categories, the good and the bad, he feels called upon to intervene.

It is interesting to note, in passing, the extent to which the officer's categories are idiosyncratic: the "decent folk" include both the elderly and servicemen looking for prostitutes. This, I will argue shortly, is one of the consequences of personal involvement. The more bureaucrats get personally mobilized—the more "it's not just a job"—the more their own preferences and value judgments are likely to transpire in how they discharge their official duties.

Before I embark on a normative appraisal of the material presented so far, let me briefly recapitulate the framework I have developed, because I will be relying on it in chapters to come (see Figure 3). I have argued that street-level bureaucrats approach clients through "modes of appraisal." Modes of appraisal are local dispositions that evolve in light of new information while also framing how bureaucrats perceive and interpret new information. They act as filters that modulate what bureaucrats can see and

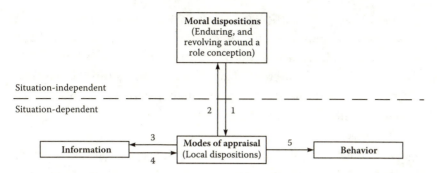

The arrows indicate the direction of influence:
1) Moral dispositions channel bureaucrats toward a default mode of appraisal
2) By controlling their modes of appraisal, and taking themselves "out of character," bureaucrats can gradually transform their moral dispositions
3) Modes of appraisal filter incoming information
4) Information can prompt changes in modes of appraisal
5) Modes of appraisal inform behavior

FIGURE 3. A two-tiered model of dispositions.

the poignancy with which they experience new cues. While modes of appraisal are situation-dependent, bureaucrats also develop more stable professional identities, or "moral dispositions," that revolve around a core set of beliefs regarding what the role consists in and what it means to perform it well ("role conceptions"). Moral dispositions inform bureaucrats' behavior indirectly by channeling them toward "default" modes of appraisal. While modes of appraisal shape how bureaucrats comport themselves with clients and what decisions they are inclined to reach at any given moment, moral dispositions shape how bureaucrats *tend to* comport themselves and what decisions they *tend to* reach across encounters.

Reductive Dispositions

Up to this point, I have been primarily engaged in a descriptive and interpretive exercise. I have tried to explain what it means, analytically, to say that street-level bureaucrats inhabit their role in a particular way, and I have provided a framework for thinking about how they do so. In the remainder of the chapter, I will be revisiting the material I have presented so far from a more normative perspective.

I want to argue, in particular, that we have good reason to think of the dispositions of indifference, caregiving, and enforcement as pathological (in a sense that will be specified shortly). The thrust of my argument will be cautionary—I will be concerned, that is, with describing three dispositions that street-level bureaucrats should be wary of rather than with sketching an ideal they should aspire to.[38] It is possible, however, to present the conclusion I hope to arrive at in a more positive light. To say that the dispositions of indifference, enforcement, and caregiving are pathological is to say that there is a danger in committing oneself unreservedly to any of them. It is to say, in other words, that street-level bureaucrats should be neither too withdrawn nor too involved; neither too suspicious nor too compassionate. Stated positively, this means that street-level work calls for a spirit of moderation. This point may seem excessively modest, but we will come to better appreciate its force in the next few chapters.

For now, it is important to note that there are at least two ways of understanding what it might mean to have a "spirit of moderation." One could think of moderation, along with Aristotle, as a "mean," or happy medium, between extremes. On such a construal, being moderate would mean finding a middle spot between indifference, caregiving, and enforcement, never venturing too close to any of these poles. But what I have in mind is a different understanding of moderation, one that owes perhaps more to Isaiah Berlin than to Aristotle.[39] Moderation, as I understand it, is about being attuned to a plurality of considerations and being sensitive to the tradeoffs and costs associated with them. It stands opposed not so much to extremism as to a certain narrowness or specialization in moral outlook.

On this construal, a moderate street-level bureaucrat is someone who recognizes the kernel of value in all three dispositions of indifference, caregiving, and enforcement and who is, for that very reason, reluctant to commit exclusively to any single one of them. It is someone who is capable, rather, of adapting his or her disposition to match the features of the case at hand. We can be more precise by distinguishing between the two tiers of dispositions—local and enduring—that I described earlier. A moderate street-level bureaucrat should be able to move back and forth between (local) modes of appraisal in light of the features of the case under consideration. Such a bureaucrat would not shy away from responding as an indifferent, as a caregiver, or as an enforcer if the situation called for it. In order to retain such flexibility, however, a moderate street-level bureaucrat would have to cultivate an (enduring) moral disposition sufficiently ecumenical or multifaceted—one could also say "conflicted"—to recognize the multiple dimensions of value pertinent to the role and to know when each mode of appraisal is called for. In order to be able to *respond* as an indifferent, as a caregiver, and as an enforcer, one must be careful not to *become* an indifferent, a caregiver, or an enforcer rigidly confined to a single way of enacting the role.

Before I turn to a discussion of the specific features of indifference, enforcement, and caregiving, I want to begin by clarifying in what sense I understand these moral dispositions to be pathological. It will be useful, as such, to distinguish them, as a group, from three other types of administrative pathologies that are more familiar to political theorists: corruption, rule breaking, and abuse of discretion.

We speak of corruption when officials exploit their position for illegitimate private gain.[40] Recall, however, that there was no indication in the two opening stories that the counselors put their private interest (in the narrow sense that involves a concern for standing, promotion, remuneration, or comfort) ahead of their professional responsibilities. On the contrary, both arguably went beyond the call of duty to do their job well and to act in line with their responsibilities as they understood them.

There was no indication either that the counselors violated existing laws or administrative regulations. Both acted within the scope of their prerogatives. Even the counselor in the second story, who was outraged at an "injustice" and who may, accordingly, have been tempted to resort to extralegal means, went a long way to act under the cover of the rules.

It is one thing, of course, to refrain from breaking existing rules, and quite another to act in their spirit. I argued earlier, in Chapter 1, that street-level bureaucrats should be held accountable on both counts. Would it be possible, then, to describe indifference, enforcement, and caregiving as abuses of discretion—as three dispositions that denature the spirit of the role by channeling bureaucrats toward impermissible modes of appraisal? I find such a charge implausible. Whether or not indifference, caregiving, and enforcement were warranted in the specific cases I discussed earlier, it is certainly possible to imagine other encounters in which they would be called for. It is a fact, after all, that some clients can be processed seamlessly; that others fall through the cracks and require an additional margin of support; and that others still conspire to take unfair advantage of existing provisions. In such circumstances, a bureaucrat would be justified in responding, respectively, as an indifferent, as a caregiver, and as an enforcer.

If the moral dispositions of indifference, caregiving, and enforcement are pathological, then, it is not because those who subscribe to them have corrupt motives, violate existing rules, or adopt modes of appraisal unbefitting of the role. These three moral dispositions are pathological in a different sense: because they lead to a narrowing of the field of moral perception and to a truncated receptivity to normative considerations. The dispositions are pathological insofar as they are *reductive*. They limit what bureaucrats can see and what dimensions of value they are attuned to.

I suggested earlier that, in order to be justified, the modes of appraisal that bureaucrats adopt must match the relevant features of the case at hand. In doing so, I relied on a standard of assessment common in contemporary moral philosophy. I assumed that modes of appraisal should be "reason-responsive": that they are adequate to the extent that they track the reasons for action that bureaucrats encounter in the course of their interactions with clients. When faced with a client trying to cheat the system, a bureaucrat would, *pro tanto*, be justified in leaning toward enforcement. If the client is, instead, trying to file a routine application, the same bureaucrat would, all else equal, be more justified in leaning toward indifference. There should be a close match between the nature of the case at hand and the mode of appraisal of the bureaucrat who handles the case.

The difficulty, however, is that street-level bureaucrats do not have unmediated access to reasons. At any given time, their access to reasons and to the features of a case is always filtered through the mode of appraisal they happen to be in. This mode of appraisal will shape what reasons they can recognize, what counts as a reason, and how weighty these reasons are. Enduring moral dispositions are crucial in this respect because they channel bureaucrats preferentially toward a "default" mode of appraisal that shapes how they initially apprehend clients.

The worry about moral dispositions is that by setting such a default they might contribute to a skewed perception of incoming cases and, therefore, to an inadequate response to such cases. The danger is one of systematic bias: if bureaucrats cannot easily revise or update their default mode of appraisal, they will tend to treat clients more indifferently, compassionately, or suspiciously than their case deserves. The problem of systematic bias is compounded when we factor in role conceptions. The latter provide a truncated understanding of what the role calls for—one that gives systematic, and at times unwarranted, priority to one dimension of the role over others.

While the risk of bias is unavoidable whenever bureaucrats settle, as they must, for a certain style of work, it becomes a matter of serious concern the more their moral dispositions are specialized. The more bureaucrats think of themselves as indifferents, as caregivers, or as enforcers, the more likely they will be to approach clients on these terms. This is a cause for concern because, as we saw in the opening stories, such modes of appraisal involve hermeneutic outlooks, modes of affective attunement, and normative sensibilities that are highly targeted and that tend to exclude or disregard information that is not resonant. Recall how, by the end of the first story, the counselor was entirely taken by the upholsterer's needs, and how she came to interpret any token of reticence or hesitation from him as a sign that he needed more help. Recall as well how, by the end of the second story, the other counselor had become entirely absorbed in defending the rights of a silent, rule-abiding majority, and how he came to regard any new piece of information as a vindication of the paraplegic's poor moral character. Reductive moral dispositions are troubling not because of what they let through, but because of what they screen out: the more targeted they are, the more they constrain street-level bureaucrats' capacity to adequately perceive, and thereby respond to, the specificities of the cases they encounter.

The Indifferent, the Enforcer, and the Caregiver

Reductive dispositions truncate not only the moral perception of street-level bureaucrats, but also their normative sensibility. Such dispositions fail to do justice to the full range of considerations that frontline workers must remain attuned to. Which considerations are these? I argued earlier that street-level bureaucrats must remain attuned to at least four types of demands as they fulfill their role. They must be as fast and economical as

> L) As long as these 4 demands are met, they should be able to practice discretion.

99 ·

possible in processing cases—a criterion of *efficiency.* They must be attentive to the particularities of the case at hand and to the individual circumstances of clients—a criterion of *responsiveness.*[41] They must allocate their resources equitably and treat everyone impartially on the basis of similar standards— a criterion of *fairness.*[42] They must, finally, treat clients with *respect.*[43]

This last requirement—respect—overlaps with the previous ones but is not fully covered by them. To be treated with respect means, in part, to be treated according to fair standards and with proper attention to the specificity of one's case. But it also means being treated in a way that is neither insulting, demeaning, nor infantilizing.[44] It is worth fleshing this out further.

To be treated in an insulting way is to be treated without proper regard for one's standing. In the context of the bureaucratic encounter, this means not being treated as an equal, since all citizens should have the same standing before the state. As Jonathan Wolff points out, "insulting" treatment can take the form of a lack of common courtesy or of a failure of trust.[45] A lack of common courtesy involves, for instance, being kept waiting, ignored, ridiculed, or shouted at. A failure of trust involves being treated in an overly suspicious manner, with the presumption that one has bad intentions.

To be treated in a demeaning way is to be required to act in ways, or to disclose information, that could reduce one's standing vis-à-vis others or the level of respect one has for oneself.[46] This could happen if one were required to publicly reveal one's weaknesses and to acknowledge them as such as a condition, say, for receiving assistance.[47]

To be treated in an infantilizing way, finally, is to be treated without regard for one's autonomy, as someone who is not able to take decisions for his or her own self.[48] As these remarks indicate, respect is a highly composite notion.

The fundamental problem, of course, is that the four considerations I have just laid out (efficiency, responsiveness, fairness, and respect) often point in conflicting directions. The demands of fairness and responsiveness can clash, especially when resources are scarce; there is no guarantee that the pursuit of efficiency—as measured, say, by the number of cases processed—will be reconcilable with either. All three, finally, can sometimes come in conflict with one of the many facets of respect.

To be sensitive to all of these considerations is not to deliver on all of them, all of the time, since this would be impossible, but to keep them in mind in the course of everyday work and to remain attuned to the difficult tradeoffs that must be made between them. To say that a disposition is reductive is to say that bureaucrats who adopt it fail to do *that*—that they are sensitive only to a subset of the range of considerations that they ought to be sensitive to. Those who adopt reductive dispositions, then, are not entirely in the wrong: they capture something essential about the role and pursue it with great dedication, but they do so by turning a blind eye to other, equally important, dimensions of value. They take what is a necessary component of performing the role well and treat it as if it were a sufficient one.

Let me now turn to the three dispositions of indifference, caregiving, and enforcement, with a view to showing both what aspect of the job they successfully deliver on and at what cost such specialization comes.

Indifference

We can begin to appreciate the virtues of indifference by noting that street-level bureaucrats do not interact with clients as private individuals but as public officials, and that this constrains the range of considerations that should be permitted to influence their actions. We expect civil servants, as agents of the state, to behave in a person-neutral way.[49] They should not let their own values, projects, commitments, and relationships interfere with how they fulfill the role.[50] The requirement of person-neutrality is closely related to the ideal of impartiality, which is one of the core promises of the modern bureaucratic state. It is also meant to protect citizens from being subjected to the arbitrary use of power by public officials. Differences in treatment between clients should occur only on the basis of criteria specified in the law and not on the basis of the bureaucrat's own preferences or views.[51]

Withdrawal is arguably the easiest way to achieve person-neutrality. By refusing to get personally involved, bureaucrats can put aside their own biases and inclinations and abstract away from their particular selves. This capacity for "self-denial" has often been praised.[52] Arthur Applbaum writes, for instance, that "the epithet 'faceless, nameless bureaucrat' is in this sense a virtue: actions of an official should not depend on her identity, attributes, or values."[53] Weber goes further and says that bureaucracy "develops the more perfectly the more [it] is 'dehumanized,' the more completely it succeeds in eliminating from official business love, hatred, and all purely personal, irrational, and emotional elements which escape calculation. This is the specific nature of bureaucracy and it is appraised as its special virtue."[54]

There are several other advantages to withdrawal. Bureaucrats who remain indifferent tend to be more rapid and efficient than their colleagues—they process cases faster because they resist the urge to get entangled in their intricacies. They do not hesitate to cut their clients' stories short. They are scrupulous about meeting their targets. On every quantifiable metric, they perform just as well, if not better, than those of their colleagues who feel imbued with a sense of mission.

Indifference also brings its own share of psychological benefits. Street-level work is emotionally draining. Every account of it is punctuated by stories of workers who had to leave because "they could no longer take it." In such an environment, withdrawal offers a welcome—and perhaps even necessary—protection from emotional burnout.[55] Withdrawal can also serve to preempt "decision fatigue." By doling out an undifferentiated response to most ("I don't bother going out of my way," the French immigration agent says), those who remain indifferent can preserve their "decisional energy" for cases that demand more tailored attention.[56] Finally, the very fact that indifferent bureaucrats lack a strong sense of commitment, the very fact that they are dispassionate, can be a blessing in disguise: it allows for some measure of moderation and perspective. Disengagement is a shield against the radicalizing tendencies of an ethic of "ultimate ends"—a unilateral commitment to ridding the streets from the "animals" or to helping out all those who are in need. Much like Weber's politician, street-level bureaucrats need a sense of proportion, an "inner concentration and calmness" that can only be achieved by developing a certain "distance" from "things and men."[57]

There would not be much to say *against* indifference if bureaucratic rules were always sound and if they always yielded a determinate answer. But they do not. As we saw in Chapter 1, street-level bureaucrats inherit a considerable margin of discretion and are expected to make use of it. The problems with indifference are, in this respect, similar to the problems with the compliance model of bureaucratic responsibility: they stem from a failure to recognize that the role itself *demands* the exercise of individual judgment.

It is important to note, first, that indifference is *not* a neutral stance. Since rules are indeterminate, bureaucrats who remain indifferent must effectively be resolving indeterminacies by resorting to *some* rules of thumb. The fact that these rules are not consciously chosen does not make one less responsible for selecting them. One of the dangers of indifference is that it reduces the salience of these choices and renders them less visible. The other danger is that those who remain indifferent fail to do precisely what they are expected to do with their discretion: namely, to bring abstract principles to bear on particular cases. To apply the same rule of thumb to everyone, in a space that is left open precisely to make room for particularization and differentiated treatment, is to effectively refuse to fulfill a central requirement of the role.

The capacity to remain attuned to differences among clients is important not just because administrative categories do not capture all relevant distinctions, but also because clients differ in their capacity to present themselves in terms of administrative categories. Street-level bureaucrats are, in large part, translators; it is up to them to extract information from clients and to assist them in portraying themselves. To refuse to discriminate among clients is to refuse to recognize that some people are less equipped to deal with bureaucracy than others and that these differences often track class, race, and gender lines.

It is worth pointing out, second, that complete disengagement is not necessary to meet the requirement of person-neutrality. One can strive to be "person-neutral" without being dehumanized—that is, without altogether abandoning one's values, commitments, and affective responses. If there are obvious dangers to bringing one's personal body to work (with all the reflexes and values that have been ingrained in it by socialization), there are also significant benefits: personal reactions and the emotions associated with them can serve as "triggers" or "signals" that break the spell of the routine and that indicate that the case at hand might require special attention.[58] So long as this "attention-grabbing" function is not seen as a sufficient justification for treating the case differently, it is possible to bring one's personal body to work without abandoning the ideal of impartiality or person-neutrality.

We should note, finally, that while indifference has psychological advantages, it can also be dangerous: it is conducive, in particular, to a dilution of responsibility. By standing at a remove from one's role and focusing exclusively on adhering to existing rules or on attaining mandated targets ("I aspire to meet my target and nothing more," the agent says), one places too much trust in the goodness and soundness of hierarchical directives. We have reason to be worried about the readiness of the indifferent bureaucrat to apply rules or work toward targets without considering whether they are fit or appropriate and without feeling that the decision, or the action, is ultimately *his* or *hers*.

This critique of withdrawal indicates, by contrast, the positive attributes of involvement, be it in the form of caregiving or enforcement: a greater attention to the particularities of the case at hand and a greater sense of ownership and responsibility for the decisions and actions that one takes. Yet to the extent that one veers too much in either of these directions, one begins to encounter the dangers that withdrawal was meant to address: partiality, emotional and cognitive burnout, and a lack of willingness to compromise.

Caregiving

We can best appreciate the virtues of caregiving by thinking about the particular setting and circumstances in which street-level bureaucrats interact with their clients. Bureaucracies can be alienating and difficult to navigate.[59] They operate according to a logic and pace that are often ill adapted to the needs of clients and in a language frequently inaccessible to them. Given their familiarity with the bureaucratic process and their standing as gatekeepers, street-level bureaucrats are uniquely positioned to reassure and guide clients who are often panicked, lost, and ill informed about their rights. By virtue of being the face of institutions that people typically solicit in the last resort, street-level bureaucrats also find themselves, at times, in situations where clients have no one else to turn to. Seen from this perspective, caregiving might seem like a morally sensitive response to a situation where one party is placed in a precarious and unfamiliar situation while the other is in a position to offer precious assistance and comfort. It is a response that is made possible by the power differential between the two parties and that might be called for because of that.

Unlike bureaucrats who remain indifferent, caregivers are attentive to the particularities of individual clients' circumstances and try, insofar as possible, to be responsive to them. They also deliver on an important dimension of respect by bringing a humane and courteous face to institutions that often appear daunting and forbidding to outsiders. With them, clients are no longer "cases" or "numbers" but individuals who are treated with the compassion and attention they deserve.

Despite its virtues, however, caregiving raises a host of serious concerns. As we saw earlier, respectful treatment involves more than courtesy and consideration. It also involves not calling on clients to demean themselves. Caregiving, however, gives clients a perverse incentive: it rewards them for letting their despair be visible. The problem is not only that this gives people a way of "gaming the system," but more seriously, perhaps, that it encourages them to present themselves in the most unfavorable and helpless light—in a way that may, unintentionally, contribute to undermining their own sense of self-respect.[60]

Treating people respectfully also means being mindful of their autonomy and nurturing their capacity for self-reliance. The danger with caregiving, however, is that it can easily morph into paternalism—an unequal relationship in which bureaucrats treat clients as if they could not be trusted to make decisions for themselves.[61] Recall how the counselor gradually stepped in on behalf of the upholsterer, how she came to speak for him and substitute her judgment for his. While such a mode of engagement may at times be justified, it can, if left unchecked, confirm the client in his or her helplessness and usher in a form of personal dependence.[62] For all its shortcomings, one of the promises of the modern bureaucratic state was to eradicate this sense of personal dependence of one citizen on a particular other.[63]

From the standpoint of respect, then, caregiving presents mixed results. It has other drawbacks too. For one, it is resource intensive: it takes time, effort, and emotional energy. This means that caregivers will, on average, be slower than their peers. But it also means that caregiving is, for that very reason, an approach that does not universalize well. Caregivers simply do not have the resources necessary to offer the same level of dedication and service to everyone. They will, therefore, be forced to discriminate sharply between cases that need tailored attention and those that can be processed more rapidly.[64] The same—we will see shortly—is true of enforcement. The problem is that this distinction, between cases that deserve care and those that do not, serves as a haven for rampant stereotypes and idiosyncratic biases. Recall how much attention the first counselor gave, in her story, to the client's attire and demeanor, and to the fact that he was a "rescuer." This is, of course, a serious worry at the front lines of the state, because citizens may end up being subjected to their peers' biases as well as to their moralizing, and potentially normalizing, judgment.[65]

It is worth noting, finally, that caregiving—much like enforcement—is an ethic of ultimate ends: workers set themselves an objective (to help all those in need, or to clean the streets from the bad guys) that they will never attain in full. Some experience the gap that inevitably arises between achievements and aspirations as a personal failure, which puts them at risk of emotional burnout. Others come to see it, rather, as a vindication of past efforts and a sign that more needs to be done. They may suffer from exhaustion and frustration but tend to rest in the confidence that they, unlike their coworkers, are in the right. This sense of self-righteousness is psychologically necessary given the setbacks that caregivers and enforcers are bound to experience and the resistance they stand to face from those of their peers who are less willing to put themselves on the line. If they are to be sustainable in the long run, caregiving and enforcement must effectively become vocations or "moral missions" of sorts. Those who conceive of the role in such terms will, on the whole, be more intransigent and less inclined to engage in the everyday compromises between different dimensions of value that are an unavoidable feature of the job when resources are tightly constrained. *✻Applying ethics in decisionmaking*

Enforcement

It is relatively easy to make a *prima facie* case for caregiving, because the sentiments that animate the caregiver cohere with our beliefs about what it means to act in a morally praiseworthy way as private individuals. To capture the merits of enforcement, however, we must remember that bureaucrats interact with clients as *agents of the state*. This official status confers upon them standing and power (in the form of symbolic insignia, access to resources, or even, in the case of the police, a right to use violence), but it also comes with its own breed of responsibilities. To put it simply, street-level bureaucrats must distribute resources, services, and sanctions that are not properly speaking *theirs.*

In a private capacity, they may be inclined to offer generous help to people in need; as welfare officers, however, they are bound to be more cautious and suspicious. When walking by a bar, they may prefer to ignore an insult or to look the other way if a fight is about to start; as police officers, however, they may be compelled to intervene and perhaps even to resort to violence. As Applbaum puts it, "moral prescriptions can be *relative to the role* of the agent, in that occupants of particular institutional or social roles face particular moral reasons for action that others, outside the role, do not face, and they are directed to ignore moral reasons for action that others, outside the role, may not ignore."[66] This "role relativity" can justify a certain margin of suspicion, reluctance to help, or readiness to use force that would not be warranted if one were acting in a private capacity.

As agents of the state, street-level bureaucrats are responsible for upholding existing laws, program requirements, and eligibility criteria, and must not shy away from enforcing those strictly when necessary.[67] And yet, the nature of their relationship with clients can make this difficult. As we saw in the opening stories, bureaucrats often have protracted face-to-face encounters with clients and become acquainted with them on a personal level. Clients are no longer strangers or anonymous others but particular beings who can elicit sympathy and compassion. This is precisely why enforcement, as a disposition, can be helpful, because it enables bureaucrats to resist the pull of their moral sentiments and prepares them to take their duties as agents of the state seriously.

Unlike bureaucrats who remain indifferent, enforcers do not merely abide by the letter of the law but feel responsible for preserving and protecting its spirit. They strive to discern between clients who are genuinely entitled to benefits and assistance and those who seek to take advantage of public services by extracting more than their fair share. There is much to be said for such an attitude. By distinguishing between those who are the proper recipients of public programs and those who are not, enforcers preserve valuable public resources for their intended beneficiaries. They also deter "free riders" and fraudsters, and by doing so contribute to preserving the trustworthiness of the institution in the eyes of the public (the presumption that people take unfair advantage of public services is often used as a justification for cutting them down). Someone, after all, has to prevent abuse and enforcers, to their credit, are not afraid of getting their hands dirty.

Despite these merits, however, enforcement comes with serious drawbacks. If enforcers are keen on preserving the overall fairness of the system, their suspiciousness renders them blind to considerations of need and distress and makes them susceptible to engage with clients in a way that is overly confrontational and insufficiently courteous. It is important to note, as well, that while suspicion may be warranted toward those who take unfair advantage of public resources, it can be insulting and overly intrusive toward everyone else who acts in good faith. Lack of trust is particularly unseemly when it is directed at clients who are already part of society's most disadvantaged groups.[68] As Jonathan Wolff argues, we have good reason not to be exceedingly preoccupied with catching free riders once we recognize the cost, in terms of respect and privacy, that this may impose on everyone else.[69] There are good reasons, in other words, not to aspire to a completely foolproof system.

Like caregiving, enforcement is also resource intensive. To be suspicious and to follow through on one's suspicion takes time and detracts from the fast pace of everyday work. Given that resources are limited, an attitude of suspicion cannot be applied equally to all, and enforcers will have to discriminate sharply between clients who will get the benefit of the doubt and those who will be subjected to further scrutiny. Since this sorting process stems from the personal initiative of the bureaucrat and is not regulated by official guidelines, it can serve as a haven for stereotypes and biases.[70] Recall that part of the counselor's suspicion toward the paraplegic stemmed from the fact that he had acted irresponsibly in his youth—a fact that is irrelevant from a strictly administrative standpoint. This is, of course, a serious cause of concern: one of the reasons we have an impersonal administrative apparatus is to insulate citizens from the moralizing and discriminatory judgment of their peers.

It is worth noting, finally, that enforcement, like caregiving, is an ethic of ultimate ends in which workers set upon a mission ("to protect the system from the bad guys") that they are unlikely to ever attain in full. Enforcers are destined to experience a sense of shortcoming that can, in the long run, become psychologically untenable. Since they are convinced that they hold

I have argued that we cannot properly grasp the ethical challenges that street-level bureaucrats face if we restrict our attention to the moment of ethical decision-making and to the process of moral reasoning that immediately precedes it, but that we must look, more broadly, at the dispositions that bureaucrats adopt. Such a shift, from the study of decisions to that of dispositions, is necessary for two reasons: because dispositions convey something about the manner of conduct of bureaucrats, and because they shape how bureaucrats tend to perceive the morally salient features of individual cases and what considerations they are inclined to prioritize when responding to them.

The shift from decisions to dispositions brings to light a range of normatively troubling ways of inhabiting the role. Indifference, caregiving, and enforcement are pathological not because they are departures from the role that street-level bureaucrats are meant to play, but because they are reductive takes on it. Ideally, we would want street-level bureaucrats to be able to adapt their modes of appraisal in light of the features of the cases they encounter. We would want them to be flexible enough to respond as indifferents, as caregivers, or as enforcers when the situation calls for it. Bureaucrats who settle for reductive moral dispositions, however, approach new cases with a tunneled vision and a truncated understanding of their responsibilities. Their capacity to adapt their mode of response in light of the merits of individual cases and to do justice to the plurality of values that we need them to remain sensitive to is thereby limited. Reductive dispositions are insidious: those who inhabit the role in these ways can fail to live up to their responsibilities even as they remain well intentioned, civic-minded, and within the scope of their prerogatives.

This cautionary tale leaves us with two questions: Why is it that street-level bureaucrats tend to gravitate toward reductive moral dispositions? And what, if anything, can we do to counteract such a drift? The following chapters address these questions from three separate but complementary perspectives: that of the individual bureaucrat, that of the peer-level group, and that of management and public policy.

CHAPTER THREE

A Gymnastics of the Self
Coping with the Everyday Pressures of Street-Level Work

Despite the early hour, the waiting room of the Norville Service Center teems with people of all ages and ethnicities. Some have sunk into their chairs with a look of resignation or wariness. Others seem more anxious, holding on nervously to folders or plastic bags filled to the rim with paperwork. The heavy silence is punctuated by the voice of the receptionist, DeShawn, who alternates between addressing clients ("Please take a seat and fill out this form"; "Someone will be with you shortly, Ma'am"), and answering the phone, which never stops ringing.

An elderly woman, visibly exasperated, walks up to the desk. She tells DeShawn that it is her third visit to the center in as many days. She explains at length that she had met with a case manager the day before and that she was instructed to come back with additional documents. She seems exhausted and out of breath; her eyes are tired and her voice plaintive.

Over the course of the interaction, DeShawn alternatively leans forward, as if to create an intimate space with the woman in the midst of the crowded room, and reclines in his swivel chair, looking away to a nonexistent horizon, seemingly inattentive and unconcerned by what he hears. He switches between a warm and compassionate mode of address and a more distant and impersonal one. He takes turns apologizing on behalf of the organization ("I am terribly sorry") and providing instead a detached, unapologetic summary of the rules in place ("I am not authorized to take your documents myself; you must reschedule another appointment with the staff member you saw yesterday").

Further into the building, another encounter takes place in a room filled with cubicles. A client from the Caribbean inquires about the services her disabled daughter might be entitled to. The case manager, a middle-aged Hispanic woman, risks a smile, as if to encourage the client to open up and tell her more, and promptly takes it away, effectively cutting her story short. She makes eye contact, then interrupts it and glances at her computer screen, clicking aimlessly, as if to recuperate for a moment and gather her thoughts.

Her colleagues, who are busy assisting other clients, mobilize a similar array of gestures. They look away at opportune moments, suddenly reach out for their smartphone, or remember, conveniently, that they forgot to say something to a previous client. When an interaction heats up they exchange looks of support, encouragement, or complicity with one another. They take cigarette or coffee breaks at key moments and know when to step away to "fetch a file" or to allegedly solicit their supervisor's advice. Over the course of the encounter, and depending on the demeanor that they adopt, the desk takes the allure of a shared and intimate space where a proximate and genuine encounter can take place, or reemerges as a formidable boundary—one that, in the words of Hungarian novelist George Konrád, apportions "the roles as unmistakably as a whipping post or a guillotine."[1]

The scenes I am describing are ones I witnessed on a daily basis while conducting participant observation at the Norville Community Development Initiative. My proximity to frontline staff allowed me to observe in detail their interactions with clients and the everyday gestures they mobilize during such interactions. To the extent that such gestures are discussed in the scholarly literature, they are seen either as tactics used to control the flow of the conversation and the image that one projects in it, or as palliative strategies used to protect oneself from the risk of burnout.[2] These interpretations, though at least partly accurate, fail to acknowledge that these gestures can also serve as intentional and voluntary practices that do moral work on the agents who perform them. They can function as *exercises* or *practices of the self,* through which bureaucrats can shape, adjust, or, as I will prefer to say, calibrate and modulate their own dispositions toward clients.

These practices have a long, if somewhat overshadowed, lineage in the history of moral philosophy—one that has garnered renewed attention under the auspices of Pierre Hadot and Michel Foucault. Building on this tradition, I will argue that mastering such practices is essential for street-level bureaucrats to confront the challenges of everyday work.[3] Retaining a balanced moral disposition at the front lines of public service— one that avoids the pitfalls of indifference, enforcement, and caregiving— calls less for the development of a set of unchanging character traits (i.e., of virtues) or for the cultivation of a form of autonomy from one's environment than for the gradual mastery and judicious deployment of a set of situationally specific practices of the self. These practices are necessary, or so I will argue, to enable street-level bureaucrats to face up to the dissonance they are bound to experience if they remain sensitive, as they should, to the plural and conflicting demands of street-level work in a context where resources are severely constrained.

Before I start making this case, however, let me resume the discussion where I left it in Chapter 2. I had promised to explore why street-level bureaucrats are drawn toward reductive dispositions and what can be done to counteract such a drift at the level of the individual agent, of the peer-level group, and of managerial practices. This chapter aims to deliver on the first leg of that promise.

To understand how to counteract the drift toward reductive dispositions, we must try to explain, first, what accounts for their existence. There is a long line of research on the adverse effects of bureaucracy as an organizational form on the moral faculties of bureaucrats. I review this literature rapidly in the first section but argue that—however enlightening it may be for "back-office" bureaucrats—it is of limited help in explaining the challenges faced by frontline workers.

I show, in the second section, that the work of social psychologists on cognitive dissonance and coping mechanisms offers a more promising entry into the predicament of frontline workers. The problem with street-level bureaucracy is not so much that it creates a setting that is inhospitable to moral personhood but that it forces its agents to contend poignantly with several irreconcilable and often conflicting demands. Social psychologists have shown that in such settings individuals tend to redefine their role, often unconsciously, in ways that reduce the salience of moral conflict and that make the job more bearable. I argue that the reductive dispositions of indifference, caregiving, and enforcement perform, each in their own way, precisely such a function.

How, then, should individual agents resist the imperceptible drift toward such dispositions? In the third section, I reconstruct two possible answers to such a question that stress, respectively, the cultivation of virtue and the attainment of personal autonomy. I argue, however, that both of them fall short of addressing the specific challenges of street-level work. I offer as an alternative a third approach, which puts the accent on everyday practices of the self. I argue that those who manage to retain balanced moral dispositions do so, in part, by deploying a regime of such practices—a kind of gymnastics of the self—through which they mitigate their exposure to dissonance and thereby reduce the cognitive distortions it induces. I begin to develop this account in the third section and flesh it out further in the fourth.

I should stress at the outset that while this chapter is written with a concern for street-level bureaucrats as individual moral practitioners, it is not my intention to downplay the importance of institutional architecture. I do not mean to suggest, in particular, that street-level bureaucrats will *always* succeed in retaining balanced moral dispositions through their own efforts. The literature on street-level bureaucracy has shown time and again how fragile individual responses can be, and how permeable the moral personalities of workers are to changes in structural and organizational parameters.[4] My goal, rather, is to make sense of the fact that *given a particular organizational setting*, some bureaucrats tend to respond more successfully to the challenges of street-level work than others. I turn to moral philosophy and moral psychology to understand why this might be the case.

Bureaucracy and Moral Personhood

There is a widely held view in the history of political thought—a view that goes back at least to Plato and Aristotle—according to which the social and political environment in which we evolve is in large part formative of the kind of moral agents we are. If it is common to read the history of political thought as an extended attempt to specify the political conditions under which our moral faculties can flourish, it is also possible to read it against the grain—as an attempt to expose, in various times and places, the social and political conditions that lead to moral degeneration. From Plato and Ibn Khaldun to Rousseau and Hegel, we have no shortage of illustrations of the ways in which a particular kind of culture, or the requirements imposed by a given social role, can impede, pervert, or overwhelm our moral faculties.

In the twentieth century, the question of the relationship between social and political environment and moral breakdown posed itself perhaps most poignantly in the aftermath of World War II, as the extent of the Final Solution, and the contours of the bureaucratic machinery that had been marshalled to effect it, slowly came to view. Hannah Arendt suggested famously that one of the most pressing questions the Holocaust forced upon us was to understand how "an average, 'normal' person, neither feeble-minded nor indoctrinated nor cynical, could be perfectly incapable of telling right from wrong."[5] How, she wondered, could sensitive people all of a sudden become complicit in mass murder?

This question became a rallying cry for a generation of scholars across disciplines. One of the most influential lines of research that emerged in response to Arendt's challenge sought to investigate whether bureaucracy— that quintessentially modern form of social and political organization— could itself be at the root of the problem.[6] This suspicion led scholars to revisit, with more cautious eyes, those very same attributes of bureaucracy— hierarchy, division of labor, limited discretion, proliferation of rules, and standard operating procedures—that were once seen, in the rational systems perspective I laid out in Chapter 1, as the secret of its success. In what follows, I reconstruct the generic critique of bureaucracy that emerged from this line of thinking and explain why it is of limited relevance to the case of street-level bureaucrats.

As early as 1940, Robert Merton had already warned that bureaucracies could have adverse consequences on bureaucrats' capacity to think and act independently.[7] Merton thought that the capacity to exert independent judgment was not an inalienable property of human beings but a faculty that had to be cultivated and practiced. Bureaucracies, however, offer few opportunities to exert such a faculty. They tend, rather, to simplify the tasks that bureaucrats must perform, to standardize them, and to encode them in procedures that must be followed to the letter. Merton went further. He argued that the reliability and regularity of bureaucracies depend on bureaucrats' capacity to *suspend* their judgment and on their readiness to cultivate an inclination to follow rules and procedures almost instinctively. Such an inclination is instilled through training and reinforced by a system of rewards and incentives designed to promote compliance. According to Merton, then, the problem with bureaucracies is not simply that they fail to provide positive opportunities for proper habituation but that they effectively encourage a kind of *improper habituation* (Merton refers to Thorstein Veblen's concept of *trained incapacity*), as a result of which bureaucrats gradually surrender their capacity for independent judgment.

This bureaucratic propensity to stop relying on one's own self in order to comply with directives issued from above purportedly leads to an erosion of individual agency. To be an agent is to be the author of one's actions and to understand oneself as such. There are different ways of spelling out what this means. On one view, authorship means that the actions performed must bear the mark of the agent who carries them out—they must be expressive, say, of some distinctive features of the agent's character or beliefs, and the agent must recognize them as such. It is not difficult to see why the routine of bureaucratic work may threaten this conception of agency. Bureaucrats are encouraged to refrain from acting on the basis of considerations that are distinctive to them. They must aspire, on the contrary, to be interchangeable with their peers. Bureaucratic work leaves little space for the expression of individuality; it demands actions that bear no distinctive connection to the agents that perform them.[8]

There is an alternative conception of agency that places the emphasis not on any substantive affinity between the actions and the agent, but on the procedural condition that the actions must result from the agent's own deliberation. Effective agency presupposes, on this view, agents who are in possession of the reasons on the basis of which they act. Bureaucracies, however, often deny bureaucrats access to such reasons. By institutionalizing a rigid hierarchical chain through which a unidirectional flow of information trickles, bureaucracies place low-level bureaucrats at an epistemic disadvantage. They create situations like those studied by Stanley Milgram, in which such bureaucrats, not fully informed of the aims of the organization or of the rationale behind established procedures, are systematically driven to impute more knowledge and expertise to their superiors and to defer to their authority without being able to assess its merits. Bureaucrats are deprived, that is, of the *grounds* on the basis of which they could deliberate. They are effectively encouraged to entrust this process to someone else.

Given the hurdles that bureaucrats purportedly face in understanding themselves as agents, it is not surprising that they would come to see themselves as mere "spectators" to their own deeds, much like workers on a factory chain. Seen from this perspective, the lifeless mechanical analogy that bureaucrats often use to represent themselves (a "cog in a machine" that neither "deliberates" nor "wills" nor "judges") cannot be dismissed as a facile trope used for the purposes of self-exculpation. It must be seen, rather, as conveying something of the phenomenology of everyday work.

The most serious consequence of this erosion of agency, if we are to trust the generic critique of bureaucracy, is that it leads to a dilution of moral responsibility.[9] If bureaucrats do not consider themselves the authors of their actions, how can we expect them to feel personally responsible for what they do? This loss of responsibility is facilitated by the parcelization of work. Because of the detailed division of labor, bureaucrats are directly responsible for, and typically only aware of, an infinitesimal portion of what the organization actually does. Both of these conditions—a collective endeavor in which responsibility is spread over "many hands" and a lack of immediate awareness of the end product—are conducive to a dilution of individual responsibility.[10]

Bureaucracies have also been faulted for impeding what Jonathan Glover has called our human responses—movements of sympathy and respect that pull us toward others and pose restraints on how we interact with them.[11] This happens through routinization and distancing. Routinization desensitizes bureaucrats and numbs their moral sentiments.[12] It can also lead to what psychologists have called "compassion fatigue."[13] How much empathy can one realistically have in store when confronted day in, day out, with a steady stream of cases, each more harrowing than the last?

Bureaucracies, finally, create distance: they separate bureaucrats from the people whose lives they directly affect. Most bureaucrats never meet their clients, nor do they witness the consequences that bureaucratic decisions have for them and their families. This lack of sight and contact was notorious in the case of desk bureaucrats who played a major role in the Holocaust while rarely encountering their victims. It is interesting to note the moral high ground, they may also be more reluctant to compromise than those of their peers who are less personally involved.

This brings to a close my critique of indifference, caregiving, and enforcement. I hope to have shown, in the preceding pages, that these three moral dispositions are pathological in a special sense. They are not to be seen as *transgressions* or *deformations* of the role: they do not introduce into the practice of public service provision something foreign or alien to it (in the way in which corrupt officials, say, bring their own personal gain to bear on the conduct of public affairs). These dispositions are pathological, rather, insofar as they are *reductive* takes on the role: they collapse the plural demands internal to the role onto a single dimension and ignore the rest. By doing so, they effectively dispense with the need to make difficult, context-sensitive tradeoffs between different dimensions of value—which, as we saw in Chapter 1, is one of the main reasons for having discretion in the first place. The problem with indifferents, caregivers, and enforcers is that they have largely settled the question of how to act in advance of their encounter with particular cases.

Conclusion

Given their position at the front lines of public service and law enforcement, street-level bureaucrats effectively serve as the face of the state. Since such bureaucrats wield a significant margin of discretion, it matters a great deal to ordinary citizens how they go about fulfilling their responsibilities. In this chapter, I have provided a framework for thinking about how street-level bureaucrats inhabit their role. I did so by relying on three concepts— "modes of appraisal," "moral dispositions," and "role conceptions." A mode of appraisal is a composite notion that captures an agent's hermeneutic outlook, mode of affective attunement, and normative sensibility at any given moment in time. A moral disposition refers to a more stable style of work, anchored around a "role conception." Moral dispositions channel bureaucrats towards "default" modes of appraisal, which can be updated depending on what transpires in any particular encounter.

that when such encounters did occur, even those who were most un-flinching in their commitment to the Final Solution were typically re-pelled by what they witnessed and could not bear the sight. If physical proximity ordinarily amplifies sentiments like sympathy, pity, or compas-sion, distance tends, on the contrary, to weaken them.[14]

Distance, of course, is not only sensory but also symbolic. Bureaucra-cies widen the gap between bureaucrats and their clients both by instituting linguistic barriers (clients' names are replaced by numbers and their prob-lems are given remote, unfamiliar names) and by stripping clients of their individuating features and reducing them to generic and interchange-able "cases." The rift created between the two parties makes respect—a response predicated in large part on our commonality as human beings—more challenging. By inhibiting our "human responses" of sympathy and respect, bureaucracies reduce the likelihood for what Glover calls "break-throughs"—moments where we are spontaneously drawn, through a move-ment of sympathy or indignation, to rethink our moral commitments and reevaluate our dispositions.

We can now summarize the barrage of criticism I have just laid out: by reducing our capacity for independent judgment, eroding our individual agency, diluting our sense of individual responsibility, and blocking our human responses, bureaucracies, so the argument goes, create an environ-ment that is inhospitable to moral personhood. It is important to note that this charge is meant to apply to bureaucratic organizations with some gen-erality and not simply to Nazi bureaucracies. The latter are simply thought to have taken to an extreme, and thus to have rendered visible, tendencies latent in *any* bureaucratic organization.

Given how damning this critique of bureaucracy is, it is important to set its scope right. We must add, to this effect, two necessary qualifications, which together limit the applicability of the critique to the realm of street-level bureaucracy. It is crucial to note, first, that the arguments presented above presuppose a model of bureaucracy that is directly drawn from the rational systems perspective on organizations that I challenged in Chapter 1. According to this model, bureaucracies operate following a strict hierarchical principle and on the basis of clear and detailed standard operating procedures that leave little room for discretion. They provide bureaucrats with specific goals, monitor their performance closely, and are able to sanction those who fail to comply.

But is this model of bureaucracy fact or fiction? Several scholars have taken issue with the implicit portrait of bureaucratic life that the critique presupposes. They have shown that even in Nazi Germany (a limit case, if any), the structure of rules and regulations was often looser, the goals more vague, and the penalties for not complying weaker than commonly thought.[15] They have argued, more generally, that bureaucratic life frequently involves more creativity and that it requires more judgment and initiative than is commonly acknowledged. This was the case, at any rate, for the officer who has become, for better or worse, the paradigmatic figure of the Nazi bureaucrat: Adolf Eichmann. As Hannah Arendt herself acknowledged, and notwithstanding the way he portrayed himself, Eichmann was not merely following directives but also showed ingenuity and creativity in fulfilling his role.

I have tried to show, in Chapter 1, that this departure from the rational systems model of bureaucracy is neither exceptional nor reserved to high-ranking officials like Eichmann. It is also characteristic of the experience of street-level bureaucrats. I argued, there, that the routine of street-level work involves a substantial margin of discretion and that it depends, as such, on the bureaucrats' capacity to exert independent judgment. I showed, moreover, that these judgments are not simply technical in nature but also value-laden. It is hard to see, accordingly, how the charge of *improper habituation* could be persuasive at the street level. Far from impeding frontline workers' capacity for independent judgment, street-level bureaucracies are utterly dependent on it.

It also seems unlikely that street-level work would lead to an erosion of agency for the two reasons mentioned earlier—by undercutting one's capacity to deliberate independently and by preventing the expression of one's individuality. Given that street-level bureaucrats occupy the last stage in the process of policy implementation, they inherit and must resolve all the ambiguities and conflicts that were not, or could not, be resolved by their superiors. They must also juggle a variety of normative considerations that often pull in competing directions. All of this requires them to deliberate independently. Street-level work, moreover, does not only call for decisions. As we saw in Chapter 2, the discretionary spaces that frontline workers inhabit allow them to develop different styles of work through which they can express their distinctive selves.

We should note, too, that while street-level bureaucrats might gradually lose their sense of individual responsibility, such loss cannot be imputed to the parcelization of labor. This is because street-level bureaucrats occupy a special position in the division of labor: their role involves bringing to bear the final "decision" of the bureaucracy on the client. They are better placed than their peers to see what the bureaucratic output actually amounts to. It is under their watch, after all, that the countless little decisions that had to be taken in the back office finally take a recognizable form (as an arrest, a check, a denial of entry, etc.).

This brings me to the second important qualification to the generic critique of bureaucracy: it presupposes bureaucrats who do not interact directly with clients but solely with files and "cases." The distance at which these bureaucrats stand from clients is central to explaining why the human responses of sympathy and respect are attenuated.

Yet one of the defining characteristics of street-level work is that it involves direct, typically face-to-face, contact with clients. Street-level bureaucrats are able to witness firsthand the impact of their actions; they are able to sense, and sometimes even to be stirred, by the distress, joy, or anger of the people with whom they interact. On a psychological and phenomenological level, such proximity to clients makes their job fundamentally different from that of their peers in the back office.[16] The element of proximity also allows clients to behave in a less scripted manner. There is no guarantee that they will abide by established symbolic distinctions or remain quiescent. Some of them will, inevitably, disrupt the routinized nature of the encounter and openly refuse to be slotted into ready-made administrative categories. Breakthroughs may not be frequent but, in such conditions, they are certainly possible.

All of this is not to say that street-level bureaucrats are immune to an erosion of moral agency, to a loss of responsibility, or to a numbing of human responses. As a matter of fact, one of the reductive dispositions I discussed in Chapter 2—indifference—exhibits all three of these features. What I mean to suggest, however, is that we cannot explain such shortcomings by appealing to the generic critique of bureaucracy, because this critique does not do justice to the distinctive character of street-level work. At any rate, if this critique were valid, we would expect indifference to be the only widespread pathology at the street level. But it is not. Bureaucrats frequently adopt two other types of reductive dispositions, caregiving and enforcement, that seem to go against the thrust of everything that has been said so far. These dispositions exhibit not a depletion of moral agency, responsibility, or human responses, but an excess of all three.

Indifference, Caregiving, and Enforcement as Adaptive Responses

If the generic critique of bureaucracy fails to explain why street-level bureaucrats tend to gravitate toward the three reductive dispositions of indifference, caregiving, and enforcement, what else can? I argue, in the following pages, that research in social psychology on adaptive responses to cognitive dissonance can provide us with a better grasp on the predicament of frontline workers. To see why this is the case, we must begin by identifying the specific challenges that street-level bureaucrats confront on a recurring basis, and by attempting to understand how they cope, or adapt themselves, to such challenges. This represents an important shift in emphasis from the line of critique discussed so far. The aim is no longer to find out how the objective features of a "work situation" directly impede the moral faculties of bureaucrats but to highlight how the adaptive responses that such bureaucrats develop to their work situation can, in and of themselves, be morally troubling. One of the advantages of this approach is that it sheds light not just on one of the reductive dispositions but on the common logic that underpins all three.

The theory of cognitive dissonance is, at heart, very simple. As it was first described by Leon Festinger, dissonance is a state that occurs whenever an individual jointly holds two cognitions (attitudes, beliefs, perceptions, emotions) that are psychologically inconsistent.[17] Since the occurrence of dissonance is presumed to be unpleasant or uncomfortable, individuals strive to reduce it either by adding new "consonant" cognitions or by changing one of the two cognitions to make them consonant with one another.[18] Cognitive dissonance can, accordingly, serve as a powerful motivator for change in human thought and behavior. The greater the inconsistency, the stronger the drive to reduce it, and the more pronounced the changes we can expect to witness.[19]

While the theory was initially thought to apply to *any* two conflicting cognitions, further research showed that dissonance is particularly severe when our self-image is at stake.[20] This finding prompted the development of self-affirmation theory, which starts from the premise that most of us are motivated to maintain an image of ourselves as good and appropriate persons.[21] According to this theory, dissonance is caused not so much by an inconsistency between our cognitions, but by behavior that threatens our positive self-image. The resulting state is psychologically uncomfortable because it forces us to face the gap that exists between who we think we are and how we have in fact behaved. There are three ways to alleviate such dissonance: (1) by changing our behavior to bring it in line with our self-image (accommodation), (2) by revising our self-image to bring it in line with our behavior, or by adding new "cognitions" to reduce the gap between the two (direct psychological adaptations), or (3) by finding alternative sources of self-affirmation that help us reinstate a positive image of ourselves (indirect psychological adaptations).[22]

In practice, however, it turns out that avenue (1) is frequently closed, either because the dissonant actions are performed in public or because they are hard to amend, retract, or deny. This is typically the case for street-level bureaucrats, who act in view of clients and colleagues and who make administrative decisions that cannot easily be revised. In such cases, Philip Zimbardo writes, "the pressure to change is exerted on the softer elements of the dissonance equation, the internal, private elements—values, attitudes, beliefs and even perceptions."[23]

Interestingly, researchers have found that the intensity, and hence the effects, of dissonance typically *decrease* the more one can resort to external justifications to explain one's behavior.[24] An individual will experience less dissonance when given strong external incentives (i.e., an order, or a large sum of money) to perform an action that conflicts with his or her self-image than when given little inducement to do so. An element of choice or freedom will, on the contrary, tend to *increase* the level of dissonance ex-post.[25]

The theory of cognitive dissonance, suitably updated to take heed of the insights of self-affirmation theory, can help us understand the three reductive dispositions of indifference, enforcement, and caregiving as adaptive responses to the psychological pressures of everyday work.

There are two primary sources of dissonance at the front lines of public service. The first received much attention in Michael Lipsky's classic study. From their very first day on the job, street-level bureaucrats must confront the discrepancy that exists between the ideal of public service that drove many of them to the public sector and the grim realities of everyday work.[26] If anything, this discrepancy has augmented in the thirty-five years that have elapsed since the publication of Lipsky's study, with the reforms brought about by New Public Management pressuring street-level bureaucrats to do even more with less. Given how limited bureaucratic resources are, frontline workers cannot provide all clients with the level of service, quality of treatment, or degree of attention they deem appropriate. They are often reduced to being front-row witnesses to deep social problems to which they can provide no more than "patchwork" solutions. If they are to preserve a positive self-image or retain a minimum of satisfaction on the job, they must, accordingly, find a way to reduce the gap that exists between their expectations as to what public service should accomplish and the limited capabilities they can marshal in practice.

To this first challenge, we must add a second, which becomes palpable when bureaucrats face up to the necessity of acting under limited resources. Even as they are to deploy limited capabilities, street-level bureaucrats must remain sensitive to a plurality of normative considerations that are central to our democratic political culture: they are to be efficient, responsive, respectful, and fair. The problem, however, is that these requirements often pull in conflicting directions. For conscientious bureaucrats, who aspire to retain a rich and multifaceted conception of their role and responsibilities, the terrain is, so to speak, mined. Since the requirements are impossible to reconcile, any resolution is bound to create dissonance. Whatever they decide to do, the chosen course of action—even if it is a good one—will smack of compromise: it will be short of optimal on at least one of the dimensions that matter.

The sense of shortcoming that is bound to result from these two challenges—the feeling that one is always betraying, or falling short of, the ideals that one holds dear—is certainly not exclusive to street-level bureaucracy. It is a feature of our everyday moral lives, one that does not always lead to profound attitudinal change. What is special about frontline work in public service, however, is that it amplifies and dramatizes such internal conflict to the point where it cannot be easily ignored or shrugged away. It is important to remember, in this regard, that many of the clients with whom street-level bureaucrats interact belong to the most disadvantaged segments of society, and that it is only in the last resort that many of them turn to public agencies. Given how much is at stake for such clients in the bureaucratic encounter, and given the proximity at which they stand to frontline workers, any deviation from the ideal of public service—any half-measure or compromise—will have real costs, and will manifest itself in a particularly vivid way.

A few examples may help convey this. The discrepancy between aspirations and capabilities means, for instance, that a case manager at the NCDI may have to bring herself to turn away clients who have been waiting in line for hours because she will not be able to see them before closing time despite her best efforts. It means that a teacher who does not have enough resources to provide sufficient attention to all the students in her overcrowded classroom may have to watch, powerless, as some of them slide behind. The need to make difficult tradeoffs between competing considerations means, in turn, that a counselor may have to choose between pausing to voice a few words of support to a client who has just disclosed a sensitive personal problem and following up, immediately, with the next question on the roster because the waiting room is full and the clock ticking fast. The expeditious option may sting the client; the compassionate one may do a disservice to those stranded in the waiting room. Whatever the counselor does, there is no easy way out.

To measure the full force of the psychological strain that street-level bureaucrats experience—and hence, to appreciate the reach of the transformations it can induce—it is important to note two additional factors. The first is that street-level workers must face the aforementioned tensions and challenges on an ongoing basis. They cannot "suffer through" dissonance once but must develop an adaptive response that will work for the long haul: this is not a sprint but a marathon. The second is that street-level work involves a significant margin of discretion. This discretion is limited, of course, both formally and informally, but it is nevertheless substantial. Street-level workers are, within certain limits, "free" to choose. As we have seen, though, this only increases the intensity of the dissonance they are bound to experience.

To recapitulate: street-level bureaucrats are placed on a recurring basis in choice situations that are bound to threaten their self-image as dedicated and capable public servants. They experience an ongoing tension between their lofty aims and their limited capabilities, and between their aspiration to "do a good job" and the conflict that is bound to arise, especially when resources are scarce, between the various normative demands to which they must attend. This setup is structurally bound to generate dissonance. This dissonance will, in turn, be experienced vividly because the stakes are high, the clients proximate, and the decisions discretionary.

In such conditions, the theory of cognitive dissonance predicts that street-level bureaucrats will either find the tensions unbearable and quit their job, or develop adaptive responses by narrowing their understanding of their role and responsibilities to bring them in line with existing capabilities (thus developing reductive moral dispositions, or what Lipsky calls "private conceptions of the job").[27] The theory also suggests that street-level bureaucrats may try to reduce the extent to which they feel personally responsible for their behavior and that they may try to find alternative sources of self-affirmation.

These predictions bear out in practice. Burnout is a significant problem in the human services, in education, and in the police, and it is one of the strongest predictors of employee turnover and intention to leave.[28] The literature on street-level bureaucracy suggests, moreover, that many of those who remain do indeed gravitate toward reductive dispositions. As we saw in Chapter 2, three such dispositions are particularly common: indifference, caregiving, and enforcement. I have already described these dispositions at length. It will suffice here to recall some of their distinctive traits to explain why they succeed in reducing dissonance, and at what cost they do so.

Indifference is an attitude of withdrawal that makes possible a people-processing mindset. It is the response of bureaucrats who make peace with the conflicts inherent to the job by convincing themselves that they exert less discretion—that they have less freedom or agency—than they actually do. Indifference is a form of "bad faith." Those who adopt such a disposition come to believe that they are merely responsible for complying with the directives, or seeking to attain the targets, that are handed down to them. As we saw in Chapter 1, however, such an understanding of bureaucratic responsibility is inaccurate descriptively, and untenable as a normative ideal. Hierarchical directives are often too vague, ambiguous, and conflicting to fully govern the behavior of bureaucrats.

This delusional belief, however, and the reductive conception of work responsibilities that it makes possible, allows bureaucrats to reduce the extent to which they feel personally on the line. They come to conceive of the job as an act that they put on, a mask that does not involve their "true" or "deep" selves. This coping mechanism—known to psychologists as "compartmentalization" or, in severe cases, as "doubling"—involves a splitting of one's existence into separate realms (work, and everything outside of work) that do not communicate with one another.[29]

Along with this split personality comes a perception of clients as a dull, anonymous "mass" that must be processed and kept at bay. Clients and their problems are, after all, "only work." This conception of clients comes with a silver lining: it allows bureaucrats to move through cases fast without getting drawn into their intricacies. Emotional distance allows for a certain measure of pragmatism. As we saw in Chapter 2, "indifferents" see themselves as guardians of public resources and strive to attain their targets in the most economical way. Efficiency is their rallying call.

If indifference is an adaptive response that capitalizes on withdrawal and emphasizes efficiency, the other two responses, caregiving and enforcement, make room for more personal involvement, but at the price of an equally unimodal understanding of what the job calls for. Caregivers come to conceive of their role as one that requires providing tailored assistance to those in need. They focus on responsiveness and respect, often at the expense of fairness and efficiency. Enforcers, on the other hand, take it upon themselves to ensure that resources are distributed fairly and that no one takes advantage of the system. This concern comes to eclipse considerations of respect and efficiency. Both caregivers and enforcers see themselves as acting on behalf of a certain constituency—those too needy to fend for themselves, or the silent majority that are too honest, quiescent, or afraid to stand up for their rights and denounce free riders. They develop specialized modes of affective attunement revolving, respectively, around compassion and suspicion.

Caregiving and enforcement are resource intensive. It can take a considerable amount of time and effort to provide adequate support to a client in need or to expose a free rider. As such, these responses cannot be applied equally to all. Caregivers and enforcers rationalize distinctions in treatment by adding consonant cognitions: they create a split between "deserving" and "undeserving" clients.

Even this split, however, is not enough to render the job fully manageable. Enforcers and caregivers are still bound to fall short of attaining their lofty aims—to help all those in need, or to protect public resources from being improperly used. Those who manage to retain such dispositions do not see this as a personal failure but rather as a confirmation that their resolve needs to be strengthened further. Caregivers and enforcers think of their role as a moral mission. They respond to adversity with further radicalization; even failure becomes an occasion for self-affirmation.

Each of the three dispositions I have just described alleviates dissonance, but does so at the cost of cognitive distortions and of a reductive understanding of the role. Indifference reduces dissonance by enabling bureaucrats to feel less responsible for their actions; caregiving and enforcement do so by radicalizing bureaucrats and providing them with opportunities for self-affirmation. Above all, however, the three dispositions reduce dissonance by truncating bureaucrats' understanding of what they are responsible for so that it more closely matches the capabilities at their disposal.[30] Instead of being torn between competing demands, reductive dispositions entice bureaucrats to focus on a single dimension of the role, to the exclusion of others.

I have detailed the costs of such reductive dispositions in Chapter 2 and will not rehearse them here. There are, however, three other characteristics of indifference, caregiving, and enforcement that are worth noting. The first is that such dispositions, once adopted, are hard to dislodge, because they come with a specialized hermeneutic grid and mode of affective attunement. Research on motivated reasoning and confirmation bias suggests that those who adopt such dispositions are likely to search for information that validates their presumptions and to discount information that is discordant with their outlooks.[31]

It is also worth noting that indifference, caregiving, and enforcement are emergent responses. We do not need to presume that the individuals who enter public service agencies are strongly predisposed toward such dispositions. The radicalizing tendencies are not to be found in what agents bring *to* work, but in the conflicts and tensions that are latent *at* work.[32]

It is important to note, finally, that our discussion of adaptive responses to dissonance reveals "in negative," or by contrast, an essential aspect of what street-level work must be like for those who *do not* succumb to the drift toward indifference, caregiving, or enforcement. The challenge for such bureaucrats is to find a way to cope with the conflicts inherent to their role without adopting a reductive conception of their responsibilities; it is to retain a commitment to a multifaceted ideal of public service in the face of psychological pressures that constantly threaten to reduce or narrow such a commitment. Achieving this involves finding a sustainable way of living with dissonance without yielding to it.

There is an element of tragedy in street-level bureaucracy, and it is this: experiencing dissonance, however distressing it may be, is a sign that one is doing the job well—that one has indeed remained sensitive to a plurality of normative considerations. It is the absence of dissonance, a state of harmony or peace with oneself, that should have us worried, because it suggests that one may have settled for a reductive conception of the role.

Virtue, Autonomy, Practices of the Self

There are two ways to respond to the dissonance-induced drift toward indifference, caregiving, and enforcement. One is to accept the prevalence of these dispositions as a byproduct of the work environment and to think not about the shortcomings of any given bureaucrat but about the way in which these bureaucrats, *put together,* might be able to work in a sensible manner. The aspiration, in other words, would be to create an organizational culture in which bureaucrats from all three "strains" balance each other out. I will explore this avenue in Chapter 4.

The other, which I will explore in the rest of this chapter, is to think about how individual bureaucrats may, through their own efforts, resist being drawn to reductive dispositions. This approach starts from the observation that not all bureaucrats succumb to the three reductionist tendencies described above. How—through what kind of moral practice or training—do these individuals manage to hold their ground?

It is necessary to pursue both of these avenues in tandem. We need to focus on individual bureaucrats because clients typically interact with a single bureaucrat, not with a group average. But since the outlooks and dispositions of individual bureaucrats depend in large part on their everyday interactions with peers, we also need to have an organizational culture that makes the best of the individual differences that are, nevertheless, bound to arise.

I suggested at the close of the previous section that a central challenge for street-level bureaucrats is to retain a rich and balanced moral disposition in the face of unrelenting psychological pressure toward specialization. Meeting such a challenge is not trivial. To do so, street-level bureaucrats must learn to live with internal conflict and compromise. They must acquire a substantial margin of control over their own selves so as to remain in charge of their own affective, interpretive, and valuational sensibilities despite the transformative pull of dissonance.

This is an exercise in moral psychology, and there are two programs of moral formation (*Bildung*) that immediately come to mind as potentially holding promise for street-level bureaucrats: the development of personal autonomy and the cultivation of virtue. Both autonomy and virtue would, presumably, allow workers to preserve a margin of self-control or equanimity in the face of situational pressure. I will describe these two programs of moral formation and their limitations first, before explaining why I believe that a third program of moral exercise—one that focuses on the mastery and deployment of a range of everyday practices of the self—is better adapted to the challenges of street-level work.

Programs of moral formation that revolve around personal autonomy start from the presumption that bureaucrats may be too exposed, or too permeable, to their environment. If only bureaucrats could stand at a remove from their everyday routine, with enough detachment or perspective, they would—allegedly—become more resilient as moral persons.

Hannah Arendt made an argument of this sort in her writings on the trial of Eichmann.[33] If Eichmann had lost his moral compass, it was not because of shortcomings in character, but because he had become incapable of thinking for himself. Arendt kept emphasizing this "thoughtlessness" throughout the trial. Eichmann, she wrote, "was genuinely incapable of uttering a single sentence that was not a cliché"; all he said was "empty talk."[34] "The longer one listened to him," she added, "the more obvious it became that his inability to speak was closely connected with an inability to think."[35] Arendt was intent on showing—rather controversially—that Eichmann was not a sadistic person with evil thoughts but someone whose principal fault was to have relinquished his capacity to think autonomously.[36]

Arendt did not spend much time in *Eichmann in Jerusalem* explaining what Eichmann's thoughtlessness consisted in. She took up the task in a series of lectures delivered a few years later under the title "Some Questions of Moral Philosophy."[37] There, Arendt returned to the Greeks, and more specifically to Socrates, to present thinking as an activity, as an internal conversation with oneself. Thinking men, she said, "are two-in-one, not only in the sense of consciousness and self-consciousness . . . , but in the very specific and active sense of [a] silent dialogue, of having constant intercourse, of being on speaking terms with themselves."[38]

But if thinking involves, or rather if thinking requires, being on speaking terms with oneself, then there is implicit in the very activity of thinking a kind of moral safeguard.[39] There are certain things that someone who thinks—someone who keeps engaging in dialogue with oneself and who has grown to appreciate this relationship—will simply refuse to do, because they would endanger one's capacity to remain on speaking terms (i.e., in some degree of harmony) with oneself. "If I disagree with other people," Arendt explains, "I can walk away; but I cannot walk away from myself."[40] "I cannot do certain things," she writes, "because having done them I shall no longer be able to live with myself."[41]

We can restate Arendt's argument somewhat more systematically: (1) thinking involves entertaining and cultivating a dialogue with oneself; (2) individuals who think (in this way) will refrain from performing certain deeds, because they would no longer be able to live with themselves if they performed them ("no one can want to live with a criminal"); (3) Eichmann performed such deeds, and thus we can infer that he must have stopped thinking (in the relevant sense); (4) this is coherent with what we could observe from the trial, where Eichmann demonstrated that he was incapable of thinking independently. The conclusion to draw, then, is (5) if only Eichmann and others like him had kept thinking, if only they had retained and nurtured their special relationship to themselves, they would have preserved a minimal sense of moral direction—enough, perhaps, to place a limit on the unspeakable evil they perpetrated.

The problem with Eichmann had to do with a loss of moral autonomy, and such autonomy had to be understood, in turn, as the correlate of an internal activity—an ongoing exercise in dialogue—that Eichmann had not sufficiently attended to. Eichmann's failure, according to Arendt, was not one of character but one of practice. The third approach that I present below—the one that I come to favor—is very much aligned with this part of Arendt's argument.

There is, however, more to Arendt's take on Eichmann than the emphasis on moral practice. There is also a commitment to a form of personal autonomy and to the idea that the drive to retain self-harmony (under the guise of the question "Could I live with myself if I did *this?*") can offer valuable moral guidance. Both of these features limit the applicability of Arendt's argument to the challenges of street-level bureaucracy. Let me mention three difficulties.

The first is that Arendt begins with a diagnostic of the problem—a loss of autonomy—that only does partial justice to what street-level bureaucrats actually experience. Of the three dispositional pathologies I discussed in Chapter 2, only indifference can be said to display the symptoms of a loss of autonomy (disengagement, uncritical reliance on rules, and lack of initiative). Caregivers and enforcers, whatever else they may lack, are certainly not short on that front. As we saw in Chapter 2, with the stories of the upholsterer and the paraplegic, they are often willing to tweak or selectively invoke the rules in place, often at some risk to themselves, so as to act in line with their own conception of their role and responsibilities.[42]

The second difficulty in transposing Arendt's argument to street-level bureaucracy is that the criterion of self-harmony does not always provide much guidance in ordinary circumstances. It is easy to see why such a criterion may have worked for Eichmann. Considering the two options he presumably had to face—to evade orders, or to be complicit in mass murder—it is clear how he should have acted had he wanted to remain on "speaking terms" with himself. The fear of spending the rest of his life with a criminal may have provided him, moreover, with the motivational strength required to make this choice, despite the hefty price that he would (putatively) have had to pay. Eichmann's choice was morally easy but motivationally difficult.

Street-level bureaucrats, however, must generally make the opposite type of choices—choices that are less challenging motivationally but more complex morally. They operate in situations where the correct course of action is, from a moral point of view, far from obvious. Indeed, if my description of street-level work is correct, they have to constantly juggle various considerations that point in different directions. They are in the business of negotiating compromises. Given the nature of the job, it is unavoidable for well-balanced workers to experience some level of disharmony or dissonance, whichever way they ultimately decide to act. As I argued earlier, such dissonance is actually indicative of a proper disposition—it suggests that workers have indeed remained sensitive, as they ought, to a plurality of competing considerations.

While self-harmony can provide guidance in the face of enormities like the Holocaust, it is hard to see how it could be of much help in the murkier situations that street-level bureaucrats have to confront. How can self-harmony serve as a criterion of differentiation between several courses of action, if all of them are bound to generate some measure of disharmony? The worry is not only that the criterion may be practically useless, but also that it may be potentially misleading. The very idea that being in harmony with oneself is a state of being that one should aspire to is tendentious when one occupies a social role that necessarily involves getting one's hands dirty.[43]

It is important to note, as well, that the question that Arendt enjoins us to ask before acting ("Could I still live with myself after doing *that?*") can only yield a negative answer. As Arendt herself acknowledges, "the only recommendation we are entitled to expect from the 'It is better to be at odds with the whole world than being at odds with myself,' will always remain entirely negative. It will never tell you what to do, only prevent you from doing certain things, even though they are done by everybody around you."[44] It is easy to see how a maxim like this can yield "whistleblowers"—lone persons who can stand out from a group and refuse to be complicit. But it also clear that such a maxim, and the frame of mind that comes with it, will not be able to provide much help in more ordinary circumstances—circumstances in which street-level bureaucrats must distinguish not between what is permissible and impermissible, but between various shades of gray.

There is a third and last problem with approaches that stress the importance of personal autonomy, although Arendt is less guilty of it than others: these approaches tend to be overly rationalistic. In placing the emphasis on the capacity of individuals to disconnect themselves from their routine, to step back and reflect upon what they are about to do, personal autonomy effectively creates a rift between individuals and the world that surrounds them. It enjoins bureaucrats to subject their emotions and spontaneous responses to rational assessment.[45]

The problem is that street-level bureaucrats can get much valuable guidance from their moral sentiments—sentiments like empathy, compassion, or indignation—that lose much of their force when subjected to dry rational scrutiny.[46] While such sentiments should not be allowed to unilaterally determine the actions of bureaucrats, there is a danger in relegating them to a subservient role where they are viewed with suspicion and summoned to justify themselves in the language of reason. The danger with personal autonomy is that it can put bureaucrats at risk of severing their ties with those very sentiments that sometimes force them to reconsider their dispositions—those sentiments that can make for "breakthroughs," to return to Glover's fitting term.

There is a second approach to the challenges of street-level work that puts the emphasis not on the development of personal autonomy but on the cultivation of virtue. Virtues are generally understood to be deeply rooted character traits acquired and perfected via habituation.[47] They are, to use a formulation provided by Martha Nussbaum, "settled patterns of motive, emotion, and reasoning that lead us to call someone a person of a certain sort (courageous, generous, moderate, just, etc.)."[48] Someone who possesses a virtue will display a propensity to act in a particular way, a certain constancy of behavior across settings and situations. An honest person is, *among other things,* someone who can be relied upon to speak the truth unless there is a sufficiently weighty reason not to do so. A virtuous agent should be able to identify the morally salient features of a situation and to respond to them appropriately. He or she knows when to behave in a trait-relevant way (courageously, honestly, with benevolence, etc.) and how to do so without falling into either excess or deficiency.[49]

The cultivation of virtue might seem like a plausible solution to the challenges in moral psychology that street-level bureaucrats confront. The latter must navigate judiciously between a variety of extremes: between overzealous involvement and excessive withdrawal; between outright suspicion toward clients and inordinate compassion. They must develop a sense of balance and self-control in the face of psychological pressure, while remaining sensitive to the particularities of individual clients and cases.

Despite its *prima facie* attractiveness, however, the virtue-based approach runs into three difficulties. As I mentioned above, virtues are often thought to be stable or robust character traits. Once someone has acquired a virtue via training or habituation, it is supposed to travel, with them, from one setting or situation to another. This very assumption, however, has been challenged by a significant body of work in "situationist" social psychology.[50] A number of studies have shown that minor situational changes—changes involving the level of ambient noise, whether one is in a hurry or not, whether one has just found a dime on the street, etc.—tend to have considerable effects on behavior in morally charged situations.[51] If such trivial alterations, which should arguably carry little to no moral weight, can make the difference between decent and appalling behavior, how could we have confidence in the robustness of our character traits?

It is difficult for those who insist on the cultivation of virtue to respond to this charge—of excessive inconsistency—without limiting the reach of their own aspirations. One option would be to claim that virtue is rare and that one cannot expect to find it widely instantiated in a random sample of the population. Such a claim to exclusivity, however, would undercut the appeal of virtue as a general program for moral formation. If virtue is indeed rare and hard to attain, why not focus, instead, on developing a more modest and less demanding form of moral training—one that may be more accessible to bureaucrats whose cognitive and emotional capacities are already stretched thin?[52]

The difficulty of attaining virtue and its rarity also raise questions about its standing *as an ideal* toward which moral formation should tend. One cannot object to an ideal, of course, simply on the grounds that it is difficult or demanding to reach. The worry, rather, is that bureaucrats who pursue an ideal that they are not likely to attain may fall prey to the "problem of second best." By trying to reach virtue but falling short of it, they may end up with a disposition that is less desirable than the one they would have reached had they opted for a more modest goal in the first place.

The acquisition of virtue calls for a process of rigorous habituation typically performed under the guidance of a role model. This training is meant to equip the practitioner not only with a set of character traits or "natural abilities," but also with the practical wisdom required to instantiate these traits correctly in specific situations, and with the capacity to handle adequately conflicts between them.[53] The danger with practitioners who strive to be virtuous but do not succeed is that they may be left with character traits they are committed to instantiating, but without the practical wisdom they need in order to be sensitive to context and competing considerations. The risk with virtue is that it can fail ungracefully. Should that be the case, it would yield dispositions that are overly rigid and insensitive to conflict.

It is worth noting, finally, that there is another way in which situationism cuts against virtue ethics. I have focused so far on how minor situational changes can account for morally troublesome *inconsistencies* in behavior. Situationist findings, however, also raise the possibility that praiseworthy *consistencies* in behavior—of the kind we typically attribute to virtuous character traits—may in fact be better explained by reference to situational factors, or to context-specific practices.[54] The point is not the familiar one that the environment in which individuals are placed is necessary for the acquisition of virtue; it is, rather, that virtuous behavior must be sustained *on an ongoing basis* by features of the environment and by everyday practices that the environment makes possible.[55] This finding, if correct, runs against what many consider to be a central tenet of virtue ethics, namely, the idea that "the possession of the motivational structure of virtue . . . be, in maturity and under normal circumstances, independent of factors outside oneself, such as particular social relationships and settings."[56]

The implications for moral formation are significant. Instead of encouraging bureaucrats to develop character traits that would render them impervious to their surrounding environment, the findings of social psychologists suggest that bureaucrats should be encouraged, rather, to identify and promote situational factors and environmental conditions that support the behavior or disposition to which they aspire.[57] Whether this is seen as a challenge to virtue ethics or as a friendly amendment depends on whether one is willing to depart from the conception of virtue as a robust character trait that becomes, once acquired, independent from external factors.

As an alternative to the cultivation of virtue and to the fostering of personal autonomy, I believe that it is possible to sketch a third line of response to the problems in moral psychology that are at the heart of street-level bureaucracy. This approach takes inspiration from the work of Pierre Hadot and Michel Foucault on Hellenistic practices of the self. It draws in important ways on the two programs of moral formation that we have seen so far, but it takes heed of the difficulties that plague them.

I use the phrase "practices of the self," like Foucault, to refer to a wide range of everyday exercises (in self-examination, moral imagination, recollection, etc.) through which individuals can fashion their own moral dispositions. Such exercises draw on resources that exist in the practitioner's environment and are typically performed within a community of peers. Practices of the self have a long lineage in the history of moral philosophy. They form an essential part of the teachings of the four Hellenistic schools (Stoicism, Epicureanism, Cynicism, and Skepticism); they feature prominently in Eastern philosophical traditions; they appear in the guidebooks composed by Christian thinkers like Benedict and Loyola and in the writings of more modern philosophers like Montaigne, or the Descartes of the *Meditations;* and they are still very much alive, albeit in a somewhat impoverished form, in the widely popular self-help literature. More recently, these practices have been the subject of much experimental research in the field of "positive psychology," and their effectiveness appears to be largely corroborated.[58]

It is sometimes said that the resurgence of philosophical interest in questions of moral character around the 1950s arose out of a conviction that modern ethics had preoccupied itself exclusively with the question "What ought one to do?" and had unduly neglected the ancient question "What kind of person ought one to be?" We can read Foucault and Hadot as taking this critique one step further. They seek to draw our attention not only to the ideal models of personhood that the ancients proposed, but also—and primarily—to the everyday exercises through which ancient schools enjoined their followers to become such persons. Their take on the history of moral philosophy is distinctive in that they are more concerned with capturing patterns of moral practice than with articulating normative blueprints. Their work prompts us to think of moral dispositions not as deeply ingrained character traits but rather as the correlate, or effect, of everyday practices that we engage in.

What is interesting about this focus on moral practice is that it starts from the premise that moral reasoning does not operate on its own, but that there is an interdependence of action, cognition, memory, and emotion, and that all of these elements can be worked upon to alter one's moral disposition.[59] This explains the wide range of practices that Foucault and Hadot describe in their survey of Hellenistic schools.[60] These include:

- exercises in *abstinence and endurance* (fasting, exposure to cold, deprivation of pleasures) that are meant to strengthen one's self-discipline and to increase one's confidence in one's capacity to rise above the objects that one desires;
- exercises in *concentration,* in which one strives to focus on the present moment, so as to liberate oneself from the fears or hopes associated with the past or future;
- exercises in *imagination,* where one vividly recreates the possibility of proximate death so as to live each day as if it were the last;
- exercises in *self-examination,* where one keeps a close daily account of one's actions, thoughts, and dreams (often in the form of a diary);
- exercises in *perspectival change,* which involve looking at things from a different angle, typically by replacing events that take place within one's own life in the broader scheme of nature, thereby relativizing their importance;
- exercises in *recollection,* where one repeatedly invokes certain maxims or exemplary stories to keep them fresh in mind and to prepare oneself to act upon them.[61]

For Hadot and Foucault, as for the Hellenistic schools before them, practices of the self are performed with a view to attaining a certain *telos*—a form of self-presence for Foucault, a kind of reconciliation with the universal standpoint of reason for Hadot. It is possible, however, to decouple the emphasis on practices of the self from the particular ideal of the good life that Foucault or Hadot wish to advocate. Such practices can be assembled in different configurations and made to serve different ends.

A program of moral formation that revolves around practices of the self calls for some measure of autonomy. It presupposes agents who have some degree of reflective self-awareness, who are cognizant of their own dispositions and capable of seeking to change them.

The "practices of the self approach" to moral formation also has affinities with virtue ethics. Both look beyond the standalone ethical decisions that agents take and focus instead on the moral dispositions they develop. Both recognize the importance of moral perception, moral sentiments, and self-understanding to ordinary moral life. Both aim to provide agents with some measure of equanimity and self-control in the face of situational pressure. Both, finally, stress the importance of engaging in recurring patterns of exercise so as to shape one's moral outlook.

Despite these similarities, however, the practices of the self approach and virtue ethics differ in three important ways: practices of the self address a different kind of problem than virtues; they offer a different kind of solution; and they are more modest in aspiration. *Self approach vs. virtue ethics*

According to Alasdair MacIntyre, "a virtue is an acquired human quality the possession and the exercise of which tends to enable us to achieve those goods which are internal to practices and the lack of which effectively prevents us from achieving any such goods."[62] For MacIntyre, internal goods are goods that can be achieved only by participating in a given social practice (e.g., the unique combination of skills and abilities one develops while playing chess). These stand in contrast to external goods, which are attached to the practice only by the accidents of social circumstance (e.g., the monetary reward that one may get for winning a professional chess game). When MacIntyre speaks of external goods, he typically means competitive goods such as money, power, or status.[63]

Building on MacIntyre's conceptualization, we can distinguish between two types of virtues: virtues that protect practices or institutions from being denatured by the pursuit of external goods, and virtues that promote the realization of internal goods. Many of the virtues generally discussed in administrative ethics fall under the first rubric. Bureaucrats need, for instance, the virtue of courage to refrain from passively complying with their superiors' orders when these orders are unjust or immoral; they also need the virtue of integrity to resist being tempted by bribes. Such virtues prevent the pursuit of external goods (the promise of promotion, or that of personal enrichment) from encroaching upon internal goods. As character traits, they are unmitigated blessings.

However, the type of dilemmas that street-level bureaucrats must routinely contend with—those I discussed in the second section—are of a different kind. They do not involve a conflict between internal goods and external goods but a conflict between a range of goods—such as efficiency, fairness, and responsiveness—that are all internal to the practice of public administration and central to its legitimacy. Each of these internal goods can be advanced by a distinctive character trait or virtue (respectively: industriousness, equity, benevolence). But since these goods are plural and often conflict with one another, none of the character traits that are meant to advance them should be pursued single-mindedly or uncompromisingly. The problem with caregivers, indifferents, and enforcers, as we have seen, is that they are so committed to instantiating one, admittedly praiseworthy, character trait that they fail to register the salience of other normative considerations. The point of practices of the self is to enable street-level bureaucrats to retain a dispositional outlook sufficiently broad to recognize and act upon the full range of normative considerations that are pertinent to the role.

One could say, then, that practices of the self and virtues are solutions to different but complementary moral challenges. Virtues are answers to the following challenge: What character traits should one develop to excel at attaining the internal goods of a given practice? Practices of the self are answers to another challenge, which lies upstream: How can one retain a moral disposition sufficiently broad to recognize which internal goods (of the many that might be involved in a practice) are at play in a given situation? Both virtues and practices of the self might therefore be necessary for street-level bureaucrats to perform their role well.

Practices of the self also differ from virtue ethics in the kind of response they offer to the moral challenges of bureaucratic life. Unlike virtue ethics, the practice of the self approach does not aim to foster character traits that are inscribed deep within an individual's psyche. It sees moral dispositions, rather, as the effect or result of a certain regime of situationally specific practices of the self. If one were to stop performing the practices, the dispositions would not last for long. In other words, practices of the self are necessary not just for the acquisition of moral dispositions, but also for their ongoing sustenance. The practices of the self approach, moreover, does not promise to secure moral dispositions that can travel across settings or that can insulate practitioners from their environment. On the contrary, the approach encourages practitioners to fully acknowledge their dependence on their environment and to attempt to shape it to their advantage by identifying and promoting situational factors and environmental conditions that support the dispositions to which they aspire.

It is worth noting, finally, that the practices of the self approach is more modest and preventative in its aspiration than virtue ethics and, perhaps for this reason, more fail-proof. The goal of practitioners is not to attain the kind of knowledge and experience that would enable them to act reliably well in all circumstances, but—more modestly—to find a way to retain a balanced disposition in an environment that tends to truncate their moral sensibilities. The goal, to put it more colloquially, is not to always get it right, but to protect oneself from getting it systematically wrong by becoming aware of one's biases and proclivities and finding ways to counteract them.[64]

In what follows, I use the concept of "practice of the self" as an interpretive lens through which to revisit the everyday world of street-level bureaucrats. My aim is not to identify and propose new exercises nor to offer a self-help manual, but to give intelligibility and coherence to a wide range of seemingly disparate practices that street-level bureaucrats already perform. What this interpretive exercise will reveal is that those who succeed in retaining a balanced approach to their role engage in a complex moral craft, a gymnastics of the self, through which they constantly examine, calibrate, and modify their own dispositions. It is the mastery of this craft that serves as a bulwark against the drift toward reductive moral dispositions.

A Gymnastics of the Self

In this section, I reconstruct some of the everyday practices, or exercises, that street-level bureaucrats deploy to monitor and adjust their dispositions on an ongoing basis. Those who succeed in retaining a balanced approach to the role must walk a thin line. They must be careful not to expose themselves too much or shield themselves entirely, not to become overly suspicious or overly compassionate. They must come to accept internal conflict as an unavoidable part of the job, but they must learn to tune it down to a level they can sustain in the long run. One could say, to go back to the discussion in the second section, that such bureaucrats must effectively develop their own preemptive response to dissonance. By moderating the level of tension they experience, they can deflate the force of such dissonance and mitigate the cognitive distortions it induces. As we will see, this leads them to develop over time a more modest and realistic role conception—one that allows them to put up with the difficult compromises that the job calls for.

I have found helpful to group the practices of the self that street-level bureaucrats mobilize into three categories: exercises in *self-examination*, exercises in *calibration*, and exercises in *modulation*. We can visualize these categories by returning to the diagram I had presented earlier in Chapter 2 (see Figure 4). Exercises in self-examination enable street-level bureaucrats to uncover their own proclivities and biases (this amounts to identifying one's starting position on the diagram). Exercises in calibration allow them to regulate their level of personal involvement with clients (navigating the vertical axis). Exercises in modulation, finally, help them shape the nature of such involvement, negotiating a path between the two poles of caregiving and enforcement (navigating the horizontal axis). These last two categories of exercises enable bureaucrats to counteract the proclivities or biases they discover in themselves via self-examination.

In the following pages, I describe such practices of the self schematically and illustrate them with concrete vignettes drawn from a range of empirical studies, from literary sources, and from my fieldwork at the NCDI. When drawing on the latter, I will rely on the example of Maria, a senior case manager from Puerto Rico who was held as a role model within the agency for her success in skillfully balancing the plural demands of the role.

It is worth bearing in mind, as I describe these practices of the self, that their effects range over both local and enduring dispositions ("modes of appraisal" and "moral dispositions," to use the terminology of Chapter 2). Within the context of any particular encounter, practices of the self give bureaucrats some control over their modes of appraisal. When repeated over a number of encounters, however, such local interventions can have

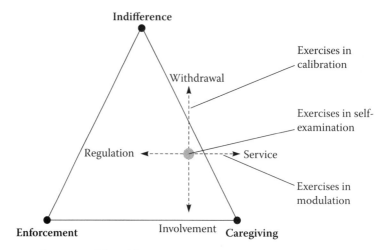

FIGURE 4. Practices of the self.

more lasting effects on bureaucrats' moral dispositions. By mitigating the force of dissonance in particular encounters, bureaucrats can reduce its distorting effects over time on their moral dispositions. Bureaucrats can also engage in projects of self-reform by voluntarily adopting modes of appraisal that are out of tune with their moral dispositions. They can take themselves "out of character" in the hopes of gradually effecting a change in their character.

Exercises in Self-Examination

Self-examination is a necessary prelude to self-reform: one must first know one's inclinations and biases before one can attempt to counteract them. It is for this reason that the Stoics enjoined their students to keep a diary—a daily record of their own thoughts and deeds. While diaries can be, and sometimes have been, used in street-level bureaucracies to good results, frontline workers tend to examine themselves in a less formulaic way.[65] They often do so in the course of informal debriefing sessions at the end of the workday, taking a few minutes with their colleagues to revisit their actions and assess their performance.[66]

An important component of the process of self-examination is comparative. Frontline workers situate themselves vis-à-vis the sample space constituted by their peers. They come to know their colleagues' dispositions and gradually identify, in contradistinction, the contours of their own. An intake worker interviewed by Vincent Dubois says of her colleagues:

> We're different, Sylvie, she's a lot more confrontational, she shakes people up a lot more. . . . She explains things in a more technical way so people don't really understand, either. . . . Lionel is very socially-minded. When someone comes in who doesn't have accommodation anymore, he's going to call the municipality, the social worker to find a place. In terms of language he puts himself in people's shoes more. He's going to do everything to have people sorted out. . . . I think I'm somewhere in between, myself.[67]

Frontline workers can also find a valuable source of information regarding their own proclivities in the feedback they obtain through formal institutional channels, via performance reviews and conversations with supervisors. For Maria, such feedback proved crucial in her early career. "Your problem," one of her supervisors once told her, "is that you treat clients like friends, and friends like family." This remark stuck with her as a cautionary tale about the excesses of caregiving and her own proclivity to give in to it.

Interestingly, the various targets, metrics, and performance reports, which have been making inroads into public institutions from the private sector, can also play an important part in the process of self-examination, provided they are not used exclusively for the purposes of evaluation.[68] At the NCDI, staff members were given access to a sophisticated case management software that displayed detailed information about the number of clients that individual case managers had served and the types of services such clients had received. This data provided staff members with a quick and easy way to compare their pace of work to that of their peers. A significant difference could throw light on one's tendency to get too involved or to be overly expeditive. For Maria, the availability of these numbers was a welcome addition to the more formal feedback sessions she had with her supervisor. Given her inclination to listen to clients at length, and her susceptibility to become emotionally involved while doing so, her numbers—which were on the lower side of the acceptable range—provided a constant reminder not to give in to the temptations of caregiving.

It is important to note, of course, that the capacity to engage in self-examination, and the motivation to do so, may not come naturally to frontline bureaucrats. Self-examination takes effort and requires a supportive environment. Maria was first prompted to examine her inclinations because of the feedback she received. She has since continued to do so by drawing on the various resources that her workplace makes available to her (from formal meetings and informal gatherings to monthly reviews and daily statistics).

Exercises in Calibration

Once bureaucrats have become cognizant of their own inclinations, they can attempt to counteract them. Exercises in calibration help bureaucrats regulate the extent of their involvement with clients. How much of themselves will they put on the line? Are they too exposed? Or have they become exceedingly withdrawn? These exercises contribute to moderating the poignancy with which bureaucrats are exposed to psychological strain.

Exercises in calibration come in three variants. I call them, respectively, exercises in heightening / dampening of one's moral perception, exercises in crystallization / dissolution of one's moral agency, and exercises in consolidation / compartmentalization of one's moral identity. These exercises can be put to use in both directions: to increase one's level of involvement or to decrease it. In this regard, the moral craft I seek to capture is importantly different from the one described by Foucault, where the objective is always to attain a greater sense of presence and agency. This has to do with the specific challenges posed by street-level bureaucracy, where it is possible to go wrong both by lack of involvement and by excess of it (see Chapter 2).

The scenes at the NCDI with which I opened this chapter illustrate the first family of exercises—exercises in heightening / dampening of one's moral perception. These exercises allow bureaucrats to regulate how intimate their interactions with clients are. Frontline workers mobilize their body language. They alternatively lean forward, make eye contact, and force themselves to listen attentively, thus exposing themselves further; or choose instead to lean back, look away, and allow themselves to be distracted by other tasks, thus reducing the likelihood that they will be moved by, or drawn into, the stories they hear.

Street-level bureaucrats also make use of the particular architectural setting within which the encounter takes place. When they meet their client in an office, the computer screen often serves as a shield—an item accessible only from within their own field of vision, which allows them to evade the searching eyes of the client and to slow or accelerate the rhythm of the encounter. They can also interrupt conversations that become too emotionally draining by stepping outside, under the pretense of fetching a file, or by soliciting the support and complicit gaze of their colleagues. In the words of a welfare worker:

> Sometimes we go out of our office, supposedly to check out a file, then either we breathe a little, or we scream . . . our colleagues are used to it. When you're too . . . you have to get out.[69]

This capacity to interrupt a conversation, to force oneself to "stop looking" or "stop seeing," is key for those who tend to get too involved. Those who are too distant will, on the contrary, have to exert themselves to maintain contact.

The importance of regulating one's moral perception is often revealed in negative, by seeing what happens to those who are no longer able to do so. Halfway through George Konrád's novel, *The Caseworker*—a novel inspired by Konrád's own experience as a street-level bureaucrat—the narrator, a frontline worker for child protection services, laments:

> I can't tear my eyes away from what I see day after day. . . . My defensive reflexes are slack, more and more often the blows hit me in the stomach; it's what happens to aging wrestlers who are baffled by the new techniques and keep finding themselves flat on the mat. Other people's sufferings have been affecting me lately; my head is full of their stories, my dreams are live with them . . . : I strongly suspect that those of my acquaintances who manage to live day after day with equanimity are sleight-of-hand artists.[70]

If the caseworker can no longer bear his work, it is because he has lowered his guard too much—he can no longer "tear his eyes away." It is telling that the narrator resorts to the language of wrestling: his failure is a failure of practice. He hasn't sufficiently exerted his defensive reflexes.

The second family of exercises in calibration—exercises in dissolution / crystallization of one's moral agency—enable bureaucrats to regulate the extent to which they feel personally responsible for their actions. One of the distinctive features of street-level bureaucracy is that it involves a large number of rules and regulations, the precise reach of which is typically unknown to clients. This allows bureaucrats to seek shelter behind the protective shield of the rules. They can deflect criticism under the guise of the familiar formula "I am simply doing my job."

The availability of this excuse, and the ease with which it can be put to use, allows some bureaucrats to gradually dissociate themselves from their actions and to experience difficult discretionary decisions with less poignancy or agony. Some may even develop, over time, a secondary set of rules or heuristics that they can apply automatically, and through which they can handle discretionary decisions without experiencing them as such. Like factory line workers, they effectively train themselves to "zone out." As Vincent Dubois puts it:

> "Bureaucratic over-conformity'. . . plays an important role in allowing for self-protection in the face of difficult situations. . . . A retreat towards bureaucratic rules should not be confused with the individual's "passive identification" to an externally imposed role. It can be understood, rather, as an anonymizing tactic: if in a given situation a reception agent seeks to fit the administrative mould, it is because this mould provides a shelter, a means for protection.[71]

While retreating behind rules or behind the automatism of self-imposed heuristics is sometimes advisable for bureaucrats who become too involved with clients, the converse is true for those where inclinations point the other way. Bureaucrats can "prebind" themselves to experience the full weight of their decisions.[72] Some of the case managers I observed at work at the NCDI did not hesitate, for instance, to disclose the exact limits of their discretion to clients. By doing so, they effectively committed themselves ex-ante to justifying any discretionary decisions they would take, and encouraged clients to hold them personally accountable for such decisions.[73]

The third family of exercises in calibration—exercises in consolidation/compartmentalization of one's moral identity—pertain to the boundary between private and professional life. Frontline workers often find that they can cope with the pressures of everyday work only by establishing a clear separation between work and home. Some measure of compartmentalization allows them to return refreshed the next day and may be necessary for those who have a tendency to get too involved. Yet learning to make a clean break ("leaving work at work") takes practice. One has to learn to "empty oneself" of the frustrations one has experienced during the day and to divert one's attention from matters and memories pertaining to work. One has to develop the capacity, moreover, to drop the emotional shield that one has constructed at work, only to put it up again the next morning.

Failure to effect such a break can come at great cost. A welfare worker who had to quit her job because she could no longer bear the psychological strain said, "There was a moment when life outside and work formed a whole." She added, "I relived my workday every night." One of her colleagues, alerted to the problem, offered the following diagnostic: "She's too uncompromising. . . . We all have problems, you have to be able to keep your chin up, and maintain boundaries in your professional life."[74]

The theme of boundaries is one that kept surfacing in my conversations with Maria. During one of our regular meetings, she pulled from her bookshelf an imposing, 400-page volume titled *Empowerment Skills for Family Workers*. While the volume had signs of wear, the pages were largely unmarked with the exception of a short section, three to four pages long, which was heavily highlighted and underlined and to which yellow Post-it stickers were attached. The section was titled "How to Avoid Families Becoming Dependent on You," and the subsection to which Maria drew my attention was called "Setting Healthy Boundaries."

In guiding me through it, Maria kept emphasizing that it provided valuable advice and that she had the habit of sharing it with new colleagues (as she was doing with me). The section contained a variety of rules or principles of conduct for frontline case managers. One sentence, which stood out from the rest of the text in bold font, read, "The ability to know what your own abilities are and to not push yourself beyond that limit; that's a skill that needs to be developed." Another paragraph offered the following counsel: "It's often hard to say no when asked to help. . . . But saying no helps keep the relationship from becoming unbalanced. . . . It also keeps feelings of resentment from growing in you and getting in the way of the relationship." Yet another said, "By expressing feelings and sorting out what's going on, workers can remain empathetic with the family, but detached enough to clearly see the family's situation and needs. These workers care about the families, but don't live their lives for them.

The workers have full personal lives of their own." In pointing out these excerpts to me, Maria insisted that she found it helpful to read them again and again, to refresh her memory—an exercise which is reminiscent of the Stoic practice of memorizing maxims and of constantly recalling them to mind. "It's a constant reminder that I have," she said; "I need to revisit it from time to time."

Other workers start at the opposite end of the spectrum. Instead of being overly empathetic, they are overly distant. Such workers do not need to build additional boundaries but lower the ones they have already established. They do so, in part, by trying to foster a more intimate connection between their personal and professional lives so as to let some of their private sensibilities filter through in their encounters with clients. For some case managers at the NCDI, attending the local church on Sunday played an important part in such a process of decompartmentalization. At church, they would run into their clients, but in a setting where the psychological and symbolic boundaries erected in the office were less salient. As one of my colleagues of Cape Verdean descent told me, to see clients with their families at church is to remind oneself of the community that one belongs to and of the reasons why one became a case manager in the first place. This serves as a check against the drift toward indifference.

Exercises in Modulation

In addition to calibrating their level of involvement, street-level bureaucrats can deploy practices of the self to modulate the nature of such involvement. To the extent that they do get involved, which way do their sympathies point? How can they moderate these sympathies so as to retain a balanced perspective—a workable compromise between the outlook of a caregiver and that of a guardian of public resources?

Bureaucrats modulate their involvement through exercises in recollection and moral imagination. Let us start with recollection. Frontline workers keep in mind a repertoire of "war stories" recounting encounters that marked them, or encapsulating important lessons. These stories, much like the ones I discussed in Chapter 2, present a certain picture of the client, a description of the encounter that took place, and a *dénouement*—an ending that can be either a success or a failure. By selecting these stories and revisiting them periodically, bureaucrats participate in shaping their own moral sensibilities.

Take the example, once again, of Konrád's caseworker. He prepares himself for the job by rehearsing a series of stories drawn selectively from his previous encounters.[75] In these stories, clients whom he had treated with compassion eventually turned out to be undeserving of his trust, while clients he had treated harshly turned out to have been victims of circumstances they could not have foreseen or prevented. For the caseworker, recollecting such stories is not merely an exercise in repentance. It serves, as well, to generate a complex and nuanced portrait of clients, and some measure of skepticism regarding his capacity to tell the deserving apart from the undeserving. It is such a portrait that enables the caseworker to mitigate his own tendency to make quick judgments and that helps him refrain from veering too much toward either compassion or suspicion.

Interestingly, this is not a lesson that can be learned once and for all, but one that the caseworker suspects he may forget. To assist and stimulate his memory, he has preserved small objects (a file, a picture, a letter) that remind him of the individual stories, and he keeps them ready at hand in a drawer in his office. With a simple pull, the caseworker can thus activate his memory selectively, bringing to mind the kinds of stories he needs to counteract or moderate his inclinations.

Street-level bureaucrats also make use of exercises in moral imagination to alter the standpoint from which they appraise clients. Some insist on putting themselves in the position of the people whom they serve. As one of the case managers I interviewed said:

> you've got to understand that people see things in a different way, . . . you can't judge them or say that they are right or wrong . . . I wouldn't like someone to do that to me. So when I have people here, I try to think of myself sitting in their chair and imagine what it must be like. It's hard to ask for help.

By asking themselves, "How would I feel if *I* were lining up for a welfare check, or if *I* were asking the police to intervene in a domestic quarrel?" frontline workers can sometimes retrieve, from within their own life experiences, the memory of past difficulties they had to face—a memory that might allow them to muster some measure of sympathy for their clients. Others insist on sticking to their own viewpoint and on assessing the choices of their clients in light of their own present circumstances—a decision that might, given the social, economic, and cultural gap that sometimes separates the two parties, incline them toward enforcement.

Frontline workers also resort to exercises in moral imagination to alter the nature of their relationship to clients. Some workers conjure up mental associations between their clients and people they are personally related to. They exert themselves to think of clients as "friends" or "family" who are in trouble. Others take the opposite approach. They refuse such intimacy altogether and train themselves to resist any drive toward identification, often by cutting the conversation short. As one case manager put it to me, "I need to know why you [the client] are here, but I don't want to hear the back story, what led you to being in a situation where you have no money."

The significance of these exercises can be captured in terms of Michael Walzer's *Spheres of Justice*.[76] We are all involved in different social spheres and the sort of treatment we believe we owe to others depends on which sphere we think they belong to. Exercises in moral imagination allow frontline workers to transfer their clients across such spheres. They can come to see them as strangers plundering public resources, or as close acquaintances in need.

Conclusion

I have tried to show, in this chapter, that the bureaucrats who are able to stand the test of street-level work—those who manage to retain a balanced approach to their role by withstanding the pull toward reductive dispositions—are far from passive. They engage in a delicate moral craft, a silent gymnastics of the self, through which they constantly monitor, modulate, and calibrate their moral dispositions by making creative use of the resources (collegial, informational, architectural, etc.) that their environment makes available to them.

Like any other craft, the moral gymnastics that I have described leaves room for individual variation across bureaucrats. There is no "correct solution"—no single disposition or regime of practices—that will work for all. Some will lean more toward enforcement, others toward caregiving, and others still toward indifference, and the practices they will have to deploy will vary accordingly. Behind this diversity, however, there is one constant: practitioners must learn to reconcile themselves, however reluctantly, with the twin virtues of moderation and restraint. When dissonance has structural roots that lie deep in the nature of the social role that one occupies, the most one can do—short of institutional reform—is to mitigate its force. Bureaucrats who succeed in controlling the tensions latent in their work eventually gravitate toward a conception of their role that is modest yet sustainable over time. Konrád's caseworker sums up this attitude toward the end of the novel, as he castigates in the same breath those who turn to caregiving and to indifference:

> I repudiate the high priests of individual salvation and the sob sisters of altruism, who exchange commonplace partial responsibility for the aesthetic transports of cosmohistorical guilt or the gratuitous slogans of universal love. I refuse to emulate these Sunday-school clowns and prefer—I know my limitations—to be the skeptical bureaucrat that I am. My highest aspiration is that a medium-rank, utterly insignificant civil servant should, as far as possible, live with his eyes open.[77]

Bureaucracies, the caseworker seems to tell us, are no place for grand vocations. And yet his own resolution, sobering as it is, is far from a sigh of despair. To exchange grand aspirations for partial responsibility; to become aware of one's limitations; to be able to live as far as possible with one's eyes open: if my description of the work that street-level bureaucrats have to perform is anywhere close to correct, this—we will have to concede—is no small feat.

CHAPTER FOUR

When the Rules Run Out
Informal Taxonomies and Peer-Level Accountability

When I began my fieldwork at the NCDI, I was intent on observing the nature of ordinary moral deliberation among street-level bureaucrats. I wanted to know how questions of moral significance were brought up, discussed, and resolved in the thick of everyday work. I suspected, in line with much of the literature on organizational behavior, that workers would be engaged in ongoing conversations about practice, and I assumed that I knew, roughly, what such conversations would be like and what they would be about.

Since street-level bureaucrats inherit directives that are often vague and conflicting, I imagined that I would see them debate at length how to best interpret the demands of their role. What does it mean to treat someone with respect? How should one balance considerations of efficiency with those of responsiveness? When is it acceptable to make an exception to standard operating procedures? I thought that these questions, and others like them, would be a topic of ongoing discussion, involving an exchange of arguments and prompting those involved to articulate and defend their role conceptions to one another. I suspected that these debates would be driven less by a desire for theoretical clarity or consistency than by practical disagreements about particular cases. Yet I assumed, perhaps betraying my own biases as a political theorist, that in order to understand the source of these disagreements and to resolve them, frontline workers would have to elevate the conversation to a somewhat more abstract level. They would have to appeal to such things as their understanding of the organization's mission, their sense of professional identity, their conceptions of justice and fairness, and so on.

Several months into the job, however, I had not observed a single exchange that conformed to these expectations. To the extent that my colleagues interacted and disagreed with one another on questions of value, they did so in a very different way. Their exchanges were brief, terse, and practical. They rarely involved drawn-out arguments, and they practically never touched on questions of principle. Particular controversies were addressed, or so it seemed, without the mediation of more abstract or fundamental precepts. Besides being highly targeted, the exchanges I observed were often hard to decipher, because they assumed familiarity with a specialized lexicon that no one in the organization seemed willing or able to define with any precision. Take the following interaction as an example:

Flora, yelling to Laura, who is in a different office: "Anna called again. She was supposed to come in yesterday but missed it. She wants to reschedule. She's called five times. I told her that I would get back to her tomorrow 'cause I'm too busy now, and she's still calling. This lady has a serious attitude!"

Laura, shouting back: "Yeah. . . . Well, you know, she has issues."

Flora, sounding incredulous: "She has issues?"

Laura, walking over to Flora's office and leaning against the door: "Oh, you didn't know? She didn't tell you? She has a situation too. You know what, I'll do it."

How should we interpret such an exchange? What does it mean for someone to have an "attitude," a "situation," or "issues"? This chapter began as an attempt to grapple with these interpretive questions; it later expanded considerably when it became clear that the answers to such questions uncovered a host of serious normative issues about discretion and accountability at the front lines of the democratic state.

Introduction

While discussing the importance of practices of the self in Chapter 3, I focused on the experience of individual street-level bureaucrats taken largely in isolation from their peers. But such bureaucrats do not work alone. Whether they spend their days behind counters, in offices, cubicles, classrooms, or patrol cars, they are almost always in close proximity to colleagues. They exchange greetings, jokes, and stories with one another; they ask each other questions and look to each other for emotional support and advice; they encourage, challenge, and pass judgment on one another; they are each other's closest confidants and most relentless critics. In this chapter, I try to capture something of the dense patterns of interaction that take place between peers during a regular workday, and I argue that such horizontal exchanges play a central role in the proper moral functioning of our bureaucracies.

The argument I make in what follows is the converse of the one I offered in Chapter 3. I argued there that street-level bureaucracies must guard against excessive moral specialization at the individual level. I try to show here that a certain degree of diversity or pluralism in moral dispositions at the group level—and hence, some measure of moral specialization at the individual level—can be desirable. This will be an argument in favor of an "organized heterogeneity" in moral dispositions at the front lines of public service.[1] If I am correct, then the argument of this chapter, taken together with that of Chapter 3, shows that street-level bureaucracies must guard against two types of dangers: they must tread a path between excessive specialization at the individual level and excessive homogeneity at the group level.

The benefits of organized heterogeneity become visible, or so I will try to show, when we look at street-level bureaucrats not as isolated moral agents but as participants in a dense network of informal relationships. I draw on my experience at the NCDI to show that such relationships, and the everyday interactions that accompany them, play a central role in shaping the moral perception of individual bureaucrats and in setting the assumptions on the basis of which their moral reasoning takes place. When these interactions occur against a background of organized heterogeneity, they also set the stage for an informal regime of accountability that is well adapted to overseeing the moral tasks that street-level bureaucrats must perform and that can serve as a check against the reductionist tendencies I described in Chapters 2 and 3.

The significance of peers, and the importance of the ongoing conversations that take place between them in the thick of everyday work, have not been lost on political theorists. Legal scholars have long recognized, for instance, that the process of interpreting the law and applying it to specific cases is dependent on the existence of "interpretive communities."[2] These communities play a central role in constraining the process of legal interpretation, in establishing shared assumptions among practitioners, and in providing them with an understanding of the nature and purpose of the practice they participate in. Writing in a different tradition and with a different set of concerns, virtue ethicists have also underscored the role that communities of peers play in giving practical content to abstract moral requirements and in shaping the moral virtues of individual members.[3] Deliberative democrats, finally, have called attention to the importance of reciprocal practices of reason-giving that accompany the work of formal political institutions and that tie public officials to each other and to citizens in complex webs of justificatory relationships.[4] They have shown that, when such practices are properly structured, they can transform the outlook of individual participants and serve as useful fora for everyday accountability.

The importance of horizontal interactions among peers has also been recognized in organization theory and in the literature on street-level bureaucracy. John Brehm and Scott Gates have argued, for instance, that the decision to work, shirk, or sabotage among low-ranking bureaucrats depends much less on the coercive capacities of supervisors than on the influence of fellow employees.[5] According to Brehm and Gates, bureaucrats look to their peers both for informational cues about the proper course of action and for recognition or approval.

In stressing the importance of peers, Brehm and Gates could find support in a long tradition of research in organization theory running back to Chester Barnard's critique of Scientific Management for its reductive fixation on the coercive capacities of supervisors, and to the work of the human relations movement on the role of informal group dynamics and shared cultural norms in organizations.[6] Brehm and Gates could also draw, in political science proper, on Herbert Kaufman's classic work on forest rangers.[7] In a study that prefigured much of the literature on street-level bureaucracy, Kaufman showed that the Forest Service's success in running a decentralized operation was tributary to the existence of a strong corporate ethos that informed the behavior of individual field officers. Like others before and after him, Kaufman stressed the role of peers in propagating such an ethos and in socializing new members.[8]

More recently, Michael Piore has argued that what distinguishes street-level bureaucracy from other organizational forms, such as hierarchies or markets, is the extent to which it combines extensive discretion for line officers with reliance on organizational culture and everyday conversations among peers (as opposed, say, to economic incentives or hierarchical directives) to guide the exercise of such discretion.[9] It is not surprising that one would find, peppered throughout the literature on street-level bureaucracy, references to the Toyota Production System—a management approach that delegates authority to the base of the organizational hierarchy and that relies heavily on shared cultural norms, group-level dynamics, and teamwork.[10]

My argument in this chapter builds on this rich body of work. It seeks to expand our appreciation of the importance of informal interactions among peers beyond the domains of efficiency, innovation, and effectiveness, which have been the primary concern of organization theorists and scholars of public administration, to that of morality. The chapter also seeks to draw attention to the microdynamics of organizational life, which are often buried under—and obscured by—the abstract language of "informal norms" and "organizational culture." We know that peers matter, but how, precisely, do they matter? It is by being on the lookout for ethnographic detail that we can begin to see, for instance, that "organizational culture" is often a mystifying term—one that glosses over the centrality of disagreement between workers who have different ways of inhabiting their role. In the picture of street-level work that I will draw in the following pages, it is not just culture that matters, but how the various subcultures or subgroups that exist within a given organization negotiate their disagreements on an ongoing basis.

I build my argument—about the importance of informal interactions among peers and the need for a plurality of moral dispositions at the front lines of public service—by focusing on one of the key moments at which street-level bureaucrats are solicited as moral agents, namely, when the formal rules they have at their disposal run out. As I will explain at length in the body of the chapter, street-level bureaucrats are known to develop informal moral taxonomies that allow them to distinguish between clients and cases in a way that is more granular than the official rules provide for. They resort to such taxonomies, in part, to fill the gaps that arise when the rules are not precise or decisive enough to yield determinate guidance.

While informal moral taxonomies are not democratically sanctioned, they effectively mediate the implementation of public policy. They also serve to anchor a distinctive form of moral reasoning—an "everyday casuistry"— that differs from the top-down application of rules that we often associate with bureaucratic rationality. I will show that such casuistry can play a valuable role in the implementation of public policy. I will argue, as well, that peers can influence how such casuistry unfolds, and that—when the right conditions obtain—they can also hold each other accountable for how they engage in casuistic reasoning.

By stressing the importance of everyday casuistry and peer-level accountability, one of my aims is to show that street-level bureaucracies are home to a complex moral ecosystem that is largely opaque to hierarchical scrutiny and control. The proper functioning of these organizations—on a moral plane—is largely parasitic on a dense web of informal relationships and practices whose importance is not sufficiently recognized, and which often end up being the intended or unintended casualty of attempts at institutional reform.

The reasons for this neglect or lack of appreciation are plain to see. The form of moral reasoning that I will describe under the label of "everyday casuistry" is convoluted, messy, and attains at most local coherence. To outside observers, it may look muddled, haphazard, and arbitrary. The type of horizontal accountability that I will depict is also likely to be viewed with suspicion. It relies on unofficial sanctions, is not always dependable, and remains largely opaque to hierarchical oversight. What's more, everyday casuistry and informal accountability run counter to at least two widely accepted principles of institutional design: the requirement of transparency, and the need for articulate consistency (namely, for a relatively high degree of principled coherence in the way in which a public organization and its officials behave toward the public).[11]

While these concerns are justified, I argue that it would be a mistake to downplay the many ways in which everyday casuistry enables frontline workers to meet the demands of their role in a sensible and responsible manner. It would be wrong, moreover, to equate lack of transparency or articulate consistency with absence of accountability. To acknowledge the positive contributions that everyday casuistry and peer-level account-ability make to the functioning of our public institutions is not to relin-quish altogether our commitment to established principles of institutional design. It is, rather, to attain a more nuanced appreciation of the tradeoffs that are involved when one attempts, in the name of such principles, to press for changes in policy and management that are likely to shake up other valuable facets of an organization's moral ecosystem.

Informal Moral Taxonomies: "Situations," "Issues," and "Attitudes"

Street-level bureaucrats are responsible for bringing laws and policies to bear on specific cases. This is an exercise that may, at first sight, appear to be merely subsumptive. A subsumptive model of policy implementation would proceed roughly as follows: frontline workers inherit from their su-periors a body of rules that have a proper democratic pedigree; when con-fronted with a new case, they look to see which of those rules the case falls under; the relevant rule indicates the various considerations that ought to be taken into account in adjudicating the case, and their respective weight; the resulting calculus determines, finally, the appropriate course of conduct to follow. If such a model always held true, street-level bureaucrats would be able to approach clients as undifferentiated individuals, as theories of the modern rational-legal state often presuppose. It is in the process of applying the law, and on the basis of criteria specified in the law, that clients would be sorted into categories and that an appropriate response to each would be found.

The subsumptive model of policy implementation sometimes hits the mark. There are cases that are unambiguously picked out by a rule, and there are rules that yield determinate guidance. As a general guide to bu-reaucratic behavior, however, such a model is deeply misleading. Simply put, it overstates the capacity of bureaucratic rules to provide guidance that is both dispositive and exhaustive. I described the reasons why the subsumptive model breaks down in Chapter 1. Let me briefly review four of them here.

First, the subsumptive model does not recognize that rules frequently come into conflict with one another. When a case falls under more than one rule (say, A and B), and when these rules point in conflicting directions, frontline workers must be able to assess which of them should take precedence. The answer will involve drawing distinctions between various types of cases (those for which A prevails over B and vice versa) that are not contained in the rules themselves.

The subsumptive model also ignores the fact that frontline workers inherit not only rules but other types of legal norms as well, such as "factors" and "standards." Unlike rules, factors and standards point to considerations that must be taken into account but that are not given a clear weight, or to thresholds that must be met but that do not have a well-defined cutoff point (e.g., standards of "reasonableness"). Frontline workers must determine how to weigh these considerations (for factors) and where to draw the line (for standards). This too will depend on establishing judicious distinctions between various types of cases.

The subsumptive model assumes, moreover, that the rules that street-level bureaucrats inherit will yield determinate guidance—that they will single out a particular course of action. But rules can be vague or ambiguous and leave open a range of possibilities. In the case of street-level bureaucrats, rules often specify *what* action must be taken without exactly specifying *how* such an action ought to be taken. Frontline workers are often responsible, as such, for deciding which style of delivery will be most appropriate for any given type of client or situation.

The subsumptive model fails, finally, to take into consideration the special constraints placed by limited resources. When resources are scarce, cases that ought to be treated identically in theory may have to be handled differently in practice. If clients cannot all be given the level of treatment they should ideally receive, there may be good reasons to prioritize some over others.

In all the situations I have just described, the guidance provided by the rules that street-level bureaucrats inherit effectively runs out. To fulfill their role in a responsible manner, such bureaucrats are effectively compelled to develop distinctions between clients and cases that are more granular than those formally sanctioned by the policy or law being implemented. Street-level bureaucrats tend to meet such a challenge by developing informal moral taxonomies: classification schemes that enable them to distinguish between different types of clients and situations and to deliver an appropriate response to each.[12] Unlike standard operating procedures, such taxonomies are typically developed from the bottom up. They are conceived, transmitted, monitored, revised, and regulated by peers. While they lack a proper democratic pedigree, they effectively constitute an important, if often overlooked, layer that mediates the implementation of public policy and the enforcement of laws.

The use of informal taxonomies has attracted some attention, though perhaps not as much as it deserves, from scholars of street-level bureaucracy and policy implementation.[13] The case of the police is illustrative. In an influential article titled "The Asshole," the organizational ethnographer John Van Maanen has shown that police officers tend to distinguish between three types of citizens: "suspicious persons," "assholes," and "know-nothings."[14] Suspicious persons are those whom the police have reason to believe may have violated the law. Assholes are those who openly challenge the authority of police officers by casting doubt on their motives, questioning their right to intervene, or disputing their definition of the situation. Know-nothings, finally, are members of the public who do not belong to either of the first two categories and who usually come into contact with the police via their request for services.

The ability to distinguish between these three categories of citizens and to know how to respond to each is part of the "commonsense wisdom" of police officers—a set of skills honed by years of experience that can make the difference between a good cop and a bad one. Telling "suspicious persons" apart from "know-nothings," for instance, allows officers to focus their limited time, attention, and effort on tracking, observing, and interrogating those most likely to have violated the law. Distinguishing between these two categories and "assholes" helps them pick a suitable demeanor— soft-spoken or assertive, friendly or inquisitive, conciliatory or confrontational. Given that an officer's capacity to do his or her job well depends on having an aura of authority and on seeming to be in control, there may be good reason to be more firm or brusque with someone presumed to be an "asshole" than with a "know-nothing" even though neither is suspected of having broken the law.

While informal taxonomies can be useful or even indispensable to frontline practitioners, they should also give us cause for concern. For one, such taxonomies are not democratically sanctioned, nor is their application democratically controlled. They can therefore serve as a haven for implicit biases and stereotypes. This raises serious questions about accountability—as to the nature of the categories and their application to specific cases. Such worries are crystallized in a category such as that of the "asshole." As Van Maanen points out, one can legitimately wonder whether such a label ought to feature at all in the lexicon of a state representative, let alone one who has the right to use violence, and whether the attributes that the label picks out do in fact warrant special treatment.

I will engage in a more thorough normative discussion of informal taxonomies in the second half of the chapter, and I will have a chance to explain there how we might be able to mitigate the risks they pose. Before I do this, however, I would first like to examine, with the aid of a detailed case study drawn from my fieldwork, how these taxonomies are structured and how they shape the moral deliberation of street-level bureaucrats.

The case I want to discuss relates to missed appointments—a frequent occurrence at the NCDI. Whenever clients failed to show up at the agreed time, they would usually call or stop by later to see if they could reschedule their meeting for an alternative date. Case managers were not allowed to deny such requests; they were instructed, rather, to reschedule the appointment for the next available spot on their calendar.

Though simple in appearance, this directive opened a substantial space for discretionary judgment. Like most other frontline workers in the public services, case managers at the NCDI were understaffed and were almost always operating with a considerable backlog of tasks to perform. They could always fill an opening in their calendar by reaching out to new clients, by tracking the progress of existing cases, or by catching up with the mountains of accumulated paperwork. In light of the never-ending supply of things to do, determining the next *available* spot on one's calendar was a matter of prioritization: one could pick the next free spot or a later one.

This gave case managers some leeway in deciding when to reschedule a missed appointment. They could effectively choose among three responses that I will label, for ease of reference, "administrative," "responsive," and "punitive." The "administrative" response consisted in scheduling the client for the next free spot on one's calendar. Given that at certain times of the year such a response could entail lengthy delays, case managers could, alternatively, try to be more "responsive" by making themselves available before the next official slot. By working at a somewhat faster pace, shortening their lunch breaks, or staying overtime, they could reshuffle their calendar so as to "squeeze" the client between two other appointments. The "punitive" response was less common than the other two. It consisted in delaying the makeup appointment by prioritizing other activities. The client would thus be made to pay an unofficial penalty for having missed their designated slot.

In addition to setting the *when* of the appointment, case managers could also determine the *how* of the interaction. They could decide what tone or demeanor to adopt in responding to the client's request. Here too, case managers tended to choose between three approaches—"transactional," "therapeutic," and "pedagogical." The "transactional" approach consisted in handling the client's request as a routine procedure, without letting any emotion or value judgment filter through and while keeping the conversation to a bare minimum. The "therapeutic" approach took the missed appointment as an opportunity to inquire into the client's well-being (How where things going? Why was the appointment missed? Was something wrong?), to lend them a supportive ear, and to share with them a few reassuring words. The "pedagogical" approach, finally, seized on the occasion to give the client a moralizing lesson of sorts by reminding them of the need to uphold commitments, by stressing the dangers of "dependency," and by emphasizing that they were expected to play an active role in moving their own administrative case forward.

Case managers had different ways to handle missed appointments. Depending on their moral dispositions—whether they were, to use the typology I proposed in Chapter 2, indifferents, caregivers, or enforcers—they were more likely to adopt certain decisions or demeanors than others. It is helpful to think of missed appointments and similar events (such as clients being late or coming with incomplete paperwork) as "discretionary openings" that allow street-level bureaucrats to express their own distinctive sensibilities and styles.[15] Such openings are significant not only for clients, who are likely to be treated differently depending on whom they interact with, but also for bureaucrats and their sense of self. It is in such moments that it truly matters that they—as specific individuals—are the ones doing the job, not someone else.

Despite their different proclivities, however, case managers tended to approach the problem of rescheduling a missed appointment in a broadly similar fashion. To determine when to see a client and how to interact with them, they relied on a three-part taxonomy: they sought to assess whether the client had a "situation," "issues," or an "attitude."

Clients with a "situation" were, by and large, those who needed prompt attention. This included clients who had an official deadline coming soon as well as those who were in urgent need of services (clients whose heating, for instance, was in danger of being cut off). But the label "situation" was also applied more broadly to refer to clients who, while not effectively constrained by time, exhibited the signs of distress, anxiety, and alarm that are usually associated with looming and momentous deadlines. Clients who were unduly nervous or anxious were prime candidates for having a "situation." As a case manager once told me, blurring the boundaries of the category even further, the label was meant to pick out those clients "who would not be fine coming back" at some later date as opposed to "those we know will be fine."

Clients with "issues" were those facing serious personal difficulties that were not likely to be resolved in the near future. While not urgent or necessarily manifest, these latent problems could affect their capacity to cope with ordinary affairs. Having "issues" could help explain, for instance, why a client was aggressive, rude, or brash. Someone had "issues" if they had ongoing marital difficulties, if their immigration status was not fully regularized, if one of their family members had a disability or illness (e.g., an autistic child), or if they were in the midst of trying legal proceedings. Clients could also have "issues" if they or one of their family members were "constantly getting into trouble"—a phrase that could refer to anything from an inability to rein in one's spending to a propensity to have run-ins with the law. Much like having a "situation," having "issues" did not refer to a narrow range of cases with well-defined boundaries but to a variety of situations that bore a vague family resemblance.

Besides "situations" and "issues," case managers also sought to ascertain whether clients had an "attitude." This label referred to clients who acted in ways that were, to the bureaucrat's mind, "inappropriate" or "out of place." Clients with an attitude were often rude, loud, or inconsiderate. At times,

Style

		Therapeutic	Transactional	Pedagogical
	Responsive	Issues & Situation		
Timing	Administrative		No Issues & No Situation	
	Punitive			Attitude; No Issues & No Situation

FIGURE 5. Rescheduling a missed appointment (1 / 2).

the label was also used to designate clients who felt unduly entitled and who were not seriously trying to "get their act together": clients who appeared to be lazy, irresponsible, or uncooperative. The category included a hodge-podge of negative attitudinal traits, and its boundaries were fluid. Unlike clients with "issues," however, those with an "attitude" lacked a valid excuse for their behavior and did not elicit much compassion from case managers. For some of my colleagues at the NCDI, the test of professionalism was to control one's hostile feelings and to treat such clients in a courteous and respectful manner. Others believed, on the contrary, that it was their responsibility to correct or reform such clients, both for their own good and to pave the way for smoother interactions in the future.

The three categories I have just described, which together make up an informal moral taxonomy, share several properties. First, these categories are action guiding. It is by determining whether a client has a "situation," "issues," or an "attitude" that case managers select an appropriate response to the request for rescheduling (see Figure 5). Clients with neither issues nor situations (the middle cell) can expect to receive an administrative and transactional response. Clients with both issues and situations (the top left cell) are more likely to be treated in a responsive and therapeutic manner. Finally, clients with an attitude who cannot claim mitigating issues or situations are likely to either receive a punitive and pedagogical response or to be treated in an administrative and transactional manner—depending on which case manager they happen to see.

Style

		Therapeutic	Transactional
Timing	Responsive	Issues & Situation	Situation & No Issues
	Administrative	Issues & No Situation	No Issues & No Situation

FIGURE 6. Rescheduling a missed appointment (2 / 2).

We can gain a more granular picture by focusing on "situations" and "issues" (see Figure 6), and leaving aside for the time being the more contentious category of "attitude." The top left and bottom right quadrants of the matrix in Figure 6 appeared already in Figure 5: clients with both situations and issues are likely to be treated in a responsive and therapeutic way, while those with neither situations nor issues are likely to have their requests handled in an administrative and transactional manner. As for clients who belong to one of the two categories but not to the other, they can expect a hybrid response. For those with a situation but no issues (top right), speed is of the essence; such clients have an immediate problem or crisis that needs to be resolved. Case managers will place the emphasis, accordingly, on providing them with a quick appointment, but will see no reason to drop their professional distance. They will be responsive but transactional. Clients with issues but no situation (bottom left) will receive the opposite kind of response: case managers will lend them a supportive and therapeutic ear, but since their problems are not pressing, they will be made to wait for the next free spot on the calendar. The response will be therapeutic but administrative. In both matrices, the default answer to a request for rescheduling is administrative and transactional. "Situations," "issues," and "attitudes," if and when they are detected, can motivate a departure toward other modes of response.

In addition to being action-guiding, "situations," "issues," and "attitudes" all stand at the margins of the formal structure of rules and regulations that govern the NCDI. The three categories do not feature in rulebooks or in training programs. Senior members of the hierarchy, moreover, refrain from using them and from conferring upon them, by that token, some measure of official recognition and legitimacy.

Besides being informal, "situations," "issues," and "attitudes" also differ from the systems of classification that usually prevail in bureaucracies. As we saw earlier, these three categories do not have sharp boundaries, nor do they have clear criteria for membership. Even if such boundaries and criteria once existed, they appear to have been gradually breached by a process of accretion—with the categories growing out of their original scope to accommodate cases that resemble one another. It is not simply that the categories were not formalized; in the state in which I witnessed them, it is hard to see how they possibly could be. This may explain why case managers, despite my multiple probings, either seemed reluctant to define the boundaries of the categories in analytic terms or were incapable of doing so in a way that they found satisfying. They could tell me whether any given client had a "situation," "issues," or an "attitude," but they could not specify in the abstract what conditions were necessary and sufficient for someone to belong to one of these categories.

This lack of analytic sharpness did not mean, however, that the categories were amorphous. They were organized according to a different logic— around central cases or paradigms. When I asked case managers what it took for a client to have a "situation," "issues," or an "attitude," they would invariably respond by describing a particular case. By way of explaining, for instance, what it meant for someone to have both a situation and issues (a possibility captured by the top left quadrant in Figures 5 and 6), one case manager said:

> So I have this client, who comes in, and who's acting rude . . . and then you find out that her child is autistic and is at home, and that they don't have a job, and they're threatening to close down their heat.

Cases like this are not merely examples drawn randomly from the relevant category; they are *exemplars,* selected because they are unmistakable members or perfect embodiments (be they real or constructed) of the category. The other members of the category radiate outward, so to speak, from these central cases through chains of analogies.

This way of thinking about categories, as radiating outward from central cases through chains of family resemblance, departs from the traditional understanding of categories as defined by a shared nuclei of proper-ties that belong to all their members.[16] The notion of centrality, in particular, according to which some cases are more essential members of a category than others, is important to keep in mind when interpreting Figures 5 and 6. It is for such central members that the action-guiding consequences that I described are seen as most appropriate. As we depart from these central cases, the level of confidence with the associated response diminishes. A case manager would rarely hesitate to reshuffle their calendar to see a client whose heating is about to be cut, but he or she may think twice before doing so for someone whose heating is not immediately at risk but who appears to be unduly worried about that prospect.

"Situations," "issues," and "attitudes" have one last attribute in common: they can be difficult to ascertain. Not all clients are eager to disclose their personal problems, and those who do are not always the ones in greatest need. To apply the proper label to an incoming client, case managers must take a close look at the particularities of the case at hand. They must be at-tuned to signs of nervousness, to expressions of despair, to any hints in the conversation that may suggest deeper issues or problems. As we will see in the next section, this is an exercise in moral perception.

A proper allocation of clients to categories also depends on the avail-ability of private and sensitive information that clients are often reluctant to volunteer. To gather such information—pertaining to income, health, disability, or family abuse—case managers must cultivate some level of trust and intimacy with their clients. This requires a skillful mastery of the con-versation, a careful ordering of the questions (so as to transition smoothly from mundane topics to more sensitive ones), and a display of emotional empathy in the form of properly timed smiles, sighs, frowns, expressions of surprise, etc.[17] This is an exercise in moral excavation.[18]

Everyday Casuistry

Let me briefly summarize where we are so far. We have seen that when the rules run out, case managers tend to respond to clients on the basis of in-formal moral taxonomies. These taxonomies expand outward from central or paradigmatic cases through chains of analogies. When new clients ar-rive, frontline workers attempt to discern which category they belong to and how close they fall to that category's central or paradigmatic cases. It is by sorting clients as such that frontline workers decide how to answer their requests.

This way of approaching new cases is known as casuistry.[19] Casuistry is often used as a synonym for case-based moral reasoning: instead of starting with abstract principles and rules and then trying to see what particular response such rules call for, casuistic reasoning starts with the case and tries to relate it, through analogies, to other cases that have been resolved in a satisfactory way. We can think of categories, in this regard, as functioning like classes of equivalences, grouping together cases that are relevantly alike and separating cases that are relevantly dissimilar.

Casuistry has a long and fraught history. Tracing its origin back to Aristotle, it reached its peak with the Jesuits.[20] Its most salient characteristic, perhaps, is its distrust for large-scale, ambitious theories.[21] Casuistry takes root when practitioners have more confidence in how to handle specific cases than in the general principles or rules that should govern their conduct.[22] These cases end up serving as paradigms or fixed points around which moral reasoning operates. They connect morally salient features of a client's circumstances to an appropriate response. A client who has just lost his job and who lacks any other source of income must, for instance, be seen urgently. What makes these paradigmatic cases different from principles is that they do not aspire to have a wide range of applicability. They prescribe a response that holds with full confidence only for the specific case at hand. By focusing on paradigmatic cases rather than principles, casuists can refrain from committing themselves to abstract rules of behavior that are laid in advance and used to settle a wide range of novel cases before such cases are actually encountered.

Yet casuistic reasoning is not altogether devoid of principles. When a new client comes in, case managers must engage in a process of analogical reasoning. They must first discern the morally salient features of the case at hand, then relate these features to the paradigmatic cases that are already available so as to capture relevant similarities and differences. They must subsequently determine how to respond to the case—they must decide, for instance, whether a client whose salary has been steeply reduced should be treated like a client who has lost his job or not. To settle such a question, case managers must distill what it is that makes the two cases alike. This implies trying to find a common, and slightly more abstract, description of the two cases that can account for their similarity. The principle at work could be, for example, that all clients who are in "dire financial need" have a situation and that they must, accordingly, be seen as fast as possible—a formulation that can cover both clients who have lost their job (the paradigmatic case) and clients whose salary has been slashed (the new case). What is distinctive about casuistry, then, is not the absence of principles altogether but the fact that these principles operate at a relatively low level of abstraction. Casuistry makes use of principles only to the extent that they are necessary to resolve the practical matter at hand, without attempting to offer a fully systematized account of how all the decisions and paradigms fit together. It shuns the realm of high theory and is content with providing local (as opposed to full) coherence regarding how cases are handled.[23]

The principles involved in casuistry have another important characteristic: they are not given in advance of the process of analogical reasoning but are produced by the process itself.[24] Casuists do not approach new cases with a clear understanding of what will be analogous to what.[25] The relevant principles, or midrange abstractions, tend to emerge, rather, as they compare and contrast cases with one another. This stance, which gives primacy to the case over the principle, betrays an epistemological commitment—an openness to the fact that one may learn something by looking closely at the particularities of individual cases, and a belief that one's working principles must be malleable enough to change accordingly.

Casuistry involves two major steps. The first is an exercise in moral perception and excavation.[26] When confronted with a new case, and before they can begin to reason about it, frontline workers must be able to perceive its morally salient attributes. Case managers must be able to register, for instance, whether a client is in distress or danger; they must know whether an aggressive tone is a sign of belligerence or anxiety or both. As we will see in the next section, being able to draw these distinctions and to perceive these saliences accurately calls for a variety of sensibilities that agents must cultivate.[27]

The second step involved in casuistry is that of analogical reasoning. Once the moral saliences have been registered—once it has been established, say, that the new case (A) has features x, y, and z—case managers must relate it to existing paradigmatic cases (P1, P2, P3, etc.). Recall that each of these paradigmatic cases can be understood as connecting a set of moral saliences to an adequate response. If there is a perfect match between the saliences associated with (A) and those associated with one of the paradigmatic cases (say, P1), then the same response can be offered to both. What makes analogical reasoning difficult, however, is that such a perfect match rarely occurs. In most cases, the match is only partial, and the case manager has to assess whether (A) is *sufficiently* close to P1 to justify a similar response. This depends on whether a plausible midrange principle can be discovered or created to explain why a similar treatment is warranted despite the differences.

While it is useful for expository purposes to divide casuistic reasoning into two analytically distinct steps, with the first (moral perception and excavation) providing the raw input into the second (analogical reasoning), it is important to bear in mind that this is a simplification. As several scholars have argued, the process of perception is in part an exercise in pattern recognition: we perceive things by recognizing them as analogous to others we already know.[28] To put it differently, perception depends on the categories we already have at hand.[29] It is in part through analogies that we obtain the propositional data (i.e., the moral saliences x, y, and z) on the basis of which we then engage in analogical reasoning. This observation is important because it suggests that the moral taxonomy that case managers have in mind, and the set of paradigmatic cases with which they are equipped, play an important role in shaping what it is that they can "see" in the first place.

We should be cautious, of course, before imputing to real-world agents a mode of reasoning—such as casuistry—that we cannot directly observe in practice. Unlike common-law judges or the Jesuit priests under which casuistic reasoning flourished, street-level bureaucrats do not leave behind written records of their moral deliberation, nor do they assemble compendia of cases that can be used by other practitioners. In probing their thinking, we are limited to what we can hear them say to one another, to what we can glean from the devices they use to describe and sort cases, and to what we can infer from the decisions we observe them taking.

With these limitations in mind, I believe we nevertheless have good reason to think that the framework of casuistic reasoning does in fact capture how street-level bureaucrats tend to engage with cases when the rules run out. First, casuistic reasoning can help us make sense of the absence of principled and abstract discussions, which I mentioned earlier in the chapter. If such discussions are absent, it is because they are largely unnecessary. Casuistry provides case managers with a structured way to discuss cases and resolve disagreements without having to go back to fundamental questions. The framework of casuistic reasoning can also help us explain the open-ended and fluid structure of the categories that case managers utilize (since these categories can be understood to have been built up over time through chains of analogies) as well as the fact that no one feels the need to delineate these categories analytically (since such an analytic specification is not required in the process of casuistic reasoning). The framework allows us to understand, finally, why the decisions of street-level bureaucrats, while not lacking in structure, are sometimes hard to predict, and why they often lump together cases that may—to an outside observer—look rather dissimilar (this is because casuistic reasoning lacks the global coherence that we can find in more principled approaches to case resolution).

The Virtues of Casuistry

The informal moral taxonomies that proliferate at the front lines of public service are not isolated aberrations; they cannot be dismissed, either, as the result of malicious or unauthorized maneuvering by public officials seeking to expand their autonomy, substituting their own will for the law, or giving voice to their prejudices. Such taxonomies must be understood, at least presumptively, as sensible responses to a real problem: namely, a mismatch between the coarseness of the rules that street-level bureaucrats inherit and the differentiated character of the responses that they can, or must, offer.

The normative task, however, remains ahead of us. Even if we accept that informal moral taxonomies arise for a sensible reason, we must still ask whether there should be any room for them at the heart of the state. For one, these taxonomies are not democratically sanctioned. They constitute a layer that mediates the implementation of public policy, yet one that lacks a proper democratic pedigree and that seems to circumvent, by its very informality, the standard channels of bureaucratic oversight. By what right do street-level bureaucrats develop and deploy such taxonomies, and what guarantees, if any, do citizens have that they will do so in a way that is measured, reasonable, and sensitive to core democratic values? Given the potential risks associated with informal moral taxonomies—risks that involve arbitrary treatment, particularism, discrimination, and abuse of authority—we must ask at least three questions: Can we dispense with the need for such taxonomies altogether by closing the spaces of discretion in which they flourish? If not, are there other, better ways for street-level bureaucrats to make use of their discretion? And finally, if it turns out that informal taxonomies are unavoidable, or that there are good reasons to preserve them, how can we make sure that bureaucrats will be held accountable for how they develop and deploy such taxonomies? I will tackle the first two of these questions here and return to the topic of accountability in the next section.

Informal taxonomies and casuistic reasoning are one way in which street-level bureaucrats can cope with gaps in standard operating procedures. But there are at least three plausible alternatives. The most obvious, perhaps, is formalization: the creation, by a political or administrative act, of additional rules that close the aforementioned gaps and remove, by that token, the need for discretionary decision-making. If successful, formalization would drive street-level bureaucrats back to a subsumptive model of policy implementation.

Formalization is sometimes an appropriate response to the proliferation of discretion at the front lines of public service. Some decisions are too sensitive, important, or error prone to be left to the discretion of street-level bureaucrats. But formalization is an ex-post remedy. It can be used to fill gaps in the rules once such gaps have been identified, but it cannot prevent such gaps from arising in the first place.[30] This is because we cannot anticipate all the contingencies that street-level bureaucrats will face, nor transmit to them, through language, standards of behavior that will settle every contingency in advance. Formalization also comes with its own vices: it stifles innovation and reduces flexibility, adaptability, and responsiveness. The difficulty is not only theoretical, but practical: the more detailed the rules become, the less useful they are as guides for action and the more likely they are to come into conflict with one another, thus opening further spaces for discretionary judgment. Scholars of bureaucracy have long observed that attempts to eradicate discretion by increasing the length of standard operating procedures tend to backfire or to simply displace the locus of discretion.[31]

If formalization cannot serve to patch up all the gaps that exist in the structure of rules and regulations, then we must examine how street-level bureaucrats ought to think when the rules run out. This question is similar, in spirit, to the one that legal philosophers have had to address when thinking about the process of adjudication. By looking at the literature on jurisprudence, we can identify at least two alternatives to casuistic reasoning—one associated with legal positivism, the other with legal interpretivism.

Legal positivists understand the law as a body of rules and principles that are binding because they can be traced back to an authoritative social act. When addressing a new case, a judge must first look at the guidance contained in the law. If such guidance is not dispositive, the judge has no choice but to effectively promulgate new law by making a decision that will have power of precedent for others. A decision of this sort is weighty. The judge has to ground it in the best and most general moral principles or reasons available to him or her while keeping in mind the rights of citizens as well as their welfare.[32] As a lawgiver of sorts, he or she should be able to explain, by reference to a well articulated body of beliefs and principles, why *this* decision (as opposed to the other possible ones) was the most appropriate one to take, not just in his or her own personal opinion but "in the name of society."

Ronald Dworkin has offered an alternative picture of adjudication that moves us away from the image of the judge as lawgiver. According to Dworkin, the law does not consist only of rules or principles that can be traced back to authoritative social acts but also includes the moral principles that undergird such socially sanctioned norms and that best explain and justify them.[33] As one commentator has observed, this means—in contradistinction to legal positivism—that "even when social guidance runs out, the law does not, for moral guidance does not."[34] On such a view, the process of figuring out where the law falls on any given case is thoroughly interpretive: the judge must resolve the case in accordance with the principles of political morality that provide the best constructive interpretation of a community's legal practice. This process of constructive interpretation serves to guarantee a normative ideal of the "law as integrity": new decisions must fit with previous ones as though they had been pronounced by a single voice and as if they flowed from a single, coherent moral and political theory.

When transposed to the front lines of public administration, these two theories of jurisprudence give us two contrasting normative ideals: that of the street-level bureaucrat as lawgiver and that of the street-level bureaucrat as constructive interpreter. Despite their differences, these two models have much in common. Both stress the importance of moral reasoning in the process of adjudication. Both call on bureaucrats to step back from the case at hand and to offer decisions on the basis of principles that could be articulated, justified, and employed to resolve future cases. Both assume, finally, that it is the responsibility of frontline workers, as legislators or interpreters, to reconcile their decisions in particular cases to a more abstract body of beliefs and principles—a theory of sorts—that could help explain why their decisions are appropriate and how they fit with each other. Both models are, in this regard, theoretically ambitious: they require street-level bureaucrats to be in possession of a fully fledged moral or political theory that could motivate, explain, legitimize, and harmonize their choices.

However accurate or desirable these two models may be in the realm of jurisprudence, I believe that they do not capture, even in essence, the way in which street-level bureaucrats actually approach the resolution of specific cases, and that they fail to offer, moreover, a desirable ideal for how they should do so. I have tried to show in the preceding two sections that frontline workers are neither legislators nor political theorists but casuists, and I will try to argue in the rest of the chapter that it is a good thing for them to be.

Casuistry assigns street-level bureaucrats a task that is far more modest theoretically than that which they would inherit under the legal positivist or interpretivist models of adjudication. Casuistic reasoning effectively decouples the everyday work of frontline officials from the realm of high theory: it allows street-level bureaucrats to decide "hard cases" without having to trace their decisions back to fundamental moral principles. It does so by operating on the basis of analogies to paradigmatic cases, which can be motivated and justified by appeal to low- or midrange principles. As I explained in the second section, this provides a framework for moral reasoning that is structured enough to do justice to the relevant differences and similarities between cases, but that neither needs nor aspires to offer a fully coherent and integrated moral theory. Casuists typically refrain from engaging in abstract arguments, because they do not need such arguments to resolve cases; they tend to refrain, as well, from making bold pronouncements that look like policies or laws because such pronouncements would commit them, in advance, to a particular course of action in the future, and would prevent them from being as responsive as possible to new situations. This is a luxury that street-level bureaucrats have because their decisions do not have power of precedent. Such a stance has several advantages over more theoretically ambitious approaches.

For a start, casuistry is less cognitively demanding than the two alternatives I have just described. When faced with a new case, frontline workers can triangulate an appropriate answer based on the existing repertoire of paradigms. They do not need, like Dworkin's judge Hercules, to reason their way back to fundamental moral principles; nor do they need to strive to attain a reflective equilibrium between their intuitions regarding the case and their more basic moral commitments. By relying on analogical reasoning and being content with local coherence, they can decide cases faster and with less cognitive expense.

Another advantage of casuistry is that it allows street-level bureaucrats to resolve cases in a structured manner without having to pronounce themselves on questions of policy. Such humility befits their lack of democratic credentials. Since frontline workers are responsible for handling particular cases, one could argue that they should treat gaps in the law not as occasions to proclaim their own policies but as invitations to handle the particularities of the case at hand in the most responsive and nuanced way possible without feeling obligated to follow a preestablished rule of behavior. For surely, if elected representatives or their duly authorized agents had wanted to resolve the matter with a rule or policy of sorts, they could have done so of their own accord.

Casuistry also encourages street-level bureaucrats to focus their limited attention and resources on the task that is most distinctively theirs in the division of moral labor: namely, grasping and responding to the particularities of individual cases. The realities of the social world will always be more granular and complex than administrative rules and categories. As intermediaries between citizens and the state, street-level bureaucrats are uniquely positioned to perceive the morally salient features of a case and to know which of these features are not adequately captured by the rules in place. One of the advantages of casuistry, as compared to more theoretically ambitious forms of moral reasoning, is that it puts the emphasis squarely on the process of moral perception—on the capacity of frontline workers to individuate moral saliences. Instead of encouraging such workers to improve their capacity to reason deductively from first moral principles or to become more rigorous in developing a systematic and coherent theory, casuistic reasoning puts the accent on a different virtue— that of discernment: the capacity to perceive a case accurately and to register its subtle similarities and differences to other such cases. Cultivating such a virtue is a way to acknowledge and accommodate the specific moral demands placed on street-level bureaucrats because of the position they occupy at the interface of state and society.

Two other features of casuistry are useful given the role that street-level bureaucrats play as mediators between citizens and the state: its flexibility and revisability. Casuistic reasoning is flexible because it does not require street-level bureaucrats to deliver off-the-shelf responses to cases on the basis of binary criteria. It allows them, rather, to calibrate their response based on a case's *degree* of proximity to one or more existing paradigms. This allows for more granular and nuanced responses. In addition to being flexible, casuistic reasoning is easily revisable because it aims only for local coherence. This means that new paradigmatic cases can be added to the existing repertoire and old ones removed without having to revise the entire structure of one's moral thinking as one would if one were operating on the basis of a systemic moral theory. This allows street-level bureaucrats to rapidly correct prior mistakes, to experiment with new ways of responding to clients, and to adapt themselves to changing conditions.

The last, and perhaps most important, advantage of casuistry is that it allows street-level bureaucrats with different moral dispositions and role conceptions to work with each other without having to relinquish or align their distinctive moral commitments. One of the payoffs of casuistry's skepticism toward the realm of high theory is that it can foster what Cass Sunstein has called "incompletely theorized agreements": it allows people to reach consensus on practical questions even though they disagree on other, more fundamental issues.[35] Instead of forcing street-level bureaucrats to pit their basic commitments against one another and to negotiate their differences so as to achieve a common theoretical framework, it drives their attention to the resolution of specific problems. As pragmatists and deliberative democrats keep reminding us, people can often agree on how to resolve practical problems even if they disagree on more fundamental matters. At the NCDI, for instance, caregivers, enforcers, and indifferents all agreed that someone who had a "situation" ought to be seen rapidly. They agreed on this even as they disagreed about which role conception or moral disposition was most appropriate for the job and which client in particular had a situation.

By allowing individuals with different moral dispositions to work together without forcing them to align their views on questions of fundamental principle, casuistry allows for a plurality of approaches to the role to coexist within bureaucratic agencies. Instead of shunning the pluralism that is characteristic of our political culture, it makes room for it within the administrative state. This comes with three benefits: it creates a state that better reflects the society we live in; it sets up an administrative body that is less likely to trample upon some moral values or to be oblivious to some moral saliences, because advocates for those values and saliences will exist within the administration itself; and it helps secure a much-needed place for diversity which, as we will see in the fifth section, is a necessary precondition for an effective regime of peer-level accountability.

The Problem of Accountability

We have seen so far that formalization cannot entirely eliminate the need for informal moral taxonomies, and that when it comes to using discretion, casuistic reasoning is a sensible response to the demands of street-level work—a response that has several advantages over more theoretically demanding models of reasoning. This leaves us with the thorny question of accountability. The informal moral taxonomies I have described so far are not democratically sanctioned. What guarantees, if any, do we have that they will be deployed in a way that is sensitive to the plurality of normative values that are characteristic of our political culture? What safeguards do we have against the dangers of arbitrariness, prejudice, or particularism? These questions are crucial, for unless we can secure some margin of accountability, it may be preferable to forego the advantages of discretionary decision-making altogether and to compel street-level bureaucrats to follow a preestablished course of action. Rigidity and lack of responsiveness are a price many would be willing to pay to avoid the risk of arbitrary treatment at the hands of the state.

When using informal moral taxonomies, street-level bureaucrats must be held accountable on two fronts: for the nature of the moral taxonomy that they use (Why these categories? Why these paradigmatic cases?) and for how they apply such a taxonomy to specific situations (Does this client really have an attitude? Is the response proportionate?). The first worry—about the moral taxonomy—has to do with the standards set by the peer-level group; the second—about the application of the taxonomy—has to do with assessing the behavior of individual bureaucrats against the standards set by the group.

Although the question of accountability poses itself whenever public officials hold discretionary power over their fellow citizens, it is particularly pressing in the case of informal taxonomies because casuistic reasoning has a rather unflattering reputation. According to the Collins English Dictionary, casuistry refers to "reasoning that is specious, misleading, or over-subtle." The Oxford Dictionary of English points, for its part, to "a quibbling or evasive way of dealing with difficult cases of duty." Such a reputation is partly deserved. Casuistic reasoning can be criticized on at least two counts: for being lax, and for being opaque to external scrutiny. These charges are intimately connected to casuistry's virtues—they are, so to speak, the flip side of its flexibility, focus on particularity, skepticism toward high theory, and openness to pluralism.

The charge of laxity was voiced most forcefully by Pascal in his *Provincial Letters,* a series of scathing attacks on the Jesuits, who were at the time the main proponents of casuistic reasoning.[36] As we saw earlier, casuistry relies on chains of analogies. The problem with analogical reasoning is that no two cases are exactly alike, and almost any two cases have *something* in common. By parsing out cases in a way that is sufficiently subtle and drawing chains of analogies that are sufficiently long and complex, one can relate those that are most dissimilar and pull apart those that are most alike. Since casuistry does not specify in advance which similarities are relevant and which are not, and since it does not offer a systematic theory to which practitioners can turn for guidance, it lends itself all too easily to misuse and abuse. Casuistry is lax insofar as it does not impose enough constraints on the process of moral reasoning—it gives individual practitioners too much leeway to proceed as they see fit.

What should give us even more cause for concern, however, is that none of the three dominant models of accountability on which public bureaucracies rely to control the exercise of discretionary power by line agents—hierarchical, direct, and professional accountability—can provide adequate oversight for the use of informal moral taxonomies.[37] Casuistic reasoning is hard to assess when one does not belong to the immediate community of practice.

Hierarchical accountability is the form of answerability that features most prominently in public bureaucracies. As low-ranking employees, street-level bureaucrats can be called upon at any moment by their supervisors to explain and justify their discretionary decisions. Since subordinates know that they may have to account for their actions, they have an incentive to act in ways they can explain and justify.[38]

Hierarchical accountability plays a central role in the everyday operation of bureaucracies, but its reach is limited when it comes to informal moral taxonomies. For a start, such taxonomies are *informal*—they are circulated among peers and are not typically disclosed to supervisors, for fear that the latter may disapprove of them or cancel the spaces of discretion in which they flourish. As a consequence, supervisors may not know what such taxonomies are, nor when they are being used. Even if such taxonomies were disclosed, however, it is unlikely that supervisors would be able to evaluate them properly. Supervisors work in conditions that are different from those of their subordinates; they are often unaware of the practical needs and constraints that drive street-level bureaucrats to distinguish between clients. At the NCDI, for instance, frontline workers were convinced that their supervisors understood neither the basis for the distinctions that they had so carefully erected nor the need for such distinctions. They viewed the advice that such supervisors offered as hopelessly out of touch with the realities of street-level work. On the subject of informal moral taxonomies, authority and hierarchy parted ways. As one case manager put it to me:

> Sometimes we know the clients, we know some of them keep coming to bother us, so we know when to put an end to it—we're like "no, go home, do this," and then the director walks out and is like why didn't you give her the time. . . . So there's a disagreement, but since we know the clients we sometimes try to swerve around it. . . . So it's a never ending. . . . He [the director] can talk to us about it, and sometimes it can leave our mind . . . we're like pffff, who cares, kind of a thing.

Besides not being qualified to evaluate the merits of informal taxonomies, supervisors are not well positioned either to assess how such taxonomies are applied. Casuistic reasoning relies on moral perception and judgments of similarity, the quality of which can be difficult to appraise unless one has independent access to the case at hand. And yet, supervisors do not typically interact with the clients their subordinates encounter. The little information they do receive is unreliable, for it is relayed by the very subordinates whose actions they seek to appraise.

Supervisors, in short, are too foreign to the realities of street-level work to properly evaluate moral taxonomies, and too distant to monitor their application. This is not to say, however, that hierarchical accountability is useless. Far from it. By keeping tabs on the actions of their subordinates and the services provided to clients (*who* gets *what, when,* and *how*), managers are in a good position to identify statistical biases that may result from the adoption of informal taxonomies even though they are not well placed to directly observe these taxonomies in use.

Public service agencies typically supplement hierarchical accountability with a regime of direct accountability. They enlist the help of those who have most at stake in the bureaucratic encounter—clients—to monitor the behavior of bureaucrats. While the oversight provided by supervisors is meant to be continuous like that of a "police patrol," the oversight provided by clients can be more episodic: they are meant to sound a "fire alarm" in case a specific problem arises.[39] Clients have a variety of ways to hold bureaucrats accountable. They can question frontline agents directly; they can ask to speak to a manager; they can file a formal complaint; and they can, in the last resort, contact their political representatives or take the matter to court.[40] The thought, here as well, is that the fear of sanctions and the possibility that one may have to account for one's decisions publicly would motivate bureaucrats to make sound use of their discretion.

When it comes to informal taxonomies, however, direct accountability fares no better than hierarchical accountability. Since such taxonomies are not public, clients, like supervisors, are in the dark: they do not know when the taxonomies are being employed nor what they are. This prevents them from adequately challenging or questioning the decisions of street-level bureaucrats. There are good reasons, moreover, why informal moral taxonomies should not be publicized to clients. If clients were told that they would get preferential treatment for having a "situation," and if they knew exactly what to say to be labeled as such, they would be in a position to reliably "game the system." Publicizing informal moral taxonomies would defeat their purpose.

In addition to supervisors and clients, public service agencies also depend on the help of professional communities to hold bureaucrats accountable. Such communities develop and police their own codes of ethics, and members found guilty of breaching them can be subject to punishment or exclusion.[41] Such codes are particularly useful when members of a profession must abide by moral standards that differ from those of the public at large (e.g., lawyers in adversarial systems), or when a proper assessment of a member's conduct requires expertise that only members of the profession possess (e.g., medical malpractice).

Unlike hierarchical and direct accountability, professional accountability relies on peers who are closer to their colleagues and better placed to assess their behavior. It nevertheless suffers from two limitations. First, not all street-level bureaucrats actually belong to organized professions. Second, and most importantly, professional codes of ethics, though well suited to some tasks, are too coarse for others. In particular, such codes tend to prescribe sanctions only for behavior that is unethical or unprofessional. As instruments of accountability, they are primarily designed to distinguish between members who fulfill the social role that the profession claims to occupy (and from which it draws its legitimacy) and members who trespass the boundaries of that role.

The problem, however, is that many of the controversies that surround the use of moral taxonomies fall within the ambit of professional behavior. To put it simply, there are various ways of fulfilling one's professional responsibilities—various ways of being in-role—and street-level bureaucrats must be held accountable for those too and not simply for when they act unprofessionally. And yet, codes of ethics are usually silent on matters of style. Organized professions can rein in bureaucrats who are incompetent or who lack in integrity, but they will not call into question those who are too lenient in finding "situations" or too inclined to uncover "attitudes." They might expel police officers who are unnecessarily violent or corrupt, but they will not single out those who are too eager to apply the label "asshole." This leaves us in a bind: hierarchical and direct accountability cannot probe deep enough into the informal world where moral taxonomies proliferate, while professional accountability is not sufficiently fine-grained to be of much use except in cases of misconduct.

Peer-Level Accountability and Organized Heterogeneity

If it is true that neither supervisors nor clients nor professional communities are well positioned to directly monitor and police the use of informal moral taxonomies, then we must turn our attention to peers and see if they can in any way supplement these channels of accountability.[42] Unlike supervisors, who are often outnumbered or distant, peers are practically always within sight. Unlike clients, they are fully aware of the contours of existing taxonomies. Peers are "in the know"; it is through them that informal norms are relayed from one generation of practitioners to the next. They are ideally situated, moreover, to appraise their colleagues' working styles, to overhear their conversations with clients, and to know when to intervene and how to do so.

The observations I collected while working at the NCDI do indeed suggest that the use of informal moral taxonomies is not an individual affair, but one that bears the distinctive mark of the group. In the course of everyday work, peers relentlessly observe and probe each other's working styles. They intervene directly to praise, criticize, mock, or confront one another. They raise questions, give advice, demand explanations, and pass judgment. Peers serve as a constant, panoptic presence. Their influence is both disciplining and formative, and it makes itself felt at each step of the process of casuistic reasoning: in determining what is morally salient about a situation, in deciding what label is most appropriate, and in assessing what to do once a label has been assigned.

In what follows, I draw on my fieldwork to illustrate the patterns of interaction among peers around the use of informal taxonomies. I hope to show that such interactions amount to a distinctive regime of accountability that can serve to supplement the hierarchical, direct, and professional models described earlier. I will argue, as well, that the motor for such a regime of accountability is diversity in moral dispositions and role conceptions. To the extent that street-level bureaucrats are held accountable for how they deploy informal moral taxonomies, it is because they have to do so in the presence of peers who disagree with them and who have ways to make their discontent heard and felt.

In Chapter 2, I had shown that street-level bureaucrats respond to new cases in a way that is colored by their moral dispositions. Workers with different dispositions tend to perceive moral saliences differently, and to disagree about which paradigmatic cases to adopt as a foundation for casuistic reasoning. In a workplace that is sufficiently diverse, the use of informal taxonomies occurs against the backdrop of such divergences and disagreements. Frontline workers are caught in a field of competing horizontal pressures. Some of their colleagues see themselves as guardians of certain moral saliences: they encourage those who see and think like them and keep a close watch on those who do not. These pressures serve as a safeguard against reductionism; they discourage workers from developing moral dispositions that are overly specialized. The narrower one's sensibilities become—the more one moves, say, toward the three poles of indifference, caregiving, or enforcement—the more resistance one is bound to encounter from colleagues who have competing commitments. When moral dispositions are sufficiently diverse, they keep each other in check. I believe that there is an important organizational lesson in this: if bureaucracies cannot avoid relying on informal moral taxonomies, and if they are to do so without relinquishing altogether on the promise of accountability, then they must foster a working environment in which a plurality of moral dispositions can develop, and in which individual workers are sufficiently committed to their own ways of inhabiting the role to act as lively advocates for them.

Consider, once again, the exchange with which I opened this chapter, and which we are now in a position to decipher:

> *Flora, yelling to Laura, who is in a different office:* "Anna called again. She was supposed to come in yesterday but missed it. She wants to reschedule. She's called five times. I told her that I would get back to her tomorrow 'cause I'm too busy now, and she's still calling. This lady has a serious attitude!"
>
> *Laura, shouting back:* "Yeah. . . . Well, you know, she has issues."
>
> *Flora, sounding incredulous:* "She has issues?"
>
> *Laura, walking over to Flora's office, and leaning against the door:* "Oh, you didn't know? She didn't tell you? She has a situation too. You know what, I'll do it."

This is the kind of conversation—brief, terse, barely articulate, and loaded with presuppositions—that one would expect between two colleagues who work within proximity, and who have grown accustomed to one another's presence. The conversation assumes that both parties are familiar with the informal moral taxonomy being used; "situation," "issues," and "attitude" are here employed as technical terms.

In substance, the exchange is simple. A case manager (Flora) voices her frustration at a client's incessant phone calls and solicits her colleague's sympathy. Instead of acquiescing, the colleague (Laura) proceeds to contest her coworker's reaction. She alleges that Flora mistook the client's insistence for an "attitude" when it was, in fact, the symptom of a "situation" and "issues." As per the matrix in Figure 5, this change in categorization calls for a different response to the client's request: instead of putting other tasks ahead of the makeup appointment (as Flora did), the client should be seen as soon as possible (as Laura volunteers to do).

By challenging her colleague's take on the situation, Laura corrects what she takes to be an improper application of the moral taxonomy. The disagreement between the two colleagues hinges, at least in part, on a question of moral perception. Where Flora sees unnecessary phone calls, Laura sees a sign of distress that has to be addressed urgently. Laura feels confident challenging Flora's reading of the situation because she knows the case more intimately. She has access to information—about the client's situation or issues—that Flora is not aware of. This lack of knowledge, however, is precisely what Laura reproaches her colleague for. The charge, implicit in her rhetorical question ("She didn't tell you?"), is that Flora should have known better. Had she (Flora) been more attentive and discerning while interacting with the client, she would have been able to detect signs of a "situation" or of latent "issues." Perhaps she was too focused on meeting her targets to see that something was wrong? Perhaps she sounded overly distant and judgmental in the course of the encounter? Perhaps she didn't listen to the client closely enough to know what questions to ask? As Laura sees it, it is Flora's responsibility to know whether or not the client requires special attention. "Not knowing" is less an excuse than a confession of failure.

Laura's intervention is both disciplinary and formative: it points at a mistake and suggests a more appropriate response. Justified or not, her criticism also sends a signal, namely, that colleagues are keeping a close watch on the labels that their peers assign to clients and that they will not hesitate to intervene if such labels are applied in a way that they deem improper.

What makes Laura's intervention significant is that it is not an isolated event but one among dozens, if not hundreds, of similar exchanges taking place on a daily basis. Laura and Flora were not alone in negotiating their differences. They were involved in a dense network of crisscrossing relationships with a variety of other colleagues who had their own moral sensibilities, role conceptions, and normative priorities. If Laura could observe, criticize, and challenge, so could all the others—and so they did. This added up to a form of decentralized oversight. When it came to assigning labels to clients, case managers could not act as they wished: they had to take into account the sensibilities of their colleagues lest they expose themselves to criticism, reprimand, or confrontation.

It is worth emphasizing that this horizontal regime of scrutiny is as informal as the taxonomy it oversees. Colleagues are not formally compelled to police one another and have little to gain from doing so. If they do intervene, it is on their own initiative. When Flora expressed her frustration at the client's incessant phone calls, Laura could have easily shrugged or nodded in approval. If she took the risk, instead, of reprimanding her colleague and if she eventually decided to take on additional work, it is, at least in part, because she must have felt *responsible* for doing so—out of a sense of obligation to the client, or out of commitment to a certain conception of her role and responsibilities. If she gave in to this motivational impulse, it is perhaps also because she suspected that there were others in the organization who shared her commitment and who would have backed her up if the interaction with Flora had taken a confrontational turn.

The influence that peers exert on each other is most visible, in both its formative and disciplining guises, in the interactions they have with interns or new recruits. As newcomers to the organization, the latter must undergo a process of organizational socialization in which they are introduced to shared assumptions and sensibilities that go largely unspoken between more seasoned workers.[43] Newcomers also tend to be seen by their peers as blank slates who are not yet wedded to a moral disposition and who can therefore be more easily rallied to one's own. For both of these reasons, newcomers serve as a focal point where competing sensibilities and pedagogical undertakings are on display.

Take the following exchange, which unfolded before me:

An intern is in the process of helping an old African American man apply for a federally funded fuel assistance program to cover heating expenses during the winter. Upon checking the papers that the client has brought in, the intern realizes that one of the required documents is missing. The client apologizes, rifles through a bag filled with papers and envelopes, and after a few futile attempts, despairs of finding the right document. He asks the intern in a meek and subdued tone if he can come back later in the week to drop off the missing piece of paper. The intern immediately denies the request and explains that the schedule is fully booked for the following two weeks. She reminds the client that he had been explicitly told what to bring and hands him back his incomplete documents. She then turns to her computer screen, seemingly unperturbed by his increasingly agitated and helpless expression. At that moment, Paulina, a more experienced case manager, jumps in from the adjacent cubicle. She takes the documents back from the client, places them on her desk, and tells him that he should come back whenever he finds the missing piece of paper. She promises that she will be able to see him then.

In this brief interaction, a frontline worker is, once again, interrupted by a colleague for responding improperly to a client's request. Here as well, the disagreement between the case manager (Paulina) and the intern is about the morally salient aspect of the situation. Where the intern sees a standard bureaucratic case that needs to be addressed routinely, the more experienced case manager discerns the contour of a "situation." The client is old, confused, helpless, and worried; he is one of those who "would not be fine" coming back. By taking over the interaction, Paulina not only reverses the outcome of the encounter but also challenges the intern's judgment in view of all. Her intervention is both corrective and disciplining.

Interestingly, when I later asked Paulina why she felt compelled to intervene, she did not fault the intern for making a poor decision but for not having the right disposition. The problem, she explained, is that the intern was so absorbed by the rapid pace of work and so preoccupied with procedural correctness that she failed to register some important features of the situation that ought to have been salient to a more discerning eye. This focus on disposition underscores a connection that has been observed by theorists of virtue and moral psychologists—namely, that our moral perception is related to our sensibilities, and by that token, to our character or moral identity.[44] To improve one's capacity to perceive a range of moral saliences is to change, albeit slightly, the kind of person that one is.

The pedagogical approach that Paulina and other senior case managers employed when interacting with newcomers seemed informed by such a realization. It consisted in stimulating the moral sentiments and moral imagination of their younger colleagues, often by redescribing the situation in slightly more dramatic terms that accentuated certain features of it (e.g., "See how lost he was with that huge bag of papers?"; "He didn't know what was going on, didn't have a clue"; "seemed like he'd never make it back").[45] In doing this, case managers effectively assumed, in their capacity as colleagues, a function that would appear familiar to students of ancient philosophy—namely, that of rhetors, who took it upon themselves to arouse around them the emotions and images that were required to transform the dispositional states of their peers.[46]

The discussion so far has focused on how peers observe, assess, and question each other's perception of incoming clients, and how they intervene to shape the dispositional states that undergird such perception. But as I indicated earlier, and as evidenced in the interaction between Laura and Flora, properly applying the labels of a moral taxonomy does not only depend on moral perception. It also calls, at times, for a process of moral excavation. Case managers can be required to extract information that is not readily volunteered by clients. In order to gather such information, they must know what questions to ask and how to sequence them. They must also be able to create a modicum of trust with their clients. This involves knowing how to communicate and how to listen so as to put the other party at ease.

Unsurprisingly, given the diversity of moral dispositions within the NCDI, the questions attending such an active "ethics of listening"—How should I formulate queries? How should I express concern? For how long? With what tone?—were a source of contention. Paulina, for instance, was keen on coaching her colleagues to engage with clients properly. When she felt that a case manager had cut a client short or had not probed sufficiently deep, she would take them aside and voice her concerns. She described her own approach as such: "I listen. I ask clients, 'How are you doing?' And I sit down, and let them speak, and I listen, and as I listen, I collect information." As for her attitude toward colleagues:

> I give a lot of feedback to others. . . . It's primarily about communication. . . . We need to be careful about the way we say things . . . and we need to be attentive to how clients feel. . . . So when I give feedback to others, it's primarily about how things are being said, about whether they are making proper eye contact, about their body movement and how they handle themselves.

This approach to listening and communicating has consequences for a case manager's propensity to depart from the default standard of treatment. The more, the harder, and the longer one looks for "situations" and "issues," the more likely one is to find them. The question, of course, is whether this time and attention would be better devoted to other tasks. For all her zeal in coaching and pressuring others, Paulina was herself a frequent target of criticism. She was regularly teased by some of her peers for wasting too much time listening to clients. There was a running joke among receptionists that anyone who had been stranded in the waiting room for a long period of time must have been there to see her, for she could get so entangled in the intricacies of a case that she would sometimes forget about her other appointments. The joke served as a comic, if somewhat cruel, reminder that some sensibilities (e.g., to the plight of the person across the desk) can effectively block others (e.g., to the needs of those who are not within sight).

Paulina was not singled out for ridicule. The line of criticism to which she was exposed took aim at all those who shared her approach to the role. Laura, for instance, with whom I opened this section, was also faulted by some for being too sensitive to clients' special circumstances and not enough to the requirement of efficiency. DeShawn, a receptionist who sometimes doubled as case manager, made it a point to regularly stop by her office to say, sarcastically, "Ah, it's very nice here; I see it's not too busy." By this, he insinuated that instead of taking her time with individual clients, Laura would do well to see a greater number of them. Since the demand for services was always high, DeShawn felt that "not being busy" meant that one was shirking one's responsibilities.

The examples and anecdotes I have related, filled as they are with signals, hints, insinuations, words of counsel, and displays of disapproval, are meant to illustrate the pressure that peers exert on each other. Such pressure is not only constant but also multidirectional: peers pull in as many directions as they have moral dispositions. Case managers go about their work knowing that they will have to contend with the expectations of their colleagues and their variegated sensibilities.

There are three important points to take away from the material presented thus far. First, the informal patterns of interaction that I have been describing effectively amount to a regime of accountability—if by accountability we mean, as Mark Philp puts it, that there is an institutional relation or arrangement by which A (peers) can require B (individual case managers) to inform and explain / justify their conduct with respect to C (clients).[47] This regime of peer-level accountability differs from the hierarchical, direct, and professional models I presented earlier insofar as peers lack the formal authority to *demand* an account from each other. To the extent that they can "require" others to provide such an account, it is because they can threaten them with informal sanctions—it is because peers can shun, mock, criticize, ostracize, and confront one another. As with other sanctions, these threats don't need to materialize to be effective. It is the expectation that one *may* be observed, that one *may* have to answer for one's actions, and that one *may* be subject to sanctions that induces self-discipline.

It is worth noting, second, that while peer-level accountability and professional accountability both rely on horizontal oversight by peers, the former provides a level of scrutiny that is far more granular and penetrating than the latter. Notice that none of the exchanges I described in this section were prompted by behavior that was blatantly incompetent or that clearly violated the spirit of the role. Peers are not simply on the lookout for gross misconduct; they keep a close watch on each other's propensities and sensibilities—they inspect each other's choice of words, tone of voice, body posture, emotional involvement, and degree of attentiveness. They hold each other accountable not only for acting in line with the role but also for the specific way, or style, in which they go about fulfilling the demands of the role.

Third, and most importantly perhaps, we have seen that the motor for peer-level accountability is diversity in moral dispositions. It is because peers have different role conceptions, affective sensibilities, and normative priorities, that they disagree with each other. It is because they are committed to their own ways of inhabiting the role, moreover, that they are motivated to engage with those of their colleagues who have a different approach than theirs. But there is an important caveat here. It is one thing to be motivated and another to act on such a motivation. If peers are to take it upon themselves to breach the cohesiveness of the group and to risk alienating their colleagues, diversity and commitment are necessary but not sufficient. Peers must also know that they have like-minded allies in the organization who can provide them with reassurance that their view is sensible, and with the social backing necessary to take on others. Peer-level accountability requires not only a diversity of moral dispositions but also a diversity of subgroups within the organization that can nurture these dispositions and provide their carriers with social and informational support.[48] The existence of heterogeneous clusters reduces the pressure toward conformity and can serve as a valuable check against some of the other pernicious dynamics that are known to affect groups—such as groupthink, shared information bias, group polarization, and amplification of bias.[49]

If heterogeneity in moral dispositions can set into motion a regime of accountability fit to oversee how informal taxonomies are applied, I want to suggest in what follows that it can also stimulate street-level bureaucrats to question, test, and revise the very taxonomies that are in use.[50] Diversity in moral dispositions—or, to be more precise, the existence of heterogeneous clusters of colleagues aligned along distinctive moral dispositions—can serve as an institutional irritant of sorts that prompts the group to question, from within, the very standards it employs to assess individual behavior.[51]

Take the category of clients with an "attitude." As I mentioned in the first section, the proper response to such clients was a matter of controversy. Some case managers, like Paulina, believed it was their duty to exhibit maximal self-restraint when confronted with such cases. They took it upon themselves to see past the client's anger or confrontational tone and attempted, insofar as possible, to treat the case in a cool and dispassionate way. Others in the agency saw things differently. They believed that in order to be treated with courtesy and respect, clients had to behave properly too—it was up to them to act "like adults" and to demonstrate a readiness to cooperate with frontline workers. In DeShawn's words, "Some individuals come in to the office and they *demand* things; I mean you really have to set them straight sometimes." He went on to say, "I have little patience for attitudes; I have an attitude of my own . . . , so sometimes . . . a client has come in, and I know off the bat I'm not going to assist them."

The disagreement between Paulina and DeShawn differs in kind from the ones we have seen so far. At issue is not whether a particular client has an attitude, but what the response to an attitude ought to be. Notice that there are two ways to understand the dispute: as a disagreement about the paradigmatic response that should be offered to a central member of the category "attitude," or as a disagreement about the very need for such a category. Which interpretation is correct depends on how we understand Paulina's view. One could read her as conceding that "attitudes" deserve special treatment, but as disagreeing with DeShawn about what such treatment ought to be. Should clients with "attitudes" be treated more severely than regular clients (DeShawn), or should they be accorded greater patience (Paulina)? But it is also possible to interpret Paulina as claiming that clients with an attitude should be treated just like everyone else. This view cuts deeper than the first. It suggests that whether or not a client has an attitude should be irrelevant: the label ought to be discarded from the moral taxonomy altogether. On both interpretations, the disagreement involves the moral taxonomy itself, not just its application.

These two approaches to "attitudes" coexisted uneasily within the organization and sometimes came into conflict. Laura told me about an incident that pitted her against an experienced intern who had been working at the NCDI for close to a year. The intern had helped a client, a single Hispanic mother, file an application for citizenship, which Laura had then carefully reviewed for correctness. A week later, the client came back with additional documents and met with another staff member. In the course of that meeting, the client accused the intern of having made mistakes in filing the original application. She claimed that the intern was inexperienced and that she had incorrectly transcribed her housing situation and marital status. Upon hearing these accusations, the intern, who was sitting nearby, became furious. She stormed into Laura's office and said, "Oh, now she's making it seem as if I didn't do my job. I want to go out there; if only I spoke Spanish, I would go out there and tell her this and that [expletives]."

As Laura recounts the story, she had to intervene to calm the intern and persuade her to be more lenient in handling attitudes. She reminded her that clients lived volatile lives and that they often changed their minds about their filing status. Accusing the staff of a mistake was a way to "save face," an attempt to conceal inner turmoil from public view. There was nothing to be gained by confronting such clients and exposing their lies—there was no valuable "lesson" to be taught. It was better to just make the change and move on.

One could debate, of course, the relative merit of these two views on how to handle attitudes. What is more important for our purposes, however, is the fact that such debates do indeed occur in the workplace itself, and that they are fueled by the ongoing friction between various moral sensibilities and role conceptions. In a sufficiently diverse environment, informal moral taxonomies are alive: the labels that make up such taxonomies and the paradigmatic cases on which they are built are constantly being tested, challenged, and revised.

Interestingly, the category "attitude" itself appeared to be a relatively new addition to the taxonomy in use at the NCDI. Clients who exhibited an "attitude" were often derided by case managers for being "stuck with the old welfare mentality," according to which they would be granted assistance automatically and indefinitely as long as they met certain income categories. But these expectations no longer corresponded to reality. With the passage of the Personal Responsibility and Work Opportunity Reconciliation Act (PRWORA) in 1996, the old welfare program, Aid to Families with Dependent Children (AFDC), was replaced by a more restrictive one, Temporary Assistance for Needy Families (TANF). The new program features a sixty-month cap on welfare assistance and makes such assistance conditional upon the fulfillment of certain work requirements. Welfare provision is no longer simply about dispensing resources to those in need. It has taken on the additional mission of reducing dependency on the state by encouraging clients to become "personally responsible." Recipients are now expected to cooperate with case managers to develop the skills necessary to reenter the workforce; it has become incumbent upon them to exert effort, show initiative, and demonstrate proper motivations.

While clients' "attitudes" were largely irrelevant in the old system of welfare provision, their standing under the new program is far more ambiguous. Are case managers responsible for policing and sanctioning attitudes? Which attitudes should they sanction, and which not? How, precisely, are they supposed to sanction them? One can understand the debate over the place of "attitudes" in the informal moral taxonomy as a debate over how to answer these questions, and how to interpret, by that same token, the spirit of the new welfare policy. So long as these questions are not authoritatively settled through democratic means, this is a debate that case managers should indeed be having—and one that will be far richer and more balanced if the organization is home to a plurality of competing views that can impose a healthy justificatory burden on each other.

Van Maanen concludes his article on "The Asshole" on the following note: "When it comes to the asshole, police actions are not governed at all, given the present policies of allowing the watchers to watch themselves."[52] He ends by calling for a police force that is "accountable." These statements can be interpreted broadly or narrowly. If we take Van Maanen's remark as a general statement—to the effect that frontline workers who are allowed to govern themselves and to oversee the application and content of their own informal taxonomies are in effect unaccountable—then I hope to have shown that such a conclusion is unduly alarmist and pessimistic. Under conditions of organized heterogeneity, a group can actively participate in policing itself; peers can and do hold each other accountable both for the application and the content of the informal moral taxonomies they deploy.

But if Van Maanen's conclusion is unwarranted as a general statement about the futility of peer-level accountability, it must be taken seriously as a specific observation about the police, and about the category of the asshole in particular. Some police departments are known for having a strong and cohesive culture that can stifle dissent and diversity and encourage conformism.[53] To the extent that this is true, such departments will lack the kind of organized heterogeneity that I have described as a condition of possibility for informal accountability. There is something to be said, as well, about the label "asshole." Since the police are known for having a fraught relationship with the public—one frequently marred by accusations of brutality—it may be dangerous to allow officers of the law endowed with the power to use violence to routinely slot people into disparaging categories. Such a practice not only breaks with the most basic rules of common courtesy but also makes the interaction with citizens unmistakably confrontational, thereby paving the way for escalation and, potentially, for abuse of authority.

Van Maanen's study of the police exposes the limits of the regime of peer-level accountability I have described. It reminds us that such a regime can work well only under certain conditions and that in the absence of such conditions the influence of peers could well be detrimental. This should serve as a word of caution against relying on informal moral taxonomies when the culture of an agency is overly cohesive, when it is marked by hostility or distrust toward its surroundings, and when the costs of failure are ones we would be unwilling to accept. In such conditions, managers may have no choice but to intervene directly into the thick of street-level work by closing up the spaces of discretion in which informal taxonomies flourish. This may come at the cost of effectiveness, flexibility, and responsiveness, but in some settings, this may be the only way to counteract the risk of arbitrariness.

The case of the police also reminds us that there are serious normative concerns that peer-level accountability cannot address. Peers can hold each other accountable when they have different ways of inhabiting the role. Yet there is always the possibility, which has been in the public eye recently with the controversy over the stop-and-frisk program in New York City, that members of a profession may share implicit biases that cut across differences in moral dispositions and role conceptions. These biases may arise in response to the particular work situation in which officers are placed, they may reflect existing prejudices within society at large, or they may be distinctive of those who self-select into the force. Irrespective of their origin, there is little that peers can do to detect and dislodge such biases if they are indeed shared by most.

This is why I have insisted that peer-level accountability is meant only to *supplement* other channels of accountability, not to replace them. In the case of implicit bias, hierarchical accountability may actually serve us better because it involves collecting and aggregating data across a number of workers and interactions. It is in such large statistical samples that implicit biases become most acutely visible.

Given how much is at stake for clients in the bureaucratic encounter, public service agencies cannot afford to rely on a single form of oversight. They must deploy a plural regime of accountability that multiplies the number of safeguards on the use of discretion.[54] Even as peers police each other, it is important that clients keep reporting behavior that they find unacceptable and that they have adequate channels to do so; that supervisors keep asking questions and continue intruding occasionally on the discretionary spaces of their subordinates; and that professional communities keep probing and overseeing the behavior of their members.

Conclusion

I began this chapter by describing how street-level bureaucrats approach cases when the guidance provided by standard operating procedures runs out. I showed that frontline workers tend to fill the gaps that inevitably arise by deploying informal moral taxonomies and by engaging in an everyday form of casuistry. Casuistry works from the bottom up: it puts the emphasis on moral perception and excavation, proceeds through analogies, and shuns the realm of high theory. It remains largely opaque to hierarchical scrutiny and achieves at most local coherence. As a consequence, it lacks the consistency and systematicity that we have come to expect from bureaucratic norms.

I have argued that such shortcomings can also be virtues. Everyday casuistry plays a central role in enabling street-level bureaucrats to fulfill their role in a sound and responsible manner. Casuistic reasoning has the advantage of concentrating the limited resources that frontline workers have at their disposal on the task that is most distinctively theirs in the division of moral labor—that of responding to the particularities of individual cases. Casuistry has several other virtues to recommend it over more principled approaches to discretionary decision-making: it is flexible enough to permit workers to respond in a nuanced way to new situations; it can be easily revised to accommodate the need for further (or lesser) distinctions between cases; it is modest in its aspirations and hence realistic in the demands that it places on frontline workers; and, finally, it allows peers to work together and agree on specific outcomes while maintaining their commitment to different moral dispositions. These features are particularly valuable for frontline officials who are obligated, by virtue of the social role that they play, to reconcile, accommodate, or patch two worlds—the regimented realm of administration and the unwieldy realities of social life—that are often out of step.

In addition to laying out the structure of everyday casuistry and its merits, I also showed that casuistic reasoning is marked at each step by the influence of peers. Individual moral deliberation bears the trace of the group. For such a relation between group and individual to be symbiotic, at least one condition must obtain: the group must be heterogeneous. It must comprise clusters of individuals whose moral dispositions vary. Heterogeneity at the group level serves three related purposes. It stimulates the moral perception and reasoning of individual bureaucrats; it serves as a check against the drift toward overly narrow moral dispositions; and it spurs a regime of informal accountability that is well adapted to probe into the intricacies of casuistic reasoning.

If I insisted, at several junctures in the chapter, on using the phrase "*organized* heterogeneity," it is to underscore that such heterogeneity cannot be left to chance. Public managers must take care to foster it. As we will see in Chapter 5, they can do so through recruiting, by selecting new entrants with diverse predispositions and professional backgrounds; and through education and training, by socializing workers into different ways of inhabiting the role; or through career advancement, by making sure to promote workers with different sensibilities at each step of the hierarchy. Public managers can also promote heterogeneity by making available to their subordinates different repertoires of normative justification and by carefully orchestrating misalignments in the incentive structure they design.

The complex formed by everyday casuistry and informal accountability can come under threat from two directions. One is the elimination of the organized heterogeneity on which the symbiotic relationship depends. This could occur directly—through the passing of measures, or the promotion of an organizational culture, that actively endorses a single, uniform type of "ideal" employee—or indirectly, through the design of policies or incentive structures that effectively make certain moral dispositions untenable (more on that in Chapter 5).

The second threat to everyday casuistry and informal accountability comes in the guise of two normative principles that are meant to apply to public institutions: the requirement of transparency and that of articulate consistency. Transparency is typically used as a synonym for openness. According to Amitai Etzioni, it is "generally defined as the principle of enabling the public to gain information about the operations and structures of a given entity."[55] This involves giving them access to the grounds—rules, principles, factors, standards, and so forth—that govern the behavior of institutions and institutional actors.

Articulate consistency aims, for its part, to constrain what those grounds can be. It requires that public institutions and public officials be able to account for their actions on the basis of a consistent and coherent set of principles. As Dworkin puts it, the principle of "articulate consistency" stems from the belief that it would be "unfair for officials to act except on the basis of a general public theory that will constrain them to consistency, provide a public standard for testing or debating or predicting what they do, and not allow appeals to unique intuitions that might mask prejudice or self-interest in particular cases."[56]

Both of these desiderata—for transparency and articulate consistency—are often subsumed under the heading of publicity. As I understand it, the demand for publicity involves two negations: it stands in opposition to secrecy—that is, to a willful obstruction of what there is to see—but also in opposition to opacity—that is, to an excessively convoluted, unclear, or idiosyncratic way of doing things.[57]

Everyday casuistry falls short of the principle of publicity on both dimensions. Casuistry does not take place in the open. Informal moral taxonomies operate without being officially proclaimed or disclosed. They remain largely hidden from supervisors and clients and are discussed freely only in the company of peers. In addition to being secretive, everyday casuistry is also opaque. Even if it were to occur before the eyes of the public, it would lack the well-defined criteria, sharp boundaries between categories, and principled coherence that would allow external observers to easily assess and oversee the behavior of frontline workers.

It is no surprise, then, that public service agencies would often choose, in the name of publicity, to close the spaces of discretion where casuistic reasoning can flourish. While such a choice may at times be warranted, I hope to have shown that it should not be taken lightly. Casuistry has something important to contribute to a more adequate fit between the state and the street: something by way of flexibility, adaptability, revisability, and sensitivity to the particularities of individual cases. I have tried to argue, moreover, that our worries about accountability can be alleviated when we take into account the existence of informal interactions among peers, and when we recognize that it is possible to influence these interactions by controlling the degree of "heterogeneity" that exists within the organization. We may not be able to dictate what informal labels frontline workers choose to use, nor how they apply them, but we can shape the environment and the colleagues in the presence of which they will have to do so—and this is quite different from giving them free license.

The argument I have offered is not one for doing away with hierarchical, direct, and professional accountability, nor for relinquishing our commitment to transparency and articulate consistency. My claim is more modest: it is that we need an approach to policy implementation that—to reuse Charles Lindblom's celebrated phrase—permits some measure of moral "muddling-through" to coexist with the rigid structure of rules and guidelines that frontline officials inherit.[58] Informal taxonomies and everyday casuistry are not perversions that need to be excised, but sensible responses to problems that a specific social role—at the juncture of state and society—makes unavoidable.

CHAPTER FIVE

Impossible Situations
On the Breakdown of Moral Integrity at the Front Lines of Public Service

This chapter examines how public policy and managerial practices inform the moral dispositions of street-level bureaucrats. I argue that if we want such bureaucrats to remain sensitive to a plurality of normative considerations—if we want to guard against the twin dangers of excessive specialization and excessive conformity in moral outlooks—we need to reproduce the desired pluralism within the organizational environment in which they evolve. As I will show in the following pages, this calls for some measure of misalignment between managerial signals. When properly orchestrated, conflicting managerial demands can serve to expand the range of values to which bureaucrats are attuned, while curbing the drift toward reductive ways of inhabiting the role.

I also want to argue, however, that there is such a thing as *too much misalignment*. There is a point beyond which exposure to conflicting demands becomes incapacitating. If we are to understand when that threshold is crossed and why, we need to remain attentive to the experience of the frontline workers who must live amid conflicting signals. My goal, then, will be to examine how conflicting demands can both enable and constrain the deployment of moral agency at the front lines of public service.

I take as my guiding thread a grievance frequently voiced by frontline workers across public service agencies, namely, that they find themselves caught in "impossible situations" in which they can no longer fulfill the demands placed on them. I address three related questions: What does it mean, conceptually, to say that a situation is "impossible"? Under what conditions are such situations likely to arise? And how can those who are caught in such situations respond to them? I aim to show that impossible situations are not simply ethical dilemmas that individual officials must face alone, but that they are a matter for public concern. These situations capture and dramatize tensions between competing aspirations for public policy that come to the fore during periods of policy change and administrative reform.

Consider the following three stories:

Story 1

On March 3, 2012, the *New York Times* published an op-ed titled "Confessions of a 'Bad' Teacher."[1] The author, William Johnson, a special education teacher from New York, wrote that his job, which was already "extremely difficult," had gotten much more demanding over the previous 18 months as his school started enforcing new requirements for teacher accountability. According to these requirements, which were introduced with the No Child Left Behind Act, teachers were to be monitored closely and regularly by their principals and were to be assessed based on their students' performance on standardized, state-designed exams.

In one of the recurring rounds of evaluation mandated by the new policy, Johnson's teaching was rated "unsatisfactory"—a rating that placed his career in limbo. Johnson, who had only recently been nominated for a citywide award for "classroom excellence," was not the only teacher to receive such a rating. The psychological effects were devastating for him and his colleagues. "I've seen a teacher with 10 years of experience," he wrote, "become convinced, after just a few observations, that he was a terrible teacher. A few months later, he quit teaching altogether. I collaborated with another teacher who sought psychiatric care for insomnia after a particularly intense round of observations."

As a seasoned teacher, Johnson understood the rationale for standardized tests and greater accountability, but he could not help but wonder whether the new regime of scrutiny, and the punitive measures associated with it, were really called for. The truth, he wrote, is that "teachers care a great deal about [their] work." Part of what they do involves exposing students to "new and exciting ideas," and "planting seeds that wouldn't bear fruit in the short term"—"the sort of thing that doesn't show up on high-stakes tests." Since he received the "unsatisfactory" rating, however, with administrators "breathing down his neck," and with the imperative to train his students to perform well on standardized exams, "the students became a secondary concern." He added: "I simply did what my principal asked me to do. . . . In all honesty, my teaching probably became close to incoherent."

To avoid being a "bad teacher" in the eyes of his administration, Johnson effectively became a bad teacher in his own. He could not bear this for long. He quit his job, and transferred to another school.

Story 2

With the enactment of the Personal Responsibility and Work Opportunity Reconciliation Act (PRWORA) in 1996 and the creation of the Temporary Assistance for Needy Families (TANF) program, welfare agencies in the United States went from "delivering the routinized, depersonalized, 'people sustaining' product of cash assistance" to offering more "supportive," "people-transforming" services aimed at helping clients reintegrate the workforce.[2] This transformation had two primary consequences for caseworkers: it enlarged the scope of their discretion and heightened the pressure to reduce caseload—such a reduction being seen, in most cases, as a proxy for success (i.e., as a sign that clients had regained economic self-sufficiency and were no longer in need of public assistance).[3]

Soon after PRWORA was passed, policymakers realized that some of the new requirements mandated by the policy (such as the strict 60-month time limit on benefits, mandatory work requirements, and child support enforcement) might endanger women attempting to flee abusive relationships. They therefore passed an amendment to the Act, the Family Violence Option (FVO). The FVO effectively allowed states to waive TANF program requirements "if these would endanger a woman or were beyond her current ability to comply because of domestic violence."

While the FVO was adopted by a majority of states, researchers subsequently found that few women were actually benefiting from the types of assistance provided through it. A study of welfare caseworkers in Louisiana revealed that the emphasis on reducing caseload worked at cross-purposes with the attempt to implement the FVO.[4] Those interviewed explained that it had become extremely difficult to find enough time to build the personal relationships and the level of trust that were required before clients would "open up" and disclose sensitive information about their private lives. As one worker put it, "you just don't have time to pull [domestic violence] out of somebody, unless they come here with visible observations [bruises], which doesn't happen often."[5]

The study also found that the increased pressure to reduce caseload was a source of significant stress and anxiety among workers, many of whom believed that the agency's goal—as officially proclaimed—was to assist individuals in becoming genuinely independent, not just in getting them off the rolls. One worker expressed the frustration that he and his colleagues felt in the following words: "It's just mind boggling how we're doing such a number game, and then we try to be a people person. You can't do both."[6]

Story 3

On April 23, 2010, Arizona governor Jan Brewer signed into law what was then the strictest immigration bill in the United States' recent history.[7] Among other provisions, the law required law enforcement officials to check the residency status of any individual whom they suspected to be in the country illegally. While some sections of the law were subsequently struck down by the Supreme Court, the portion allowing state officials to investigate immigration status during a "lawful stop, detention, or arrest" (known as the "show me your papers" provision) was upheld.

Several police officers and unions were openly critical of the law. "We're way too busy," said Sgt. Ross Charlton, who patrols the south side of Tucson. "We don't have enough officers on the street to look for other stuff like that. If they're not doing anything, they're just being normal people. Why would I do that [question them about their immigration status]?"[8] As Sgt. Charlton saw it, after 30 years on the force, his job was "to investigate crimes and help people who need help," not to arrest peaceful individuals minding their own business. For Martin Escobar, another patrolman from Tucson who sued Arizona to block the law, the problem was not simply that the law would deflect scarce resources away from essential police activities, but that it would lead to racial profiling and make people more hesitant to report crime, share information with police, and serve as witnesses.

According to Karthick Ramakrishnan, an expert on law enforcement, the reason why several police officers felt so strongly about the bill that they were willing to voice their objections publicly had to do with the recent history of policing: "The biggest trend in policing in the past two decades has been community policing in which cops walk the local beat and spend much time gaining the trust of the people. [The immigration reform] puts that trend entirely in jeopardy—it is a very big deal for them, indeed."[9] Joel Jacobsen, an assistant attorney general in the criminal appeals division in New Mexico, pressed the point further: "[The immigration law] obviously puts police in an impossible situation because it requires them to pursue two goals simultaneously: to enforce the immigration laws; and to enforce the criminal laws, keep the peace, provide assistance, and all the other ordinary tasks of police officers. Which goal should they pursue?"[10]

These three stories chronicle well-known problems in policy implementation. The first shows what takes place when accountability standards, instead of serving to measure progress toward an independently specified goal ("student learning"), become themselves a surrogate for that goal. The second describes what happens when a pressing concern for "numbers" displaces other aspects of an organization's mandate. The third, finally, illustrates a case where the pursuit of new objectives undermines the attainment of older ones.

Seen from the perspective of frontline workers, however, these stories have much in common. In all three, we hear street-level bureaucrats—teachers, welfare caseworkers, and police officers—voice a sense of frustration and distress in the face of new, or looming, organizational transformations. In each, the workers claim that they have been, or that they will be, placed in a situation where it is no longer possible for them to do their job well. The grievances share a similar structure: a teacher explains that the requirements for greater accountability effectively prevent him from being a "good teacher"; welfare caseworkers claim that the "numbers game" jeopardizes their commitment to being people persons and to helping their clients become independent (*"you can't do both,"* one of them says); police officers, finally, complain that the new immigration law would undermine their capacity to operate according to the premises of community policing. Frontline bureaucrats experience these professional difficulties acutely, with a sense of agony. They are, to use the words of Jacobsen, placed in an "impossible situation." The tension generated by such a situation is such that it leads to a form of agential breakdown. The role becomes untenable: Johnson quits his job, caseworkers burn out or become desensitized, and police officers break the ranks to engage in open conflict with their peers.

One of my goals in this chapter is to shed light on the nature of the impossibility that lies at the heart of an "impossible situation." How should we interpret the grievances voiced above? On one reading, the testimonies simply betray the workers' frustration at having to accomplish tasks that are difficult, unrewarding, or conflicting. This much is certainly true—but what if the grievances went deeper? What if the workers meant to indicate that there was a *real* impossibility at play: that a teacher like William Johnson *cannot* live up to the school's accountability requirement *and* be a good teacher; that caseworkers *cannot* both play the numbers game *and* be "people persons"; that police officers *cannot* fulfill the core requirements of policing *and* apply the "show me your papers" clause? What would the workers have meant if they had meant to say *that*?

The questions I raise here are inspired by the opening pages of Jonathan Lear's *Radical Hope*.[11] There, Lear seeks to explore the possible philosophical meaning of an obscure utterance by the last great chief of the Crow nation, Plenty Coups: "After [the Buffalo went away] nothing happened." Much like Lear in his study of the Crow, I cannot pretend to know with any certainty what the frontline workers actually meant when they told their stories and voiced their complaints. I am interested, rather, in trying to articulate a plausible and philosophically coherent understanding of what they *may* have meant. As Lear would say, this is in an inquiry into a possibility.[12]

Yet unlike Lear, who repeatedly says that the "end of happenings" is a possibility that could affect not just the Crow but everyone else, my analysis of "impossible situations" is more contextually specific. While "impossible situations" could, in theory, confront us all qua moral agents, the story I want to tell revolves primarily around bureaucracies. I want to show that impossible situations, if not exclusive to bureaucracies, are at least particularly likely to arise there. "Impossible situations," as I will describe and analyze them here, are a bureaucratic pathology that leads to a breakdown in individual moral agency. They are not the *only* type of bureaucratic pathology, nor the *only* kind of situation that could lead to agential breakdown—but they are troubling and frequent enough to deserve to be better understood and conceptualized.

I will work my way in the chapter toward an increasingly detailed characterization of impossible situations. The conclusion I will arrive at is that such situations arise when frontline workers find themselves required to act in ways that run against the professional moral identity or role conception they had been encouraged to adopt up to that point. This form of conflict leads to a breakdown in moral agency insofar as it makes it impossible for workers to act in ways they deem justified. It involves a form of self-betrayal that many find unbearable.

Impossible situations are sometimes the regrettable, but unavoidable, byproduct of policy change or of transformations in organizational culture. But they can also be the consequence, anticipated or not, of asking public service agencies to do, or to be, too many things at once. As such, they can reveal the existence of tensions and conflicts between aspirations for public policy that ought to be discussed, and possibly resolved, in a legislative arena, but which are ignored, passed along, and relegated to the front lines of public service.

Whichever their origin, impossible situations should give us pause. The sight of workers who break down or burn out reminds us that street-level bureaucrats are not simply the strategic actors presupposed by rational choice theory, who can swiftly change their way of performing the role in response to changes in incentives, but that they also form moral commitments to particular ways of performing the role, and that these commitments change at a far slower pace than the political priorities of the day. This is a fact that reformers must take at heart and, if at all possible, work around, lest they deprive themselves of the very workforce they depend upon to implement change.

Varieties of Impossibility

The phrase "impossible situation" captures in a concise and evocative way the predicament of the frontline workers whose stories we just heard. What follows—in the next three sections—is an exercise in disambiguation. Can we formulate an account of "impossible situations" that does justice to the three opening stories on both an analytic and phenomeno-logical level?

When the phrase "impossible situation" appears in ordinary discourse, it is used, variously, to denote the predicament of an agent who is (1) re-quired to perform an action that he or she literally cannot do, (2) asked to meet an objective that is unattainable, (3) asked to work toward two or more objectives that are incompatible in principle, or (4) required to act in a way that is antithetical to the requirements of the social role that he or she oc-cupies. We also use the phrase "impossible situation," at times, in a figura-tive sense, as a shorthand for a situation traversed by deep, unbridgeable conflicts: a situation where one is exposed to a variety of incongruous demands. Impossibility, as such, can refer to incapability, unattainability, incompatibility, irreconcilability, or incongruity. None of the first four meanings, however, adequately captures the kind of impossibility at work in the opening stories, and the fifth is not specific enough. Let us examine them in turn.

The label "impossible situation" can be used to refer to the predicament of an agent who is required to undertake an action that he or she is inca-pable of performing. This may be due to the presence of external impedi-ments to action ("a caseworker cannot provide assistance to an eligible client because the agency has run out of funds") or to internal impediments ("due to his fear of heights, a police officer cannot get himself to cross the bridge to follow a fugitive").[13] In either case, it is the agent's inability to perform the action, coupled with an understanding that the action is required, that can result in a feeling of distress.

This sense of "impossibility as incapability," however, does not capture what is at stake in the opening stories. None of the workers that featured in them were required to undertake actions they could not perform. On the contrary, the grievances voiced by both teachers and caseworkers stemmed from the fact that they were indeed successful in altering their everyday behavior so as to implement the new directives. The same goes for police officers: if they are dissatisfied with the new immigration law, it is, in part, because they can all too easily imagine themselves enforcing it. To the ex-tent that there is a breakdown in moral agency, it does not occur because actions are impossible to perform, but in response to actions that can be performed.[14]

The phrase "impossible situation" may also be used when an agent is asked to meet objectives that are unattainable. In studies of welfare reform, for instance, it is common to find workers voicing complaints of the following sort: "When they changed . . . the performance measures to [a caseload mandate of] 90 to one, it was like, that's impossible. There is no way someone can manage 90 cases."[15] The problem, here, is one of unrealistic expectations: there is simply not enough time, given the average duration of a visit, for a single worker to manage ninety clients.

Unattainable objectives certainly form an important part of the opening stories. Teachers, caseworkers, and police officers all claim that they are being asked to do too much. Taken alone, however, "unattainability" is not sufficient to explain what is distinctive about the stories for the simple reason that unattainable objectives are endemic to street-level bureaucracy. In the public services, demand is elastic and typically rises to meet supply. Caseworkers, police officers, and teachers will always have more clients to see, laws to enforce, and students to help than they possibly could. This is not to belittle the stress that unattainable objectives can cause, but to note that, since they are such a staple of life at the front lines of public service, it would be surprising if the stories above—with the seemingly qualitative shift in experience they relate and the radical reactions they involve—were simply responses to *that*.

It is also important to note that the "unattainability" of objectives does not capture an important aspect of the workers' grievances. Sgt. Charlton's worry is not only that the immigration law will prevent him from attaining his other objectives, but also that the law requires him to perform actions that are difficult to relate to the activity of policing as he understands it ("*Why* would I do that?" he asks). The same goes for William Johnson, the teacher: the problem with accountability measures is not that they require him to do more, but that they do not properly track what it is that a good teacher is supposed to do (as a teacher, he says, his job involves "planting seeds that wouldn't bear fruit in the short term"). For a situation to be "impossible," then, the "unattainability" of objectives is neither necessary nor sufficient. What is more crucial, it appears, is the *character* of the objectives, and how they relate to the self-understanding of those who are asked to pursue them.

One might also describe a situation as "impossible" when agents are asked to pursue two objectives that are incompatible in principle—two objectives, that is, that cannot be attained simultaneously. If police officers were to fully implement the immigration law, they would destroy the tissue of trust necessary for community policing. Similarly, if caseworkers focused exclusively on reducing caseload, they would not be able to conduct conversations intimate enough to identify cases of domestic violence.

Goals that are incompatible at the limits, however, do not necessarily yield the kind of practical distress that frontline workers relate in the opening stories. In the thick of everyday work, one does not face an all-or-nothing choice between two objectives that are mutually exclusive, but a more tractable problem of prioritization. Caseworkers must choose between spending a bit more time trying to "pull" a case of domestic violence and pushing ahead until they have sufficiently reduced their caseload. Even if two goals cannot be reconciled *in principle*, it may still be possible to attain a working compromise between them in practice. In essence, this is no different from the compromises that frontline workers must strike on an ongoing basis, when managing the tension between treating people fairly and responding to individual needs, between being efficient and being respectful.

What motivates the workers' grievances, therefore, cannot simply be an abstract concern for the fact that their objectives are impossible to attain simultaneously, nor a worry about the need to make compromises between such incompatible objectives (they must have been making compromises all along), but it must involve the realization that such a *modus vivendi* is no longer workable. The testimony of the welfare caseworker in the second story gives us a precious cue. In saying that you cannot be both a people person and a numbers person, he points to a sense of conflict that leaves him unable to settle for an identity. The incompatibility, to the extent that it exists, is not between objectives *per se*, but between the different identities, or role conceptions, that workers need to adopt if they are to pursue these objectives.

The phrase "impossible situation" may also be used to describe the predicament of an agent who is torn between his or her responsibilities as a role incumbent and other responsibilities external to the role. This is a form of "impossibility as irreconcilability" between two kinds of moral demands. These are the sorts of dilemmas that are central to the literature on role morality.[16] A caseworker may be torn, for instance, between the impetus to give special attention to a family member in need and the requirement of impartiality that comes with public office; or between the urge to provide unreserved care to a fellow human being in distress and the requirement of public office to offer assistance only on the basis of principles that could be scaled up and universalized.

This kind of "impossibility as irreconcilability," however, does not feature in the opening stories. In all three, workers are concerned with balancing demands *internal* to their role as frontline officials. The practical dilemma that police officers face is between applying the immigration law and fulfilling their ordinary tasks of order maintenance and criminal law enforcement; teachers are torn between performing well on accountability metrics and teaching lessons that may be more useful to students in the long run; caseworkers, finally, must decide whether to see a greater number of clients or to increase the quality of service they provide to those they do manage to see. To the extent that such workers experience a conflict that touches upon their identity, such a conflict is not—as in the bulk of the literature on role morality—between the demands of their role as public officials and demands that are external to the role, but between a variety of demands that are internal to the role.

What makes this conflict particularly distressing, moreover, is that the various internal demands are all, in varying degrees, "legitimate"—that is, they carry some moral weight. Frontline workers, after all, have a presumptive moral obligation to obey existing policies, especially when they have a democratic pedigree (immigration law) and when they are backed up by a sensible rationale (accountability measures are intended to motivate better performance; the focus on reducing caseload is meant to encourage a more efficient allocation of limited public resources). But frontline workers also have an obligation to act according to their professional understanding of what the role requires, and in light of their assessment of what clients need. Street-level bureaucrats are both subordinates and professionals. This reflects the fact that public administration derives its legitimacy from at least two distinct sources. It is both an arm of the legislative that implements the "general will" (input legitimacy), and a direct provider of services advancing the "general interest" of the public (output legitimacy).[17] The first requires street-level bureaucrats to be faithful subordinates; the second enjoins them to act as professionals.

It is important to add, of course, that the moral obligation that street-level bureaucrats have to obey the law can drop if the latter is unjust, or if the process through which it was arrived at lacks democratic legitimacy. In such cases, we would say that the law loses its moral force, and that bureaucrats might be justified in obstructing or subverting it. Note, however, that none of the bureaucrats in the opening stories goes as far as to make such a claim. Even the police officers, who would arguably be most justified in adopting such a stance, do not take issue with the immigration law on the grounds that it is unjust, but on the grounds that it detracts from certain tasks that they consider more pressing. While they may not be fully persuaded by the merits of the law, they nevertheless appear to acknowledge its authority, and their obligation to abide by it.

It is important to recognize, as well, that while the three opening stories involve a conflict between moral demands, prudential considerations play a critical role in determining how this conflict is resolved. If teachers change their lessons in light of new accountability requirements, and if caseworkers devote more attention to reducing their caseload than to building relations of trust with clients, it is, in part, because they would put their careers at risk if they did otherwise.

This brings us to yet another—perhaps the most common—way in which the phrase "impossible situations" appears in ordinary discourse. The phrase is often used as a shorthand for a kind of "incongruous situation," a situation where agents have to contend with several conflicting practical demands that all pertain to the role they occupy, and that all have a legitimate claim on them. This is a phenomenon that has been studied by scholars of organizational behavior under the name "role conflict"—an umbrella term meant to designate the predicament of an agent who is subjected, on a day-to-day basis, to a variety of demands or expectations that push and pull in different directions.[18] Role conflict is known to cause some amount of "tension, dissatisfaction, and psychological withdrawal" among workers.[19]

Are "impossible situations," then, another word for role conflict? Not quite. The relationship between conflict and agency is not always antagonistic. While conflict can at times be incapacitating, it can also be empowering: the existence of a plurality of competing standards of value and sources of authority can give bureaucrats access to a range of repertoires of normative justification that they can use, play against each other, and combine in creative ways. Impossible situations, therefore, must involve a particular kind of conflict—one that is, in a sense yet to be specified, "intractable."

I will parse out this sense of intractability in the section after next. Before proceeding further in that direction, however, it will be useful to examine more closely the relationship between conflicting demands and individual moral agency. I will do so by drawing on a set of observations from my fieldwork. This will take us momentarily away from the focus on "impossible situations"—indeed, the framework that I will try to develop below is intended to have wider relevance—but it will ultimately allow us to better capture how such situations emerge.

On Conflict and Moral Agency: John's Visit

It is around 2 PM on a Wednesday afternoon at the end of January. The day so far has been relatively quiet when Isabel, the director of the Norville Hispanic Center, rushes into the reception area. She stops abruptly in the middle of the room, looks around, then leaps into a frenzy of activity. In a few brief and brusque movements, she rearranges the piles of informative fliers into neat stacks, moves the garbage bin into a less visible spot, replenishes the lot of plastic cups for the water cooler, and readjusts the inclination of the giant Miró poster on the wall. I look at her from behind the reception desk, somewhat perplexed. "John's coming," she says in response. "My boss is coming."

This was not my first encounter with John. As director of operations for the agency, he was responsible for coordinating and supervising the work of several neighborhood centers like ours. John was known for making surprise visits to the various sites. This time, however, his call had caught Isabel at a particularly bad moment: she was about to leave for an important personal appointment that had been scheduled weeks earlier. And for once, John took longer than expected to show up. Isabel waited for him as long as she could but eventually left.

In the forty minutes that elapsed between her departure and John's arrival, the Center witnessed a sudden rush of clients. The reception area, which had been largely empty since the morning, filled up completely. I went around the office, trying to fetch additional chairs, but the space was too small to accommodate everyone and a few clients were left standing. At that time on Wednesdays, with Isabel gone, there was only one case manager on duty at the Center—Flora.

Of all the clients in the reception area, it turned out that only two had appointments scheduled for that afternoon. The rest had simply walked in on the off chance that a case manager would be available to see them. This practice of "dropping in" was one that Isabel frowned upon in private but did little to curtail in practice. The fact that clients would repeatedly miss their appointments and show up unannounced on a different day was, in her words, "a cultural thing." As she once put it, "they just don't show up, they do that all the time; sometimes they can't find transportation, sometimes, they just have something more pressing to do. It's a culture." This, according to her, was a fact that case managers had to accept and accommodate; the Center had to adapt itself to the ways of the community—a community that she, as a Hispanic young mother and resident of the neighborhood, knew very well. Appointments were understood, by both staff and clients, to be more suggestive than binding, and despite the occasional complaint, neither side seemed particularly intent on questioning the status quo, and no penalties were enforced for no-shows.

Isabel's readiness to adapt to the mores of the community fit squarely within her broader approach to the role, one that stressed the importance of being warm to clients and of offering personalized service. As director of the Center, she made sure that everything in the office—from the soft yellow and orange colors that she selected for the walls to the family pictures that adorned her desk—felt welcoming and intimate. She created an environment in which clients and case managers were comfortable addressing each other as "mi amor," where embraces were frequent, and where clients would stop by, occasionally, to give the staff generous samplings of their latest culinary achievements. These clients, Isabel told me, were pushed around all day long, sent from one office to another, and given the impression that no one cared for them. "I want this place to be different, to be welcoming, inviting, a place where people feel they can come to get help when they need it, and where someone will actually listen to them." It was not all that surprising, therefore, that the waiting room was crowded with clients who had decided to "drop in" at the last minute. Isabel's lenient and easygoing attitude had, if not exactly encouraged this, then at least made it possible.

When John finally opened the front door, he took the sight in disbelief. The ten seats or so were occupied, and clients were standing past the reception desk, in the hallway leading to Flora's office. He turned to me and asked, visibly displeased, "Why are so many clients waiting? Where is Isabel? Why don't you have enough chairs?" Before I could answer, he had already stormed past the desk, looking severely at a group of three children who were chasing each other in the room, and entered Flora's office. I heard him repeat the same questions there.

John's disapproval did not catch me or Flora by surprise. His favorite metaphor—the animating image he wanted all sites to strive for—was that of a doctor's office. The space had to be clean and orderly, case managers punctual and competent. Clients had to be treated with courtesy, but with professional distance, and according to clear rules. The ultimate aim of the agency, as he understood it, was to put an end to dependency. One of my coworkers summed up John's approach as such: "We're not their friends, and we will not treat them like babies; they must take care of themselves."

This made John suspicious of the personalized relationships that Isabel aimed to foster, and it made him prefer a more "bureaucratic" approach to the scheduling of appointments. Clients had to show up on time, and case managers had to hold them accountable for doing so, if need be by issuing light punishments. The agency was not merely responsible for providing services; it also had to teach clients lessons, to impart them with the kind of norms and behavioral expectations they would need to succeed in the world "out there."

Since John was a senior figure in the organization, his visit and ensuing criticism were a source of worry for both Flora (who did not know how to break the news to Isabel) and Isabel (whose reputation and standing as a manager were on the line). It served as fodder for conversation between the three of us over the following weeks.

As staff members of the Hispanic Center, Flora and I, as well as the other interns and case managers who were absent on that day, were exposed to both Isabel's and John's competing visions of what the office ought to look and feel like. These visions had their own languages, vocabularies, and animating metaphors. Each of them offered a coherent and plausible "lifeworld"—a sensible, if partial, way of seeing, experiencing, and interpreting the demands of the role.[20] Each of them also derived from a clear source of authority (the chief of operations, and the director of the site), who had at their disposal various means to influence behavior.

Yet these two visions or lifeworlds (for simplicity, I will say "worlds" in what follows) were not the only ones on offer. As frontline workers, we were also in constant contact with clients and their specific requests. Whether on the phone or in person, we had to interact with a never-ending flow of people who—out of dire need, helplessness, or momentary panic—demanded immediate assistance. At least a third of the several hundreds of calls I fielded while working at the Hispanic Center involved some kind of "emergency," with clients claiming they had to speak to a case manager right away.

In such circumstances, it was hard to resist the impression that what clients wanted, at the end of the day, was neither "warmth" nor "professionalism," but rapid assistance with the particular problem they happened to have, whenever they happened to have it. This called for an emergency-response mode of operation, and for rapid transitions from one crisis to the next. Such an approach, however, was at odds with John's preference for predictable appointments, and it was tangential, in spirit, to Isabel's penchant for a friendly atmosphere where personal relationships could flourish.

While the three "worlds" I have just described—anchored, respectively, in visions of pastoral care, professionalism, and rapid responsiveness—informed how I and others approached the role, none of them featured prominently in the official data that the organization recorded, and on the basis of which individual performance was formally evaluated. Such data, which had to be entered into a specialized case management software at the end of every encounter, tracked the number of clients served, their profile, and the type of services provided to them.

The case management software gave everyone in the organization access to a tab, aptly titled "director's view," that provided an up-to-date record of the performance of each individual worker, and summary statistics for each site. Workers and site managers could thus keep track of their "numbers" and compare them to those of their peers. The atmosphere in the agency was not particularly competitive, but workers were keenly aware of their standing, and the pressure to catch up—for those who were behind—was fairly acute. While the "numbers game" had an affinity with the "emergency-response" approach, the two were not always aligned. The director's tab was not designed to keep track of whether any particular client's problem was resolved, but rather to ensure that the organization was on track toward meeting its overall targets.

As workers, then, we had to contend with at least four different "worlds" or visions of what street-level work ought to be like, which had, at heart, different animating spirits. These worlds corresponded not just to normative outlooks but also to spheres of influence. Each had at its disposal the means to reward bureaucrats or to impose sanctions on those who strayed away too far. As director of operations, John was in charge of performance reviews and promotions—he also had the power to expand or curtail each worker's sphere of autonomy (a currency that is particularly valuable because it allows workers to give expression to their own "styles" of work).[21] Isabel had control over the day-to-day life of the office and the allocation of tasks—she could make one's job interesting, stressful, or boring. Clients could express gratitude or voice their dissatisfaction—they could "make" your day or ruin it. Numerical targets, finally, were the only objective criterion of evaluation, and failure to meet them could put one in a precarious position.

One might expect the daily friction between such a plurality of competing worlds within a single organization to be incapacitating. One might imagine line agents being pulled in a variety of directions, not knowing what to do, and being unable, in the long run, to develop coherent moral dispositions or role conceptions. Interestingly, though, the pluralism I encountered at the Norville Hispanic Center, while certainly a source of tension, did not lead to paralysis or inaction. It served, rather, to open up a space where bureaucrats could develop a variety of individual styles of work (much like those I described in Chapter 2). Far from constraining agency, the existence of a plurality of standards gave bureaucrats access to a range of motivations for action, and to several repertoires of justification that they could use, pit against each other, and combine in creative ways. Each of the worlds provided a set of resources—metaphors, reasons, precedents, as well as role models and allies—that bureaucrats could leverage to motivate their actions in any given encounter and explain them to others.[22] More importantly, perhaps, on a long-term basis, the lack of alignment between the various worlds gave bureaucrats space to craft a diverse range of moral dispositions, some leaning closer to one world than others.

Such flexibility, of course, had its limits. Bureaucrats knew very well that they would get in trouble if they consistently fell short on any of the four sets of criteria—and as I explained earlier, in reference to the possibility of "sanctions," this was not an idle threat. The system had a built-in elasticity of sorts: it would allow workers to move between the four poles but not stray too far from any of them. The existence of a plurality of nonaligned normative worlds served, therefore, both to open up a space for moral agency and to delimit its scope.

The observations I have been making here—that occupants of organizational roles are exposed to a variety of normative worlds, or "economies of worth"; that they develop partial identifications and allegiances to these worlds; and that their agency derives in part from their capacity to deploy these worlds against each other and to use them to develop complex forms of justification—will not strike sociologists as new. Similar thoughts have been pressed by Luc Boltanski and Laurent Thévenot among others, as an alternative to more narrow conceptions of agency.[23] As Boltanski and Thévenot have been at pains to argue, the behavior of agents cannot be explained simply by reference to calculating self-interest: it also betrays a concern for justifying one's conduct to others by appealing to normative principles that command respect. There is no direct mapping, moreover, between the personal dispositions of agents and the social or organizational environment that surrounds them. While the environment shapes the possibilities that are available to agents, they also play a part in picking their allegiances and constructing their dispositions.

While not novel per se, these observations on agency deserve to be made for two reasons. The first is to rectify an imbalance in the sorts of questions that political theorists have thought worth asking about the morality of roles. The bulk of the literature on role morality is concerned with two types of problems: conflicts between the demands of a role and the demands of ordinary morality, and conflicts between the demands of two separate roles that one individual occupies at the same time. The questions that have attracted most attention are of the following sort: What should I do if the role requires me to perform actions that I would otherwise be morally reluctant to undertake (as a public bureaucrat, say, should I follow orders that conflict with my religious beliefs, or should I step outside the role and disobey)?[24] Or, alternatively, what should I do if the various roles I occupy place conflicting demands on me (say, as a soldier who must be ready to put his life at risk, and as a son who has to care for his aging mother)?

While these questions are undoubtedly important, our fixation on answering them makes it seem as though being "in-role" involves applying a set of standards that are clear and well defined. In the examples above, it is assumed to be obvious what I should do as a soldier, son, or bureaucrat. The only question that remains is whether I should actually do such things on balance. Our discussion so far, however, should serve as a reminder that role-incumbents often find themselves at the intersection of various realms of expectations that promote different normative values and different rationales for action *even as they remain within the confines of a single role.* Part of what it means to occupy a role is to figure out how to balance these various considerations and how to create a workable compromise between them. To recover F. H. Bradley's famous title, it is no easy task to go from one's station to one's duties.[25]

The other reason to stress the relationship between the plurality of normative worlds that exist within an organization and the dispositions of individual moral agents is to underscore the crucial role of management. The choices that managers and institutional architects make effectively shape the environment within which individual bureaucrats live their everyday moral lives. If we think of organizations as complex ecosystems—which encompass a variety of normative worlds, each with its own representatives, rewards, sanctions, and animating imagery—then a central task of managers and institutional architects is to orchestrate the diversity, overlap, and conflict between these worlds.

It bears emphasizing, as I mentioned above, that the various worlds make available both repertoires for the justification of individual decisions and resources for the development of a sense of self (i.e., a professional moral identity or role conception). By adjusting the configuration of these worlds within the organization, managers can influence not only the decisions workers are likely to make but also the kinds of moral dispositions they are likely to develop. They can make some dispositions easier (or harder) to maintain than others. By increasing numerical targets and the cost of not reaching them, for instance, organizations will drive more workers toward indifference. By giving case managers more autonomy, and recruiting those with a background in social work, they will end up with more caregivers.

This way of looking at management—not simply as a matter of wielding sticks and carrots in the form of money or status but as an attempt to orchestrate a configuration of normative worlds that will then inform the moral dispositions available to workers—forces us to be attentive to the entire spectrum of tools, soft and hard, that public service managers have at their disposal. Managers can utilize these tools to select which normative worlds are represented within the organization; to regulate the extent to which these worlds are aligned or not; and to calibrate their relative strength.

As managers, John and Isabel can advance a particular vision of street-level work by utilizing standard instruments of organizational control. They can give people and projects visibility, they can deliver informal praise or blame, and they can influence the design of performance evaluation processes. They can also play a part in shaping the culture of the organization by choosing the language in which organizational goals are couched; by selecting the metaphors that will be used in internal communications; and by setting an example for their subordinates through their own conduct.

Managers can also regulate the degree to which their subordinates are exposed to normative worlds they do not directly control. John and Isabel cannot dictate what clients say, nor whether they smile or frown, but they can arrange how such clients come in contact with workers by crafting protocols for interaction, or making changes to the interior architecture of the space (Will interactions happen in person or over the phone? Can caseworker offices be accessed directly, or do clients have to stop by a reception desk? What is the shape of this desk, and how much does it shield the receptionist from direct contact with clients?). Similarly, managers cannot directly control the informal exchanges that take place among peers, but they can influence where, when, and between whom such exchanges take place, and whether to facilitate or impede them (Do workers take their lunch break at the same time? Is there a common area or coffee machine? Is it in full view of the entire office or in a more secluded place where semiprivate conversations can actually take place?).

Managers can also weigh in on how aligned the various normative worlds are with one another. Instead of putting the accent on professionalism, John—had he wanted to play a "numbers game"—could have consistently emphasized the importance of meeting numerical targets, thereby aligning himself with the organization's formal evaluation system. He could, moreover, have decided to promote a middle manager also committed to numbers instead of an independently minded one like Isabel. He might, finally, have required the various sites to implement policies that would have shielded frontline workers further from clients. All of these measures would have contributed to a greater alignment between the various worlds and would have reduced the range of viable moral dispositions.

Managers can, finally, play a role in determining the relative force of the various normative worlds. How pressing are the directives issued by these worlds, and how serious are the consequences of ignoring them? Will John content himself with a verbal remark of disapproval to Flora (as he did), or will he take more serious measures to transform the operations of the Hispanic Center? Will Isabel be openly confrontational with workers who are less caring and warm than she is, or will she be tolerant of the existence of various styles of work?

Some contributors to the literature on street-level bureaucracy have argued recently that public management has been fixated on "hard" questions of rules and incentives, and should instead pay closer attention to governing the behavior of frontline agents through the "softer" terrain of organizational culture.[26] My argument is in line with theirs. I aim to show, however, that the reference to a single "organizational culture" can sometimes obfuscate promising possibilities for managerial intervention. Organizations, in the most general case, do not have a single culture, but a variety of subcultures aligned around various poles or "worlds." Part of what a skilled manager needs to do is to orchestrate such diversity so as to encourage bureaucrats to remain attentive to a plurality of normative considerations as they exercise their discretion. This is an approach to management that recognizes that moral judgment is necessary and that seeks to inform the considerations that go into it.

Managers who rely on such an approach must settle two questions. They must figure out which normative worlds should be represented within the organization. And they must know when the conflict between these worlds is productive, contributing to a healthy pluralism, and when it leads, on the contrary, to a form of agential breakdown, such as we find in impossible situations.

We can begin to address these questions by looking back at the Norville Hispanic Center as an example of a street-level bureaucracy where conflict was properly orchestrated. The first thing to note about the Center is that the various normative worlds—professionalism, pastoral care, responsiveness, and efficiency—all promoted normative considerations that were relevant to the job at hand. This is not always the case. Bureaucracies can go wrong by accommodating a spectrum of normative worlds that is too narrow or too wide: too narrow if some considerations that are relevant are left out (imagine what would happen if both John and Isabel abandoned their concern for professionalism and pastoral care and rallied behind "the numbers"), too wide if some considerations that are extraneous to the role are included (imagine what would happen if public servants decided, for instance, to hand out services on the basis of their own conception of desert).

The other feature of the Center that stands out, and that provides the beginning of an answer to the second question (when does conflict bolster agency, and when does it stifle it?), has to do with the relative strength of the various normative worlds. The reason why it was possible for workers to move flexibly between repertoires of justification, and to draw on a variety of resources to craft distinctive moral dispositions, is that none of the worlds completely towered, in importance and influence, over the others. Each of the worlds effectively provided workers with considerations—reasons that they had to take into account when deciding how to act. Depending on the circumstances, some of these considerations carried more weight than others, but none of them systematically overpowered the rest. It was left to frontline workers to determine how precisely to balance these considerations in light of the particularities of a case or situation.

But this, of course, does not always obtain. Sometimes the pressure to comply fully with one of the worlds is so intense, and the costs of noncomplying so high, that bureaucrats are effectively no longer provided with considerations for action but with an imperative of sorts. Such a world comes to dominate the others, collapsing the pluralism necessary for the proper implementation of public policy, and with it the space for flexibility and judgment that workers had at their disposal.

This brings us closer to an understanding of impossible situations. Such situations arise when organizations encourage workers to draw on a variety of normative worlds to construct their moral dispositions, but where only one of these worlds effectively governs their actions. Bureaucrats thus find themselves forced to undertake actions on a repeated basis that are at odds with the sense of self they have developed.

Impossible Situations: A Phenomenological Characterization

Impossible situations involve a sense of conflict between a variety of legitimate demands that are internal to the role that street-level bureaucrats occupy. This type of conflict perturbs workers to such an extent that they find themselves reevaluating their commitment to their job and struggling to find escape solutions. What is the nature of the conflict that prompts such distress? Moral and political philosophers have provided us with a variety of ways to think about conflict between moral demands: conflict between *prima facie* obligations, conflict between incommensurable or unsubstitutable values, and tragic conflict. Can any of them do justice to the three opening stories?

There is a view of morality, one often associated with utilitarianism, according to which a conflict between moral demands is always, in the last resort, a conflict between *prima facie* obligations. Upon proper reflection, when all parameters are taken into account, one obligation always prevails over the other. When that happens, the obligation that has been defeated drops and no longer exerts any claim. It may still be difficult to determine what one ought to do, especially in the presence of uncertainty, but the nature of the difficulty would be epistemological rather than moral. According to this view, an agent may justifiably experience torment or distress in coming to a resolution to act; but if the choice that the agent makes is correct, and if the agent knows it, the torment should subside. Any lingering form of distress or regret would be unjustified.

This view of moral conflict has been criticized on several counts: as being untrue to the kind of moral reactions we do have, as being unable to account for the existence of long-term principled commitments, and as resting on an unjustified belief in the ultimate harmony between our values.[27] More importantly for our purposes, this view of conflict does not square well with the first two opening stories. In neither of them do workers make a mention of uncertainty. The torment they experience, moreover, does not stem from the difficulty of forming a resolution to act; it arises, rather, after their actions have already been taken. Something must keep haunting them still. How can we account for such disquiet?

We can begin to make progress on this front by recognizing alongside philosophers like Isaiah Berlin, Bernard Williams, and Joseph Raz that real moral conflict—conflict that is not merely apparent—is possible. According to such thinkers, our values are mediated by the contingencies of history and society, and there is no reason to suppose, a priori, that they will always be in agreement.[28] The fact that one of two conflicting obligations prevails does not mean that the weaker obligation disappears. When we sacrifice one value for another, there is a real loss—a genuine moral cost—that it is important to register in the form of "regret" after the choice has been made and the action performed.

This view of conflict can help us offer one possible interpretation of the torment that workers relate: it is a form of regret that is bound to arise because they are placed in a situation where moral conflict is unavoidable. Indeed, in each of the stories, workers are forced to pick between two options or values that both exert a moral claim on them. Whichever option they choose, a sense of loss would seem appropriate. A caseworker who decides to play the numbers game and to serve as many clients as possible would have reason to regret not being sufficiently attentive to the needs of those who may be victims of domestic violence; but a caseworker who resolves to scrupulously check whether clients are eligible for the FVO would also have reason to regret not being able to provide assistance to the far greater number of those he or she could have seen in the interim.[29] The obligation to make most efficient use of limited public resources comes into conflict with the obligation to be as responsive as possible to the needs of specific individuals. In such conditions, it may be appropriate for workers to feel regret whatever they do. It is a sign that they remain attuned to a plurality of considerations and that they retain a "sensibility to moral costs"—a quality that is particularly important for public officials who must confront such dilemmas frequently.[30]

Are impossible situations then merely a shorthand for the kind of difficult tradeoffs involved in situations such as these? The problem with such an interpretation is that it eliminates any real sense of impossibility. It locates the difficulty in the taking of decisions that frontline officials effectively can and do take on an ongoing basis. Such workers must constantly make hard tradeoffs between various normative considerations. If this is all it took for frontline workers to have an emotional breakdown, to quit their job, or to raise a lawsuit, public agencies would have effectively ceased to function long ago. The stakes in an impossible situation must be higher.

There are at least two ways to up the stakes. The first consists in making the two options available to the agent more dramatic. The second consists in making the choice between these options more momentous for the agent's sense of self or identity. Let us take them in turn. The first possibility leads us in the direction of tragic conflict. As Martha Nussbaum defines it, tragic conflict occurs when none of the alternatives available is morally acceptable: both options involve "serious moral wrongdoing."[31] A tragic conflict, as such, is not necessarily one where it is difficult to decide which option is preferable to the other. What is difficult, however, is living with the choice when one has made it. In Nussbaum's words, "the tragic question registers not the difficulty of solving the obvious question [of how to act, or what to do], but a distinct difficulty: the fact that all the possible answers to the obvious question, including the best one, are bad. . . . In that sense, there is no 'right answer'."[32]

As a way to make sense of the opening stories, however, such an account seems inadequate. In none of the stories are workers forced to commit "a serious moral wrong" (with the possible exception of the police in the immigration case, but even they do not put the issue in such terms). To be sure, the workers are placed in situations where they are forced to act in ways that we may describe, following Williams, as "morally disagreeable." Yet to compare the decisions they have to make to the type of decisions that are usually given to illustrate cases of tragic conflict (where, say, one can save only one of two drowning children) would be overly sensationalistic. The fact is, impossible situations can be prompted by actions that may not seem particularly momentous to a third-party observer.

There is another way to account for the personal torment that impossible situations provoke without resorting to the unavoidable occurrence of a "serious moral wrong." Instead of increasing what is at stake in the options that are available to the agent, one can increase how much a choice between these options means to the agent. This way of approaching conflict points us to a slightly different understanding of tragedy—one that appears most clearly in the writings of Hegel.[33]

In his interpretation of Sophocles's *Antigone,* Hegel places the accent on the fact that both protagonists, Antigone and her uncle Creon, are immersed in a specific sphere of life that intimately informs their sense of self. As a sister, Antigone is determined to stage a proper burial for her brother, Polyneices, who died fighting in Thebes's civil war. As a ruler, Creon is determined to uphold an edict according to which Polyneices must be punished for his role during the hostilities, his body left unburied on the battlefield, "a corpse for birds and dogs to eat." The choice that Antigone has to make—about whether to bury her brother or to abide by the rules of her king—is not just a choice between two abstract duties or obligations; it is a choice, rather, that entirely implicates her sense of self. The same is true for Creon, whose authority as a king is on the line.

Interestingly, neither Antigone nor Creon hesitates in deciding how to act. Antigone resolves to bury her brother in spite of Creon's prohibition, and the latter does not flinch in enforcing the law. There are two ways to read this lack of hesitation on Antigone's and Creon's parts. It is possible to take it as a sign that they are not sensitive to competing moral claims, such as the need to obey the law (for Antigone) or the need to fulfill one's familial and religious obligations (for Creon). This is a view that Martha Nussbaum attributes to Hegel. Antigone and Creon, on such an interpretation, are "narrow" moral figures who consider only one sphere of value and neglect the claim of the other.[34] According to such a reading, the two protagonists do not themselves experience tragic conflict; the conflict, rather, is experienced by the spectators (or the chorus) who, standing at a distance, are able to feel the pull of both normative worlds. This line of thought would be of little help in explaining the kind of disquiet that the workers (our protagonists) experience in the opening stories.

But there is another way to look at Antigone and Creon. Their lack of hesitation might simply indicate that they have arrived at a clear resolution about how to act. This, however, does not necessarily mean that they are blind to the force of the other normative sphere to which they also belong (that of family, for Creon; that of political authority, for Antigone). Indeed, Hegel argues that a tragedy finds its most complete development when:

> the individuals engaged in conflict . . . appear in each case essentially in-volved in one whole, so that they stand fundamentally under the power of that against which they battle. . . . Antigone, for example, lives under the political authority of Creon; she is herself the daughter of a king . . . so that her obedience to the royal prerogative is an obligation. But Creon also, who is on his part father and husband, is under obligation to re-spect the sacred ties of relationship. . . . In consequence of this we find immanent in the life of both that which each respectively combats, and they are seized and broken by that very bond which is rooted in the com-pass of their social existence.[35]

This view of tragedy goes some way toward capturing what is at stake in the opening stories: namely, that participants are torn between the demands of two normative spheres, both of which have some claim on them. If they are troubled, it is not so much because their actions amount to serious wrongdoing, but because they find themselves bound to act in ways that violate or undermine an important aspect of their distinctive moral identities—of whom they take themselves to be.

There are several differences, however, between the case of Antigone and the opening stories. To the extent that Antigone faces tragic conflict, this conflict is between two separate roles that she occupies—that of a cit-izen and that of a sister. In the opening stories, however, the conflict oc-curs within the bounds of a given social role: the workers are conflicted over how they should behave *as street-level bureaucrats*.

More importantly, and unlike Antigone, the frontline workers who figure in the opening stories take heed of the prudential considerations at play. They do not act in line with their professional moral identity or role conception, but against it. The teacher ends up prioritizing accountability standards over his understanding of the mission he is supposed to play; caseworkers focus on reducing caseload even though the FVO is essential to their idea of helping clients become independent.

There is a third difference. The conflict that Antigone experiences is spurred by the fact that she has to make a single momentous decision (should she bury her brother or not?). In the first two stories, however, there is no such "fateful moment"—workers seem to look back, rather, at a series of actions they have already performed. The personal torment they experience does not occur while they act, but after they have acted; it is in retrospect that the significance of their past behavior becomes clear.

There is another model of tragedy in Hegel's work that can help us better capture this last feature of impossible situations. This is the model of tragedy that appears in Sophocles's two other Theban plays—*Oedipus Rex* and *Oedipus at Colonus*.[36] What is tragic about Oedipus, according to Hegel, is that the protagonist has to take personal responsibility for having performed actions that seem contrary to the kind of person he is, and whose significance he was not properly aware of. It is only after he has murdered his father and married his mother that Oedipus understands the words of the Oracle and realizes what he has done. Likewise, it is only once he has slowly and repeatedly breached his conception of what a teacher ought to do that William Johnson realizes, looking back, that he is no longer the teacher he thought he was. A few actions that are out of line with one's sense of self can be dismissed as exceptions. It is only when the departures start to form a recognizable pattern that the conflict can no longer be ignored. Impossible situations do not always confront an agent frontally; they can creep in silently, and one may find oneself already enmeshed in them.

We are now—at last—in a position to characterize what an impossible situation is and capture the kind of impossibility that lies at the heart of it. Such an impossibility is, effectively, a kind of performative self-contradiction. It is impossible for an agent, who embraces a certain moral identity, to retain this self-understanding while continuing to systematically and consciously perform actions that are contrary to it. If my interpretation is sound, the teacher's complaint effectively amounts to something like this: "You cannot expect me, as a teacher, to keep doing what I need to do to meet the accountability requirements. As a teacher (according to how I understand this term and myself), it is impossible for me to do so. Of course, I, as an individual, could still perform the actions that you require of me. But I would effectively no longer be a teacher in my own eyes. What I cannot do is hold on to the identity and to the actions at the same time."

If this kind of self-contradiction grips bureaucrats at such a profound level, it is because developing a role conception and a professional moral identity are deeply transformational processes.[37] In the course of organizational socialization, and in the process of developing their own styles of work, bureaucrats come to believe in a set of values and excellences that pertain to the role; they develop a set of emotional responses, a manner of interpreting new phenomena, and a way of prioritizing values.[38] For most people, inhabiting a role is not something one can keep at arm's length; it involves a change in how one understands and sees oneself.[39] When "impossible situations" force agents to take actions that are irreconcilable with their role conception, they force them to jeopardize *that*. Such situations put workers in conflict with their own selves. An impossible situation threatens one's sense of moral integrity.

Impossible Situations: A Structural Characterization

What I have offered up to now is a first-person, phenomenological characterization of an impossible situation. In what follows, I want to argue that while impossible situations serve to designate an experiential bind, their causes are in large part structural. This will be the occasion to explain why such situations are prone to arise in bureaucracies.

Impossible situations result from a mismatch between an agent's self-understanding and his or her actions. Bureaucracies are prone to creating such situations because they can fix both sides of the equation. Bureaucracies are, by design, social arrangements meant to extract patterns of action from people. There are various ways in which bureaucracies can make bureaucrats act. All the "hard" tools of management—rules, standard operating procedures, incentive systems, and so on—are meant to do just that.

But bureaucracies also play a part in shaping the moral identity and role conception of individual workers. They imbue bureaucrats with a sense of mission, with a moral sensibility, and with a set of metaphors to use when looking at the world. All the "soft" tools of management, and the attempts to orchestrate organizational culture, are deployed for that purpose.[40]

Bureaucracies, therefore, operate at two distinct levels: at the level of requirements for action (which may be perceived as "external" obligations that bureaucrats have to contend with, but that do not directly affect their sense of self), and at the level of dispositions and identities (which affect bureaucrats more intimately, "from within"). Impossible situations arise when these two levels are at odds with one another: when the actions that are required and the sense of self that is fostered cannot be reconciled.

This is where the framework I proposed in the second section can be useful. I suggested there that there are various normative worlds at work within an organization. These worlds provide bureaucrats with both resources to craft their own moral dispositions and incentives to act in particular ways. Impossible situations emerge when several of these worlds participate in shaping the moral dispositions of bureaucrats, but where one of them effectively silences the others when it comes to action. Instead of supplying bureaucrats with one consideration among many, such a world effectively issues "imperatives" that trump other considerations. Bureaucrats find themselves committed to moral dispositions that they have, in part, been encouraged to adopt by the organization, while being at the same time compelled to act in ways that disregard, and sometimes even undermine, such dispositions.

Let me try to illustrate this point by expanding, somewhat speculatively, on the first of the opening stories. As a teacher, it is likely that William Johnson would have been encouraged during his professional training to develop a concern for expanding his students' worldview and for equipping them with useful skills. This professional ethos, and the sense of mission associated with it, would also have been relayed at school by peers and administrators, repeated in staff meetings, and stressed in internal communications. Under normal circumstances, such influences would have contributed to shaping Johnson's personal sensibilities and his vision of what teaching is about.

When the new requirements for teacher accountability are introduced, they come to bolster measures for performance evaluation that had existed all along. However, they make such measures far more stringent. The importance of standardized tests become such, and the costs of noncompliance so high, that Johnson finds himself spending more and more time preparing students for them.

The first time he has to cancel an important lesson to "teach for the test," Johnson consoles himself by thinking that this is an exceptional measure. He does this the second, third, and fourth time. But at some point, he looks back and notices what has taken place. He realizes that while he has been faithful to the new policy requirements, he is no longer acting in line with the role conception he had formed and that he is unable, accordingly, to offer a compelling moral justification for what it is he has done and must continue to do. He finds himself stuck in an impossible situation. From then on, every lesson he must teach will stand in contradiction to his sense of professional identity. His moral integrity is endangered: either the actions have to stop, or the identity has to go.

"Impossible situations," as I have presented them here, bear a close resemblance to the theory of the "double bind" first described by Gregory Bateson in his work on the theory of schizophrenia.[41] In everyday parlance, the term "double bind" refers to a situation where one is exposed to conflicting demands. For Bateson, however, the term has a more specific meaning. It refers to a situation in which the following four premises obtain:

(1) The agent is given a primary negative injunction, issued by an authoritative figure, typically in the form of a command backed by a threat (e.g., "Do not do such and such, or I will punish you").
(2) The agent is given a secondary injunction, issued by the same authoritative figure and also backed by a threat, that is more abstract than the first and that conflicts with it (e.g., "Do not submit to my prohibitions, or else something bad will happen to you").
(3) The agent is exposed to these two conflicting injunctions on a repeated basis.
(4) There is a third injunction or practical constraint that makes it impossible for the agent to escape the field delimited by the first two.

The agent is caught in a predicament from which there is no good way out. The example that Bateson gives is that of a mother who tells her child that she loves him while shrinking away in disgust at the child's touch. The mother effectively sends two conflicting signals. At an explicit level, she says, "I love you, and I expect you to respond to me as a loving mother; otherwise I will punish you." Her body language, however, says, "I cannot stand your displays of affection, and if you continue showing your love, I will punish you (by withdrawing from you)." A successful response to either signal is a failed response to the other. If the child is to respond to the first hint that his mother gives him—that of love—he will arouse her anxiety and disgust. If he is to respond to the second signal and withdraw, he will be punished for not being sufficiently affectionate. As a result, Bateson hypothesizes that the child, who is punished whatever he does, will not develop the capacity to properly discriminate between the various signals he receives—a failure which is, according to Bateson, at the heart of schizophrenia.

The merits of the double bind *as a theory of schizophrenia* are suspect and need not concern us here.[42] What is important for our purposes is that repeated exposure to two authoritative and conflicting signals at different levels of abstraction can lead—as it does in an impossible situation—to a psychologically traumatic experience for the agent. Interestingly, Bateson's work has been used to discuss conditions of psychological alienation in the context of colonialism and gender—two instances where the occurrence of a double bind can be traced not to the idiosyncrasies of an individual parent but to broader structural dynamics.

Sandra Bartky, for instance, relies on the notion of the double bind to develop a phenomenological account of a particular form of "psychological oppression" that women and colonial subjects experience.[43] This form of oppression arises when one is denied possibilities for self-realization that are open to others while being assured, at the same time, that *of course* one is a human being like everyone else ("*of course* women are persons; *of course* blacks are human beings").[44] As Bartky puts it: "To be psychologically oppressed is to be caught in the double bind of a society which both affirms my human status and at the same time bars me from the exercise of many of those typically human functions that bestow this status."[45] This double bind leads to a form of psychic alienation: confronted with practical signals that point at their inferiority, and with other, more abstract messages that deny categorically that such inferiority has to do with generic categories like gender or race, members of oppressed groups have no choice but to accept that they—as particular individuals—must be the source of the problem. In Bartky's words: "I may reject entirely the belief that my disadvantage is generic; but having still to account for it somehow, I may locate the cause squarely within myself, a bad destiny of an entirely private sort—a character flaw, an 'inferiority complex,' or a neurosis."[46]

Bateson's theory of the double bind, and Bartky's use of it, are both relevant to our discussion of impossible situations. They describe forms of individual breakdown that must be characterized in phenomenological terms but that have structural roots. As in the double bind, agents who are caught in an impossible situation face two injunctions that are both authoritative and that operate at distinct levels: one that requires them to act in a particular way ("reduce caseload") and another, more abstract, that enjoins them to act in line with long-term moral commitments ("continue being a people person committed to the welfare of your clients"). The conflict between these injunctions occurs repeatedly, and as in Bartky's case, it does not arise because of the peculiarities of any single individual, but because of policy choices or managerial practices that play a part in maintaining and reinforcing both types of signals.

Responses to Impossible Situations

Much like the double bind, impossible situations drive street-level bureaucrats toward a variety of pathological coping responses. I review these responses below and explain why they are normatively troubling. The point of this exercise is to show that there is no good way for individuals to confront impossible situations on their own. If a remedy is to be found, it has to be structural in nature. It is the managerial practices and public policies that give rise to such situations that have to change.

In thinking about how bureaucrats respond to impossible situations, it is important to keep in mind the distinction I established in the previous two sections between structural and phenomenological levels of analysis. This distinction is important because not all bureaucrats who are placed in a situation that *is impossible* experience that situation *as impossible.* To experience a situation as impossible, one must be personally committed to some aspect of the role that one is then forced to betray. If we are to trust popular representations of bureaucracy, however, not all bureaucrats are committed to their role in such a way. Some remain detached and do not take pride in doing their job. This shields them from the sense of self-betrayal associated with impossible situations.

There are two observations to make in relation to detachment—one psychological, the other normative. The psychological observation is that detachment is difficult to maintain in practice. Studies of organizational behavior suggest that agents tend to develop a considerable degree of identification with the organizations to which they belong.[47] They form moral commitments, and their sense of self enlarges to encompass the role they occupy.[48] Their successes, failures, and difficulties at work become their own. We have good reasons, in short, to suspect that detachment is less common among bureaucrats than popular writings on bureaucracy make it to be.[49]

The other normative observation is that detachment—even if it were possible to maintain—is not a desirable disposition at the front lines of the state. It is important for bureaucrats to develop long-term personal commitments to their role and to not be entirely pliant to the turns and twists of hierarchical directives. The best safeguard against overly volatile management and rapid changes in political priorities is having bureaucrats who feel committed to a certain mission, and who are willing to devote themselves to it. It is precisely such bureaucrats, however, who are susceptible to being caught in impossible situations.

For those who feel the force of impossible situations, a variety of responses are available. They can be captured under the familiar headings of exit, voice, and loyalty.[50]

Exit. Bureaucrats who are caught in impossible situations sometimes quit their jobs, either because they can no longer find them fulfilling or because they are unwilling to compromise their sense of moral integrity. This was the response of William Johnson, and it seems to recur with some frequency across public service agencies.[51]

There are two problems with "exit." The first is that such a response may appear overly self-indulgent to those concerned.[52] The more they are committed to their job—the more they feel the weight of impossible situations—the more they will be worried about vacating their position, knowing that they may be replaced by someone who could be far less scrupulous or conscientious. The second, more troubling problem with exit is that it effectively weeds out those bureaucrats who care enough about their role that they are unwilling to part with their approach to it. The ones who leave are often those who have the best motivations and intentions. This is a loss we should be reluctant to accept.

Voice. Bureaucrats who refuse to quit under the pressure of impossible situations may try to relay the nature of their predicament to their superiors in the hope that the latter would enact appropriate structural reform. But resorting to "voice" when one belongs to the lowest rungs of an organization is difficult and potentially risky. The complaints of subordinates are frequently ignored or lost in the sea of information that managers must filter through. Those who would like to speak up also fear that they may alienate their superiors and potentially put their own careers at risk.[53]

For "voice" to be a viable option, proper procedures and protections must be put in place: procedures that encourage mutual trust and openness between various levels of the bureaucratic hierarchy and that provide lower-ranking personnel with guarantees that they will not be penalized for expressing their concerns.[54] Since the demands that managers place on their subordinates are partly a reflection of the policies they inherit, there must also be channels of communication between senior bureaucrats and policymakers. For voice to "work," policy implementation must be treated not merely as a technical affair subsidiary to policymaking but as a valuable source of feedback into policymaking.

Loyalty. The sourness of exit and the risk of voice both militate in favor of loyalty—that is, of staying within the organization and attempting to face up to impossible situations. Loyalty comes in a variety of flavors. Some refuse to compromise on their moral integrity altogether and continue acting as they believe they ought, regardless of the pressures they face. These "tenacious" individuals are often depicted on the screen as lone (and typically male) mavericks—the likes of Harry Callahan in *Dirty Harry* or Jimmy McNulty in *The Wire.* They manage to stay true to themselves against all odds, braving unsupportive colleagues and a hostile boss, and putting their careers repeatedly at risk.

Tenacity, however, is not without its problems. The first is that such a response is not open to everyone, but only to those with a certain temperament. Tenacity is also precarious: those who settle for such a disposition are likely to overstep the mark at some point, and to be fired or sidelined. Most importantly, perhaps, tenacity is troubling in itself. In order to resist an environment that is stacked against them, those who decide to stay true to themselves must radicalize their own commitment so as to make it unassailable to criticism. The problem with Dirty Harry and Jimmy McNulty is that they are both highly reductive figures. They are incapable of recognizing that those who disagree with them are sometimes in the right, and that some measure of compromise might be called for.

While some respond to impossible situations by becoming more steadfast, others take the failure to harmonize their actions with their self-understanding as a personal failure—as a sign of their own incapacity to live up to the demands of the job. They blame themselves rather than the situations they are caught in. The structural roots of impossible situations are often opaque to those who are enmeshed in them—so much, in fact, that self-blame is a central component of the psychological oppression that Bartky describes in the context of gender and colonialism. Recall that in the opening story, William Johnson's colleague becomes convinced that he is a "terrible teacher." Those who go down that path end up like the teacher. They suffer from burnout—a reaction that involves overwhelming emotional exhaustion and a sense of ineffectiveness, and one that paves the way for exit.[55]

An equally troubling, though arguably more common, response to impossible situations is self-deception. Workers can fool themselves into thinking that the conflict they first perceived between their actions and their self-understanding is not as pronounced as they initially made it to be. Self-deception is sustainable, but it comes at the cost of a distorted moral perception, or of a deformed self-understanding. It is important to note, moreover, that self-deception does not exempt bureaucrats from acting. Even if they no longer *feel* the pull of competing considerations, their behavior must effectively give priority to some of these considerations over others. Self-deception is a form of bad faith, and it amounts, as such, to a denial of responsibility.

The only avenue left open to frontline workers is cynicism: to give up on the idea that public agencies are a space amenable to moral commitments and to resign themselves to accepting the conflicting requirements of the job without attempting to reconcile them. Cynicism leads us back where we started, namely, to detachment and indifference toward role and clients—attributes that are hardly desirable in public officials who wield discretionary power over some of the most vulnerable members of society.

Conclusion

Periods of policy change and administrative reform are often fraught with drama.[56] Those who have the most at stake, of course, are the recipients of public services and the targets of law enforcement. Yet the frontline bureaucrats who must enact policy reform—the often-vilified face of the state—do not emerge unscathed either. They sometimes find themselves caught in impossible situations that pit them against themselves. I have tried to show that taking the grievances of these bureaucrats seriously reveals a disquieting truth, to wit, that their plight is not a private or professional tragedy but a public one. Street-level bureaucrats do not merely burn out; they effectively break down on the altar of our evolving or conflicting democratic aspirations.

Impossible situations are sometimes the regrettable byproduct of an evolution in democratic preferences. They arise when street-level bureaucrats have built their role conceptions around aspirations for public policy we once had, and are now trying to change. At heart is a mismatch in temporalities: role conceptions change at a far slower pace than requirements for action. Changing such requirements may, in fact, be one of the ways in which managers try to induce workers to change their role conceptions, effectively "resocializing" them. Doing so may, on occasion, be necessary. The role conceptions and moral dispositions of frontline workers could, for some reason or another, have become inadequate or out of tune with the values and priorities of the democratic public.

Even in such circumstances, however, impossible situations should give us pause. Given the psychological strain they occasion, they should prompt us to think seriously about whether there may be other, more gradual, ways to change how street-level bureaucrats inhabit their role. This is, in part, to acknowledge our responsibilities toward frontline workers—especially if the identities we are now asking them to abandon are ones we had once actively encouraged them to adopt. Exploring alternative pathways to organizational change is also warranted on more pragmatic grounds: if requirements for action shift too abruptly, they may not so much resocialize or reform workers as effectively break them down, thus preventing them from working toward policy goals, whatever those may be.

Impossible situations, however, do not emerge only during periods of sustained change in democratic aspirations. They can also arise when we ask public agencies to do or be too many things at once without giving them adequate resources to do so. Bureaucrats may hold role conceptions that encapsulate aspirations for public policy that are still very much ours, but that conflict with more recent policy measures we have also passed. Here, being attuned to the grievances of such bureaucrats, especially if they recur with some frequency, may reveal tensions between competing aspirations for public policy that need to be addressed. The bureaucrats who break down on this account are reflections of the state of our democracy. In their desperate attempts to fulfill their social role in a responsible manner, they expose the inconsistencies and incompatibilities of the mandate we give them, and with this sad spectacle, some hard questions that are in the last resort political—questions about objectives, priorities, and resource allocation—are thrust back upon us. These are questions that must be settled, not at the front lines of public service, but in a legislative arena. It is perhaps because these questions are politically contentious that they are often ignored, postponed, or papered over, and that the ambiguities and inconsistencies are passed down to the front lines of public service, where the responsibility for making difficult tradeoffs, and the liability associated with it, can be delegated no further.

By trying to make sense of impossible situations, this chapter has brought together several of the themes developed throughout this study. The first, and most important perhaps, is the need to put the moral dispositions and role conceptions of bureaucrats at the center of our thinking about bureaucratic behavior. Bureaucrats are not simply strategic and self-interested decision-makers. They also develop distinctive ethical commitments to a certain way of performing the role, and these do not change as rapidly as the political priorities of the day.

I have tried to describe the relationship between organizational environment and moral dispositions by resorting to the language of normative "worlds." One can typically find, within any given organization, a range of such worlds, anchored around distinctive cores of values and beliefs, and offering a coherent way of experiencing the job and of making sense of it. Each of these worlds is relayed by its own group of advocates within the organization, who have at their hands the capacity to dispense sanctions and rewards. Organizations comprise a number of such worlds, pulling in various directions. It is the configuration of these worlds that shapes the field of moral dispositions that are open to bureaucrats. Three parameters are central: Around what values are these worlds organized? To what extent are they aligned or misaligned? And what is their relative strength? Depending on how these three parameters play out, some moral dispositions will become more appealing; others will become harder to maintain; and others yet will become untenable.

Managers have at their disposal a range of tools to fine-tune these three parameters. This allows them, in turn, to channel the moral dispositions of their subordinates. In doing so, they must keep the following four considerations in mind. They must make sure that the worlds represented within the organization actually capture and reflect the plural normative demands of street-level work; that these worlds are sufficiently misaligned to enable bureaucrats to develop a diverse range of moral dispositions; that they pull sufficiently strongly that bureaucrats cannot afford to ignore any one of them entirely; but that they do not pull so strongly apart that it becomes effectively impossible to live by their joint demands.

This is a delicate equilibrium to attain, and managers do not have free rein; their hands are usually tied by the policy objectives they inherit. Striking a proper balance between a plurality of normative worlds—one that prompts organizational agents to retain a rich and multifaceted approach to their role—is a task that requires both good management and sound policies. The costs of getting such a balance wrong are significant. If the worlds do not pull sufficiently apart, or if any one of them towers in importance over the others, street-level bureaucrats will be driven toward reductive dispositions, and the diversity in moral dispositions, upon which the regime of everyday casuistry and informal accountability described in

Chapter 4 depends, will collapse. If, on the other hand, the worlds pull too far and too strongly apart, bureaucrats risk being caught in "impossible situations": situations where they can no longer operate as integrated moral agents because their actions and self-understanding are at odds with one another.

Conclusion

It is through our encounters with bureaucracies and bureaucrats that most of us come to know the state. It is then—when we apply for a driver's license or for public assistance; when we are questioned by a police officer or searched by an immigration agent—that the state ceases to be an elusive abstraction, and takes concrete form before us. It is during such encounters, as well, that we come to realize most acutely that we are governed not just by laws, but by laws and by man.

For all the emphasis that theorists of the modern state have placed on its impersonal character—on the separation between person and office— the state, when we encounter it, does have a face.[1] It is the face of a very particular person, one that changes with every procedure and agency. It is a face we can grow to appreciate or to fear, one whose expressions we scrutinize closely and whose reactions we try to anticipate; one we try to please, sway, or distract; one to whom we express our gratitude or vent our frustration.[2] It is a face whose bearer we suspect may have some influence over how our case will unfold, though how much, we do not know for sure. If we are lucky enough to belong to those segments of society who do not directly depend on the state, it is a face that can make or break our day. If we are part of society's most disadvantaged groups, it is a face that can make or break our lives.

This study has taken us into the eventful routine of those whose job it is to be the face of the state—the frontline public workers, or street-level bureaucrats, who are responsible for implementing public policy and enforcing the law. Such bureaucrats make decisions on a day-to-day basis that are highly consequential for ordinary citizens. Their demeanor also contributes to shaping what citizens think of their state, and of their own standing in it. In the preceding pages, I have tried to shed light on how street-level bureaucrats perceive the situations and clients they encounter and how they understand themselves as moral agents. I have also attempted to assess how well their actions and dispositions measure up against the normative values that lie at the heart of our democratic political culture.

We have seen that such bureaucrats are not merely compliant operators, carrying out precise directives inherited from above, nor technical experts, looking for effective means to attain prespecified ends. They are also solicited by their respective agencies as moral and political agents who must give practical content to hierarchical directives that are often vague, ambiguous, and conflicting, and who must strike sensible compromises between a plurality of normative considerations that frequently pull in competing directions.

Such tasks would be challenging in any context. But street-level bureaucrats must perform them in working conditions that are particularly strenuous. On any given day, they must cope not only with drastic limitations in resources and a chronic shortage of staff, but also with incompatible objectives, unrealistic targets, and an endless stream of emotionally trying encounters with clients. When experienced day in, day out, the psychological pressures fomented by such an environment tend to erode their moral sensibilities and to truncate their understanding of their role and responsibilities.

This leaves us with the predicament that this study has sought to explore and unravel: namely, that while public service agencies actively depend on the moral agency of street-level bureaucrats, they place these bureaucrats in working conditions that tend to undermine that very agency. This is a serious worry at the front lines of the state, for if we are indeed governed by ordinary men and women endowed with discretionary power over us, we must take an interest in making sure that they evolve in conditions where it is possible for them to fulfill their role adequately—if only because we would be the ones to pay the price of their failure to do so.

Moral Agency and Its Environment

In the course of exploring how such a predicament plays out, what reasons lead to it, and what responses can be offered to it, I have made a series of claims that build on each other.

I began by arguing, in Chapter 1, that street-level bureaucrats wield a significant margin of discretion; that this discretion is not merely technical, but normatively charged; and that there would be good reasons to preserve it even if institutional reform were possible. The proper implementation of public policy requires far more than compliance with hierarchical directives. It calls for street-level bureaucrats who can give sensible content to vague mandates, who can make reasonable compromises between competing demands, and who can improvise suitable responses to unforeseen dilemmas. It calls for bureaucrats, that is, who can operate as full-fledged moral agents.

The existence of discretion at the front lines of public service makes it possible for street-level bureaucrats to inhabit their role in a variety of ways. Whichever style of work they adopt, however, such bureaucrats must remain sensitive to a plurality of normative considerations. The implementation of public policy involves more than the provision of services and the enforcement of laws. It also raises the question of *how* the state and its officials should interact with citizens. While street-level bureaucrats must strive to be efficient in performing their duties, they must also use their discretionary power in a way that is fair, respectful, and as responsive as possible to the particularities of individual cases. When assessing how well the bureaucratic encounter unfolds, we must take all of these desiderata into account. While the criterion of efficiency is one that public workers share with their peers in the private sector, the other three are particularly salient in the public domain because citizens in democracies have distinctive moral and political claims on their state.

To properly understand the challenges that street-level bureaucrats face in attending to these four desiderata, we must look beyond the moment of ethical decision-making, and consider more broadly the moral dispositions they adopt on the job. These dispositions come with an interpretive grid, a mode of affective attunement, a normative sensibility, and a way of conceiving of one's role and responsibilities. The shift from the study of decisions to that of dispositions is necessary for two reasons. The first is that dispositions precede and inform individual decisions by shaping how bureaucrats perceive moral questions and what weight they confer to various normative considerations. The second is that dispositions convey something about the demeanor or manner of conduct of bureaucrats, which is normatively significant in its own right. To reiterate a point made earlier, *how* one is treated by the state matters as much as *what* one gets.

The shift from the study of decisions to that of dispositions can help us throw light on how the pressures of everyday work truncate the moral dispositions of street-level bureaucrats. The problem is not that bureaucrats lose their capacity for moral reasoning, but that the moral perception and role conception that feed into such reasoning become narrower and more targeted. This brings into focus a range of pathological dispositions—such as indifference, enforcement, and caregiving—that are troubling because they are reductive takes on the role. These dispositions are more insidious than the well-known problems of corruption, rule breaking, abuse of discretion, and incompetence, because bureaucrats can fall into them even as they remain wholeheartedly dedicated to their mission, within the scope of their prerogatives, and in full mastery of the technical skills necessary to fulfill their role.

Reductive dispositions are best understood as adaptive responses to the pressures of everyday work. The environment in which bureaucrats operate does not directly erode or truncate their moral personality. It exposes them, rather, to a variety of psychological pressures that threaten what psychologists call their "self-integrity"—their conception of themselves as good, moral persons. It is in trying to cope with these pressures while retaining a modicum of self-worth that bureaucrats gravitate, sometimes consciously though often not, toward reductive moral dispositions. The drift occurs because these dispositions provide, each in its own way, some measure of psychological relief from the pressures of everyday work. Since bureaucrats do not have the capabilities to satisfy all the demands of the role, they narrow their understanding of these demands to bring them in line with the capabilities they can marshal in practice.

It is important to note, however, that while the environment in which bureaucrats are situated makes certain moral dispositions harder to maintain and others easier to flow into, it does not unilaterally determine which dispositions they settle for. Individuals can respond in various ways to the pressures exerted upon them. Bureaucrats who gravitate toward reductive dispositions proceed along different paths, veering toward indifference, enforcement, or caregiving. And, of course, not all bureaucrats do settle for reductive dispositions: some respond better than others to situational pressure. If we are to understand the moral dispositions that emerge at the frontlines of public service, we must look at both the structural pressures to which bureaucrats are exposed, and at the everyday practices they deploy to modulate the effect their environment has on them.

Counteracting the drift toward reductive moral dispositions is an effort that requires a combination of agential practices at the individual and group level, and the orchestration of a suitable institutional environment at the managerial level. As individuals, street-level bureaucrats are exposed to the transformative pull of dissonance. Such a pull is occasioned by the conflicting requirements inherent to the job, and by the gap that exists between what street-level bureaucrats believe they ought to do in principle and what they can actually achieve in practice. To retain a balanced moral disposition, such bureaucrats must find a way to regulate their exposure to dissonance so as to mitigate the cognitive distortions it would otherwise induce. I have tried to show, in Chapter 3, that they can do so by deploying a regime of everyday practices of the self.

But while street-level bureaucrats must exert themselves, as individuals, to resist the pull toward overly specialized moral dispositions, I argued in Chapter 4 that they must strive, as a group, to retain a range of dispositions that are sufficiently diverse. If the danger at the individual level is the pull toward moral specialization, the danger at the group level is the pull toward uniformity. The existence of a diverse array of moral dispositions within bureaucratic agencies serves two salutary functions. The first pertains to moral perception. Peers with contrasting sensibilities prompt each other to pay attention to a variety of cues or normative considerations that they might otherwise have ignored. The second has to do with informal accountability. Peers with diverging moral commitments place a healthy justificatory burden on each other: they observe, probe, and question one another's working styles and act as a safeguard against behavior that is arbitrary or systematically biased.

The task for managers is to tread a path between the two pitfalls of excessive specialization and uniformity. It is to create an environment in which street-level bureaucrats can develop and maintain a diverse range of balanced dispositions. In order to do so, managers can utilize an array of tools, both "hard" and "soft." They can shape the incentive structure that bureaucrats must navigate as well as the discourses and repertoires of normative justification they have at their disposal. This exercise involves a delicate balancing act, for in order to entice bureaucrats to remain sensitive to a plurality of normative considerations, managers must carefully orchestrate an array of managerial signals that pull in competing directions. The failure to properly orchestrate such signals can lead to the creation of impossible situations—situations in which bureaucrats are pulled in directions that are so antithetical that they can no longer operate as integrated moral agents.

We can tie the previous points together as such: if the implementation of public policy is to respond to a plurality of normative demands, as I believe it should, it must be enacted by bureaucrats who are themselves sensitive to such demands. For this to happen, the desired pluralism must be reflected within the organizational environment in which bureaucrats evolve. As I argued in Chapter 5, the capacity of street-level bureaucrats to operate as balanced moral agents is predicated on the coexistence of a plurality of normative worlds within the organization. It is the lack of alignment between these worlds that provides bureaucrats with the space and resources necessary to craft their own moral dispositions. And it is their relative strength that determines the range of dispositions that are sustainable in the long run.

The capacity of street-level bureaucrats to properly fulfill their role also depends on a web of informal practices. Neither the practices of the self I described in Chapter 3 nor the everyday casuistry I examined in Chapter 4 have formal standing and protection within public service agencies, yet they both play a crucial role in helping street-level bureaucrats live up to their responsibilities.

If I stress the importance of informal practices and pluralism, it is because both can be put in jeopardy by attempts at institutional reform. If their significance is not properly appreciated, informal practices, such as the exercises of the self I described in Chapter 3, could be seen as a waste of time and resources to be excised. Others, like the casuistry I described in Chapter 4, could be deemed a threat to the values of "transparency" and "accountability." Even pluralism is sometimes at risk. The central idea underpinning New Public Management is that the use of a market-oriented approach within the public sector would lead to greater cost-efficiency in the implementation of policy, and would go some way toward addressing long-standing issues within public administration (e.g., red tape, lack of flexibility, absence of transparency). As critics of NPM have noted, however, the reform agenda's fixation on emulating the private sector in terms of efficiency may come at the cost of other normative considerations that should also govern the provision of *public* services—considerations such as fairness, responsiveness, and respect.

A related worry, which I have tried to substantiate in this study, is that such reforms may have adverse effects on the moral dispositions of street-level bureaucrats. If one of the normative worlds that exists within the organization comes to tower in importance over the others, street-level bureaucrats will be driven toward it. They will be less likely to resist such a pull if they are denied access to competing repertoires of normative justification, to like-minded peers, and to alternative sources of motivation. This is a serious matter, for if we are indeed governed by ordinary men and women equipped with discretionary power, we must make sure that their moral personalities are something that we—as a democratic polity—would recognize ourselves in, not a lopsided instantiation of the values we stand for.

By sounding these cautionary notes, I do not mean to imply that public service agencies are beyond reproach—far from it. What I wish to emphasize, rather, is that the proper delivery of public services depends on the existence of a fragile moral ecosystem within bureaucracies, one that involves a delicate equilibrium between a competing array of normative pulls. In thinking about institutional reform, we must keep this ecosystem in mind and try to anticipate how it may be affected by new policies, and how it may, in turn, affect the moral dispositions of bureaucrats. We must remain attuned, in particular, to the possibility that reforms that may seem attractive from the perspective of one normative criterion may have unintended costs along other dimensions. Looking at institutional reform through the prism of moral dispositions gives us a distinctive way to appraise the costs and benefits of policy proposals. It also helps us think anew about the goals of institutional design: not to replace discretion with formal structure, but to orchestrate the environment in which individual agents develop self-understandings and exercise discretion.

Stepping back from street-level bureaucracy and onto a more abstract plane, the claims I have offered, taken together, stress the importance of thinking about moral agency in conjunction with its surrounding environment. As I hope to have shown throughout this study, this is a two-sided endeavor. It involves, on the one hand, teasing out the ways in which the environment informs, sustains, and, at times, erodes, the moral dispositions of individual agents; and on the other, examining how these agents can creatively mine, "colonize," or draw upon their environment to support the moral dispositions they deem appropriate. Articulating more precisely the connections between moral agency and its environment—as I have tried to do for a particular category of social actors operating in a specific kind of organizational context—opens up a vast and exciting field of inquiry, one that brings political theory and moral philosophy into conversation with psychology, sociology, and anthropology.[3]

Revisiting Administrative Rationality

A proper appreciation of the nature of street-level work, and of the extent to which such work involves discretionary judgment over questions of normative significance, has far-reaching implications for our understanding of the administrative state. The first such implication is that public policy continues to be made as it is being administered. To put it more precisely, the implementation of public policy is suffused by moments of policymaking. By the time administrative directives and standard operating procedures reach frontline workers, their content is often still underdetermined: it is up to such workers to fill the gaps left in them, to resolve any ambiguities and conflicts they contain, and to give practical content to the abstract standards that should guide their application. In so doing, street-level bureaucrats effectively contribute to shaping public policy.

That policy implementation cannot be neatly separated from policymaking is old news to political scientists, but it is a fact that political theorists have been slow to take on board, at least judging by the relative paucity of studies on policy implementation. And yet, the significance of such a fact is obvious. If policymaking takes place at all levels of the bureaucratic hierarchy, down to the front lines of public administration, then no normative theory of the state would be complete that did not attend to the process of policy implementation in some detail and to the agents responsible for it. We need a more thorough political theory of implementation, and I hope that this study will be seen as an early and tentative contribution to it.

Our inquiry into the everyday moral life of street-level bureaucrats should also prompt us to revise our understanding of the kind of rationality that is characteristic of the administrative state. As I showed in Chapter 1, it is common to think of bureaucracy as exhibiting a technical rationality, and of the bureaucratic encounter as a moment in which a well-formed body of law is applied to particular cases. Yet this is at best a partial character-ization of what takes place when the state meets the street.

Since the laws and policies that street-level bureaucrats inherit are often not fully determinate, and since they lend themselves, accordingly, to a va-riety of possible interpretations and enactments, the moment at which these laws are applied to particular cases is one in which their meaning takes shape. The process is not merely one of application but one of con-cretization: by coming into contact with particular cases, the law takes one of several possible instantiations it could have taken.

The street, as such, is not simply a passive target or receptacle for the law; it contributes to shaping what the law means. The relationship between the two is dialectical, and the agents who must carry out such a dialectic—the street-level bureaucrats who must "think the case with the law"—are not simply performing a technical exercise, but one that requires practical wisdom. They must give countenance to the law in light of their considered judgments about particular cases. It is through the intervention of such bureaucrats, as well, that the abstract normative standards that are em-bedded in our laws, and that guide their application—considerations like respect, fairness, responsiveness, and efficiency—are given concrete shape, and that the tensions between them are worked out in light of the demands of concrete situations. Street-level bureaucracy is a site of *institutionalized phronesis,* one where universal norms encounter particular cases and acquire practical meaning.[4]

If I am correct in claiming that bureaucracy is as much a site of phro-nesis as it is a haven for technical, means-end rationality, then we have reason to be cautious about analyses that draw too stark a distinction be-tween how the state sees and thinks and how other social actors do. Take the case, for instance, of James Scott's *Seeing Like a State,* one of the most celebrated accounts of administrative (ir)rationality at work.[5] Scott draws a contrast between the high-modernist approach that often underpins the workings of the state, with its top-down way of seeing, its emphasis on formal rules and well-ordered categories, and its attempt to master contingency, and the ancient Greek notion of "mētis," a kind of practical knowledge or intelligence that is typically local and informal, and that allows one to respond with flexibility to changing situations. Scott argues and demonstrates with the aid of compelling case studies that states who ignore mētis do so at their own peril.

But while the distinction between high-modernist rationality and mētis can indeed account for the failure of various statist interventions, we should be careful not to take it as expressing something essential about how states "see" or "think" in general. Our inquiry into the world of street-level bureaucracy should remind us that policies designed in planning offices, however formal and rigid they may be, do not encounter the street directly. The implementation of such policies is mediated by layers upon layers of bureaucrats who leave their imprint too. When we inquire into how states see or think, we must take these intermediary actors into consideration. We must remain attuned, in particular, to the possibility that their behavior may be influenced by a variety of factors that are foreign to the design of policy planners, and that it may differ quite substantially from what such planners originally intended.

As we have seen in this study, bureaucrats are not inert conduits for standard operating procedures, but moral agents in their own right with distinctive moral dispositions. It is from the standpoint of these dispositions that they appraise the policies they inherit, that they decide what meaning they will attribute to them and how they will resolve the ambiguities and gaps that inevitably remain in them. The moral dispositions of bureaucrats are shaped by the environment in which they work and by the role they must fulfill.

For street-level bureaucrats, both working environment and role are marked by their proximity to the street—not an abstract construct, but a vibrant collection of individuals, each with their own stories, temperaments, aspirations, and anxieties. If the upper echelons of bureaucracy can afford to simplify, to categorize, and to formalize in order to govern, street-level bureaucrats are reminded, day in, day out, of the complexity and shifting nature of social problems and of the limits of ready-made categories and formal solutions. The closer we get to the street, the more the mismatch between the formal logic of administration and everyday reality becomes palpable, and the need to patch them more pressing. The closer we get to the street, moreover, the more the sense of worth, fulfillment, and integrity of bureaucrats will depend on how well they can attend to its complex realities.

Caught between an impersonal, formal world to which they owe allegiance and a personal, shifting realm that demands tailored attention, street-level bureaucrats respond as best as they can: they develop an array of context-specific practices that enable them to cope with the dual demands of their superiors and of the street; they find a way to be as responsive as possible to the needs of their clients by tweaking existing rules, interpreting them creatively, and playing them against each other; they construct informal taxonomies to crystallize their practical knowledge; and they come up with creative rationales to distinguish between cases in a way that is more granular than official rules allow for. In short, they resort to mētis and, thereby, cushion the encounter between the universal, formal norms embedded in law and the fluid realities of social life.

While these reflections may seem to run against Scott's argument, I believe they are in line with his broader point. It is arguably because the distinction between formalism and mētis does not neatly map onto the separation between state and society; because the state, when seen from the bottom up, does indeed make room for some measure of practical know-how and informal processes; because it endows its agents with a margin of discretion to attend to the complexity and shifting nature of their environment—it is because of all these reasons that the state tends to be more resilient and durable than the high-modernist projects it sometimes tries, and fails, to implement. To put it more concisely, it is perhaps to the extent that states are more than rules and procedures—to the extent, that is, that they depart from how they describe and legitimize themselves— that they are ultimately so resilient.

Political Theory from the Bottom Up

When political theorists write about the democratic state, they generally focus on the design of democratic institutions and on the merits of particular policy schemes. The approach I have adopted in this book starts at the other end of the political process, with how the state manifests itself to ordinary citizens at the moment of service provision or law enforcement. What does this shift in perspective add to our capacity to interpret, criticize, and evaluate the workings of the democratic state? What new vistas does it offer for political theory?

One upshot of looking at the state from below is that it puts some of the abstract concepts of interest to political theorists under a magnifying glass. As the psychologist Tom Tyler and others have shown, it is in large part through the everyday interactions that citizens have with their state that their perception of the legitimacy of public institutions, and their belief in their standing as equal members of the polity, is produced or undermined. By examining such interactions up close, we can arrive at a better understanding of the considerations that drive people's understanding of legitimacy and equal citizenship and of the failings they take to be particularly damning. Studying the state from below allows us to think the big (legitimacy, citizenship) in the small (everyday interactions), and serves to bring a healthy dose of concreteness to discussions that are usually highly abstract.

This is not to say, of course, that the abstraction characteristic of political philosophy will altogether dissolve to make way for interpretive social science, nor should it. Understanding what clients and bureaucrats think is legitimate, and what they perceive to be failures of legitimacy, will not, on its own, give us a compelling theory of legitimacy. Normative arguments are not settled by field observations or interviews any more than they are by counting heads. People might be mistaken, or deluded, or unreasonable. But they often are not. Examining their views and observing the nature of their encounters with authority might alert us to important considerations and nuances that would otherwise have escaped our attention.

Another reason to look closely at the state from the perspective of the bureaucratic encounter is that the content of public policy is in part settled there, in function of the meaning that bureaucrats and clients assign to it.[6] Policy statutes leave room for discretion and the way in which bureaucrats make use of their discretion depends on how they understand their role and responsibilities. Meaning, in other words, is a crucial mediating link between public policy, as it is formulated, and public policy, as it is effectively enacted.

Attending to the meaning of public policy is also crucial from the vantage point of clients. Whether they deem a policy respectful or insulting, whether they see it as enabling or disciplining, are considerations that matter for our understanding and appraisal of the policy in question. Looking at the state from below invites us to take into account the symbolic and expressive dimensions of policy when evaluating its successes and failures.

Studying the state from the bottom up can also serve to unmask political projects or dimensions of political conflict that would otherwise remain hidden.[7] Public policy necessarily undergoes transformations as it is being implemented. While some of these transformations are innocuous, others exhibit political bias. These biases, however, can be difficult to detect because they typically result from managerial choices that purport to be merely "technical." By exposing the political significance of such choices, we can make visible forms of politics that take place—intentionally or not—behind our backs, and open them up to scrutiny and critique.

Consider, for example, the United States' welfare-to-work reform of 1996, known as TANF (Temporary Assistance for Needy Families).[8] At the policy level, the reform package embodied a political compromise between two approaches to welfare: a formative one, centered on providing clients with personalized assistance to reenter the labor market, and a more disciplinary one, striving to attain the same objective by penalizing nonwork and withholding benefits. While the policy itself was ambivalent between these two orientations, the reforms were accompanied by governance provisions inspired by New Public Management, including devolution, contracting, and performance-based management. As Evelyn Brodkin and Flemming Larsen have argued, these provisions altered the working practices of street-level bureaucrats in ways that ultimately favored the disciplinary approach. This happened for a number of reasons—one of them being that it proved easier to roll out performance metrics that could track the disciplinary dimensions of welfare (e.g., number of cases closed) than metrics that could track the enabling ones (e.g., did clients receive adequate training? Were they directed to jobs that were suitable for them?). The case of TANF reminds us that decisions taken in the course of implementation can tilt the nature of public policy by altering the conditions of street-level work.

I have highlighted so far the contributions that a bottom-up approach to the state can make to strands of political theory that are primarily interpretive and critical: those concerned with elucidating the meaning of the political concepts that we use and with unmasking political projects that conceal themselves under a different guise. I want to suggest, in what follows, that studying the state from below can also provide us with a distinctive entry point into *normative* political theory.

In a democracy, the state and its policies are meant to embody the values and principles that citizens have chosen to regulate their life in common. Studying the state from below gives us an opportunity to reassess these values and principles by seeing what they entail in practice. As is well known, the legal documents that articulate our collective political project—statutes, regulations, ordinances, or even constitutions—are often vague, ambiguous, and ridden with conflicts. This is one of their virtues: by papering over disagreements between various political factions and covering tensions between our own values, they make compromise possible and allow public institutions to function without requiring us to have a perfectly well-ordered set of preferences. But it is also one of their weaknesses: they give us the illusion that we have resolved certain conflicts or controversies when we have, in fact, just buried them under words.

At the front lines of public service, however, the ambiguities and conflicts contained in our laws can no longer be concealed behind clever turns of phrase. They must translate into action. For that reason, observing the practices of street-level bureaucrats can serve to reveal tensions between our values and aspirations that were until then obscured. At times, this may force us to recognize the pluralism that is inherent to our political culture and the tragic conflicts that result from it; at others, it may prompt us to confront our hypocrisies and oversights, placing us before the need to make hard tradeoffs that we thought we might have been able to avoid. In this respect, studying street-level bureaucracy is tantamount to holding a mirror to ourselves as a polity—a mirror that will often be more truthful than our laws because it involves deeds rather than words.

But there is more. Studying the *experience* of street-level bureaucrats, not just their behavior, is akin to observing an "experiment in living."[9] It shows us what happens to people who try to live by the conflicting values and principles that we have enshrined in legislation. This can serve as a test of whether these values, and the vision of society they embody, are indeed right for us. This is the significance of the "impossible situations" I described in Chapter 5. Seeing street-level bureaucrats break down while trying to deliver on the mandate they inherit suggests that the conflicts and tensions latent in such a mandate may have reached a point where they need to be addressed.

Seeing the state from the perspective of street-level bureaucracy, finally, opens up a different starting point for normative inquiry. Instead of starting with policymaking and institutional design and thinking about policy implementation as a derivative problem to be addressed further down the line, it invites us to flip things around—that is, to start with an account of how we would want the state to interact with its citizens and to use this as a criterion to guide or constrain how our institutions ought to be designed and what policies they ought to pursue.

This is the approach I have adopted in this book, arguing, first, that street-level bureaucrats ought to remain sensitive to a plurality of normative considerations as they go about implementing public policy, and trying to articulate, thereafter, the kind of organizational environment they would need to be able to do so. This is also the approach that proponents of basic income often take. They start from the presumption that entrusting decisions about welfare eligibility to street-level bureaucrats will inevitably lead to encounters that are intrusive, demeaning, and arbitrary. They proceed, from this assessment of the conditions of service provision, to advocate a change in policy: the adoption of an unconditional basic income that would, in principle, do away with such unwelcome uses of discretion.[10]

These attempts suggest that it might be possible and useful to articulate in much greater detail than I have done here what one might call a "bottom-up normative theory of the state"—one that begins with the moment of service provision and that works its way up, from there, to questions of policymaking and institutional design. To be sure, thinking about how the state should interact with citizens at the moment of service provision will not tell us what substantive policies the state ought to pursue. But it may rule out some options and, more importantly, it may condition the answers we are willing to accept.

Political Theory with an Ethnographic Sensibility

I would like to close on a methodological note. I have attempted, in this study, to combine an attention to questions in normative political theory with an ethnographic sensibility to the experience of ordinary moral agents.

To adopt an "ethnographic sensibility" is to be interested not just in what people do, but also in why they do it.[11] It is to be concerned with how they perceive, think about, and ascribe meaning to the contexts that surround them. The enterprise is descriptive and interpretive at once: it involves both observing how people respond to specific situations and trying to make sense of what these situations look like to them—interpreting their interpretations of the social world.[12]

This has led me to draw extensively on empirical research and, in particular, on organizational ethnography and open-ended interviews with street-level bureaucrats. Some of this material I gathered myself; the rest of it came from secondary sources in anthropology, sociology, and political science. Where possible, I opened the chapters with close descriptions of street-level work. It is from these accounts that I attempted to tease out the normative challenges that street-level bureaucrats face and the nature of the answers they offer to them. Only then did I subject these answers to a more detached form of normative scrutiny.

I am not the first, of course, to try to bring moral and political theory into closer contact with ethnography. The latter has long served as a valuable companion to interpretive, critical, and conceptual strands of political theory. By drawing our attention to the experience of ordinary people, ethnography has played a part in unmasking hegemonic discourses, in uncovering conceptual blind spots, and in revealing political biases implicit in the workings of our institutions.[13] By forcing us to come to grasp with cultures and institutions different from our own, it has also given us an external vantage point from which to criticize the functioning of our own societies and to interrogate their unsubstantiated claims to universality.[14]

I believe that ethnography has something important to contribute to *normative* strands of political theory as well.[15] It can do so in at least four ways. It can help us (1) map the normative demands that individuals face in certain situations or social roles; (2) diagnose the obstacles that they encounter in trying to respond to these demands; (3) evaluate whether the practices that these individuals engage in, and the institutional arrangements in which they are placed, are conducive to advancing the values that we hold; and (4) question and reflect upon these very values. The contributions, in other words, are epistemic, diagnostic, evaluative, and valuational.[16] Let me take them in turn.

An ethnographic sensibility can help us, first of all, unpack the complexity of the moral and political situations in which individuals find themselves. This allows us to map out more accurately the moral facts and demands on the basis of which we can then engage in normative reasoning. It is by looking closely at the bureaucratic encounter that we came to notice, for instance, that the interaction involves far more than the provision of services, but that it is seen, by clients and bureaucrats alike, as a moment in which a certain form of recognition is given or withheld. This lends moral and political significance not just to the decisions of street-level bureaucrats but also to their demeanor, word choice, and body language. Being attuned to the experience of real-world agents can also help us grasp the nature of the tradeoffs that arise when resources are scarce and cognitive and emotional capacities are limited. It can open our eyes, finally, to the wide range of practical meanings that abstract normative values like "respect" or "fairness" take on in particular social and cultural settings.

In all of these ways, an ethnographic sensibility can provide us with a more accurate picture of the normative considerations that bearers of a social role must take into account; of the tensions that arise between such considerations; and of the ways in which such considerations can be interpreted. Such groundwork is invaluable if one is to normatively assess how well individual agents perform their role, and how effectively our institutions support them in doing so.

Besides helping us capture more accurately the ethical situations in which individuals are placed, an ethnographic sensibility can also shed light on how individuals experience such situations. The emphasis that ethnographers place on the embodied viewpoint of individual actors, on the phenomenology of everyday experience, and on ongoing patterns of sense-making, can serve to refocus our attention on a host of ethical tasks that feed into the process of moral reasoning but that are distinct from it: how individuals come to perceive and frame moral issues, how they respond to them affectively, and how they conceive of their role and responsibilities. These are the sorts of tasks with which I was concerned throughout this study. The problem with indifferents, caregivers, and enforcers, you will recall, is not that they reasoned improperly, but that they had a biased perception of the facts on the basis of which they were meant to reason and a truncated understanding of the considerations that were supposed to guide their reasoning. By pointing us beyond moral reasoning and inviting us to adopt a more capacious understanding of moral life, an ethnographic sensibility draws our attention to a range of challenges that individuals must overcome to be able to respond adequately to the normative demands they encounter.

Because of the detailed observational work they entail, ethnographies also draw our attention to how social institutions actually function, rather than how they are supposed to function. Ethnographic research tends to highlight, in particular, the informal processes that surround, facilitate, or undercut the work of our institutions, and that are often left out from the discourses that such institutions use to describe and legitimize themselves. It is by being on the lookout for such informal processes that we were able to uncover, in Chapter 4, a regime of everyday accountability among peers that operates alongside more formal systems of oversight. By examining such infomal practices, one can also get at a more nuanced appreciation of the effect that they have and of what they mean to the parties concerned. While the tendency of frontline bureaucrats to engage in small talk with clients, for instance, might seem like a waste of time to be curtailed, a closer look reveals that it is actually a necessary step in building a modicum of trust, which facilitates the sharing of sensitive private information.

Much like literature, ethnographies can also spur our normative imagination. If we think of the characters who figure in them as moral agents in their own right we may be able to learn not just from their mistakes, but also from the responses they put together. The approach to moral formation I advocated in Chapter 3, for instance, with its emphasis on practices of the self, was inspired by observing the strategies that case managers mobilize to retain balanced moral dispositions despite the challenges of everyday work. Ethnographies present us with a field of individuals experimenting with a variety of practices, self-understandings, and coping mechanisms, some of which can be found, upon reflection, to work better than others.

Ethnographies, finally, give us an opportunity to test our commitment to a body of values and principles by showing what forms of life these values and principles yield when people try to live by them. This is the idea, which I mentioned earlier, of ethnographic research as providing a window into various "experiments in living."

If an ethnographic sensibility can serve to expand the boundaries of political theory, the latter has something important to offer in return. Contemporary political theory and the history of moral and political thought hold in their midst a broad repertoire of interpretive frames that can give intelligibility to everyday practices that may otherwise appear to be insignificant. It is by drawing on the tradition of the care of the self, for example, that we were able to give coherence to a range of disparate gestures and to show that they amount to a regime of moral exercise through which bureaucrats regulate their moral dispositions. It is by reflecting on the nature of casuistic reasoning, to give yet another example, that we were able to comprehend the significance of conversational bribes that would have been easy to dismiss, and to show that they add up to a sophisticated pattern of moral reasoning. Concepts and images drawn from political theory can thus serve as invitations to read existing ethnographies against the grain, and as opportunities to find in them new areas of significance.

In the vast number of ethnographies that anthropologists, sociologists, and political scientists have produced over the years, political theorists have a wealth of material to work with. This material can help us think in more nuanced ways about the normative demands inherent to various social roles, about the constraints that occupiers of these roles face, and about the resources they can draw upon. More importantly, perhaps, it can help us shed light on the variety of ways in which individuals experience, interpret, and reflect upon such demands, constraints, and resources. It can help us understand, that is, how they come to terms with the roles and responsibilities they inherit or take on.

This is not just a descriptive endeavor. Moral philosophers and political theorists are not alone in grappling with normative questions. Ordinary people too think seriously about what we have reason to value, what we owe to each other, and what kind of persons we should aspire to be. They too struggle to live up to moral standards in circumstances that are often challenging. To adopt an ethnographic sensibility is to open ourselves up to the possibility that we may have something to learn *from,* not simply *about,* how they answer these questions.

To be sure, there is a limit to how far existing ethnographies can take us in this direction, seeing that they were written with different purposes and concerns in mind. If political theorists were to draw on such studies, they may eventually run up against their limits. They may catch themselves wishing, as I did, that the ethnographer had looked elsewhere or had entertained a different interpretation; that he or she had probed deeper, poked more intently, or listened more closely. Perhaps this would be a blessing in disguise: an invitation to venture out into the field more frequently than we presently do, and to find out for ourselves.

Notes

1 *The New Oxford Dictionary of English,* s.v. "bureaucrat."
2 *Webster's Third New International Dictionary of the English Language Unabridged,* s.v. "bureaucrat."
3 *Dictionary.com,* s.v. "bureaucrat," http://dictionary.reference.com/ (accessed March 15, 2017).
4 David Foster Wallace, *The Pale King* (New York: Little, Brown and Co., 2011), 262.
5 Sergei Eisenstein, *Risunki=Drawings* (Moscow: Iskusstvo, 1961), 60.
6 On the relationship between bureaucracy and paperwork, see Matthew S. Hull, *Government of Paper: The Materiality of Bureaucracy in Urban Pakistan* (Berkeley: University of California Press, 2012); Ben Kafka, *The Demon of Writing: Powers and Failures of Paperwork* (New York: Zone Books, 2012).
7 See Ludwig Von Mises, *Bureaucracy* (New Haven: Yale University Press, 1944); James M. Buchanan and Gordon Tullock, *The Calculus of Consent: Logical Foundations of Constitutional Democracy* (Ann Arbor: University of Michigan Press, 1965); Anthony Downs, *Inside Bureaucracy* (Boston: Little, Brown and Co., 1967); William A. Niskanen, *Bureaucracy and Representative Government* (Chicago: Aldine, Atherton, 1971).
8 On the oligarchic affinity of bureaucracy, see Robert Michels, *Political Parties: A Sociological Study of the Oligarchical Tendencies of Modern Democracy* (Glencoe, IL: Free Press 1949). On the co-optation of bureaucracy by the "power elite," see C. Wright Mills, *The Power Elite* (New York: Oxford University Press, 1956). On the proclivity of bureaucracy to be captured by other organizations or special interests, see Philip Selznick, *TVA and the Grass Roots: A Study in the Sociology of Formal Organization* (Berkeley: University of California Press, 1949). On the tension between bureaucracy and democracy in the political science literature, see the following review: Beverly A. Cigler and Heidi L. Neiswender, "'Bureaucracy' in The Introductory American Government Textbook," *Public Administration Review* 51, no. 5 (1991).
9 See, for instance, Robert K. Merton, "Bureaucratic Structure and Personality," *Social Forces* 18, no. 4 (1940); Frances Fox Piven and Richard A. Cloward, *Regulating the Poor: The Functions of Public Welfare* (New York: Pantheon Books, 1971); Jeffrey Prottas, *People Processing: The Street-Level Bureaucrat in Public Service Bureaucracies* (Lexington, MA: Lexington Books, 1979); Ralph P. Hummel, *The Bureaucratic Experience: A Critique of Life in the Modern Organization,* 4th ed. (New York: St. Martin's Press, 1994).
10 See, among others, Sandra Morgen, "The Agency of Welfare Workers: Negotiating Devolution, Privatization, and the Meaning of Self-Sufficiency," *American*

Anthropologist 103, no. 3 (2001); Suzanne Mettler and Joe Soss, "The Consequences of Public Policy for Democratic Citizenship: Bridging Policy Studies and Mass Politics," *Perspectives on Politics* 2, no. 1 (2004); Joe Soss, Richard C. Fording, and Sanford Schram, *Disciplining the Poor: Neoliberal Paternalism and the Persistent Power of Race* (Chicago: University of Chicago Press, 2011); Didier Fassin, *La Force de l'Ordre: Une Anthropologie de la Police des Quartiers* (Paris: Seuil, 2011); David Graeber, "Dead Zones of the Imagination: On Violence, Bureaucracy, and Interpretive Labor," *HAU: Journal of Ethnographic Theory* 2, no. 2 (2012).

11 Charles T. Goodsell, *The Case for Bureaucracy: A Public Administration Polemic*, 4th ed. (Washington, DC: CQ Press, 2004), 17.

12 Peter M. Blau, *Bureaucracy in Modern Society* (New York: Random House, 1956), 13. See also the opening of Paul Du Gay, *In Praise of Bureaucracy: Weber, Organization and Ethics* (London: Sage Publications, 2000).

13 See Michael Lipsky, *Street-Level Bureaucracy: Dilemmas of the Individual in Public Services*, 30th anniversary expanded ed. (New York: Russell Sage Foundation, 2010).

14 Street-level bureaucrats, of course, do not only interact with citizens. They also come into contact with long-term residents, temporary workers, irregular migrants, and refugees. In this book, I focus primarily on citizens because from a normative standpoint, the democratic state is typically thought to have special obligations toward its citizens, and they, in turn, are understood to have special rights and powers to press against it. How far these obligations and correlative rights extend to non-citizens is a matter of debate in democratic theory, and the question remains beyond the scope of this study. On the rights and responsibilities of the democratic state toward non-citizens, see Joseph H. Carens, *The Ethics of Immigration* (Oxford: Oxford University Press, 2013).

15 See, in particular, the work of Tom Tyler and Bo Rothstein: Tom R. Tyler, *Why People Obey the Law* (Princeton, NJ: Princeton University Press, 2006); Jason Sunshine and Tom R. Tyler, "The Role of Procedural Justice and Legitimacy in Shaping Public Support for Policing," *Law & Society Review* 37, no. 3 (2003); Tom R. Tyler, "Enhancing Police Legitimacy," *The Annals of the American Academy of Political and Social Science* 593, no. 1 (2004); Bo Rothstein, *The Quality of Government: Corruption, Social Trust, and Inequality in International Perspective* (Chicago: University of Chicago Press, 2011). Tyler's findings are also helpfully discussed in Pierre Rosanvallon, *Democratic Legitimacy: Impartiality, Reflexivity, Proximity*, trans. Arthur Goldhammer (Princeton, NJ: Princeton University Press, 2011), 171–177.

16 Bo Rothstein, "Creating Political Legitimacy: Electoral Democracy versus Quality of Government," *American Behavioral Scientist* 53, no. 3 (2009): 313.

17 For an approach germane to mine from the field of anthropology which also focuses on the spaces of agency available to frontline bureaucrats, see the essays collected in Didier Fassin, ed., *At the Heart of the State: The Moral World of Institutions* (London: Pluto Press, 2015).

18 In shifting the object of inquiry from the *what* to the *how*, I take up a theme discussed by scholars of political ethics and transplant it into the realm of bureaucratic organizations. The latter have reminded us that it is important to look not just at what politicians ought to do, but at what sorts of persons we would want them to be. See, for instance, Bernard Williams, "Politics and Moral Character," in *Public and Private Morality*, ed. Stuart Hampshire (Cambridge: Cambridge University Press, 1978); Andrew Sabl, *Ruling Passions: Political Offices and Democratic Ethics* (Princeton, NJ: Princeton University Press, 2002).

19 These questions are inspired by a long-standing agenda of research in organization theory on the effect of bureaucratic organizations on the individuals who work in them. See, for instance, Chris Argyris, *Personality and Organization: The Conflict between System and the Individual* (New York: Harper & Row, 1957); Rosabeth Moss Kanter, *Men and Women of the Corporation* (New York: Basic Books, 1977); Robert Jackall, *Moral Mazes: The World of Corporate Managers* (New York: Oxford University Press, 1989).

20 Philip Pettit, *Republicanism: A Theory of Freedom and Government* (Oxford: Oxford University Press, 1997), 57–58.

21 For a review of these various institutional measures and a discussion of why they are both necessary and insufficient, see Kenneth Culp Davis, *Discretionary Justice: A Preliminary Inquiry* (Urbana, IL: University of Illinois Press, 1971), and Pettit, *Republicanism*, 63–73, 241–246.

22 See, for instance, David M. Messick and Max H. Bazerman, "Ethical Leadership and the Psychology of Decision Making," *Sloan Management Review* 37, no. 2 (1996); Max H. Bazerman and Ann E. Tenbrunsel, *Blind Spots: Why We Fail to Do What's Right and What to Do About It* (Princeton, NJ: Princeton University Press, 2011).

23 See, for instance, the seminal study by Jeffrey L. Pressman and Aaron Wildavsky, *Implementation: How Great Expectations in Washington Are Dashed in Oakland*, 2nd ed. (Berkeley: University of California Press, 1979).

24 See Niccolò Machiavelli, *The Prince*, trans. Harvey C. Mansfield (Chicago: University of Chicago Press, 1998); *Discourses on Livy*, trans. Harvey C. Mansfield and Nathan Tarcov (Chicago: University of Chicago Press, 1995). For other influential treatments of political ethics, see Max Weber, "Politics as Vocation," in *From Max Weber: Essays in Sociology*, ed. Hans Heinrich Gerth and C. Wright Mills (New York: Oxford University Press, 1979); Michael Walzer, "Political Action: The Problem of Dirty Hands," *Philosophy & Public Affairs* 2, no. 2 (1973); Dennis F. Thompson, *Political Ethics and Public Office* (Cambridge, MA: Harvard University Press, 1987).

25 To put it as political scientists John Brehm and Scott Gates do, the question is whether to work, shirk, or sabotage. See John Brehm and Scott Gates, *Working, Shirking, and Sabotage: Bureaucratic Response to a Democratic Public* (Ann Arbor: University of Michigan Press, 1997).

26 See Michael C. Jensen and William H. Meckling, "Theory of the Firm: Managerial Behavior, Agency Costs and Ownership Structure," *Journal of Financial
Economics* 3, no. 4 (1976). For the case of public bureaucracy, see Terry M. Moe,
"The New Economics of Organization," *American Journal of Political Science* 28,
no. 4 (1984). For an overview of the literature on formal models of bureaucracy,
see Jonathan Bendor, "Formal Models of Bureaucracy," *British Journal of Political Science* 18, no. 3 (1988); Sean Gailmard and John W. Patty, "Formal Models
of Bureaucracy," *Annual Review of Political Science* 15 (2012).

27 In fact, a common assumption in the formal literature on bureaucracy is that
the risks associated with delegation would be greatly reduced if principals were
able to appoint agents who are ideological clones of themselves. This is what Jonathan Bendor and Adam Meirowitz call the "ally principle." They go on to explore the conditions under which such a principle actually holds. See Jonathan
Bendor and Adam Meirowitz, "Spatial Models of Delegation," *American Political
Science Review* 98, no. 2 (2004).

28 Joseph Heath, "A General Framework for the Ethics of Public Administration,"
unpublished manuscript (2014): 30. The idea is that the legitimacy of public administration is not merely derived from the legitimacy of the elected government
that instructs it to act in certain ways. Public administration has a claim to being
democratically legitimate in its own right, either because of the problems it
solves and the values it honors, or because it embodies a different kind of democratic generality than that which can be achieved through elections, or because
it performs a distinctive constitutional function. This line of argumentation has
been developed by a range of authors with different theoretical inclinations. See
the work of the authors of the Blacksburg Manifesto, in particular: John A. Rohr,
To Run a Constitution: The Legitimacy of the Administrative State (Lawrence:
University Press of Kansas, 1986); Gary L. Wamsley et al., eds., *Refounding Public
Administration* (Newbury Park, CA: Sage Publications, 1990). See also Rosanvallon, *Democratic Legitimacy*.

29 See, for instance, James Q. Wilson, "The Bureaucracy Problem," *The Public Interest*, no. 6 (1967). Wilson adds to the concerns of "equity," "efficiency," and "responsiveness" those of "accountability" and "fiscal integrity," and argues that
"the solution to each is in some degree incompatible with the solution to every
other."

30 This idea reflects a recent turn within legal scholarship toward the study of "Administrative Constitutionalism." The guiding thought behind this burgeoning
literature is that administrative agencies play a role not just in the application of
established constitutional requirements but also in the elaboration of new constitutional understandings and in the construction of the administrative state.
See Jerry L. Mashaw, *Creating the Administrative Constitution: The Lost One
Hundred Years of American Administrative Law* (New Haven, CT: Yale University Press, 2012); William N. Eskridge and John A. Ferejohn, *A Republic of Statutes: The New American Constitution* (New Haven, CT: Yale University Press,

2010); Sophia Z. Lee, *The Workplace Constitution from the New Deal to the New Right* (New York: Cambridge University Press, 2014). For a review, see Gillian E. Metzger, "Administrative Constitutionalism," *Texas Law Review* 91 (2013).

31 Pierre Bourdieu, *La Misère du Monde* (Paris: Seuil, 1993). Bourdieu initially used the distinction to distinguish the ministries in charge of social functions (health, housing, welfare, education) from those in charge of enforcing economic discipline. Loïc Wacquant has argued, more recently, that the police and courts are also essential constituents of the Right arm of the state. See Loïc Wacquant, *Punishing the Poor: The Neoliberal Government of Social Insecurity* (Durham, NC: Duke University Press, 2009).

32 To be sure, these countries have different administrative traditions, different regimes of administrative law, and different public policy climates. Here again, it is on the commonalities, rather than on the differences, that I will focus. For a discussion of differences in administrative traditions, see Fabio Rugge, "Administrative Traditions in Western Europe," in *The Handbook of Public Administration*, ed. B. Guy Peters and Jon Pierre (London: Sage Publications, 2003). For studies of street-level bureaucracy that are attentive to national differences, see Mark Considine et al., eds., *Getting Welfare to Work: Street-Level Governance in Australia, the UK, and the Netherlands* (Oxford: Oxford University Press, 2015); Evelyn Z. Brodkin and Gregory Marston, eds., *Work and the Welfare State: Street-Level Organizations and Workfare Politics* (Washington, DC: Georgetown University Press, 2013). Both of these volumes focus on workfare reforms.

33 On how to delimit street-level bureaucracy and on the characteristic features of street-level work, see Steven Maynard-Moody and Shannon Portillo, "Street-Level Bureaucracy Theory," in *The Oxford Handbook of American Bureaucracy*, ed. Robert F. Durant (Oxford: Oxford University Press, 2010), 254–264; Peter Hupe, Michael Hill, and Aurélien Buffat, eds., *Understanding Street-Level Bureaucracy* (Bristol, UK: Policy Press, 2016), 3–24.

34 Even operating a toll booth, however, is not quite as routinized as it may seem and leaves room for discretionary openings. See Marie Szaniszlo, "Mass. Pike Toll Collector Reflects on His Last Shift," *Boston Herald*, October 30, 2016. On 911 call operators, see Maynard-Moody and Portillo, "Street-Level Bureaucracy Theory," 263; Mary E. Guy, Meredith A. Newman, and Sharon H. Mastracci, *Emotional Labor: Putting the Service in Public Service* (Armonk, NY: M. E. Sharpe, 2008).

35 Vincent Dubois speaks of the street-level bureaucrat's "two bodies," in allusion to Ernst Kantorowicz's famous study of medieval political theology. See Vincent Dubois, *The Bureaucrat and the Poor: Encounters in French Welfare Offices*, trans. Jean-Yves Bart (Burlington, VT: Ashgate, 2010), 73; Ernst H. Kantorowicz, *The King's Two Bodies: A Study in Mediaeval Political Theology* (Princeton, NJ: Princeton University Press, 1997). See also my review of Dubois's book: Bernardo Zacka, "The Two Bodies of the Bureaucrat," *Public Administration Review* 72, no. 2 (2012).

36 Rosabeth Moss Kanter and Barry Stein, eds., *Life in Organizations: Workplaces as People Experience Them* (New York: Basic Books, 1979), 176. Cited in Maynard-Moody and Portillo, "Street-Level Bureaucracy Theory," 255.

37 On the provision of reasons as an essential component of administrative legitimacy, see John W. Patty and Elizabeth Maggie Penn, *Social Choice and Legitimacy: The Possibilities of Impossibility* (New York: Cambridge University Press, 2014), 162–188.

38 For a discussion of the development, dimensions, and risks of government contracting, see Jocelyn M. Johnston and Barbara S. Romzek, "The Promises, Performance, and Pitfalls of Government Contracting," in *The Oxford Handbook of American Bureaucracy*, ed. Robert F. Durant (Oxford: Oxford University Press, 2010).

39 On the questions occasioned by the shift from government provision of public services to nonprofit organizations dependent on public funds, see Steven Rathgeb Smith and Michael Lipsky, *Nonprofits for Hire: The Welfare State in the Age of Contracting* (Cambridge, MA: Harvard University Press, 1993). On the distinctiveness of nonprofit organizations as service providers, see Lester M. Salamon, *Partners in Public Service: Government–Nonprofit Relations in the Modern Welfare State* (Baltimore, MD: Johns Hopkins University Press, 1995); Rachel Fyall, "Nonprofits as Advocates and Providers: A Conceptual Framework," *Policy Studies Journal* (2016).

40 Lipsky, *Street-Level Bureaucracy*, 216. Lipsky adds: "Also, in many street-level bureaucracies, workers' perspectives strongly reflect professional rather than administrative norms. Thus a social worker in a contracting agency may process clients very much like a counterpart employed by a state agency."

41 Ibid., note 6.

42 See, for example, Janice Johnson Dias and Steven Maynard-Moody, "For-Profit Welfare: Contracts, Conflicts, and the Performance Paradox," *Journal of Public Administration Research and Theory* 17, no. 2 (2007). The authors conclude their examination of a welfare-to-work training program as such: "Beholden not just to clients and staff but also to their stockholders, these programs are driven by financial objectives that encourage them to maximize output while minimizing expenditures. Therefore, even as they provide services to recipients, they may have a disincentive to attend to clients' entrenched employment deficits, such as low literacy levels and mental health problems. Indeed, they may be motivated to ignore them completely, particularly in cases where the cost of attending to their clients' needs is high."

43 Mark Bovens and Stavros Zouridis, "From Street-Level to System-Level Bureaucracies: How Information and Communication Technology Is Transforming Administrative Discretion and Constitutional Control," *Public Administration Review* 62, no. 2 (2002). For a review of the literature on the impacts of e-government technologies on street-level bureaucracy, see Aurélien Buffat, "Street-Level Bureaucracy and E-Government," *Public Management Review* 17, no. 1 (2015).

44　I am thinking in particular of welfare reform in the United States. See Celeste Watkins-Hayes, *The New Welfare Bureaucrats: Entanglements of Race, Class, and Policy Reform* (Chicago: University of Chicago Press, 2009). Mark Considine and his coauthors have also found that welfare workers in the UK report an increase in their perceived discretion from 1998 to 2012. The trend points the other way in Australia. See Considine et al., *Getting Welfare to Work.*

45　For the realist critique, see Raymond Geuss, *Philosophy and Real Politics* (Princeton, NJ: Princeton University Press, 2008); William Galston, "Realism in Political Theory," *European Journal of Political Theory* 9, no. 4 (2010); David Runciman, "What Is Realistic Political Philosophy," *Metaphilosophy* 43, no. 1–2 (2012). For a defense of nonideal theory, see Amartya Sen, *The Idea of Justice* (Cambridge, MA: Harvard University Press, 2009); Elizabeth Anderson, *The Imperative of Integration* (Princeton, NJ: Princeton University Press, 2010). On the distinction between political realism and nonideal theory, see Matt Sleat, "Realism, Liberalism and Non-Ideal Theory or, Are There Two Ways to Do Realistic Political Theory?," *Political Studies* 64, no. 1 (2016).

46　Yeheskel Hasenfeld, "People Processing Organizations: An Exchange Approach," *American Sociological Review* 37, no. 3 (1972).

1. STREET-LEVEL DISCRETION

1　See Lipsky, *Street-Level Bureaucracy*, 3; Aradhana Sharma and Akhil Gupta, "Introduction: Rethinking Theories of the State in an Age of Globalization," in *The Anthropology of the State: A Reader*, ed. Aradhana Sharma and Akhil Gupta (Oxford: Blackwell, 2006), 11.

2　See Herman Finer, "Administrative Responsibility in Democratic Government," *Public Administration Review* 1, no. 4 (1941); Carl Friedrich, "Public Policy and the Nature of Administrative Responsibility," in *Public Policy*, ed. C. J. Friedrich and E. S. Mason (Cambridge, MA: Harvard University Press, 1940).

3　Merriam-webster.com, *Merriam-Webster's Dictionary of Law*, s.v. "discretion," http://www.merriam-webster.com/dictionary/discretion (accessed March 17, 2017). Another meaning of discretion is the authority to take a decision that cannot be reviewed or reversed. When we say that a jury has discretion, for instance, we mean that it has "final say." This meaning of discretion will not concern us here; since street-level bureaucrats are low-ranking officials, their decisions can typically be reviewed by their superiors. They can be reprimanded for poor judgment and, in certain cases, their decisions can be overturned.

4　See Lawrence Meir Friedman, *The Legal System: A Social Science Perspective* (New York: Russell Sage Foundation, 1975), 37.

5　See, for instance, Herbert Kaufman, *The Forest Ranger: A Study in Administrative Behavior* (Baltimore: Resources for the Future, 1960), xiii–xiv, 161–200; or the more formal study by Brehm and Gates, *Working, Shirking, and Sabotage*, 47–75.

6　The distinction between "formal" discretion and "real" discretion is indicative of the wider gap that can exist between an organization's formal structure and its actual functioning. The formal structure does not serve only to guide behavior, but also to legitimate the organization in light of broader societal norms. Even when it is decoupled from actual practice, it must still be revered ceremoniously—it serves, in part, as a "façade" or "show" that the organization puts up for its relevant publics. See John W. Meyer and Brian Rowan, "Institutionalized Organizations: Formal Structure as Myth and Ceremony," *The American Journal of Sociology* 83, no. 2 (1977).

7 As Steven Maynard-Moody and Michael Musheno put it: "Rules and procedures are an essential aspect of bureaucratic life yet provide only weak constraints on street-level judgments. Street-level work is, ironically, rule saturated but not rule bound." Steven Maynard-Moody and Michael Musheno, *Cops, Teachers, Counselors: Stories from the Front Lines of Public Service* (Ann Arbor: University of Michigan Press, 2003), 10.

8 A major difference, however, is that street-level bureaucrats are not constrained by the binding power of precedent. Their decisions can, accordingly, be less consistent over time, and more variable depending on the particularities of a given case. See Richard A. Posner, *How Judges Think* (Cambridge, MA: Harvard University Press, 2008), 4.

The idea that judges "make law" is, of course, controversial. It points to a long debate in legal theory between interpretivists and positivists. To understand what is at stake in this debate, it is helpful to distinguish, following Ronald Dworkin, between weak and strong discretion. Weak discretion refers to cases where the use of discretion must respond to a standard set by the relevant authorities (to use Dworkin's example, a sergeant is ordered "to pick *his five most competent men*"). Strong discretion, on the other hand, refers to cases where the use of discretion is not governed by any such standards (the sergeant is asked to "pick five of his men").

Dworkin, the foremost proponent of legal interpretivism, argues that when legal positivists, such as H. L. A. Hart, refer to the open texture of the law—the fact that the law can sometimes fall silent—they must mean that officials have discretion in the strong sense. According to Dworkin, however, there are "principles" contained within the law that govern the use of discretion and that serve a similar function to the "external standards" given to the sergeant. The point of contention between Dworkin and positivists, then, is whether the law really falls silent and must be created anew by the judge, or whether the law still speaks via principles and must as such be "constructively interpreted" (but not created anew). See Ronald Dworkin, *Taking Rights Seriously* (Cambridge, MA: Harvard University Press, 1978), 31–34; H. L. A. Hart, *The Concept of Law*, 2nd ed. (Oxford: Oxford University Press, 1994), 123–136; Brian Bix, *Jurisprudence: Theory and Context*, 5th ed. (London: Sweet & Maxwell, 2009), 45–47, 91–98.

This debate has occupied an important place in legal theory, but it is largely tangential to the argument I develop in this book. Whether officials "make law" or "constructively interpret it," they will, in either case, have to engage in a demanding moral exercise when making use of their discretionary power. My goal in this chapter is to show that such discretion and the moral exercise it calls for are not only a prerogative of judges and top-level officials but also a necessary and desirable feature of the work of street-level bureaucrats. For simplicity, I will continue using the language of positivists (i.e. "making law," "making policy") to describe what judges and street-level bureaucrats are sometimes called upon to do. For our present purposes, nothing substantial hinges on this choice of language.

9 For a discussion of the dangers of discretion, see Robert E. Goodin, *Reasons for Welfare: The Political Theory of the Welfare State* (Princeton, NJ: Princeton University Press, 1988), 193–204. Goodin identifies four types of dangers associated with discretionary power: manipulation and exploitation of clients; arbitrariness; unpredictability of official behavior; and intrusiveness.

10 See ibid., 12. It is, in part, to reduce such a risk of personal domination that proponents of basic income call for a radical simplification of public policy programs. If eligibility criteria were simplified, there would be less need for discretionary judgment and, therefore, less risk of exposure to arbitrariness. See Daniel Raventós, *Basic Income: The Material Conditions of Freedom* (London: Pluto Press, 2007), 127; Frank Lovett, *A General Theory of Domination and Justice* (New York: Oxford University Press, 2010), 199.

11 Evelyn Z. Brodkin, "Investigating Policy's Practical Meaning: Street-Level Research on Welfare Policy" (Center for Poverty Research Working Paper Series, Northwestern University, 2000), http://www.ipr.northwestern.edu/jcpr/working papers/wpfiles/brodkin3.PDF.

12 Dennis F. Thompson, *Restoring Responsibility: Ethics in Government, Business, and Healthcare* (Cambridge: Cambridge University Press, 2005), 52.

13 Woodrow Wilson, "The Study of Administration," *Political Science Quarterly* 2, no. 2 (1887): 209–210.

14 Frank J. Goodnow, *Politics and Administration* (New York: Macmillan, 1900), 22.

15 The following discussion is indebted to W. Richard Scott, *Organizations: Rational, Natural, and Open Systems*, 5th ed. (Upper Saddle River, NJ: Prentice Hall, 2003), 33–55. The phrase "rational systems perspective" comes from him.

16 The concept of rationality at play here is a narrow functional one. Bureaucracies can pursue goals rationally, however substantively irrational these goals may be.

17 Eric Weil writes, for instance, "Administration is an instrument, a thinking instrument and an instrument of thought, but of exclusively rational and calculating thought." In Eric Weil, *Philosophie Politique* (Paris: Vrin, 1956), 152. My translation.

18 Scott, *Organizations*, 34–37.

19 Max Weber, "Bureaucracy," in *From Max Weber: Essays in Sociology*, ed. Hans Heinrich Gerth and C. Wright Mills (New York: Oxford University Press, 1979), 196–198.

20 Ibid., 208.

21 This aspect of bureaucracy is discussed in Pressman and Wildavsky, *Implementation*, 132–133. On the transaction cost approach to the study of organizations, see Oliver E. Williamson, "The Economics of Organization: The Transaction Cost Approach," *American Journal of Sociology* 87, no. 3 (1981).

22 The relation between the rational-legal structure of bureaucracy and its instrumental efficiency is a matter of controversy in the interpretation of Weber. According to early interpreters, such as Peter Blau, Weber wanted to claim that a bureaucracy's rational-legal character (its formal rationality) was directly responsible for its means-end efficiency (its practical rationality). This reading has, in many respects, been the most influential in organization theory. See Peter M. Blau and Marshall W. Meyer, *Bureaucracy in Modern Society*, 3rd ed. (New York: Random House, 1987), 22; Scott, *Organizations*, 48. Later interpreters have argued, however, that this reading is reductive. According to Stephen Kalberg, for instance, Weber was keenly aware that rationalization processes occur on different dimensions, and that these do not necessarily go hand in hand. Formal rationality does not always yield greater efficiency; it can, in fact, prove to be a constraint on efficiency. See Stephen Kalberg, "Max Weber's Types of Rationality," *American Journal of Sociology* 85, no. 5 (1980).

23 Weber, "Bureaucracy," 215–216.

24 Ibid., 228. See also his discussion of "dehumanization" on pages 215–216.

25 Scott, *Organizations*, 47.

26 Herbert Simon, *Administrative Behavior*, 3rd ed. (New York: Free Press, 1976), 45–60.

27 This is a thought usually attributed to the later Wittgenstein. For a discussion of Wittgenstein's contribution to our understanding of rules, see Charles Taylor, "To Follow a Rule," in *Bourdieu: Critical Perspectives*, ed. Craig Calhoun, Edward LiPuma, and Moishe Postone (Cambridge, UK: Polity Press, 1993).

28 The example comes from Janet Vinzant Denhardt and Lane Crothers, *Street-Level Leadership: Discretion and Legitimacy in Front-Line Public Service* (Washington, DC: Georgetown University Press, 1998), 41.

29 As Hart puts it, "Particular fact-situations do not await us already marked off from each other, and labeled as instances of the general rule, the application of which is in question; nor can the rule itself step forward to claim its own instances." Hart, *The Concept of Law*, 126.

30 The example comes from Friedman, *The Legal System*, 31.

31 Ibid.

32 I have examined elsewhere how this logic can lead us astray in thinking about questions of responsibility. See Bernardo Zacka, "Adhocracy, Security and Responsibility: Revisiting Abu Ghraib a Decade Later," *Contemporary Political Theory* 15, no. 1 (2016); Steven C. Caton and Bernardo Zacka, "Abu Ghraib, the Security Apparatus, and the Performativity of Power," *American Ethnologist* 37, no. 2 (2010).

33 Daniel P. Carpenter, *The Forging of Bureaucratic Autonomy: Reputations, Networks, and Policy Innovation in Executive Agencies, 1862–1928* (Princeton, NJ: Princeton University Press, 2001), 4.

34 Epstein and O'Halloran compare the legislature's decision to delegate authority to the "make or buy" decision of firms in the private sector. Legislators can rely on their own staff to write policy in great detail or can "buy" policy by giving agencies the discretion to fill up the details themselves. See David Epstein and Sharyn O'Halloran, *Delegating Powers: A Transaction Cost Politics Approach to Policy Making under Separate Powers* (Cambridge: Cambridge University Press, 1999).

35 Hugh Heclo, "Issue Networks and the Executive Establishment," in *The New American Political System*, ed. Anthony King (Washington, DC: American Enterprise Institute, 1978), esp. 98–105. While these arrangements have existed for a long time, they have become the norm today, with systems of governance increasingly relying on interorganizational linkages. See R. A. W. Rhodes, "The New Governance: Governing without Government," *Political Studies* 44, no. 4 (1996); Kenneth J. Meier and Laurence J. O'Toole, *Bureaucracy in a Democratic State: A Governance Perspective* (Baltimore: Johns Hopkins University Press, 2006), 1–20.

36 It is by establishing procedures to determine how these consultations take place, and in particular who gets a seat at the table, that Congress manages to retain some measure of control over the behavior of public agencies even when it delegates a substantial amount of authority to them. On the importance of these "ex-ante" forms of control, see Mathew D. McCubbins, Roger G. Noll, and Barry R. Weingast, "Administrative Procedures as Instruments of Political Control," *Journal of Law, Economics, and Organization* 3, no. 2 (1987); and Terry M. Moe, "Delegation, Control, and the Study of Public Bureaucracy," *The Forum* 10, no. 2 (2012): 8–10.

37 See Peter H. Aranson, Ernest Gellhorn, and Glen O. Robinson, "A Theory of Legislative Delegation," *Cornell Law Review* 68, no. 1 (1982–1983); John D. Huber and Charles R. Shipan, *Deliberate Discretion? The Institutional Foundations of Bureaucratic Autonomy* (New York: Cambridge University Press, 2002).

38 See Kenneth A. Shepsle, "The Strategy of Ambiguity: Uncertainty and Electoral Competition," *The American Political Science Review* 66, no. 2 (1972).

39 See Morris P. Fiorina, *Congress: Keystone of the Washington Establishment* (New Haven, CT: Yale University Press, 1977).

40 These factors led Theodore Lowi to observe that "the typical American politician displaces and defers and delegates conflict where possible; he squarely faces conflict only when he must." See Theodore J. Lowi, *The End of Liberalism: The Second Republic of the United States*, 2nd ed. (New York: Norton, 1979), 55.

41 The threat of bureaucratic capture is at the heart of Lowi's critique of "interest-group liberalism." Lowi is concerned that Congress has reneged on its responsibilities by delegating too much authority to administrative agencies which have

become captive to special interest groups. By weighing in on agency decision-making directly, these groups are able to circumvent the more public and general legislative process that ought to take place in Congress. See ibid.

42 See Jerry L. Mashaw, *Bureaucratic Justice: Managing Social Security Disability Claims* (New Haven, CT: Yale University Press, 1983), 20.

43 The Internet has also contributed to changing the character of citizens' encounters with street-level bureaucrats. For some tasks, instant messaging has replaced face-to-face interactions. On e-government and the transformation of service delivery, see Andrew Chadwick and Christopher May, "Interaction between States and Citizens in the Age of the Internet: 'E-Government' in the United States, Britain, and the European Union," *Governance* 16, no. 2 (2003); John Clayton Thomas and Gregory Streib, "The New Face of Government: Citizen-Initiated Contacts in the Era of E-Government," *Journal of Public Administration Research and Theory* 13, no. 1 (2003); and Darrell M. West, "E-Government and the Transformation of Service Delivery and Citizen Attitudes," *Public Administration Review* 64, no. 1 (2004).

44 Several barriers prevent clients from making legal claims on public service agencies. Such clients must first be aware that their rights have been violated; they must know that a remedy is available; they must have the resources available to pursue such a remedy; and they must expect the (potential) benefits associated with such a remedy to outweigh the (certain) costs. See Joel F. Handler, *Protecting the Social Service Client: Legal and Structural Controls on Official Discretion* (New York: Academic Press, 1979), 48.

45 I use the term *direct* control here, because accepting the desirability of street-level discretion does not condemn us to giving frontline officials free rein. It forces us, rather, to look for alternative ways to inform how street-level bureaucrats exercise their discretion. I show in later chapters that this involves paying attention to their moral dispositions and to the organizational culture in which they evolve.

46 James Q. Wilson, *Varieties of Police Behavior: The Management of Law and Order in Eight Communities* (Cambridge, MA: Harvard University Press, 1968), 16–22.

47 Ibid., 22.

48 *Bureaucracy: What Government Agencies Do and Why They Do It* (New York: Basic Books, 1989), 170.

49 Ibid.

50 See ibid.; George L. Kelling and James Q. Wilson, "Broken Windows: The Police and Neighborhood Safety," *The Atlantic Monthly,* March 1982; Samuel Walker and Charles M. Katz, *The Police in America,* 4th ed. (New York: McGraw-Hill, 2002), chap. 7.

51 Lipsky, *Street-Level Bureaucracy,* 165.

52 For another example of how ambiguous goals might enable street-level bureaucrats to more effectively achieve desired policy outcomes, see Michael J. Piore

and Andrew Schrank, "Toward Managed Flexibility: The Revival of Labour Inspection in the Latin World," *International Labour Review* 147, no. 1–23 (2008).

53   There are diverging interpretations over how weak or radical value incommensurability is in the work of Berlin. See Joshua Cherniss and Henry Hardy, "Isaiah Berlin," in *The Stanford Encyclopedia of Philosophy*, Winter 2016 ed., ed. Edward N. Zalta, https://plato.stanford.edu/archives/win2016/entries/berlin/ (accessed March 15, 2017).

54   I take the term from Mashaw, *Bureaucratic Justice*, 88–97.

55   See, for instance, Lipsky, *Street-Level Bureaucracy*, 27–39.

56   See the essays "The Institutional Turn in Professional Ethics" and "Hospital Ethics" in Thompson, *Restoring Responsibility*, 267–289.

57   For an early statement of such a view, see Charles Fried, "Rights and Health Care: Beyond Equity and Efficiency," *The New England Journal of Medicine* 293, no. 5 (1975): 244.

58   Mashaw, *Bureaucratic Justice*, 52.

59   Ibid.

60   Ibid., 53.

61   "Compliance Manual," ed. The U.S. Equal Employment Opportunity Commission (1995), Section 902: Definition of the Term Disability.

62   This discussion is indebted to *Bureaucratic Justice*, 61–64.

63   Lipsky, *Street-Level Bureaucracy*, 15; Denhardt and Crothers, *Street-Level Leadership*, 41.

64   This example is adapted from *Street-Level Leadership*, 39–40.

65   See Henry Mintzberg and Alexandra McHugh, "Strategy Formation in an Adhocracy," *Administrative Science Quarterly* 30, no. 2 (1985).

66   Individual bureaucrats can also shape the nature of the bureaucratic response by "framing" the environment in a way that is congenial to their interests. Michel Crozier has shown that control over the loci of uncertainty in an organization—and hence, the right to use "discretion"—is tantamount to power. Spaces of discretion are not simply a necessity imposed on organizations by their environment; they can also be wrested away by lower-level bureaucrats seeking to expand their influence. See Michel Crozier, *Le Phénomène Bureaucratique* (Paris: Seuil, 1963), 176–214.

67   See Hart, *The Concept of Law*, 129–130.

68   See Oded Na'aman, "The Checkpoint: Terror, Power, and Cruelty," *Boston Review* 37, no. 4 (2012); Zacka, "Adhocracy, Security and Responsibility."

69   Sean Gailmard and John W. Patty, *Learning While Governing: Expertise and Accountability in the Executive Branch* (Chicago: University of Chicago Press, 2013).

70   See William G. Ouchi, "Markets, Bureaucracies, and Clans," *Administrative Science Quarterly* 25, no. 1 (1980).

71   Thompson, *Restoring Responsibility*, 56.

72   Ibid.

2. THREE PATHOLOGIES

1   The most common models of decision-making in organization theory are based on rational choice. These models construe decision-making as a choice between a range of alternatives. They assume that the agent will pick the option that best advances his or her established preferences, while acknowledging that the agent's rationality and attention may be limited. For an overview, see James G. March, *A Primer on Decision Making: How Decisions Happen* (New York: Free Press, 1994), 1–55. Much of the literature in contemporary moral philosophy is similarly concerned with the moment of choice and with the process of moral reasoning that immediately precedes it. It seeks to equip individuals with normative principles that they can use to decide among various courses of action. This is perhaps most evident in the vast literature on "trolley problems" in which an agent is presented with a constrained set of options. Philosophers rely on these controlled thought experiments to tease out our moral intuitions and to develop moral principles that can serve to guide conduct in other circumstances. See, for instance, Judith Jarvis Thomson, "The Trolley Problem," *The Yale Law Journal* 94, no. 6 (1985). For an account of how the trolley problem came to be of such prominence in moral philosophy, see David Edmonds, *Would You Kill the Fat Man? The Trolley Problem and What Your Answer Tells Us about Right and Wrong* (Princeton, NJ: Princeton University Press, 2014).

2   By shifting the focus of inquiry from decisions to dispositions, I build on the work of James March. As an alternative to theories of rational choice, March has suggested that decision-making in organizations often follows a "logic of appropriateness." Decision-makers are imagined to ask three questions: (1) What kind of situation is this? (2) What kind of person am I? and (3) What should a person like me do in a situation such as this? See March, *A Primer on Decision Making*, 57–102; James G. March and Johan P. Olsen, "The Logic of Appropriateness," in *The Oxford Handbook of Public Policy,* ed. Michael Moran, Martin Rein, and Robert E. Goodin (Oxford: Oxford University Press, 2006).

The "logic of appropriateness" puts more emphasis than the rational choice model on how decision-makers construe the situation before them and how their identities and attitudes inform the decision-making process. Organizational ethicists have seized upon this framework to argue that the nature of decision-making depends in part on whether individuals think they are faced with an ethical dilemma or not. If decision-makers construe a decision as "ethical," they will likely engage in moral reasoning. If they construe the decision differently (say, as "legal" or "personal"), they will likely resort to other modes of reasoning. See Ann E. Tenbrunsel and Kristin Smith-Crowe, "Ethical Decision Making: Where We've Been and Where We're Going," *The Academy of Management Annals* 2, no. 1 (2008).

My argument here seeks to develop these insights in two ways. I aim to show, first, that we need to go beyond the dichotomous opposition between "ethical decision frames" and "nonethical decision frames," between "moral awareness" and "absence of moral awareness." We cannot simply oppose the moral to the nonmoral; we also need to be attuned to the existence of a range of "moralities." The moral dispositions I describe in this chapter are meant to show that there are multiple ways of being "morally aware" and that these have different consequences for how agents use their discretionary power. I also aim to show that moral dispositions do not just come into play after a situation has been construed (as an answer to the question "What kind of person am I?"), but also contribute to shaping how the situation is construed in the first place.

3 Maynard-Moody and Musheno, *Cops, Teachers, Counselors.*

4 Deviation from the routine is a condition that must generally obtain for a story to be worth telling. See ibid., 32.

5 Ibid., 97.

6 Ibid.

7 See Michael Herzfeld, *The Social Production of Indifference: Exploring the Symbolic Roots of Western Bureaucracy* (Chicago: University of Chicago Press, 1992), 162–167. There is also an asymmetry between the urgency with which a client needs services and the time it takes for a bureaucrat to deliver them. As Everett Hughes has observed, "One's man routine of work is made up of the emergencies of other people." See Everett C. Hughes, "Mistakes at Work," *The Canadian Journal of Economics and Political Science* 17, no. 3 (1951): 320. Javier Auyero goes further, characterizing the extended periods of time that those seeking social services spend waiting as temporal processes "in and through which political subordination is reproduced." See Javier Auyero, *Patients of the State: The Politics of Waiting in Argentina* (Durham, NC: Duke University Press, 2012), 2.

8 Tacit knowledge is knowledge that cannot be easily formalized or verbalized. See Michael Polanyi, *Personal Knowledge: Towards a Post-Critical Philosophy* (London: Routledge, 1958).

9 Dubois, *The Bureaucrat and the Poor,* 98–100.

10 Maynard-Moody and Musheno, *Cops, Teachers, Counselors,* 98.

11 Jeffrey Prottas calls this process of categorization "slotting." See Jeffrey Prottas, "The Power of the Street-Level Bureaucrat in Public Service Agencies," *Urban Affairs Quarterly* 13, no. 3 (1978).

12 Bernard Williams, *Ethics and the Limits of Philosophy* (Cambridge, MA: Harvard University Press, 1985), 140.

13 This construction will, in turn, serve to justify the actions of the bureaucrat and to throw a positive light on them.

14 Maynard-Moody and Musheno, *Cops, Teachers, Counselors,* 98–99.

15 Ibid., 99.

16 On the importance of retrospective sense-making in organizational behavior, see Karl E. Weick, *Sensemaking in Organizations* (Thousand Oaks, CA: Sage Publications, 1995).

17 See Brehm and Gates, *Working, Shirking, and Sabotage,* 47–75.

18 Pierre Lascoumes, "Normes Juridiques et Mise en Oeuvre des Politiques Publiques," *L'Année Sociologique* 40, no. 3 (1990).

19 For studies of street-level bureaucracy that engage with these questions, see Watkins-Hayes, *The New Welfare Bureaucrats;* and Dubois, *The Bureaucrat and the Poor.* Proponents of representative bureaucracy believe that if the demographic characteristics of bureaucrats matched those of the client population, bureaucratic outcomes would better track the needs and interests of clients. See, for instance, Sally Coleman Selden, *The Promise of Representative Bureaucracy: Diversity and Responsiveness in a Government Agency* (Armonk, NY: M. E. Sharpe, 1997); Lael R. Keiser et al., "Lipstick and Logarithms: Gender, Institutional Context, and Representative Bureaucracy," *American Political Science Review* 96, no. 03 (2002); Kenneth J. Meier, Robert D. Wrinkle, and J. L. Polinard, "Representative Bureaucracy and Distributional Equity: Addressing the Hard Question," *The Journal of Politics* 61, no. 04 (1999).

20 See, for example, Lauren J. Silver, "Spaces of Encounter: Public Bureaucracy and the Making of Client Identities," *Ethos* 38, no. 3 (2010).

21 See, for instance, Tristan Loo, "How to Make an Inflexible Bureaucrat See You as a Person," http://www.technoworldinc.com/negotiation/how-to-make-an-inflexible-bureaucrat-see-you-as-a-person-t20919.0.html (accessed March 15, 2017).

22 Maynard-Moody and Musheno, *Cops, Teachers, Counselors,* 139.

23 The counselor refers to himself in the third person. Ibid.

24 Ibid.

25 Ibid., 139–140.

26 Ibid., 141.

27 Ibid., 142.

28 See notes 1 and 2. Scholars working in the tradition of virtue ethics, with whom I engage in Chapter 3, are a notable exception.

29 In other words, dispositions set the grounds on the basis of which bureaucrats will then engage in moral reasoning and ethical decision-making. A more extreme claim would be that moral dispositions effectively determine the decisions bureaucrats take by shaping their quick evaluative intuitions—the instant approval or disapproval they feel when interacting with clients—while moral reasoning comes in only after the fact to offer a post hoc rationalization of the decision that has already been taken. See Jonathan Haidt, "The Emotional Dog and Its Rational Tail: A Social Intuitionist Approach to Moral Judgment," *Psychological Review* 108, no. 4 (2001).

30 This has become particularly the case since the proliferation of means-tested benefits added a regulatory component to jobs that used to be primarily about service provision and people processing. I am grateful to Joe Heath for pointing this out.

31 In his classic study of the police, James Q. Wilson distinguishes between three styles of policing—legalistic, watchman, and service—that come close, respec-

tively, to what I have called "indifference," "enforcement," and caregiving." The typology I adopt also integrates, within a single framework, two sets of distinctions put forth by Evelyn Brodkin and Celeste Watkins-Hayes with respect to welfare workers. Brodkin distinguishes between "helpers" ("caregivers" in my typology) and "enforcers," while Watkins-Hayes distinguishes between "social workers" ("caregivers" in my typology) and "efficiency engineers" (a hybrid between "indifferents" and "enforcers"). See Wilson, *Varieties of Police Behavior;* Evelyn Z. Brodkin, "Inside the Welfare Contract: Discretion and Accountability in State Welfare Administration," *Social Service Review* 71, no. 1 (1997); Watkins-Hayes, *The New Welfare Bureaucrats.*

There are, of course, many other ways to draw distinctions between street-level bureaucrats. The choice of a typology depends in large part on the concerns and questions with which one approaches the material. Sean Gailmard and John Patty distinguish bureaucrats, for instance, on the basis of how much they care about the content of the policy they are meant to enact, differentiating between "slackers" (who are policy-indifferent) and zealots (who are policy-motivated). John Brehm and Scott Gates put the accent on how dedicated bureaucrats are to implementing public policy, distinguishing between those who "work," "shirk," or "sabotage." More recently, Zachary Oberfield has distinguished bureaucrats on the basis of their attitudes to rules (those who go "by the book" or not) and their attitudes to clients (those who view client's problems as caused by structural factors, or by their character). Oberfield's study differs from the other two by being longitudinal: it traces the development of dispositions over time. See Gailmard and Patty, *Learning While Governing;* Brehm and Gates, *Working, Shirking, and Sabotage;* Zachary W. Oberfield, *Becoming Bureaucrats: Socialization at the Front Lines of Government Service* (Philadelphia: University of Pennsylvania Press, 2014).

32 This is what psychologists call "confirmation bias." For a review of the empirical literature, see Raymond S. Nickerson, "Confirmation Bias: A Ubiquitous Phenomenon in Many Guises," *Review of General Psychology* 2, no. 2 (1998).

33 On this point, see Oberfield, *Becoming Bureaucrats,* 9.

34 It would have been possible, however, to collect testimonies that are similar in spirit from workers within a single agency. This is not to deny that there might be an elective affinity between certain agencies and certain role conceptions and dispositions (e.g., between the police and "enforcers," or between counseling and "caregivers"), but this affinity only means that workers in these agencies are, *on average,* closer to one of the three poles. It is nevertheless common to find, within a single agency, individual workers or groups of workers who have different approaches to the role. For examples of intra-agency variation, see Wilson, *Varieties of Police Behavior;* Watkins-Hayes, *The New Welfare Bureaucrats;* Dubois, *The Bureaucrat and the Poor.*

35 Alexis Spire, *Accueillir ou Reconduire: Enquête sur les Guichets de l'Immigration* (Paris: Raisons d'Agir, 2008), 77. My translation.

36 Maynard-Moody and Musheno, *Cops, Teachers, Counselors*, 61–62.

37 William Ker Muir, *Police: Streetcorner Politicians* (Chicago: University of Chicago Press, 1977), 69–70.

38 For a broader discussion of what political theory can gain from closer attention to negative moral experiences and to the moral psychologies associated with them, see Jonathan Allen, "The Place of Negative Morality in Political Theory," *Political Theory* 29, no. 3 (2001).

39 I am grateful to Josh Cherniss for pointing this out.

40 This is how the term is generally used by organizations such as Transparency International. See http://www.transparency.org/what-is-corruption/#define, accessed November 24, 2015. The study of corruption has more recently taken an institutional turn. See Dennis F. Thompson, *Ethics in Congress: From Individual to Institutional Corruption* (Washington, DC: Brookings Institutions, 1995); Lawrence Lessig, "'Institutional Corruption' Defined," *The Journal of Law, Medicine & Ethics* 41, no. 3 (2013).

41 Vincent Dubois observes that individualization (along with responsibilization) has become a keyword of social policy in the past few decades, especially in Europe. See Vincent Dubois, "Towards a Critical Policy Ethnography: Lessons from Fieldwork on Welfare Control in France," *Critical Policy Studies* 3, no. 2 (2009): 224–225. The case for responsiveness, empathy, and compassion in the delivery of public services has been made compellingly by feminist theorists writing on the "ethics of care." Such theorists have also pointed out the dangers of such an ethic—namely, its capacity to foster dependence. For a more modest conception of responsiveness in public administration, with a focus on the capacity of the bureaucrat to listen actively, see Camilla Stivers, "The Listening Bureaucrat: Responsiveness in Public Administration," *Public Administration Review* 54, no. 4 (1994).

42 For a recent study in political science that treats the impartial exercise of public power as the quintessential measure of the "quality of government," see Bo Rothstein and Jan Teorell, "What Is Quality of Government? A Theory of Impartial Government Institutions," *Governance* 21, no. 2 (2008). One of the features that distinguishes public organizations from private sector ones is a concern for providing treatment on the basis of "universal" rules that are applied impartially to all. See Michael J. Piore, "Beyond Markets: Sociology, Street-Level Bureaucracy, and the Management of the Public Sector," *Regulation & Governance* 5, no. 1 (2011): 152–153.

43 Tom Tyler and his coauthors have found, for instance, that one of the main factors shaping public support for the police is procedural fairness—a mixture between impartial application of the law and respectful treatment. See Tyler, *Why People Obey the Law*; Sunshine and Tyler, "The Role of Procedural Justice and Legitimacy in Shaping Public Support for Policing." The importance of equal respect and concern is also a key theme in the literature on relational egalitarianism. See Elizabeth Anderson, "What Is the Point of Equality?," *Ethics*

109, no. 2 (1999); Jonathan Wolff, "Fairness, Respect, and the Egalitarian Ethos," *Philosophy & Public Affairs* 27, no. 2 (1998); Samuel Scheffler, "What Is Egalitarianism?," *Philosophy & Public Affairs* 31, no. 1 (2003); Timothy Hinton, "Must Egalitarians Choose between Fairness and Respect?," *Philosophy & Public Affairs* 30, no. 1 (2001).

44 For the distinction between insulting and demeaning treatment, see Wolff, "Fairness, Respect, and the Egalitarian Ethos," 107.

45 Ibid., 108.

46 Ibid., 109. Some scholars have suggested that the stigma of public disclosure is in part responsible for the underutilization of public services. See Yeheskel Hasenfeld, Jane A. Rafferty, and Mayer N. Zald, "The Welfare State, Citizenship, and Bureaucratic Encounters," *Annual Review of Sociology* 13 (1987): 401.

47 Wolff calls this a "shameful revelation."

48 In recent decades in the United States, the fostering of "self-sufficiency" among clients has become a mantra in the public discourse on welfare reform. For a critical assessment of how "self-sufficiency" is presented as an answer to the problem of "dependence" and for an ethnographic exploration of how front-line workers give countenance to the notion, see Morgen, "The Agency of Welfare Workers." The same phenomenon is happening in France under the heading of "responsibilization." See Dubois, "Towards a Critical Policy Ethnography."

49 See Arthur Applbaum, *Ethics for Adversaries* (Princeton, NJ: Princeton University Press, 1999), 64; Robert E. Goodin, *Utilitarianism as a Public Philosophy* (Cambridge: Cambridge University Press, 1995), 8–9.

50 The idea that street-level bureaucrats may be morally obligated to exclude reasons for action that one would otherwise need to include can be captured by saying that official roles sometimes provide "exclusionary reasons," or "a second order reason to refrain from acting on some reason." See Joseph Raz, "Reasons for Action, Decisions and Norms," *Mind* 84, no. 336 (1975): 487.

51 This is one of the distinguishing characteristics of the welfare state as compared to other systems of welfare provision (e.g., private philanthropy, public charity). The actions of philanthropists are voluntary, and likewise, under the Poor Laws (old and new), the dispensation of public assistance was at the discretion of the officials concerned. In the welfare state, on the contrary, the actions of officials are "compulsory": they are meant to follow *established rules* and to dispense services to which recipients are entitled *as a matter of right*. It is to insulate recipients from the potentially arbitrary decisions of frontline officials that rule-making is exercised at a safe distance from the point of service provision. See Goodin, *Reasons for Welfare: The Political Theory of the Welfare State*, 11–12.

52 Weber, "Politics as Vocation," 95.

53 Applbaum, *Ethics for Adversaries*, 64.

54 Weber, "Bureaucracy," 215–216.

55 Dubois, *The Bureaucrat and the Poor*, 123–131. Withdrawal is a strategy frequently recommended in self-help textbooks for professionals in the human

services. See, for example, Thomas M. Skovholt and Michelle Trotter-Mathison, *The Resilient Practitioner: Burnout Prevention and Self-Care Strategies for Counselors, Therapists, Teachers, and Health Professionals* (New York: Routledge, 2010).

56 See Roy F. Baumeister and John Tierney, *Willpower: Rediscovering the Greatest Human Strength* (New York: Penguin Press, 2011), 88–107.

57 Weber, "Politics as Vocation," 115.

58 Antonio Damasio has argued that emotions like empathy can draw our attention to moral issues; without them, we would be left with a "decision-making landscape [that is] hopelessly flat." See Antonio R. Damasio, *Descartes' Error: Emotion, Reason, and the Human Brain* (New York: G. P. Putnam, 1994).

59 For an illustration of how maddeningly difficult it can be to navigate the world of social services, see Andrea Campbell, *Trapped in America's Safety Net: One Family's Struggle* (Chicago: University of Chicago Press, 2014).

60 Elizabeth Anderson makes a similar point in her attack on luck egalitarianism. See Anderson, "What Is the Point of Equality?," 305.

61 The critique of the state as a "father figure" that effectively maintains women in a state of dependence is a recurrent theme in feminist theory. Dependence can be perpetuated through the provision of care. For a critical review of this literature, see Lynne Haney, "Homeboys, Babies, Men in Suits: The State and the Reproduction of Male Dominance," *American Sociological Review* 61, no. 5 (1996): 760–761.

62 Michel Foucault has described as "pastoral power" precisely this kind of paternalistic power that provides individualized treatment and can come to be a source of personal dependence. See Michel Foucault, *Security, Territory, Population: Lectures at the Collège de France, 1977–78*, trans. Graham Burchell (New York: Palgrave Macmillan, 2007), 115–165.

63 The extent of the potential dependence does not only hinge, of course, on the specific disposition of the bureaucrat and on how the client responds to it. It also depends on the scope of the bureaucrat's discretion and on whether the client has easily available "exit" options or not. See Hasenfeld, Rafferty, and Zald, "The Welfare State, Citizenship, and Bureaucratic Encounters."

64 Michael Lipsky makes a similar point. See *Street-Level Bureaucracy*, 151.

65 This worry is expressed in Friedrich A. von Hayek, *The Constitution of Liberty* (Chicago: University of Chicago Press, 1960), 95–97. See the related discussion in Anderson, "What Is the Point of Equality?," 310.

66 Applbaum, *Ethics for Adversaries*, 63.

67 This is one of the prime characteristics of Ker Muir's "professional" policeman. See Ker Muir, *Police: Streetcorner Politicians*.

68 Wolff, "Fairness, Respect, and the Egalitarian Ethos."

69 Ibid. For a similar argument in favor of erring on the side of generosity, see Goodin, *Reasons for Welfare: The Political Theory of the Welfare State*, 220–221.

70 This is one of the reasons why racial minorities are disproportionately targeted by police stops. The authors of a recent study argue that when conducting investigatory stops (of which stop-and-frisk is an example), "officers are to stop as

many people as possible so as to be able to investigate them more closely. . . . But because officers cannot possibly stop all drivers or pedestrians and scrutinize all communities, they must focus on some, and, in the context of enduring racial stereotypes of black criminality and violence, they tend to target racial minorities and their neighborhoods." See Charles R. Epp, Steven Maynard-Moody, and Donald P. Haider-Markel, *Pulled Over: How Police Stops Define Race and Citizenship* (Chicago: University of Chicago Press, 2014), 8–9.

3. A GYMNASTICS OF THE SELF

1 George Konrád, *The Case Worker*, trans. Paul Aston (New York: Penguin, 1987), 92.

2 Techniques of self-presentation are at the heart of Erving Goffman's interactionist sociology. See Erving Goffman, *The Presentation of Self in Everyday Life* (Garden City, NY: Doubleday, 1959). Palliative "coping" strategies are the subject of a voluminous self-help literature aimed at public service personnel and at those working in the helping professions. See, for instance, Skovholt and Trotter-Mathison, *The Resilient Practitioner*; Françoise Mathieu, *The Compassion Fatigue Workbook* (New York: Routledge, 2011).

3 See Pierre Hadot, *Qu'est-Ce Que la Philosophie Antique?* (Paris: Gallimard, 1995); *Exercices Spirituels et Philosophie Antique* (Paris: Etudes Augustiniennes, 1981); *La Philosophie Comme Manière de Vivre*, ed. Jeannie Carlier and Arnold Ira Davidson (Paris: Albin Michel, 2001); Michel Foucault, *Technologies of the Self: A Seminar with Michel Foucault* (Amherst: University of Massachusetts Press, 1988); *The Hermeneutics of the Subject: Lectures at the Collège de France, 1981–82*, ed. Francois Ewald and Alessandro Fontana (New York: Palgrave Macmillan, 2005).

4 See Evelyn Z. Brodkin, "Reflections on Street-Level Bureaucracy: Past, Present, and Future," *Public Administration Review* 72, no. 6 (2012): 945.

5 Hannah Arendt, *Eichmann in Jerusalem: A Report on the Banality of Evil* (New York: Penguin Books, 2006), 26.

6 See Raul Hilberg, *The Destruction of the European Jews* (Chicago: Quadrangle Books, 1961), 639–662; Zygmunt Bauman, *Modernity and the Holocaust* (Ithaca, NY: Cornell University Press, 1989). For a more recent discussion, see Jonathan Glover, *Humanity: A Moral History of the Twentieth Century* (New Haven, CT: Yale University Press, 2000), 328–354. For a critical review of this literature, see Christopher R. Browning, *Ordinary Men: Reserve Police Battalion 101 and the Final Solution in Poland* (New York: Harper Perennial, 1998), 159–190.

7 Merton, "Bureaucratic Structure and Personality."

8 See William Whyte, *The Organization Man* (New York: Simon & Schuster, 1956).

9 See Albert Bandura, "Moral Disengagement in the Perpetration of Inhumanities," *Personality and Social Psychology Review* 3, no. 3 (1999): 198.

10 See Dennis F. Thompson, "Moral Responsibility of Public Officials: The Problem of Many Hands," *The American Political Science Review* 74, no. 4 (1980).

11 Glover, *Humanity*, 22–25.

12 See Herbert C. Kelman, "Violence without Moral Restraint: Reflections on the Dehumanization of Victims and Victimizers," *Journal of Social Issues* 29, no. 4 (1973).

13 Charles R. Figley, "Compassion Fatigue as Secondary Traumatic Stress Disorder: An Overview," in *Compassion Fatigue*, ed. Charles R. Figley (New York: Routledge, 1995).

14 In the Milgram experiments, participants were much more likely to comply with the experimenter's directives to apply increasing electric shocks to a confederate once that person was no longer within physical reach but had been placed away in another room. Stanley Milgram, Obedience to Authority: An Experimental View (New York: Harper Perennial, 2004).

15 See, for instance, Browning, *Ordinary Men;* Ingo Müller, *Hitler's Justice: The Courts of the Third Reich* (Cambridge, MA: Harvard University Press, 1991).

16 As Albert Bandura points out, a rarely noted but striking result from Milgram's experiments is that "most people refuse to behave cruelly, even under unrelenting authoritarian commands, if the situation is personalized by having them inflict pain by direct personal action rather than remotely and if they see the suffering that they cause." Bandura, "Moral Disengagement in the Perpetration of Inhumanities," 202.

17 Leon Festinger, *A Theory of Cognitive Dissonance* (Evanston, IL: Row, Peterson, 1957). For a more recent restatement and defense of the theory of cognitive dissonance, which integrates various advances in the field and shows how the theory evolved in response to several waves of criticism, see Joel Cooper, *Cognitive Dissonance: Fifty Years of a Classic Theory* (Thousand Oaks, CA: Sage Publications, 2007).

18 Elliot Aronson, "The Theory of Cognitive Dissonance: A Current Perspective," in *Advances in Experimental Social Psychology*, ed. Leonard Berkowitz (New York: Academic Press, 1969), 2–3.

19 Philip Zimbardo, *The Lucifer Effect: Understanding How Good People Turn Evil* (New York: Random House, 2007), 220.

20 Aronson, "The Theory of Cognitive Dissonance."

21 Claude M. Steele and Thomas J. Liu, "Dissonance Processes as Self-Affirmation," *Journal of Personality and Social Psychology* 45, no. 1 (1983); Claude Steele, "The Psychology of Self-Affirmation: Sustaining the Integrity of the Self," in *Advances in Experimental Social Psychology*, ed. Leonard Berkowitz (San Diego, CA: Academic Press, 1988). For a more recent overview of self-affirmation theory, see David K. Sherman and Geoffrey L. Cohen, "The Psychology of Self-Defense: Self-Affirmation Theory," in *Advances in Experimental Social Psychology*, Vol. 38, ed. Mark Zanna (San Diego, CA: Academic Press, 2006).

22 See Sherman and Cohen, "The Psychology of Self-Defense," 186.

23 Zimbardo, *The Lucifer Effect*, 220.

24 Darwyn E. Linder, Joel Cooper, and Edward E. Jones, "Decision Freedom as a Determinant of the Role of Incentive Magnitude in Attitude Change," *Journal of Personality and Social Psychology* 6, no. 3 (1967).

25 For an influential application of this insight to organization theory, see Karl E. Weick, *The Social Psychology of Organizing* (Reading, MA: Addison-Wesley, 1969).

26 Lipsky, *Street-Level Bureaucracy*, 140–156.

27 Ibid., 144–146.

28 For an overview of the literature on job burnout, most of which is concerned with the experience of workers in the human services, see Wilmar B. Schaufeli, Michael P. Leiter, and Christina Maslach, "Burnout: 35 Years of Research and Practice," *Career Development International* 14, no. 3 (2009). For more tailored articles that examine burnout in social work, teaching, and the police, see, respectively, Chris Lloyd, Robert King, and Lesley Chenoweth, "Social Work, Stress and Burnout: A Review," *Journal of Mental Health* 11, no. 3 (2002); Mei-Lin Chang, "An Appraisal Perspective of Teacher Burnout: Examining the Emotional Work of Teachers," *Educational Psychology Review* 21, no. 3 (2009); Cedric Alexander, "Police Psychological Burnout and Trauma," in *Police Trauma: Psychological Aftermath of Civilian Combat*, ed. John M. Violanti and Douglas Paton (Springfield, IL: Charles C Thomas, 1999). On the relationship between burnout and turnover or intention to leave, see Michàl E. Mor Barak, Jan A. Nissly, and Amy Levin, "Antecedents to Retention and Turnover among Child Welfare, Social Work, and Other Human Service Employees: What Can We Learn from Past Research? A Review and Metanalysis," *Social Service Review* 75, no. 4 (2001).

29 On the notion of "doubling," see Robert Jay Lifton, *The Nazi Doctors: Medical Killing and the Psychology of Genocide* (New York: Basic Books, 1986).

30 Reductive dispositions are instances of "adaptive preference formation" (although the term "adaptive role conception" might be more appropriate here)—a phenomenon also known as *sour grapes*. See Jon Elster, *Sour Grapes: Studies in the Subversion of Rationality* (Cambridge: Cambridge University Press, 1983).

31 On motivated reasoning, see Ziva Kunda, "The Case for Motivated Reasoning," *Psychological Bulletin* 108, no. 3 (1990). On confirmation biases, see Nickerson, "Confirmation Bias: A Ubiquitous Phenomenon in Many Guises."

32 This is not to deny, of course, that some people have temperaments that incline them more naturally toward indifference, caregiving, or enforcement, or that some are drawn to the public sector precisely because it would enable them to act as caregivers or enforcers. My point, rather, is that even those who do not start with such propensities may find themselves drawn toward them because of the pressures they encounter at work.

33 Arendt, *Eichmann in Jerusalem*, 26.

34 Ibid., 48–49.

35 Ibid., 49.

36 Many scholars have taken issue with Arendt's portrayal of Eichmann. Richard Wolin has been at the center of the latest wave of criticism. Drawing on the work of Bettina Stangneth, Wolin has argued that anti-Semitism played a far greater role in motivating Eichmann than Arendt acknowledges. According to Wolin, Eichmann's thoughtlessness is less the expression of a bureaucratic mentality than a theatrical performance strategically put on during the trial to downplay his responsibility. See Richard Wolin, "The Banality of Evil: The Demise of a Legend," *Jewish Review of Books*, Fall 2014.

37 Hannah Arendt, "Some Questions of Moral Philosophy," in *Responsibility and Judgment*, ed. Jerome Kohn (New York: Schocken Books, 2003).

38 Ibid., 92.

39 Ibid., 93.

40 Ibid., 90.

41 Ibid., 97.

42 It is not a coincidence that Arendt's argument only addresses the problems that emerge from indifference—problems that involve disengagement, loss of agency, and dilution of one's sense of personal responsibility. This is because her analysis presupposes that Eichmann was confronted with a bureaucratic environment that more or less resembled the one proposed by the rational systems perspective on organizations that I described in Chapter 1. If bureaucracies did work like that, and only made room for a narrow margin of technical discretion, then indifference would be the only adaptive response open to bureaucrats. The other two poles could not exist. As I have been at pains to argue, however, street-level bureaucracies make room for a more substantial margin of discretion, and hence for a wider array of possible pathologies.

43 This is a recurrent problem for political ethics under moral pluralism. In such conditions, character matters. As Andrew Sabl puts it, "those who by temperament can see the complexity of the world are better than those who cannot." The practices of the self approach I discuss later examines what it might take to retain such a temperament. See Andrew Sabl, "When Bad Things Happen from Good People (and Vice-Versa): Hume's Political Ethics of Revolution," *Polity* 35, no. 1 (2002): 92.

44 Arendt, "Some Questions of Moral Philosophy," 105.

45 They must make sure, to use more technical language, that their first-order desires are in line with their higher-order preferences. See Harry G. Frankfurt, "Freedom of the Will and the Concept of a Person," *The Journal of Philosophy* 68, no. 1 (1971). Philosophers have argued extensively about how to spell out the distinction between first-order desires and higher-order preferences, and about what it is that makes higher-order preferences authoritative (Are they simply desires? Or are they long-term evaluative judgments?). By and large, however, such debates have largely presupposed, until recently at least, that emotions and sentiments belong to the first-order realm, and that they must, ac-

cordingly, be summoned to justify themselves before the faculty of reason—which is identified with our true, autonomous self. See Michael L. Frazer, *The Enlightenment of Sympathy: Justice and the Moral Sentiments in the Eighteenth Century and Today* (Oxford: Oxford University Press, 2010), 7; and Michael Stocker, "How Emotions Reveal Value and Help Cure the Schizophrenia of Modern Ethical Theory," in *How Should One Live? Essays on the Virtues*, ed. Roger Crisp (Oxford: Oxford University Press, 1998).

46 For a discussion of the role of emotions in moral deliberation and in understanding others, see Martha Nussbaum, "The Discernment of Perception: An Aristotelian Conception of Private and Public Rationality," in *Love's Knowledge: Essays on Philosophy and Literature* (New York: Oxford University Press, 1990).

47 Aristotle, "Nicomachean Ethics," in *Introduction to Aristotle*, ed. Richard McKeon (New York: Random House, 1947), 331.

48 Martha C. Nussbaum, "Virtue Ethics: A Misleading Category?," *The Journal of Ethics* 3, no. 3 (1999): 170.

49 See John McDowell, "Virtue and Reason," *The Monist* 62, no. 3 (1979).

50 See Gilbert Harman, "Moral Philosophy Meets Social Psychology: Virtue Ethics and the Fundamental Attribution Error," *Proceedings of the Aristotelian Society* 99 (1999); John M. Doris and Stephen P. Stich, "As a Matter of Fact: Empirical Perspectices on Ethics," in *The Oxford Handbook of Contemporary Philosophy*, ed. Frank Jackson and Michael Smith (New York: Oxford University Press, 2005).

51 For a review of the relevant empirical literature, see Lee Ross and Richard E. Nisbett, *The Person and the Situation: Perspectives of Social Psychology* (New York: McGraw-Hill, 1991).

52 Even proponents of virtue ethics seem to acknowledge the need for less cognitively demanding strategies of adaptation. See Rachana Kamtekar, "Situationism and Virtue Ethics on the Content of Our Character," *Ethics* 114, no. 3 (2004).

53 On the distinction between "natural abilities" and "practical wisdom" as two components of the Aristotelian conception of virtue, see Susan Wolf, "Moral Psychology and the Unity of the Virtues," *Ratio*, no. 20 (2007): 152.

54 Maria Merritt, "Virtue Ethics and Situationist Personality Psychology," *Ethical Theory and Moral Practice* 3, no. 4 (2000): 372–375.

55 On this distinction, see Lawrence Blum, "Community and Virtue," in *How Should One Live? Essays on the Virtues*, ed. Roger Crisp (Oxford: Oxford University Press, 1998).

56 Merritt, "Virtue Ethics and Situationist Personality Psychology," 374–375. Merritt suggests that the ideal of "the motivational self-sufficiency of character" is more central to some conceptions of virtue (Aristotelian) than others (Humean). Not all proponents of virtue ethics believe that the possessors of virtue should be motivationally self-sufficient and impervious to their surroundings—Alasdair MacIntyre is a notable exception—but the view is, nonetheless, common. As Lawrence Blum puts it: "One gets the impression in much virtue writing that the

social dimension of virtue—expressed in a sustaining, content-providing, or worth-conferring role—is of little consequence. Perhaps this social dimension is not actually denied; and there may be a bow in its direction. Yet—in strong contrast to MacIntyre's work—the impression is given that the virtues and a life of virtue can be understood apart from particular forms of social life." Blum, "Community and Virtue," 235–236.

57 Merritt, "Virtue Ethics and Situationist Personality Psychology," 375–382; Kamtekar, "Situationism and Virtue Ethics on the Content of Our Character," 490. This reflects a recent shift of interest in empirical moral psychology away from "personological" approaches to the moral self and toward "social psychological" approaches to the moral self. See Benoit Monin and Alexander H. Jordan, "The Dynamic Moral Self: A Social Psychological Perspective," in *Moral Self, Identity and Character: Explorations in Moral Psychology*, ed. Darcia Narvaez and Daniel K. Lapsley (Cambridge: Cambridge University Press, 2009).

58 Scholars have found, for instance, that meditation increases compassionate responses (Condon et al.); that mindfulness helps professionals cope better with stressful working conditions (Irving et al.); and that it enhances our capacity to be attentive to what happens around us (Baer). Studies have also shown that selective recollection can lead to greater prosocial behavior (Grant et al.; Gino et al.); that imagining oneself in someone else's shoes can stimulate moral action (Batson et al.); and that writing about one's emotional experiences, e.g., by keeping a diary, can have a cathartic effect and help people cope with traumatic experiences (Pennebaker). See, in order, Paul Condon et al., "Meditation Increases Compassionate Responses to Suffering," *Psychological Science* 24, no. 10 (2013); Julie Anne Irving, Patricia L. Dobkin, and Jeeseon Park, "Cultivating Mindfulness in Health Care Professionals: A Review of Empirical Studies of Mindfulness-Based Stress Reduction (MBSR)," *Complementary Therapies in Clinical Practice* 15, no. 2 (2009); Ruth A. Baer, "Self-Focused Attention and Mechanisms of Change in Mindfulness-Based Treatment," *Cognitive Behaviour Therapy* 38, no. sup1 (2009); Adam Grant and Jane Dutton, "Beneficiary or Benefactor: Are People More Prosocial When They Reflect on Receiving or Giving?," *Psychological Science* 23, no. 9 (2012); Francesca Gino and Sreedhari D. Desai, "Memory Lane and Morality: How Childhood Memories Promote Prosocial Behavior," *Journal of Personality and Social Psychology* 102, no. 4 (2012); C. Daniel Batson et al., "'. . . As You Would Have Them Do unto You'": Does Imagining Yourself in the Other's Place Stimulate Moral Action?," *Personality and Social Psychology Bulletin* 29, no. 9 (2003); James W. Pennebaker, "Writing about Emotional Experiences as a Therapeutic Process," *Psychological Science* 8, no. 3 (1997).

On the development of positive psychology more generally, see Martin E. P. Seligman and Mihaly Csikszentmihalyi, "Positive Psychology: An Introduction," *American Psychologist* 55, no. 1 (2000); Shelly L. Gable and Jonathan Haidt, "What (and Why) Is Positive Psychology?," *Review of General Psychology* 9, no. 2 (2005).

59　See Ronald M. Epstein, "Mindful Practice," *The Journal of the American Medical Association* 282, no. 9 (1999): 835.

60　These exercises are described in Hadot, *Qu'est-Ce Que la Philosophie Antique?*, 276–334.

61　See the discussion of paraskeuê in Michel Foucault, *L'herméneutique du Sujet: Cours au Collège de France (1981–1982)*, ed. Frédéric Gros (Paris: Gallimard, 2001), 301–314.

62　Alasdair MacIntyre, *After Virtue*, 2nd ed. (Notre Dame, IN: University of Notre Dame Press, 1984), 191. MacIntyre uses the term "practice" to refer to a kind of purposive social institution. I have been using the term so far in its more common sociological usage, namely, to refer to a recurring pattern of activity.

63　See Blum, "Community and Virtue."

64　This is an instance of what Jonathan Allen calls "negative morality." See Allen, "The Place of Negative Morality in Political Theory."

65　On the use of diaries, see Kaufman, *The Forest Ranger*; Piore, "Beyond Markets," 158–159.

66　Dubois, *The Bureaucrat and the Poor*, 132.

67　Ibid., 93.

68　See Piore, "Beyond Markets."

69　Dubois, *The Bureaucrat and the Poor*, 131.

70　Konrád, *The Case Worker*, 63.

71　Vincent Dubois, *La Vie au Guichet: Relation Administrative et Traitement de la Misère* (Paris: Economica, 1999), 141–142. My translation.

72　On the rationality of various forms of self-binding or precommitment, see Jon Elster, *Ulysses and the Sirens: Studies in Rationality and Irrationality* (Cambridge: Cambridge University Press, 1979).

73　It is in the same spirit, I believe—as a contribution to heightening one's sense of presence on the job—that we can understand the significance of everyday practices of rule breaking or rule bending. As James Scott argues in his discussion of "anarchist calisthenics," such practices have an effect on those who perform them that goes beyond their immediate practical aim: namely, they enable actors to experience a sense of individual agency and independence from the institutional context that surrounds them. This can be useful in a bureaucratic work environment that drives many toward disengagement and withdrawal. See James C. Scott, *Two Cheers for Anarchism: Six Easy Pieces on Autonomy, Dignity, and Meaningful Work and Play* (Princeton, NJ: Princeton University Press, 2012).

74　Dubois, *The Bureaucrat and the Poor*, 128. Similar problems arising from an incapacity to effect a break between personal and professional life have been reported among social workers, police officers, and teachers. See, respectively, Lloyd, King, and Chenoweth, "Social Work, Stress and Burnout: A Review"; Robyn R. M. Gershon et al., "Mental, Physical, and Behavioral Outcomes Associated with Perceived Work Stress in Police Officers," *Criminal*

Justice and Behavior 36, no. 3 (2009); Lora Bartlett, "Expanding Teacher Work Roles: A Resource for Retention or a Recipe for Overwork?," *Journal of Education Policy* 19, no. 5 (2004).

75 Konrád, *The Case Worker*, 7–11.

76 Michael Walzer, *Spheres of Justice: A Defense of Pluralism and Equality* (New York: Basic Books, 1983).

77 Konrád, *The Case Worker*, 168.

4. WHEN THE RULES RUN OUT

1 I borrow the term "organized heterogeneity" from Susan Silbey, Ruthanne Huising, and Salo Vinocur Coslovsky, "The 'Sociological Citizen': Relational Interdependence in Law and Organizations," *L'Année Sociologique* 59, no. 1 (2009).

2 On the importance of interpretive communities, see Stanley Fish, *Is There a Text in This Class? The Authority of Interpretive Communities* (Cambridge, MA: Harvard University Press, 1980); Ronald Dworkin, *Law's Empire* (Cambridge, MA: Harvard University Press, 1986). Fish and Dworkin disagree about the role that interpretive communities play and the extent to which legal texts and their history can constrain the process of interpretation. For the Fish-Dworkin debate, see Stanley Fish, "Working on the Chain Gang: Interpretation in the Law and in Literary Criticism," *Critical Inquiry* 9, no. 1 (1982); Ronald Dworkin, "Law as Interpretation," *Critical Inquiry* 9, no. 1 (1982).

3 See, for instance, Blum, "Community and Virtue."

4 See Amy Gutmann and Dennis F. Thompson, *Democracy and Disagreement* (Cambridge, MA: Harvard University Press, 1996).

5 Brehm and Gates, *Working, Shirking, and Sabotage.*

6 See Chester Barnard, *The Functions of the Executive* (Cambridge, MA: Harvard University Press, 1938); Elton Mayo, *The Human Problems of an Industrial Civilization* (New York: Macmillan, 1933); Fritz Roethlisberger and William Dickson, *Management and the Worker: An Account of a Research Program Conducted by the Western Electric Company, Hawthorne Works, Chicago* (Cambridge, MA: Harvard University Press, 1939).

7 Kaufman, *The Forest Ranger.*

8 See, for instance, John Van Maanen and Edgar H. Schein, "Toward a Theory of Organizational Socialization," in *Research in Organizational Behavior*, Vol. 1 ed. Barry M. Staw and Larry L. Cummings (Greenwich, CT: JAI Press, 1979).

9 Piore, "Beyond Markets." Piore writes: "The literature suggests that the decisions within a street-level bureaucracy . . . seem to be made within the framework of a set of tacit rules and procedures against which it is possible, at least in principle, to gauge the idiosyncratic component or the narrowly self-interested calculation of particular agents. These rules are embedded in the organizational culture; they evolve as that culture evolves and are passed on from one generation of agents to the next through the process of socialization that occurs when new recruits enter the service. They are reinforced on the job as the agents interact

with each other, reviewing and discussing the disposition of particular cases in the formal and informal interactions that occur on the job."

10 On the Toyota Production System, see William G. Ouchi, *Theory Z: How American Business Can Meet the Japanese Challenge* (Reading, MA: Addison-Wesley, 1981); James P. Womack, Daniel T. Jones, and Daniel Roos, *The Machine That Changed the World* (New York: Free Press, 1990).

11 On transparency and the proximate notion of publicity, see Adrian Vermeule, *Mechanisms of Democracy: Institutional Design Writ Small* (New York: Oxford University Press, 2007), 177–216. On articulate consistency, see Ronald Dworkin, "The Original Position," *University of Chicago Law Review* 40, no. 3 (1973): 512–513. As I will argue in the conclusion of this chapter, I think that the two notions are often amalgamated under the heading of "publicity." On the latter, see David Luban, "The Publicity Principle," in *The Theory of Institutional Design*, ed. Robert E. Goodin (Cambridge: Cambridge University Press, 1996).

12 March and Olsen write in this vein: "Fitting a rule to a situation is an exercise in establishing appropriateness, where rules and situations are related by criteria of similarity or difference through reasoning by analogy and metaphor. The process is mediated by language, by the ways in which participants come to be able to talk about one situation as similar to or different from another. . . . The process maintains consistency in action primarily through the creation of typologies of similarity." See March and Olsen, "The Logic of Appropriateness."

13 See, for instance, John Van Maanen, "The Asshole," in *Policing: A View from the Street*, ed. Peter K. Manning and John Van Maanen (New York: Random House, 1978); Marie Østergaard Møller and Deborah Stone, "Disciplining Disability under Danish Active Labour Market Policy," *Social Policy & Administration* 47, no. 5 (2013); Patrice Rosenthal and Riccardo Peccei, "The Social Construction of Clients by Service Agents in Reformed Welfare Administration," *Human Relations* 59, no. 12 (2006).

14 Van Maanen, "The Asshole."

15 See Fassin, *La Force de l'Ordre*, 116–117, 143.

16 On this point, see Ludwig Wittgenstein, *Philosophical Investigations*, trans. G. E. M. Anscombe, 3rd ed. (Oxford: Blackwell, 2001). For a discussion of categories that build on Wittgenstein's insights, see George Lakoff, *Women, Fire, and Dangerous Things: What Categories Reveal about the Mind* (Chicago: University of Chicago Press, 1987).

17 In this respect, emotional labor is an important part of street-level work in the public services. On emotional labor, see Arlie Russell Hochschild, *The Managed Heart: Commercialization of Human Feeling* (Berkeley: University of California Press, 1983).

18 The difficulty of extracting private information goes a long way toward explaining why protracted relationships between bureaucrats and clients are sometimes beneficial. While such relationships raise the threat of personal dependency, they also allow for bonds of trust to form over time and enable case managers to

become acquainted with clients' personal circumstances without coming across as overly inquisitive or inconsiderate.

19 The following discussion of casuistry is indebted to Cass R. Sunstein, *Legal Reasoning and Political Conflict* (New York: Oxford University Press, 1996); and Albert R. Jonsen and Stephen E. Toulmin, *The Abuse of Casuistry* (Berkeley: University of California Press, 1988).

20 *The Abuse of Casuistry*, 47–74, 137–151. Interestingly, the Jesuits, with whom casuistry is most closely associated, were in an organizational situation in many ways comparable to that of street-level bureaucrats. They were sent on faraway missions; they could not frequently consult their hierarchy for guidance; their actions could not be directly monitored; and they had to resolve concrete problems without having the authority to develop new doctrine. One can look at casuistry as a form of reasoning that responds to these constraints. I am grateful to Richard Tuck for this observation.

21 Sunstein, *Legal Reasoning and Political Conflict*, vii–viii.

22 Jonsen and Toulmin, *The Abuse of Casuistry*, 18.

23 Sunstein, *Legal Reasoning and Political Conflict*, 68.

24 Ibid., 69.

25 Jonsen and Toulmin, *The Abuse of Casuistry*, 10.

26 On the importance of moral perception and its relation to practical wisdom, see Nussbaum, "The Discernment of Perception: An Aristotelian Conception of Private and Public Rationality."

27 Lawrence Blum, "Moral Perception and Particularity," *Ethics* 101, no. 4 (1991).

28 See Douglas R. Hofstadter, *Fluid Concepts & Creative Analogies: Computer Models of the Fundamental Mechanisms of Thought* (New York: Basic Books, 1995); "Analogy as the Core of Cognition" (Stanford Presidential Lectures in Humanities and Arts, Palo Alto, CA, 2006), https://prelectur.stanford.edu/lecturers/hofstadter/analogy.html (accessed March 15, 2017).

29 Mary Douglas remarks that "sameness" doesn't exist in things "out there" but comes from the institutionalized cognitive schemes that we bring to a situation. See Mary Douglas, *How Institutions Think* (Syracuse, NY: Syracuse University Press, 1986), 59–60, 67. See also Blum, "Moral Perception and Particularity," 707.

30 This time lag is recognized by proponents of institutional experimentalism, who believe that organizations should create formal procedures to evaluate and incorporate informal routines. See Michael C. Dorf and Charles F. Sabel, "A Constitution of Democratic Experimentalism," *Columbia Law Review* 98, no. 2 (1998); Charles Sabel, "Rethinking the Street-Level Bureaucrat: Tacit and Deliberate Ways Organizations Can Learn," in *Economy in Society: Essays in Honor of Michael J. Piore*, ed. Paul Osterman (Cambridge, MA: MIT Press, 2013).

31 Robert Gregory observes, for instance, that "there is a positive correlation between the scope of administrative discretion and the thickness of bureaucratic operating manuals." See Robert Gregory, "Accountability in Modern Govern-

ment," in *The Handbook of Public Administration*, ed. B. Guy Peters and Jon Pierre (London: Sage Publications, 2003), 345.

32 Joseph Raz, "Legal Principles and the Limits of Law," *The Yale Law Journal* 81, no. 5 (1972): 847–848.

33 Dworkin, *Taking Rights Seriously*. See especially "The Model of Rules I."

34 Scott J. Shapiro, "The 'Hart-Dworkin' Debate: A Short Guide for the Perplexed," in *Ronald Dworkin*, ed. Arthur Ripstein (Cambridge: Cambridge University Press, 2007).

35 Sunstein, *Legal Reasoning and Political Conflict*, 35–61.

36 Blaise Pascal, *The Provincial Letters* (Harmondsworth, UK: Penguin, 1967).

37 For a discussion of the various regimes of accountability with which street-level bureaucrats must contend, see Peter Hupe and Michael Hill, "Street-Level Bureaucracy and Public Accountability," *Public Administration* 85, no. 2 (2007).

38 The anticipation of future accountability inclines agents to treat their decisions more objectively. See Philip E. Tetlock, "Accountability and the Perseverance of First Impressions," *Social Psychology Quarterly* 46, no. 4 (1983). For an overview of the literature on the effects of accountability on a wide range of judgments and choices, see Jennifer S. Lerner and Philip E. Tetlock, "Accounting for the Effects of Accountability," *Psychological Bulletin* 125, no. 2 (1999).

39 On the distinction between police-patrol oversight and fire-alarm oversight, see Mathew D. McCubbins and Thomas Schwartz, "Congressional Oversight Overlooked: Police Patrols versus Fire Alarms," *American Journal of Political Science* 28, no. 1 (1984).

40 Under New Public Management reforms, public service agencies are also subject to a form of market accountability, because clients are given the liberty to choose between a range of service providers. See Gregory, "Accountability in Modern Government," 346.

41 See Mark S. Frankel, "Professional Codes: Why, How, and with What Impact?," *Journal of Business Ethics* 8, no. 2/3 (1989): 113.

42 Robert Goodin has stressed the importance and distinctiveness of accountability among peers while discussing the cooperative, network-based reference groups that emerge among nonprofit organizations. I aim to show that peer-level accountability also plays an important role *within* individual organizations. See Robert E. Goodin, *Innovating Democracy* (Oxford: Oxford University Press, 2008), 155–185.

43 See Van Maanen and Schein, "Toward a Theory of Organizational Socialization."

44 Blum, "Moral Perception and Particularity," 715.

45 On the relation between perception, imagination, and the emotions, see Nussbaum, "The Discernment of Perception: An Aristotelian Conception of Private and Public Rationality," 78–81.

46 I am indebted to Don Tontiplaphol for this parallel.

47 See Mark Philp, "Delimiting Democratic Accountability," *Political Studies* 57, no. 1 (2009): 32. Also see Mark Bovens, "Two Concepts of Accountability:

Accountability as a Virtue and as a Mechanism," *West European Politics* 33, no. 5 (2010). Bovens characterizes accountability as "an institutional relation or arrangement in which an actor can be held to account by a forum."

48 This suggests that there may be some loose boundary conditions on the optimal size of the peer-level group. The group must be large enough to accommodate different clusters of moral dispositions but small enough that the members of these clusters still need to interact with one another on a regular basis.

49 Social psychologists have shown that groups often encourage conformity and convergence; focus disproportionately on shared information; take decisions that are more extreme than the inclinations of their individual members; and amplify any bias that already exists among their members. Persistent diversity in opinions helps mitigate these group pathologies. For a review of the literature in social psychology on group dynamics, see Tali Mendelberg, "The Deliberative Citizen: Theory and Evidence," in *Political Decision Making, Deliberation and Participation: Research in Micropolitics*, Vol. 6, ed. Michael X. Dellini Carpini, Leonie Huddy, and Robert Y. Shapiro (Greenwich, CT: JAI Press, 2002). On group conformity and convergence, see Solomon E. Asch, "Effects of Group Pressure upon the Modification and Distortion of Judgments," in *Organizational Influence Processes*, ed. Lyman W. Porter, Harold L. Angle, and Robert W. Allen (London: M. E. Sharpe, 2003); Irving L. Janis, *Groupthink: Psychological Studies of Policy Decisions and Fiascoes*, 2nd ed. (Boston: Houghton Mifflin, 1982). On shared information bias, see Garold Stasser and William Titus, "Pooling of Unshared Information in Group Decision Making: Biased Information Sampling during Discussion," *Journal of Personality and Social Psychology* 48, no. 6 (1985). On group polarization, see Serge Moscovici and Marisa Zavalloni, "The Group as a Polarizer of Attitudes," *Journal of Personality and Social Psychology* 12, no. 2 (1969). On the amplification of bias, see Stefan Schulz-Hardt et al., "Biased Information Search in Group Decision Making," *Journal of Personality and Social Psychology* 78, no. 4 (2000). On the capacity of minorities to resist erosion, see Bibb Latané and Martin J. Bourgeois, "Dynamic Social Impact and the Consolidation, Clustering, Correlation, and Continuing Diversity of Culture," in *Blackwell Handbook of Social Psychology: Group Processes*, ed. Michael A. Hogg and R. Scott Tindale (Malden, MA: Blackwell Publishers, 2003). On the influence that minority groups can have on majorities, see Serge Moscovici, *Social Influence and Social Change* (New York: Academic Press, 1976); Moscovici, "Toward a Theory of Conversion Behavior," *Advances in Experimental Social Psychology* 13 (1980).

50 To say that peers play a part in challenging and revising existing taxonomies is a different matter, of course, from saying where these taxonomies come from in the first place. We know that taxonomies are typically passed on from one generation of practitioners to the next, but how do they initially appear in organizations, and how does one taxonomy impose itself over others? Do they

emerge in times of crisis? Are they imported from without, or do they grow organically? To answer such questions, one would need to embark upon a more longitudinal study than the one I have conducted.

51 I borrow the term "institutional irritant" from Robert E. Goodin, "Institutions and Their Design," in *The Theory of Institutional Design*, ed. Robert E. Goodin (Cambridge: Cambridge University Press, 1996), 38–39.

52 Van Maanen, "The Asshole," 324.

53 Such cohesiveness arises, in part, because police officers have, on the one hand, a dangerous job that often brings them into direct confrontation with citizens, and because their behavior is, on the other, exposed to tight and unforgiving public scrutiny. The cohesive culture emerges because officers feel threatened and misunderstood on both ends and results in a strong ingroup / outgroup divide. See, for instance, London Policing Ethics Panel, "Ethical Challenges of Policing London," (2014).

54 On the virtues of plural regimes of accountability, see Philp, "Delimiting Democratic Accountability," 44. On the problems that can arise when one form of accountability prevails over the others, see Barbara S. Romzek and Melvin J. Dubnick, "Accountability in the Public Sector: Lessons from the Challenger Tragedy," *Public Administration Review* 47, no. 3 (1987).

55 Amitai Etzioni, "Is Transparency the Best Disinfectant?," *Journal of Political Philosophy* 18, no. 4 (2010): 1.

56 Dworkin, "The Original Position," 513.

57 It is worth noting, in this regard, that the test of publicity, as formulated by Kant, does not merely assess whether the grounds on which we act can be disclosed to the public without self-contradiction. The test also imposes some constraints on what those grounds can be in the first place: they must be maxims, that is, principles of behavior whose range of applicability is wider than the case at hand, and which have the structure of a law. See Immanuel Kant, "Perpetual Peace: A Philosophical Sketch," in *Kant: Political Writings*, ed. H. S. Reiss (New York: Cambridge University Press, 1991).

58 Charles E. Lindblom, "The Science of 'Muddling Through,'" *Public Administration Review* 19, no. 2 (1959).

5. IMPOSSIBLE SITUATIONS

1 William Johnson, "Confessions of a 'Bad' Teacher," *The New York Times*, March 3, 2012.

2 See Taryn Lindhorst and Julianna D. Padgett, "Disjunctures for Women and Frontline Workers: Implementation of the Family Violence Option," *Social Service Review* 79, no. 3 (2005): 408.

3 For a book-length treatment of the impact of welfare reform on frontline workers, see Watkins-Hayes, *The New Welfare Bureaucrats*.

4 Lindhorst and Padgett, "Disjunctures for Women and Frontline Workers: Implementation of the Family Violence Option."

5   Ibid., 423.
6   Ibid., 422.
7   Randal C. Archibold, "Arizona Enacts Stringent Law on Immigration," *The New York Times*, April 23, 2010.
8   Peter Slevin, "Arizona Law on Immigration Puts Police in Tight Spot," *The Washington Post*, April 30, 2010.
9   Daniel B. Wood, "Arizona Immigration Law Puts Police in 'Impossible Situation,'" *The Christian Science Monitor*, April 26, 2010.
10 Ibid.
11 Jonathan Lear, *Radical Hope: Ethics in the Face of Cultural Devastation* (Cambridge, MA: Harvard University Press, 2006), 1–10.
12 Ibid., 6.
13 The distinction between various kinds of impediments is important in terms of assigning responsibility. See David Estlund, "Human Nature and the Limits (If Any) of Political Philosophy," *Philosophy & Public Affairs* 39, no. 3 (2011).
14 Notice, moreover, that the new directives did not entirely close possibilities for action that were previously open to workers—they did not make actions that were previously possible impossible. No requirement for teacher accountability will be draconian enough to prevent a teacher from occasionally expanding beyond the curriculum assessed by standardized exams. Caseworkers certainly have the authority to apply the "FVO" in any specific case. Similarly, police officers surely have enough discretion to refrain from implementing the "show me your papers" clause in any particular encounter. Such actions may be hard, or discouraged; they may put workers behind in terms of "numbers" and may jeopardize their capacity to meet the newer requirements—but they are certainly not *impossible* to perform on an occasional basis (although they would probably put one's job at risk if performed repeatedly). To the extent that "impossible situations" can be characterized in terms of actions, then, they are not spurred by strict impossibility but by a change in patterns and frequency: some actions have become harder to perform; others must be performed more regularly.
15 See Morgen, "The Agency of Welfare Workers," 755.
16 See, for instance, David Luban, *Lawyers and Justice: An Ethical Study* (Princeton, NJ: Princeton University Press, 1988); Applbaum, *Ethics for Adversaries.*
17 See Fritz Wilhelm Scharpf, *Governing in Europe: Effective and Democratic?* (Oxford: Oxford University Press, 1999); Rosanvallon, *Democratic Legitimacy*, 17–59; Heath, "A General Framework for the Ethics of Public Administration."
18 Role conflict arises when organizations depart from the classical "rational" model of organizational behavior that I described in Chapter 1. In the classical model, role conflict is ruled out by the twin principles of hierarchy and unity of command—principles that refer, respectively, to the existence of a "clear and single flow of authority from the top to the bottom" of the organization, and to

the fact that for any action an individual should receive directives "from one superior only" and be held accountable by this superior alone. Taken together,
these two principles protect individuals from being caught in the crossfire of
conflicting expectations and from being torn between multiples sources of authority. However, as soon as we abandon this classical model for a more descriptively accurate portrait of organizations, we are forced to acknowledge (as I
showed in Chapter 4) that each role incumbent is often exposed to various
sources of authority and held accountable by a plurality of actors. With this
comes the possibility of role conflict. See John R. Rizzo, Robert J. House, and
Sidney I. Lirtzman, "Role Conflict and Ambiguity in Complex Organizations,"
Administrative Science Quarterly 15, no. 2 (1970): 150–151; and Mary Van Sell,
Arthur P. Brief, and Randall S. Schuler, "Role Conflict and Role Ambiguity: Integration of the Literature and Directions for Future Research," *Human Relations*
34, no. 1 (1981).

19 Van Sell, Brief, and Schuler, "Role Conflict and Role Ambiguity," 66.

20 The concept of a "lifeworld"—the world as lived and experienced, along with the
system of common meanings and categories through which one conceives of the
world and oneself—was introduced by Husserl and mobilized by a long line of
thinkers down to Habermas.

21 For an example of how managers can control their workers by granting identity
enactment opportunities, see Michel Anteby, *Moral Gray Zones: Side Productions, Identity, and Regulation in an Aeronautic Plant* (Princeton, NJ: Princeton
University Press, 2008).

22 This view of culture as a "toolkit" that agents can draw upon to justify their
"strategies of action" was proposed by Ann Swidler. See, in particular, Ann
Swidler, "Culture in Action: Symbols and Strategies," *American Sociological Review* 51, no. 2 (1986). Swidler's seminal article was written as a critique of a view
according to which culture influences actions by shaping the values that agents
hold. Swidler argued that such a view had the story backwards: "Action is not
determined by one's values. Rather action *and* values are organized to take advantage of cultural competences" (ibid., 275). More recently, Stephen Vaisey has
argued that sociologists of culture may have gone too far in following Swidler,
and that it is important to remember that culture plays a part not only in justifying behavior, but also in motivating it. See Stephen Vaisey, "Motivation and
Justification: A Dual Process Model of Culture in Action," *American Journal of
Sociology* 114, no. 6 (2009).

23 These more narrow conceptions of agency construe individual agents as strategic, calculating, and self-interested, or posit a more automatic alignment between the agent's self and the surrounding environment. The targets of Boltanski
and Thévenot are, respectively, Michel Crozier's account of the "strategic actor"
and Pierre Bourdieu's conception of habitus. See Luc Boltanski and Laurent
Thévenot, *De la Justification: Les Economies de la Grandeur* (Paris: Gallimard,

1991); Luc Boltanski, "Sociologie Critique et Sociologie de la Critique," *Politix* 3, no. 10–11 (1990). And for the targets of their critique, see Michel Crozier and Erhard Friedberg, *Actors and Systems: The Politics of Collective Action* (Chicago: University of Chicago Press, 1980); Pierre Bourdieu, *Outline of a Theory of Practice* (Cambridge: Cambridge University Press, 1977).

24 This type of question is at the heart of Arthur Applbaum's work. While recognizing the moral significance of roles, Applbaum defends the thesis that "institutions and the roles they create ordinarily cannot mint moral permissions to do what otherwise would be morally prohibited." See Applbaum, *Ethics for Adversaries*, 3.

25 F. H. Bradley, "My Station and Its Duties," in *Ethical Studies* (Oxford: Clarendon Press, 1927).

26 See, for instance, Watkins-Hayes, *The New Welfare Bureaucrats;* Piore, "Beyond Markets."

27 See Joseph Raz, *The Morality of Freedom* (Oxford: Oxford University Press, 1986), 321–366; Martha Nussbaum, "The Costs of Tragedy: Some Moral Limits of Cost–Benefit Analysis," *The Journal of Legal Studies* 29, no. S2 (2000): 1010; Bernard Williams, "Liberalism and Loss," in *The Legacy of Isaiah Berlin*, ed. Mark Lila, Ronald Dworkin, and Robert Silvers (New York: New York Review of Books, 2001).

28 Williams, "Liberalism and Loss," 95; Raz, *The Morality of Freedom*, 344.

29 Dilemmas such as these bear resemblance to the problem of "dirty hands" but are not identical to it. In its classic formulation, the problem of dirty hands arises when an agent has to commit a wrong in order to prevent an even worse outcome from occurring. The wrong is committed as a means to prevent that occurrence. In the cases I am discussing here, an agent is forced to choose between two wrongs, such that avoiding one entails committing the other. The wrong is a byproduct or "double effect" of the decision. On the problem of dirty hands, see Walzer, "Political Action: The Problem of Dirty Hands"; Bernard Williams, "Conflicts of Value," in *Moral Luck: Philosophical Papers, 1973–1980* (Cambridge: Cambridge University Press, 1981), 74.

30 See "Politics and Moral Character," 65; see also Walzer, "Political Action."

31 Nussbaum, "The Costs of Tragedy," 1007.

32 Ibid.

33 Georg Wilhelm Friedrich Hegel, *Hegel on Tragedy* (New York: Harper & Row, 1975), 1–96.

34 Nussbaum, "The Costs of Tragedy," 1012.

35 Hegel, *Hegel on Tragedy*, 73. This view of Hegel is shared by Anne and Henry Paolucci, the editors of the volume on Hegel's writings on tragedy; see their introduction to the volume, xxvi.

36 Ibid., 69–71.

37 This idea, according to which becoming a subject who inhabits a role involves not only complying with a set of external norms but also changing how one per-

ceives and relates to one's self, is central to Foucault's work on ethics. See the introduction to Michel Foucault, *The History of Sexuality, Vol. 2: The Use of Pleasure*, trans. Robert Hurley (London: Penguin, 1990). Lear draws similar ideas on subjectivity from Kierkegaard. See Lear, *Radical Hope*, 43.

38 Van Maanen and Schein, "Toward a Theory of Organizational Socialization." In *The Managed Heart*, sociologist Arlie Hochschild argues that companies, particularly in the service sector, demand more of their employees than their time: they seek to mobilize, control, and profit from their employees' emotions and feelings. The public service sector is no exception.

39 See Michael O. Hardimon, "Role Obligations," *The Journal of Philosophy* 91, no. 7 (1994).

40 See Gideon Kunda, *Engineering Culture: Control and Commitment in a High-Tech Corporation* (Philadelphia: Temple University Press, 1992); Edgar H. Schein, *Organizational Culture and Leadership*, 4th ed. (San Francisco: Jossey-Bass, 2010).

41 Gregory Bateson, "Toward a Theory of Schizophrenia," in *Steps to an Ecology of Mind* (San Francisco: Chandler Publishing Co., 1972).

42 The theory has been criticized on multiple counts and in particular for blaming the onset of schizophrenia on the child's mother.

43 Sandra Lee Bartky, "On Psychological Oppression," in *Femininity and Domination: Studies in the Phenomenology of Oppression* (New York: Routledge, 1990).

44 Ibid., 30.

45 Ibid., 31.

46 See ibid., 30.

47 Stuart Albert and David A. Whetten, "Organizational Identity," in *Research in Organizational Behavior*, vol. 7, ed. Larry L. Cummings and Barry M. Straux (Greenwich, CT: JAI Press, 1985).

48 See Piore, "Beyond Markets," 9–10.

49 This is especially true in the public sector, where employees are often driven by a public service ethos that attracts them to such jobs in the first place and that continues to motivate them thereafter. See James L. Perry, Annie Hondeghem, and Lois Recascino Wise, "Revisiting the Motivational Bases of Public Service: Twenty Years of Research and an Agenda for the Future," *Public Administration Review* 70, no. 5 (2010).

50 See Albert O. Hirschman, *Exit, Voice, and Loyalty: Responses to Decline in Firms, Organizations, and States* (Cambridge, MA: Harvard University Press, 1970).

51 See Meira Levinson, "Moral Injury and the Ethics of Educational Injustice," *Harvard Educational Review* 85, no. 2 (2015): 217–218.

52 Ibid., 219; Thompson, *Political Ethics and Public Office*, 52.

53 See Frances J. Milliken, Elizabeth W. Morrison, and Patricia F. Hewlin, "An Exploratory Study of Employee Silence: Issues That Employees Don't Communicate Upward and Why," *Journal of Management Studies* 40, no. 6 (2003).

54 In addition to studies of whistleblowing, one can draw inspiration here from private sector practices. Toyota is often cited as an example: line workers are empowered, upon discovering a quality problem that they cannot resolve, to stop the entire production line by pulling the "andon cord"—a decision that can be extremely costly for the company. A proper use of the andon cord requires a strong relational contract between workers and managers: frontline employees must exert proper judgment before deciding to pull the cord, and they must know that they will not be punished for doing so. On the Toyota Production System, see Taiichi Ohno, *Toyota Production System: Beyond Large-Scale Production* (Cambridge, MA: Productivity Press, 1988); Jeffrey K. Liker, *The Toyota Way: 14 Management Principles from the World's Greatest Manufacturer* (New York: McGraw Hill, 2004). On the use of the andon cord as an example of a relational contract, see Robert Gibbons and Rebecca Henderson, "What Do Mangers Do? Exploring Persistent Performance Differences among Seemingly Similar Enterprises" (Havard Business School Working Paper, 2012), 29–31.

55 Burnout is a significant problem in the human services—for example, in social work (Lloyd et al.), teaching (Chang) and the police (Kop et al.). It is thought to be particularly pronounced in the public service sector because of a chronic imbalance between ideals and resources (Mor Barak et al.). See, respectively, Lloyd, King, and Chenoweth, "Social Work, Stress and Burnout"; Chang, "An Appraisal Perspective of Teacher Burnout"; Nicolien Kop, Martin Euwema, and Wilmar Schaufeli, "Burnout, Job Stress and Violent Behavior among Dutch Police Officers," *Work & Stress: An International Journal of Work, Health & Organisations* 13, no. 4 (1999); Mor Barak, Nissly, and Levin, "Antecedents to Retention and Turnover among Child Welfare, Social Work, and Other Human Service Employees."

56 For a discussion of how the latest waves of public sector reform have affected the front lines of public service, see, for example, Soss, Fording, and Schram, *Disciplining the Poor;* Brodkin and Marston, *Work and the Welfare State.*

CONCLUSION

1 On the impersonality of the modern state, see Harvey C. Mansfield Jr., "On the Impersonality of the Modern State: A Comment on Machiavelli's Use of *Stato*," *The American Political Science Review* 77, no. 4 (1983); Quentin Skinner, "The State," in *Political Innovation and Conceptual Change*, ed. Terence Ball, James Farr, and Russell L. Hanson (Cambridge: Cambridge University Press, 1989).

2 For a critical analysis of "interpretive labor" in bureaucracies—the imaginative labor that clients exert to put themselves in the shoes of bureaucrats and to see the world from their perspective—see Graeber, "Dead Zones of the Imagination." Graeber argues that interpretive labor is typically unidirectional; it is the powerless who try to see the world from the standpoint of the powerful, not the other way around.

3 This harks back to a book project to which Rousseau alluded in the *Confessions* but that he never completed as such. The book sought to examine how we could arrange our environment to "keep the mind in the state most conducive to virtue." Rousseau describes the project in these terms: "It has been observed that the majority of men are often in the course of their lives quite unlike themselves; they seem to be changed into quite different people. But it was not for the purpose of establishing such a well-known fact that I planned to write my book; I had a more original and important purpose, which was to trace the causes of these changes, isolating those that depend on us in order to show how we may ourselves control them, and so become better men and more certain of ourselves. . . .

"Looking within myself and seeking in others for the cause upon which these different states depended, I discovered that they had a great deal to do with our previous impressions from external objects, and that, being continually a little changed through the agency of our senses and our organs, we were unconsciously affected in our thoughts, our feelings, and even our actions by the impact of these slight changes upon us. Numerous striking examples that I had collected put the matter beyond all dispute; and thanks to their physical basis they seemed to me capable of providing an external code which, varied according to circumstances, could put or keep the mind in the state most conducive to virtue. . . . Climates, seasons, sounds, colours, darkness, light, the elements, food, noise, silence, movements, repose: they all act on our machines, and consequently upon our souls, and they all offer us innumerable and almost certain opportunities for controlling those feelings which we allow to dominate us from their very onset . . . I made very little progress with this work, however, the title of which was *La Morale Sensitive ou le Matérialisme du Sage*." See Jean-Jacques Rousseau, *Confessions*, trans. J. M. Cohen (Harmondsworth, UK: Penguin, 1953), 380–381.

As Michael Rosen points out, what is interesting about Rousseau's approach is that it does not "seek to use reflection to increase the discretionary power of the self" but tries, rather, "to develop 'reason' (by which he means the power of the self to act, feel and judge rightly) by bringing the self into balance with its environment." See Michael Rosen, *On Voluntary Servitude: False Consciousness and the Theory of Ideology* (Cambridge, MA: Harvard University Press, 1996).

4 I borrow the term "institutionalized phronesis" from Carl K. Y. Shaw, "Hegel's Theory of Modern Bureaucracy," *The American Political Science Review* 86, no. 2 (1992).

5 James C. Scott, *Seeing Like a State: How Certain Schemes to Improve the Human Condition Have Failed* (New Haven, CT: Yale University Press, 1998).

6 The idea that the content of public policy cannot be separated from its meaning is at the heart of interpretive approaches to policy studies. See Dvora Yanow, *Conducting Interpretive Policy Analysis* (Thousand Oaks, CA: Sage Publications, 2000).

7 See Evelyn Z. Brodkin, "Work and the Welfare State," in *Work and the Welfare State: Street-Level Organizations and Workfare Politics*, ed. Evelyn Z. Brodkin and Gregory Marston (Washington, DC: Georgetown University Press, 2013); Dubois, "Towards a Critical Policy Ethnography."

8 The following account is indebted to Evelyn Z. Brodkin and Flemming Larsen, "Governance and Welfare State Politics: What Could the US and Denmark Possibly Have in Common?," paper presented at the International Conference on Public Policy, Milan, 2015.

9 See John Stuart Mill, *On Liberty* (New Haven, CT: Yale University Press, 2003), 121–138. For an elaboration, see Elizabeth S. Anderson, "John Stuart Mill and Experiments in Living," *Ethics* 102, no. 1 (1991).

10 While I am sympathetic to the concerns of the basic income movement, I have reservations about both of these claims. I worry, in particular, that they present a picture of frontline discretion that is insufficiently nuanced and unduly negative. While we may sometimes be better off curtailing street-level discretion, such discretion often exists for good reasons (see Chapter 1) and works to the benefit of clients by enabling bureaucrats to be more responsive to the particularities of their situation. I also have doubts about the extent to which simplifying eligibility criteria or removing them altogether would eliminate discretion, or whether it would in fact just displace it.

11 I borrow the term "ethnographic sensibility" from Ellen Pader, "Seeing with an Ethnographic Sensibility," in *Interpretation and Method*, ed. Dvora Yanow and Peregrine Schwartz-Shea (Armonk, NY: M. E. Sharpe, 2006).

12 See Richard Fenno, "Observation, Context and Sequence in the Study of Politics," *American Political Science Review* 80, no. 1 (1986): 4; Clifford Geertz, "Thick Description: Toward an Interpretive Theory of Culture," in *The Interpretation of Cultures* (New York: Basic Books, 1973), 9.

13 See, for example, Clarissa Rile Hayward, *De-facing Power* (Cambridge: Cambridge University Press, 2000); Mark Bevir and R. A. W. Rhodes, *Interpreting British Governance* (London: Routledge, 2003); Cressida J. Heyes, "Foucault Goes to Weight-Watchers (Redux)," in *Self-Transformations: Foucault, Ethics, and Normalized Bodies* (New York: Oxford University Press, 2007).

14 See George E. Marcus and Michael M. J. Fischer, *Anthropology as Cultural Critique: An Experimental Moment in the Human Sciences* (Princeton, NJ: Princeton University Press, 1986).

15 Works in that vein have been fewer. See, for instance, Jane Mansbridge, *Beyond Adversary Democracy* (Chicago: University of Chicago Press, 1983); Meira Levinson, *No Citizen Left Behind* (Cambridge, MA: Harvard University Press, 2012); Jennifer C. Rubenstein, *Between Samaritans and States: The Political Ethics of Humanitarian INGOs* (Oxford: Oxford University Press, 2015). Anthropology, on the other hand, has witnessed in recent years an explosion of interest in questions of ethics and morality. See Michael Lambek, ed., *Ordinary Ethics: Anthropology, Language, and Action* (New York: Fordham University Press,

2010); Didier Fassin, ed., *A Companion to Moral Anthropology* (Oxford: Wiley Blackwell, 2012); James Laidlaw, *The Subject of Virtue: An Anthropology of Ethics and Freedom* (New York: Cambridge University Press, 2014).

16 This typology and the following discussion draw on an article coauthored with Lisa Herzog. See Lisa Herzog and Bernardo Zacka, "Fieldwork in Political Theory: Five Arguments for an Ethnographic Sensibility," *British Journal of Political Science* (Forthcoming).

Bibliography

Albert, Stuart, and David A. Whetten. "Organizational Identity." In *Research in Organizational Behavior*, edited by Larry L. Cummings and Barry M. Staw vol. 7, 263–295. Greenwich, CT: JAI Press, 1985.

Alexander, Cedric. "Police Psychological Burnout and Trauma." In *Police Trauma: Psychological Aftermath of Civilian Combat*, edited by John M. Violanti and Douglas Paton, 54–64. Springfield, IL: Charles C Thomas, 1999.

Allen, Jonathan. "The Place of Negative Morality in Political Theory." *Political Theory* 29, no. 3 (2001): 337–363.

Anderson, Elizabeth. *The Imperative of Integration.* Princeton, NJ: Princeton University Press, 2010.

———. "John Stuart Mill and Experiments in Living." *Ethics* 102, no. 1 (1991): 4–26.

———. "What Is the Point of Equality?" *Ethics* 109, no. 2 (1999): 287–337.

Anteby, Michel. *Moral Gray Zones: Side Productions, Identity, and Regulation in an Aeronautic Plant.* Princeton, NJ: Princeton University Press, 2008.

Applbaum, Arthur. *Ethics for Adversaries.* Princeton, NJ: Princeton University Press, 1999.

Aranson, Peter H., Ernest Gellhorn, and Glen O. Robinson. "A Theory of Legislative Delegation." *Cornell Law Review* 68, no. 1 (1982–1983): 1–67.

Archibold, Randal C. "Arizona Enacts Stringent Law on Immigration." *The New York Times*, April 23, 2010.

Arendt, Hannah. *Eichmann in Jerusalem: A Report on the Banality of Evil.* New York: Penguin Books, 2006.

———. "Some Questions of Moral Philosophy." In *Responsibility and Judgment*, edited by Jerome Kohn, 49–146. New York: Schocken Books, 2003.

Argyris, Chris. *Personality and Organization: The Conflict between System and the Individual.* New York: Harper & Row, 1957.

Aristotle. "Nicomachean Ethics." In *Introduction to Aristotle*, edited by Richard McKeon. New York: Random House, 1947.

Aronson, Elliot. "The Theory of Cognitive Dissonance: A Current Perspective." In *Advances in Experimental Social Psychology*, edited by Leonard Berkowitz, 1–34. New York: Academic Press, 1969.

Asch, Solomon E. "Effects of Group Pressure upon the Modification and Distortion of Judgments." In *Organizational Influence Processes*, edited by Lyman W. Porter, Harold L. Angle, and Robert W. Allen. London: M. E. Sharpe, 2003.

Auyero, Javier. *Patients of the State: The Politics of Waiting in Argentina.* Durham, NC: Duke University Press, 2012.

Baer, Ruth A. "Self-Focused Attention and Mechanisms of Change in Mindfulness-Based Treatment." *Cognitive Behaviour Therapy* 38, no. sup1 (2009): 15–20.

Bandura, Albert. "Moral Disengagement in the Perpetration of Inhumanities." *Personality and Social Psychology Review* 3, no. 3 (1999): 193–209.

Barnard, Chester. *The Functions of the Executive.* Cambridge, MA: Harvard University Press, 1938.

Bartky, Sandra Lee. "On Psychological Oppression." In *Femininity and Domination: Studies in the Phenomenology of Oppression,* 22–32. New York: Routledge, 1990.

Bartlett, Lora. "Expanding Teacher Work Roles: A Resource for Retention or a Recipe for Overwork?" *Journal of Education Policy* 19, no. 5 (2004): 565–582.

Bateson, Gregory. "Toward a Theory of Schizophrenia." In *Steps to an Ecology of Mind.* San Francisco: Chandler Publishing Co., 1972.

Batson, C. Daniel, David A. Lishner, Amy Carpenter, Luis Dulin, Sanna Harjusola-Webb, E. L. Stocks, Shawna Gale, Omar Hassan, and Brenda Sampat. "'. . . As You Would Have Them Do unto You': Does Imagining Yourself in the Other's Place Stimulate Moral Action?" *Personality and Social Psychology Bulletin* 29, no. 9 (2003): 1190–1201.

Bauman, Zygmunt. *Modernity and the Holocaust.* Ithaca, NY: Cornell University Press, 1989.

Baumeister, Roy F., and John Tierney. *Willpower: Rediscovering the Greatest Human Strength.* New York: Penguin Press, 2011.

Bazerman, Max H., and Ann E. Tenbrunsel. *Blind Spots: Why We Fail to Do What's Right and What to Do about It.* Princeton, NJ: Princeton University Press, 2011.

Bendor, Jonathan. "Formal Models of Bureaucracy." *British Journal of Political Science* 18, no. 3 (1988): 353–395.

Bendor, Jonathan, and Adam Meirowitz. "Spatial Models of Delegation." *American Political Science Review* 98, no. 2 (2004): 293–310.

Bevir, Mark, and R. A. W. Rhodes. *Interpreting British Governance.* London: Routledge, 2003.

Bix, Brian. *Jurisprudence: Theory and Context.* 5th ed. London: Sweet & Maxwell, 2009.

Blau, Peter M. *Bureaucracy in Modern Society.* New York: Random House, 1956.

Blau, Peter M., and Marshall W. Meyer. *Bureaucracy in Modern Society.* 3rd ed. New York: Random House, 1987.

Blum, Lawrence. "Community and Virtue." In *How Should One Live? Essays on the Virtues,* edited by Roger Crisp, 231–254. Oxford: Oxford University Press, 1998.

———. "Moral Perception and Particularity." *Ethics* 101, no. 4 (1991): 701–725.

Boltanski, Luc. "Sociologie Critique et Sociologie de la Critique." *Politix* 3, no. 10–11 (1990): 124–134.

Boltanski, Luc, and Laurent Thévenot. *De la Justification: Les Economies de la Grandeur.* Paris: Gallimard, 1991.

Bourdieu, Pierre. *La Misère du Monde.* Paris: Seuil, 1993.

———. *Outline of a Theory of Practice.* Cambridge: Cambridge University Press, 1977.

Bovens, Mark. "Two Concepts of Accountability: Accountability as a Virtue and as a Mechanism." *West European Politics* 33, no. 5 (2010): 946–967.

Bovens, Mark, and Stavros Zouridis. "From Street-Level to System-Level Bureaucracies: How Information and Communication Technology Is Transforming Administrative Discretion and Constitutional Control." *Public Administration Review* 62, no. 2 (2002).

Bradley, F. H. "My Station and Its Duties." In *Ethical Studies*, 145–193. Oxford: Clarendon Press, 1927.

Brehm, John, and Scott Gates. *Working, Shirking, and Sabotage: Bureaucratic Response to a Democratic Public*. Ann Arbor: University of Michigan Press, 1997.

Brodkin, Evelyn Z. "Inside the Welfare Contract: Discretion and Accountability in State Welfare Administration." *Social Service Review* 71, no. 1 (1997): 1–33.

———. "Investigating Policy's Practical Meaning: Street-Level Research on Welfare Policy." Center for Poverty Research Working Paper Series, Northwestern University, 2000. http://www.ipr.northwestern.edu/jcpr/workingpapers/wpfiles/brodkin3.PDF.

———. "Reflections on Street-Level Bureaucracy: Past, Present, and Future." *Public Administration Review* 72, no. 6 (2012): 940–949.

———. "Work and the Welfare State." In *Work and the Welfare State: Street-Level Organizations and Workfare Politics*, edited by Evelyn Z. Brodkin and Gregory Marston, 3–16. Washington, DC: Georgetown University Press, 2013.

Brodkin, Evelyn Z., and Flemming Larsen. "Governance and Welfare State Politics: What Could the US and Denmark Possibly Have in Common?" Paper presented at the International Conference on Public Policy, Milan, 2015.

Brodkin, Evelyn Z., and Gregory Marston, eds. *Work and the Welfare State: Street-Level Organizations and Workfare Politics*. Washington, DC: Georgetown University Press, 2013.

Browning, Christopher R. *Ordinary Men: Reserve Police Battalion 101 and the Final Solution in Poland*. New York: Harper Perennial, 1998.

Buchanan, James M., and Gordon Tullock. *The Calculus of Consent: Logical Foundations of Constitutional Democracy*. Ann Arbor: University of Michigan Press, 1965.

Buffat, Aurélien. "Street-Level Bureaucracy and E-Government." *Public Management Review* 17, no. 1 (2015): 149–161.

Campbell, Andrea. *Trapped in America's Safety Net: One Family's Struggle*. Chicago: University of Chicago Press, 2014.

Carens, Joseph H. *The Ethics of Immigration*. Oxford: Oxford University Press, 2013.

Carpenter, Daniel P. *The Forging of Bureaucratic Autonomy: Reputations, Networks, and Policy Innovation in Executive Agencies, 1862–1928*. Princeton, NJ: Princeton University Press, 2001.

Caton, Steven C., and Bernardo Zacka. "Abu Ghraib, the Security Apparatus, and the Performativity of Power." *American Ethnologist* 37, no. 2 (2010): 203–211.

Chadwick, Andrew, and Christopher May. "Interaction between States and Citizens in the Age of the Internet: 'E-Government' in the United States, Britain, and the European Union." *Governance* 16, no. 2 (2003): 271–300.

Chang, Mei-Lin. "An Appraisal Perspective of Teacher Burnout: Examining the Emotional Work of Teachers." *Educational Psychology Review* 21, no. 3 (2009): 193–218.

Cherniss, Joshua, and Henry Hardy. "Isaiah Berlin." In *The Stanford Encyclopedia of Philosophy*, Winter 2016 ed., edited by Edward N. Zalta. https://plato.stanford.edu/archives/win2016/entries/berlin/.

Cigler, Beverly A., and Heidi L. Neiswender. "'Bureaucracy' in the Introductory American Government Textbook." *Public Administration Review* 51, no. 5 (1991): 442–450.

"Compliance Manual." Edited by the U.S. Equal Employment Opportunity Commission, Section 902: Definition of the term "disability," 1995.

Condon, Paul, Gaëlle Desbordes, Willa B. Miller, and David DeSteno. "Meditation Increases Compassionate Responses to Suffering." *Psychological Science* 24, no. 10 (2013): 2125–2127.

Considine, Mark, Jenny M. Lewis, Siobhan O'Sullivan, and Els Sol, eds. *Getting Welfare to Work: Street-Level Governance in Australia, the UK, and the Netherlands.* Oxford: Oxford University Press, 2015.

Cooper, Joel. *Cognitive Dissonance: Fifty Years of a Classic Theory.* Thousand Oaks, CA: Sage Publications, 2007.

Crozier, Michel. *Le Phénomène Bureaucratique.* Paris: Seuil, 1963.

Crozier, Michel, and Erhard Friedberg. *Actors and Systems: The Politics of Collective Action.* Chicago: University of Chicago Press, 1980.

Damasio, Antonio R. *Descartes' Error: Emotion, Reason, and the Human Brain.* New York: G. P. Putnam, 1994.

Davis, Kenneth Culp. *Discretionary Justice: A Preliminary Inquiry.* Urbana: University of Illinois Press, 1971.

Denhardt, Janet Vinzant, and Lane Crothers. *Street-Level Leadership: Discretion and Legitimacy in Front-Line Public Service.* Washington, DC: Georgetown University Press, 1998.

Dias, Janice Johnson, and Steven Maynard-Moody. "For-Profit Welfare: Contracts, Conflicts, and the Performance Paradox." *Journal of Public Administration Research and Theory* 17, no. 2 (2007): 189–211.

Dorf, Michael C., and Charles F. Sabel. "A Constitution of Democratic Experimentalism." *Columbia Law Review* 98, no. 2 (1998): 267–473.

Doris, John M., and Stephen P. Stich. "As a Matter of Fact: Empirical Perspectives on Ethics." In *The Oxford Handbook of Contemporary Philosophy*, edited by Frank Jackson and Michael Smith, 114–152. New York: Oxford University Press, 2005.

Douglas, Mary. *How Institutions Think.* Syracuse, NY: Syracuse University Press, 1986.

Downs, Anthony. *Inside Bureaucracy.* Boston: Little, Brown, 1967.

Du Gay, Paul. *In Praise of Bureaucracy: Weber, Organization and Ethics.* London: Sage Publications, 2000.

Dubois, Vincent. *The Bureaucrat and the Poor: Encounters in French Welfare Offices*, translated by Jean-Yves Bart. Burlington, VT: Ashgate, 2010.

———. *La Vie au Guichet: Relation Administrative et Traitement de la Misère*. Paris: Economica, 1999.

———. "Towards a Critical Policy Ethnography: Lessons from Fieldwork on Welfare Control in France." *Critical Policy Studies* 3, no. 2 (2009): 221–239.

Dworkin, Ronald. "Law as Interpretation." *Critical Inquiry* 9, no. 1 (1982): 179–200.

———. *Law's Empire*. Cambridge, MA: Harvard University Press, 1986.

———. "The Original Position." *University of Chicago Law Review* 40, no. 3 (1973): 500–533.

———. *Taking Rights Seriously*. Cambridge, MA: Harvard University Press, 1978.

Edmonds, David. *Would You Kill the Fat Man? The Trolley Problem and What Your Answer Tells Us about Right and Wrong*. Princeton, NJ: Princeton University Press, 2014.

Eisenstein, Sergei. *Risunki=Drawings*. Moscow: Iskusstvo, 1961.

Elster, Jon. *Sour Grapes: Studies in the Subversion of Rationality*. Cambridge: Cambridge University Press, 1983.

———. *Ulysses and the Sirens: Studies in Rationality and Irrationality*. Cambridge: Cambridge University Press, 1979.

Epp, Charles R., Steven Maynard-Moody, and Donald P. Haider-Markel. *Pulled Over: How Police Stops Define Race and Citizenship*. Chicago: University of Chicago Press, 2014.

Epstein, David, and Sharyn O'Halloran. *Delegating Powers: A Transaction Cost Politics Approach to Policy Making under Separate Powers*. Cambridge: Cambridge University Press, 1999.

Epstein, Ronald M. "Mindful Practice." *The Journal of the American Medical Association* 282, no. 9 (1999): 833–839.

Eskridge, William N., and John A. Ferejohn. *A Republic of Statutes: The New American Constitution*. New Haven, CT: Yale University Press, 2010.

Estlund, David. "Human Nature and the Limits (If Any) of Political Philosophy." *Philosophy & Public Affairs* 39, no. 3 (2011): 207–237.

Etzioni, Amitai. "Is Transparency the Best Disinfectant?" *Journal of Political Philosophy* 18, no. 4 (2010): 389–404.

Fassin, Didier, ed. *At the Heart of the State: The Moral World of Institutions*. London: Pluto Press, 2015.

———, ed. *A Companion to Moral Anthropology*. Oxford: Wiley Blackwell, 2012.

———. *La Force de l'Ordre: Une Anthropologie de la Police des Quartiers*. Paris: Seuil, 2011.

Fenno, Richard. "Observation, Context and Sequence in the Study of Politics." *American Political Science Review* 80, no. 1 (1986): 3–15.

Festinger, Leon. *A Theory of Cognitive Dissonance*. Evanston, IL: Row, Peterson, 1957.

Figley, Charles R. "Compassion Fatigue as Secondary Traumatic Stress Disorder: An Overview." In *Compassion Fatigue,* edited by Charles R. Figley, 1–20. New York: Routledge, 1995.

Finer, Herman. "Administrative Responsibility in Democratic Government." *Public Administration Review* 1, no. 4 (1941): 335–350.

Fiorina, Morris P. *Congress: Keystone of the Washington Establishment.* New Haven, CT: Yale University Press, 1977.

Fish, Stanley. *Is There a Text in This Class? The Authority of Interpretive Communities.* Cambridge, MA: Harvard University Press, 1980.

———. "Working on the Chain Gang: Interpretation in the Law and in Literary Criticism." *Critical Inquiry* 9, no. 1 (1982): 201–216.

Foucault, Michel. *The Hermeneutics of the Subject: Lectures at the Collège de France, 1981–82.* Edited by Francois Ewald and Alessandro Fontana. New York: Palgrave Macmillan, 2005.

———. *The History of Sexuality, Vol. 2: The Use of Pleasure.* Translated by Robert Hurley. London: Penguin, 1990.

———. *L'Herméneutique du Sujet: Cours au Collège de France (1981–1982).* Edited by Frédéric Gros. Paris: Gallimard, 2001.

———. *Security, Territory, Population: Lectures at the Collège de France, 1977–78.* Translated by Graham Burchell. New York: Palgrave Macmillan, 2007.

———. *Technologies of the Self: A Seminar with Michel Foucault.* Amherst: University of Massachusetts Press, 1988.

Frankel, Mark S. "Professional Codes: Why, How, and with What Impact?" *Journal of Business Ethics* 8, no. 2/3 (1989): 109–115.

Frankfurt, Harry G. "Freedom of the Will and the Concept of a Person." *The Journal of Philosophy* 68, no. 1 (1971): 5–20.

Frazer, Michael L. *The Enlightenment of Sympathy: Justice and the Moral Sentiments in the Eighteenth Century and Today.* Oxford: Oxford University Press, 2010.

Fried, Charles. "Rights and Health Care: Beyond Equity and Efficiency." *The New England Journal of Medicine* 293, no. 5 (1975): 241–245.

Friedman, Lawrence Meir. *The Legal System: A Social Science Perspective.* New York: Russell Sage Foundation, 1975.

Friedrich, Carl. "Public Policy and the Nature of Administrative Responsibility." In *Public Policy,* edited by C. J. Friedrich and E. S. Mason, 3–24. Cambridge, MA: Harvard University Press, 1940.

Fyall, Rachel. "Nonprofits as Advocates and Providers: A Conceptual Framework." *Policy Studies Journal* (2016).

Gable, Shelly L., and Jonathan Haidt. "What (and Why) Is Positive Psychology?" *Review of General Psychology* 9, no. 2 (2005): 103–110.

Gailmard, Sean, and John W. Patty. "Formal Models of Bureaucracy." *Annual Review of Political Science* 15 (2012): 353–377.

———. *Learning While Governing: Expertise and Accountability in the Executive Branch.* Chicago: University of Chicago Press, 2013.

Galston, William. "Realism in Political Theory." *European Journal of Political Theory* 9, no. 4 (2010): 385–411.

Geertz, Clifford. "Thick Description: Toward an Interpretive Theory of Culture." In *The Interpretation of Cultures*, 3–30. New York: Basic Books, 1973.

Gershon, Robyn R. M., Briana Barocas, Allison N. Canton, Li Xianbin, and David Vlahov. "Mental, Physical, and Behavioral Outcomes Associated with Perceived Work Stress in Police Officers." *Criminal Justice and Behavior* 36, no. 3 (2009): 275–289.

Geuss, Raymond. *Philosophy and Real Politics*. Princeton, NJ: Princeton University Press, 2008.

Gibbons, Robert, and Rebecca Henderson. "What Do Mangers Do? Exploring Persistent Performance Differences among Seemingly Similar Enterprises." Havard Business School Working Paper, 2012.

Gino, Francesca, and Sreedhari D. Desai. "Memory Lane and Morality: How Childhood Memories Promote Prosocial Behavior." *Journal of Personality and Social Psychology* 102, no. 4 (2012): 743–758.

Glover, Jonathan. *Humanity: A Moral History of the Twentieth Century*. New Haven, CT: Yale University Press, 2000.

Goffman, Erving. *The Presentation of Self in Everyday Life*. Garden City, NY: Doubleday, 1959.

Goodin, Robert E. *Innovating Democracy*. Oxford: Oxford University Press, 2008.

———. "Institutions and Their Design." In *The Theory of Institutional Design*, edited by Robert E. Goodin, 1–53. Cambridge: Cambridge University Press, 1996.

———. *Reasons for Welfare: The Political Theory of the Welfare State*. Princeton, NJ: Princeton University Press, 1988.

———. *Utilitarianism as a Public Philosophy*. Cambridge: Cambridge University Press, 1995.

Goodnow, Frank J. *Politics and Administration*. New York: Macmillan, 1900.

Goodsell, Charles T. *The Case for Bureaucracy: A Public Administration Polemic*. 4th ed. Washington, DC: CQ Press, 2004.

Graeber, David. "Dead Zones of the Imagination: On Violence, Bureaucracy, and Interpretive Labor." *HAU: Journal of Ethnographic Theory* 2, no. 2 (2012): 105–128.

Grant, Adam, and Jane Dutton. "Beneficiary or Benefactor: Are People More Prosocial When They Reflect on Receiving or Giving?" *Psychological Science* 23, no. 9 (2012): 1033–1039.

Gregory, Robert. "Accountability in Modern Government." In *The Handbook of Public Administration*, edited by B. Guy Peters and Jon Pierre. London: Sage Publications, 2003.

Gutmann, Amy, and Dennis F. Thompson. *Democracy and Disagreement*. Cambridge, MA: Harvard University Press, 1996.

Guy, Mary E., Meredith A. Newman, and Sharon H. Mastracci. *Emotional Labor: Putting the Service in Public Service*. Armonk, NY: M. E. Sharpe, 2008.

Hadot, Pierre. *Exercices Spirituels et Philosophie Antique.* Paris: Etudes Augustiniennes, 1981.

———. *La Philosophie Comme Manière de Vivre.* Edited by Jeannie Carlier and Arnold Ira Davidson. Paris: Albin Michel, 2001.

———. *Qu'est-Ce Que la Philosophie Antique?* Paris: Gallimard, 1995.

Haidt, Jonathan. "The Emotional Dog and Its Rational Tail: A Social Intuitionist Approach to Moral Judgment." *Psychological Review* 108, no. 4 (2001): 814–834.

Handler, Joel F. *Protecting the Social Service Client: Legal and Structural Controls on Official Discretion.* New York: Academic Press, 1979.

Haney, Lynne. "Homeboys, Babies, Men in Suits: The State and the Reproduction of Male Dominance." *American Sociological Review* 61, no. 5 (1996): 759–778.

Hardimon, Michael O. "Role Obligations." *The Journal of Philosophy* 91, no. 7 (1994): 333–363.

Harman, Gilbert. "Moral Philosophy Meets Social Psychology: Virtue Ethics and the Fundamental Attribution Error." *Proceedings of the Aristotelian Society* 99 (1999): 315–331.

Hart, H. L. A. *The Concept of Law.* 2nd ed. Oxford: Oxford University Press, 1994.

Hasenfeld, Yeheskel. "People Processing Organizations: An Exchange Approach." *American Sociological Review* 37, no. 3 (1972): 256–263.

Hasenfeld, Yeheskel, Jane A. Rafferty, and Mayer N. Zald. "The Welfare State, Citizenship, and Bureaucratic Encounters." *Annual Review of Sociology* 13 (1987): 387–415.

Hayek, Friedrich A. von. *The Constitution of Liberty.* Chicago: University of Chicago Press, 1960.

Hayward, Clarissa Rile. *De-facing Power.* Cambridge: Cambridge University Press, 2000.

Heath, Joseph. "A General Framework for the Ethics of Public Administration." Unpublished manuscript (2014).

Heclo, Hugh. "Issue Networks and the Executive Establishment." In *The New American Political System,* edited by Anthony King, 87–124. Washington, DC: American Enterprise Institute, 1978.

Hegel, Georg Wilhelm Friedrich. *Hegel on Tragedy.* New York: Harper & Row, 1975.

Herzfeld, Michael. *The Social Production of Indifference: Exploring the Symbolic Roots of Western Bureaucracy.* Chicago: University of Chicago Press, 1992.

Herzog, Lisa, and Bernardo Zacka. "Fieldwork in Political Theory: Five Arguments for an Ethnographic Sensibility." *British Journal of Political Science* (Forthcoming).

Heyes, Cressida J. "Foucault Goes to Weight-Watchers (Redux)." Chapter 3 in *Self-Transformations: Foucault, Ethics, and Normalized Bodies,* 64–88. New York: Oxford University Press, 2007.

Hilberg, Raul. *The Destruction of the European Jews.* Chicago: Quadrangle Books, 1961.

Hinton, Timothy. "Must Egalitarians Choose between Fairness and Respect?" *Philosophy & Public Affairs* 30, no. 1 (2001): 72–87.

Hirschman, Albert O. *Exit, Voice, and Loyalty: Responses to Decline in Firms, Organizations, and States.* Cambridge, MA: Harvard University Press, 1970.

Hochschild, Arlie Russell. *The Managed Heart: Commercialization of Human Feeling.* Berkeley: University of California Press, 1983.

Hofstadter, Douglas R. "Analogy as the Core of Cognition." Stanford Presidential Lectures in Humanities and Arts, Palo Alto, CA, 2006. https://prelectur.stanford.edu/lecturers/hofstadter/analogy.html, accessed March 15, 2017.

———. *Fluid Concepts & Creative Analogies: Computer Models of the Fundamental Mechanisms of Thought.* New York: Basic Books, 1995.

Huber, John D., and Charles R. Shipan. *Deliberate Discretion? The Institutional Foundations of Bureaucratic Autonomy.* New York: Cambridge University Press, 2002.

Hughes, Everett C. "Mistakes at Work." *The Canadian Journal of Economics and Political Science* 17, no. 3 (1951): 320–327.

Hull, Matthew S. *Government of Paper: The Materiality of Bureaucracy in Urban Pakistan.* Berkeley: University of California Press, 2012.

Hummel, Ralph P. *The Bureaucratic Experience: A Critique of Life in the Modern Organization.* 4th ed. New York: St. Martin's Press, 1994.

Hupe, Peter, and Michael Hill. "Street-Level Bureaucracy and Public Accountability." *Public Administration* 85, no. 2 (2007): 279–299.

Hupe, Peter, Michael Hill, and Aurélien Buffat, eds. *Understanding Street-Level Bureaucracy.* Bristol: Policy Press, 2016.

Irving, Julie Anne, Patricia L. Dobkin, and Jeeseon Park. "Cultivating Mindfulness in Health Care Professionals: A Review of Empirical Studies of Mindfulness-Based Stress Reduction (MBSR)." *Complementary Therapies in Clinical Practice* 15, no. 2 (2009): 61–66.

Jackall, Robert. *Moral Mazes: The World of Corporate Managers.* New York: Oxford University Press, 1989.

Janis, Irving L. *Groupthink: Psychological Studies of Policy Decisions and Fiascoes.* 2nd ed. Boston: Houghton Mifflin, 1982.

Jensen, Michael C., and William H. Meckling. "Theory of the Firm: Managerial Behavior, Agency Costs and Ownership Structure." *Journal of Financial Economics* 3, no. 4 (1976): 305–360.

Johnson, William. "Confessions of a 'Bad' Teacher." *The New York Times*, March 3, 2012.

Johnston, Jocelyn M., and Barbara S. Romzek. "The Promises, Performance, and Pitfalls of Government Contracting." In *The Oxford Handbook of American Bureaucracy,* edited by Robert F. Durant, 396–420. Oxford: Oxford University Press, 2010.

Jonsen, Albert R., and Stephen E. Toulmin. *The Abuse of Casuistry.* Berkeley: University of California Press, 1988.

Kafka, Ben. *The Demon of Writing: Powers and Failures of Paperwork.* New York: Zone Books, 2012.

Kalberg, Stephen. "Max Weber's Types of Rationality." *American Journal of Sociology* 85, no. 5 (1980): 1145–1179.

Kamtekar, Rachana. "Situationism and Virtue Ethics on the Content of Our Character." *Ethics* 114, no. 3 (2004): 458–491.

Kant, Immanuel. "Perpetual Peace: A Philosophical Sketch." In *Kant: Political Writings,* edited by H. S. Reiss. New York: Cambridge University Press, 1991.

Kanter, Rosabeth Moss. *Men and Women of the Corporation.* New York: Basic Books, 1977.

Kanter, Rosabeth Moss, and Barry Stein, eds. *Life in Organizations: Workplaces as People Experience Them.* New York: Basic Books, 1979.

Kantorowicz, Ernst H. *The King's Two Bodies: A Study in Mediaeval Political Theology.* Princeton, NJ: Princeton University Press, 1997.

Kaufman, Herbert. *The Forest Ranger: A Study in Administrative Behavior.* Baltimore: Resources for the Future, 1960.

Keiser, Lael R., Vicky M. Wilkins, Kenneth J. Meier, and Catherine A. Holland. "Lipstick and Logarithms: Gender, Institutional Context, and Representative Bureaucracy." *American Political Science Review* 96, no. 3 (2002): 553–564.

Kelling, George L., and James Q. Wilson. "Broken Windows: The Police and Neighborhood Safety." *The Atlantic Monthly,* March 1982.

Kelman, Herbert C. "Violence without Moral Restraint: Reflections on the Dehumanization of Victims and Victimizers." *Journal of Social Issues* 29, no. 4 (1973): 25–61.

Ker Muir, William. *Police: Streetcorner Politicians.* Chicago: University of Chicago Press, 1977.

Konrád, George. *The Case Worker.* Translated by Paul Aston. New York: Penguin, 1987.

Kop, Nicolien, Martin Euwema, and Wilmar Schaufeli. "Burnout, Job Stress and Violent Behavior among Dutch Police Officers." *Work & Stress: An International Journal of Work, Health & Organisations* 13, no. 4 (1999): 326–340.

Kunda, Gideon. *Engineering Culture: Control and Commitment in a High-Tech Corporation.* Philadelphia: Temple University Press, 1992.

Kunda, Ziva. "The Case for Motivated Reasoning." *Psychological Bulletin* 108, no. 3 (1990): 480–498.

Laidlaw, James. *The Subject of Virtue: An Anthropology of Ethics and Freedom.* New York: Cambridge University Press, 2014.

Lakoff, George. *Women, Fire, and Dangerous Things: What Categories Reveal about the Mind.* Chicago: University of Chicago Press, 1987.

Lambek, Michael, ed. *Ordinary Ethics: Anthropology, Language, and Action.* New York: Fordham University Press, 2010.

Lascoumes, Pierre. "Normes Juridiques et Mise en Oeuvre des Politiques Publiques." *L'Année Sociologique* 40, no. 3 (1990): 43–71.

Latané, Bibb, and Martin J. Bourgeois. "Dynamic Social Impact and the Consolidation, Clustering, Correlation, and Continuing Diversity of Culture." In *Blackwell Handbook of Social Psychology: Group Processes*, edited by Michael A. Hogg and R. Scott Tindale, 235–258. Malden, MA: Blackwell Publishers, 2003.

Lear, Jonathan. *Radical Hope: Ethics in the Face of Cultural Devastation*. Cambridge, MA: Harvard University Press, 2006.

Lee, Sophia Z. *The Workplace Constitution from the New Deal to the New Right*. New York: Cambridge University Press, 2014.

Lerner, Jennifer S., and Philip E. Tetlock. "Accounting for the Effects of Accountability." *Psychological Bulletin* 125, no. 2 (1999): 255–275.

Lessig, Lawrence. "'Institutional Corruption' Defined." *The Journal of Law, Medicine & Ethics* 41, no. 3 (2013): 553–555.

Levinson, Meira. "Moral Injury and the Ethics of Educational Injustice." *Harvard Educational Review* 85, no. 2 (2015): 203–228.

———. *No Citizen Left Behind*. Cambridge, MA: Harvard University Press, 2012.

Lifton, Robert Jay. *The Nazi Doctors: Medical Killing and the Psychology of Genocide*. New York: Basic Books, 1986.

Liker, Jeffrey K. *The Toyota Way: 14 Management Principles from the World's Greatest Manufacturer*. New York: McGraw-Hill, 2004.

Lindblom, Charles E. "The Science of 'Muddling Through.'" *Public Administration Review* 19, no. 2 (1959): 79–88.

Linder, Darwyn E., Joel Cooper, and Edward E. Jones. "Decision Freedom as a Determinant of the Role of Incentive Magnitude in Attitude Change." *Journal of Personality and Social Psychology* 6, no. 3 (1967): 245–254.

Lindhorst, Taryn, and Julianna D. Padgett. "Disjunctures for Women and Frontline Workers: Implementation of the Family Violence Option." *Social Service Review* 79, no. 3 (2005): 405–429.

Lipsky, Michael. *Street-Level Bureaucracy: Dilemmas of the Individual in Public Services*. 30th anniversary expanded edition. New York: Russell Sage Foundation, 2010.

Lloyd, Chris, Robert King, and Lesley Chenoweth. "Social Work, Stress and Burnout: A Review." *Journal of Mental Health* 11, no. 3 (2002): 255–265.

London Policing Ethics Panel. "Ethical Challenges of Policing London." 2014.

Lovett, Frank. *A General Theory of Domination and Justice*. New York: Oxford University Press, 2010.

Lowi, Theodore J. *The End of Liberalism: The Second Republic of the United States*. 2nd ed. New York: Norton, 1979.

Luban, David. *Lawyers and Justice: An Ethical Study*. Princeton, NJ: Princeton University Press, 1988.

———. "The Publicity Principle." In *The Theory of Institutional Design*, edited by Robert E. Goodin, 154–198. Cambridge: Cambridge University Press, 1996.

Machiavelli, Niccolò. *Discourses on Livy*. Translated by Harvey C. Mansfield and Nathan Tarcov. Chicago: University of Chicago Press, 1995.

———. *The Prince*. Translated by Harvey C. Mansfield. Chicago: University of Chicago Press, 1998.

MacIntyre, Alasdair. *After Virtue*. 2nd ed. Notre Dame, IN: University of Notre Dame Press, 1984.

Mansbridge, Jane. *Beyond Adversary Democracy*. Chicago: University of Chicago Press, 1983.

Mansfield, Harvey C., Jr. "On the Impersonality of the Modern State: A Comment on Machiavelli's Use of *Stato*." *The American Political Science Review* 77, no. 4 (1983): 849–857.

March, James G. *A Primer on Decision Making: How Decisions Happen*. New York: Free Press, 1994.

March, James G., and Johan P. Olsen. "The Logic of Appropriateness." In *The Oxford Handbook of Public Policy*, edited by Michael Moran, Martin Rein, and Robert E. Goodin, 689–708. Oxford: Oxford University Press, 2006.

Marcus, George E., and Michael M. J. Fischer. *Anthropology as Cultural Critique: An Experimental Moment in the Human Sciences*. Princeton, NJ: Princeton University Press, 1986.

Mashaw, Jerry L. *Bureaucratic Justice: Managing Social Security Disability Claims*. New Haven, CT: Yale University Press, 1983.

———. *Creating the Administrative Constitution: The Lost One Hundred Years of American Administrative Law*. New Haven, CT: Yale University Press, 2012.

Mathieu, Françoise. *The Compassion Fatigue Workbook*. New York: Routledge, 2011.

Maynard-Moody, Steven, and Michael Musheno. *Cops, Teachers, Counselors: Stories from the Front Lines of Public Service*. Ann Arbor: University of Michigan Press, 2003.

Maynard-Moody, Steven, and Shannon Portillo. "Street-Level Bureaucracy Theory." In *The Oxford Handbook of American Bureaucracy*, edited by Robert F. Durant. Oxford: Oxford University Press, 2010.

Mayo, Elton. *The Human Problems of an Industrial Civilization*. New York: Macmillan, 1933.

McCubbins, Mathew D., Roger G. Noll, and Barry R. Weingast. "Administrative Procedures as Instruments of Political Control." *Journal of Law, Economics, and Organization* 3, no. 2 (1987): 243–277.

McCubbins, Mathew D., and Thomas Schwartz. "Congressional Oversight Overlooked: Police Patrols versus Fire Alarms." *American Journal of Political Science* 28, no. 1 (1984): 165–179.

McDowell, John. "Virtue and Reason." *The Monist* 62, no. 3 (1979): 331–350.

Meier, Kenneth J., and Laurence J. O'Toole. *Bureaucracy in a Democratic State: A Governance Perspective*. Baltimore: Johns Hopkins University Press, 2006.

Meier, Kenneth J., Robert D. Wrinkle, and J. L. Polinard. "Representative Bureaucracy and Distributional Equity: Addressing the Hard Question." *The Journal of Politics* 61, no. 4 (1999): 1025–1039.

Mendelberg, Tali. "The Deliberative Citizen: Theory and Evidence." In *Political Decision Making, Deliberation and Participation: Research in Micropolitics*, vol. 6, edited by Michael X. Dellini Carpini, Leonie Huddy, and Robert Y. Shapiro, 151–193. Greenwich, CT: JAI Press, 2002.

Merritt, Maria. "Virtue Ethics and Situationist Personality Psychology." *Ethical Theory and Moral Practice* 3, no. 4 (2000): 365–383.

Merton, Robert K. "Bureaucratic Structure and Personality." *Social Forces* 18, no. 4 (1940): 560–568.

Messick, David M., and Max H. Bazerman. "Ethical Leadership and the Psychology of Decision Making." *Sloan Management Review* 37, no. 2 (1996): 9–22.

Mettler, Suzanne, and Joe Soss. "The Consequences of Public Policy for Democratic Citizenship: Bridging Policy Studies and Mass Politics." *Perspectives on Politics* 2, no. 1 (2004): 55–73.

Metzger, Gillian E. "Administrative Constitutionalism." *Texas Law Review* 91 (2013): 1897.

Meyer, John W., and Brian Rowan. "Institutionalized Organizations: Formal Structure as Myth and Ceremony." *The American Journal of Sociology* 83, no. 2 (1977): 340–363.

Michels, Robert. *Political Parties: A Sociological Study of the Oligarchical Tendencies of Modern Democracy.* Glencoe, IL: Free Press, 1949.

Milgram, Stanley. *Obedience to Authority: An Experimental View.* New York: Harper Perennial, 2004.

Mill, John Stuart. *On Liberty.* New Haven, CT: Yale University Press, 2003.

Milliken, Frances J., Elizabeth W. Morrison, and Patricia F. Hewlin. "An Exploratory Study of Employee Silence: Issues That Employees Don't Communicate Upward and Why." *Journal of Management Studies* 40, no. 6 (2003): 1453–1476.

Mills, C. Wright. *The Power Elite.* New York: Oxford University Press, 1956.

Mintzberg, Henry, and Alexandra McHugh. "Strategy Formation in an Adhocracy." *Administrative Science Quarterly* 30, no. 2 (1985): 160–197.

Moe, Terry M. "Delegation, Control, and the Study of Public Bureaucracy." *The Forum* 10, no. 2 (2012).

———. "The New Economics of Organization." *American Journal of Political Science* 28, no. 4 (1984): 739–777.

Møller, Marie Østergaard, and Deborah Stone. "Disciplining Disability under Danish Active Labour Market Policy." *Social Policy & Administration* 47, no. 5 (2013): 586–604.

Monin, Benoit, and Alexander H. Jordan. "The Dynamic Moral Self: A Social Psychological Perspective." In *Moral Self, Identity and Character: Explorations in Moral Psychology*, edited by Darcia Narvaez and Daniel K. Lapsley. Cambridge: Cambridge University Press, 2009.

Mor Barak, Michàl E., Jan A. Nissly, and Amy Levin. "Antecedents to Retention and Turnover among Child Welfare, Social Work, and Other Human Service

Employees: What Can We Learn from Past Research? A Review and Metanalysis." *Social Service Review* 75, no. 4 (2001): 625–661.

Morgen, Sandra. "The Agency of Welfare Workers: Negotiating Devolution, Privatization, and the Meaning of Self-Sufficiency." *American Anthropologist* 103, no. 3 (2001): 747–761.

Moscovici, Serge. *Social Influence and Social Change*. New York: Academic Press, 1976.

———. "Toward a Theory of Conversion Behavior." *Advances in Experimental Social Psychology* 13 (1980): 209–239.

Moscovici, Serge, and Marisa Zavalloni. "The Group as a Polarizer of Attitudes." *Journal of Personality and Social Psychology* 12, no. 2 (1969): 125–135.

Müller, Ingo. *Hitler's Justice: The Courts of the Third Reich*. Cambridge, MA: Harvard University Press, 1991.

Na'aman, Oded. "The Checkpoint: Terror, Power, and Cruelty." *Boston Review* 37, no. 4 (2012): 38–45.

Nickerson, Raymond S. "Confirmation Bias: A Ubiquitous Phenomenon in Many Guises." *Review of General Psychology* 2, no. 2 (1998): 175–220.

Niskanen, William A. *Bureaucracy and Representative Government*. Chicago: Aldine, Atherton, 1971.

Nussbaum, Martha. "The Costs of Tragedy: Some Moral Limits of Cost–Benefit Analysis." *The Journal of Legal Studies* 29, no. S2 (2000): 1005–1036.

———. "The Discernment of Perception: An Aristotelian Conception of Private and Public Rationality." In *Love's Knowledge: Essays on Philosophy and Literature*, 54–105. New York: Oxford University Press, 1990.

Nussbaum, Martha C. "Virtue Ethics: A Misleading Category?" *The Journal of Ethics* 3, no. 3 (1999): 163–201.

Oberfield, Zachary W. *Becoming Bureaucrats: Socialization at the Front Lines of Government Service*. Philadelphia: University of Pennsylvania Press, 2014.

Ohno, Taiichi. *Toyota Production System: Beyond Large-Scale Production*. Cambridge, MA: Productivity Press, 1988.

Ouchi, William G. "Markets, Bureaucracies, and Clans." *Administrative Science Quarterly* 25, no. 1 (1980): 129–141.

———. *Theory Z: How American Business Can Meet the Japanese Challenge*. Reading, MA: Addison-Wesley, 1981.

Pader, Ellen. "Seeing with an Ethnographic Sensibility." In *Interpretation and Method*, edited by Dvora Yanow and Peregrine Schwartz-Shea, 161–175. Armonk, NY: M. E. Sharpe, 2006.

Pascal, Blaise. *The Provincial Letters*. Harmondsworth, UK: Penguin, 1967.

Patty, John W., and Elizabeth Maggie Penn. *Social Choice and Legitimacy: The Possibilities of Impossibility*. New York: Cambridge University Press, 2014.

Pennebaker, James W. "Writing about Emotional Experiences as a Therapeutic Process." *Psychological Science* 8, no. 3 (1997): 162–166.

Perry, James L., Annie Hondeghem, and Lois Recascino Wise. "Revisiting the Motivational Bases of Public Service: Twenty Years of Research and an Agenda for the Future." *Public Administration Review* 70, no. 5 (2010): 681–690.

Pettit, Philip. *Republicanism: A Theory of Freedom and Government*. Oxford: Oxford University Press, 1997.

Philp, Mark. "Delimiting Democratic Accountability." *Political Studies* 57, no. 1 (2009): 28–53.

Piore, Michael J. "Beyond Markets: Sociology, Street-Level Bureaucracy, and the Management of the Public Sector." *Regulation & Governance* 5, no. 1 (2011): 145–164.

Piore, Michael J., and Andrew Schrank. "Toward Managed Flexibility: The Revival of Labour Inspection in the Latin World." *International Labour Review* 147, no. 1–23 (2008).

Piven, Frances Fox, and Richard A. Cloward. *Regulating the Poor: The Functions of Public Welfare*. New York: Pantheon Books, 1971.

Polanyi, Michael. *Personal Knowledge: Towards a Post-Critical Philosophy*. London: Routledge, 1958.

Posner, Richard A. *How Judges Think*. Cambridge, MA: Harvard University Press, 2008.

Pressman, Jeffrey L., and Aaron Wildavsky. *Implementation: How Great Expectations in Washington Are Dashed in Oakland*. 2nd ed. Berkeley: University of California Press, 1979.

Prottas, Jeffrey. *People Processing: The Street-Level Bureaucrat in Public Service Bureaucracies*. Lexington, MA: Lexington Books, 1979.

———. "The Power of the Street-Level Bureaucrat in Public Service Agencies." *Urban Affairs Quarterly* 13, no. 3 (1978): 285–312.

Raventós, Daniel. *Basic Income: The Material Conditions of Freedom*. London: Pluto Press, 2007.

Raz, Joseph. "Legal Principles and the Limits of Law." *The Yale Law Journal* 81, no. 5 (1972): 823–854.

———. *The Morality of Freedom*. Oxford: Oxford University Press, 1986.

———. "Reasons for Action, Decisions and Norms." *Mind* 84, no. 336 (1975): 481–499.

Rhodes, R. A. W. "The New Governance: Governing without Government." *Political Studies* 44, no. 4 (1996): 652–667.

Rizzo, John R., Robert J. House, and Sidney I. Lirtzman. "Role Conflict and Ambiguity in Complex Organizations." *Administrative Science Quarterly* 15, no. 2 (1970): 150–163.

Roethlisberger, Fritz, and William Dickson. *Management and the Worker: An Account of a Research Program Conducted by the Western Electric Company, Hawthorne Works, Chicago*. Cambridge, MA: Harvard University Press, 1939.

Rohr, John A. *To Run a Constitution: The Legitimacy of the Administrative State*. Lawrence: University Press of Kansas, 1986.

Romzek, Barbara S., and Melvin J. Dubnick. "Accountability in the Public Sector: Lessons from the Challenger Tragedy." *Public Administration Review* 47, no. 3 (1987): 227–238.

Rosanvallon, Pierre. *Democratic Legitimacy: Impartiality, Reflexivity, Proximity.* Translated by Arthur Goldhammer. Princeton, NJ: Princeton University Press, 2011.

Rosen, Michael. *On Voluntary Servitude: False Consciousness and the Theory of Ideology.* Cambridge, MA: Harvard University Press, 1996.

Rosenthal, Patrice, and Riccardo Peccei. "The Social Construction of Clients by Service Agents in Reformed Welfare Administration." *Human Relations* 59, no. 12 (2006): 1633–1658.

Ross, Lee, and Richard E. Nisbett. *The Person and the Situation: Perspectives of Social Psychology.* New York: McGraw Hill, 1991.

Rothstein, Bo. "Creating Political Legitimacy: Electoral Democracy versus Quality of Government." *American Behavioral Scientist* 53, no. 3 (2009): 311–330.

———. *The Quality of Government: Corruption, Social Trust, and Inequality in International Perspective.* Chicago: University of Chicago Press, 2011.

Rothstein, Bo, and Jan Teorell. "What Is Quality of Government? A Theory of Impartial Government Institutions." *Governance* 21, no. 2 (2008): 165–190.

Rousseau, Jean-Jacques. *Confessions.* Translated by J. M. Cohen. Harmondsworth, UK: Penguin, 1953.

Rubenstein, Jennifer C. *Between Samaritans and States: The Political Ethics of Humanitarian INGOs.* Oxford: Oxford University Press, 2015.

Rugge, Fabio. "Administrative Traditions in Western Europe." In *The Handbook of Public Administration,* edited by B. Guy Peters and Jon Pierre, 113–127. London: Sage Publications, 2003.

Runciman, David. "What Is Realistic Political Philosophy?" *Metaphilosophy* 43, no. 1–2 (2012): 58–70.

Sabel, Charles. "Rethinking the Street-Level Bureaucrat: Tacit and Deliberate Ways Organizations Can Learn." In *Economy in Society: Essays in Honor of Michael J. Piore,* edited by Paul Osterman, 113–142. Cambridge, MA: MIT Press, 2013.

Sabl, Andrew. *Ruling Passions: Political Offices and Democratic Ethics.* Princeton, NJ: Princeton University Press, 2002.

———. "When Bad Things Happen from Good People (and Vice-Versa): Hume's Political Ethics of Revolution." *Polity* 35, no. 1 (2002): 73–92.

Salamon, Lester M. *Partners in Public Service: Government–Nonprofit Relations in the Modern Welfare State.* Baltimore, MD: Johns Hopkins University Press, 1995.

Scharpf, Fritz Wilhelm. *Governing in Europe: Effective and Democratic?* Oxford: Oxford University Press, 1999.

Schaufeli, Wilmar B., Michael P. Leiter, and Christina Maslach. "Burnout: 35 Years of Research and Practice." *Career Development International* 14, no. 3 (2009): 204–220.

Scheffler, Samuel. "What Is Egalitarianism?" *Philosophy & Public Affairs* 31, no. 1 (2003): 5–39.

Schein, Edgar H. *Organizational Culture and Leadership.* 4th ed. San Francisco: Jossey-Bass, 2010.

Schulz-Hardt, Stefan, Dieter Frey, Carsten Lüthgens, and Serge Moscovici. "Biased Information Search in Group Decision Making." *Journal of Personality and Social Psychology* 78, no. 4 (2000): 655–669.

Scott, James C. *Seeing Like a State: How Certain Schemes to Improve the Human Condition Have Failed.* New Haven, CT: Yale University Press, 1998.

———. *Two Cheers for Anarchism: Six Easy Pieces on Autonomy, Dignity, and Meaningful Work and Play.* Princeton, NJ: Princeton University Press, 2012.

Scott, W. Richard. *Organizations: Rational, Natural, and Open Systems.* 5th ed. Upper Saddle River, NJ: Prentice Hall, 2003.

Selden, Sally Coleman. *The Promise of Representative Bureaucracy: Diversity and Responsiveness in a Government Agency.* Armonk, NY: M. E. Sharpe, 1997.

Seligman, Martin E. P., and Mihaly Csikszentmihalyi. "Positive Psychology: An Introduction." *American Psychologist* 55, no. 1 (2000): 5–14.

Selznick, Philip. *TVA and the Grass Roots: A Study in the Sociology of Formal Organization.* Berkeley: University of California Press, 1949.

Sen, Amartya. *The Idea of Justice.* Cambridge, MA: Harvard University Press, 2009.

Shapiro, Scott J. "The 'Hart-Dworkin' Debate: A Short Guide for the Perplexed." In *Ronald Dworkin,* edited by Arthur Ripstein, 22–55. Cambridge: Cambridge University Press, 2007.

Sharma, Aradhana, and Akhil Gupta. "Introduction: Rethinking Theories of the State in an Age of Globalization." In *The Anthropology of the State: A Reader,* edited by Aradhana Sharma and Akhil Gupta, 1–42. Oxford: Blackwell, 2006.

Shaw, Carl K. Y. "Hegel's Theory of Modern Bureaucracy." *The American Political Science Review* 86, no. 2 (1992): 381–389.

Shepsle, Kenneth A. "The Strategy of Ambiguity: Uncertainty and Electoral Competition." *The American Political Science Review* 66, no. 2 (1972): 555–568.

Sherman, David K., and Geoffrey L. Cohen. "The Psychology of Self-Defense: Self-Affirmation Theory." In *Advances in Experimental Social Psychology,* Vol. 38, edited by Mark Zanna, 183–242. San Diego, CA: Academic Press, 2006.

Silbey, Susan, Ruthanne Huising, and Salo Vinocur Coslovsky. "The 'Sociological Citizen': Relational Interdependence in Law and Organizations." *L'Année Sociologique* 59, no. 1 (2009): 201–229.

Silver, Lauren J. "Spaces of Encounter: Public Bureaucracy and the Making of Client Identities." *Ethos* 38, no. 3 (2010): 275–296.

Simon, Herbert. *Administrative Behavior.* 3rd ed. New York: Free Press, 1976.

Skinner, Quentin. "The State." In *Political Innovation and Conceptual Change,* edited by Terence Ball, James Farr, and Russell L. Hanson, 90–131. Cambridge: Cambridge University Press, 1989.

Skovholt, Thomas M., and Michelle Trotter-Mathison. *The Resilient Practitioner: Burnout Prevention and Self-Care Strategies for Counselors, Therapists, Teachers, and Health Professionals.* New York: Routledge, 2010.

Sleat, Matt. "Realism, Liberalism and Non-Ideal Theory or, Are There Two Ways to Do Realistic Political Theory?" *Political Studies* 64, no. 1 (2016): 27–41.

Slevin, Peter. "Arizona Law on Immigration Puts Police in Tight Spot." *The Washington Post,* April 30, 2010.

Smith, Steven Rathgeb, and Michael Lipsky. *Nonprofits for Hire: The Welfare State in the Age of Contracting.* Cambridge, MA: Harvard University Press, 1993.

Soss, Joe, Richard C. Fording, and Sanford Schram. *Disciplining the Poor: Neoliberal Paternalism and the Persistent Power of Race.* Chicago: University of Chicago Press, 2011.

Spire, Alexis. *Accueillir ou Reconduire: Enquête sur les Guichets de l'Immigration.* Paris: Raisons d'Agir, 2008.

Stasser, Garold, and William Titus. "Pooling of Unshared Information in Group Decision Making: Biased Information Sampling During Discussion." *Journal of Personality and Social Psychology* 48, no. 6 (1985): 1467–1478.

Steele, Claude. "The Psychology of Self-Affirmation: Sustaining the Integrity of the Self." In *Advances in Experimental Social Psychology,* edited by Leonard Berkowitz, 261–302. San Diego, CA: Academic Press, 1988.

Steele, Claude M., and Thomas J. Liu. "Dissonance Processes as Self-Affirmation." *Journal of Personality and Social Psychology* 45, no. 1 (1983): 5–19.

Stivers, Camilla. "The Listening Bureaucrat: Responsiveness in Public Administration." *Public Administration Review* 54, no. 4 (1994): 364–369.

Stocker, Michael. "How Emotions Reveal Value and Help Cure the Schizophrenia of Modern Ethical Theory." In *How Should One Live? Essays on the Virtues,* edited by Roger Crisp, 231–254. Oxford: Oxford University Press, 1998.

Sunshine, Jason, and Tom R. Tyler. "The Role of Procedural Justice and Legitimacy in Shaping Public Support for Policing." *Law & Society Review* 37, no. 3 (2003): 513–548.

Sunstein, Cass R. *Legal Reasoning and Political Conflict.* New York: Oxford University Press, 1996.

Swidler, Ann. "Culture in Action: Symbols and Strategies." *American Sociological Review* 51, no. 2 (1986): 273–286.

Szaniszlo, Marie. "Mass. Pike Toll Collector Reflects on His Last Shift." *Boston Herald,* October 30, 2016.

Taylor, Charles. "To Follow a Rule." In *Bourdieu: Critical Perspectives,* edited by Craig Calhoun, Edward LiPuma, and Moishe Postone, 45–60. Cambridge, UK: Polity Press, 1993.

Tenbrunsel, Ann E., and Kristin Smith-Crowe. "Ethical Decision Making: Where We've Been and Where We're Going." *The Academy of Management Annals* 2, no. 1 (2008).

Tetlock, Philip E. "Accountability and the Perseverance of First Impressions." *Social Psychology Quarterly* 46, no. 4 (1983): 285–292.

Thomas, John Clayton, and Gregory Streib. "The New Face of Government: Citizen-Initiated Contacts in the Era of E-Government." *Journal of Public Administration Research and Theory* 13, no. 1 (2003): 83–102.

Thompson, Dennis F. *Ethics in Congress: From Individual to Institutional Corruption.* Washington, DC: Brookings Institutions, 1995.

———. "Moral Responsibility of Public Officials: The Problem of Many Hands." *The American Political Science Review* 74, no. 4 (1980): 905–916.

———. *Political Ethics and Public Office.* Cambridge, MA: Harvard University Press, 1987.

———. *Restoring Responsibility: Ethics in Government, Business, and Healthcare.* Cambridge: Cambridge University Press, 2005.

Thomson, Judith Jarvis. "The Trolley Problem." *The Yale Law Journal* 94, no. 6 (1985): 1395–1415.

Tyler, Tom R. "Enhancing Police Legitimacy." *The Annals of the American Academy of Political and Social Science* 593, no. 1 (2004): 84–99.

———. *Why People Obey the Law.* Princeton, NJ: Princeton University Press, 2006.

Vaisey, Stephen. "Motivation and Justification: A Dual Process Model of Culture in Action." *American Journal of Sociology* 114, no. 6 (2009): 1675–1715.

Van Maanen, John. "The Asshole." In *Policing: A View from the Street,* edited by Peter K. Manning and John Van Maanen, 307–328. New York: Random House, 1978.

Van Maanen, John, and Edgar H. Schein. "Toward a Theory of Organizational Socialization." In *Research in Organizational Behavior,* vol. 1, edited by Barry M. Staw and Larry L. Cummings, 209–264. Greenwich, CT: JAI Press, 1979.

Van Sell, Mary, Arthur P. Brief, and Randall S. Schuler. "Role Conflict and Role Ambiguity: Integration of the Literature and Directions for Future Research." *Human Relations* 34, no. 1 (1981): 43–71.

Vermeule, Adrian. *Mechanisms of Democracy: Institutional Design Writ Small.* New York: Oxford University Press, 2007.

Von Mises, Ludwig. *Bureaucracy.* New Haven, CT: Yale University Press, 1944.

Wacquant, Loïc. *Punishing the Poor: The Neoliberal Government of Social Insecurity.* Durham, NC: Duke University Press, 2009.

Walker, Samuel, and Charles M. Katz. *The Police in America.* 4th ed. New York: McGraw-Hill, 2002.

Wallace, David Foster. *The Pale King.* New York: Little, Brown, 2011.

Walzer, Michael. "Political Action: The Problem of Dirty Hands." *Philosophy & Public Affairs* 2, no. 2 (1973): 160–180.

———. *Spheres of Justice: A Defense of Pluralism and Equality.* New York: Basic Books, 1983.

Wamsley, Gary L., Robert Bacher, Charles T. Goodsell, Philip Kronenberg, John Rohr, Camilla Stivers, Orion White, and James Wolf, eds. *Refounding Public Administration.* Newbury Park, CA: Sage Publications, 1990.

Watkins-Hayes, Celeste. *The New Welfare Bureaucrats: Entanglements of Race, Class, and Policy Reform.* Chicago: University of Chicago Press, 2009.

Weber, Max. "Bureaucracy." In *From Max Weber: Essays in Sociology,* edited by Hans Heinrich Gerth and C. Wright Mills, 196–244. New York: Oxford University Press, 1979.

———. "Politics as Vocation." In *From Max Weber: Essays in Sociology,* edited by Hans Heinrich Gerth and C. Wright Mills, 77–128. New York: Oxford University Press, 1979.

Weick, Karl E. *Sensemaking in Organizations.* Thousand Oaks, CA: Sage Publications, 1995.

———. *The Social Psychology of Organizing.* Reading, MA: Addison-Wesley, 1969.

Weil, Eric. *Philosophie Politique.* Paris: Vrin, 1956.

West, Darrell M. "E-Government and the Transformation of Service Delivery and Citizen Attitudes." *Public Administration Review* 64, no. 1 (2004): 15–27.

Whyte, William. *The Organization Man.* New York: Simon & Schuster, 1956.

Williams, Bernard. "Conflicts of Value." In *Moral Luck: Philosophical Papers, 1973–1980,* 71–82. Cambridge: Cambridge University Press, 1981.

———. *Ethics and the Limits of Philosophy.* Cambridge, MA: Harvard University Press, 1985.

———. "Liberalism and Loss." In *The Legacy of Isaiah Berlin,* edited by Mark Lila, Ronald Dworkin, and Robert Silvers, 91–104. New York: New York Review of Books, 2001.

———. "Politics and Moral Character." In *Public and Private Morality,* edited by Stuart Hampshire, 55–73. Cambridge: Cambridge University Press, 1978.

Williamson, Oliver E. "The Economics of Organization: The Transaction Cost Approach." *American Journal of Sociology* 87, no. 3 (1981): 548–577.

Wilson, James Q. "The Bureaucracy Problem." *The Public Interest,* no. 6 (1967): 3–9.

———. *Bureaucracy: What Government Agencies Do and Why They Do It.* New York: Basic Books, 1989.

———. *Varieties of Police Behavior: The Management of Law and Order in Eight Communities.* Cambridge, MA: Harvard University Press, 1968.

Wilson, Woodrow. "The Study of Administration." *Political Science Quarterly* 2, no. 2 (1887): 197–222.

Wittgenstein, Ludwig. *Philosophical Investigations.* Translated by G. E. M. Anscombe. 3rd ed. Oxford: Blackwell, 2001.

Wolf, Susan. "Moral Psychology and the Unity of the Virtues." *Ratio,* no. 20 (2007): 145–167.

Wolff, Jonathan. "Fairness, Respect, and the Egalitarian Ethos." *Philosophy & Public Affairs* 27, no. 2 (1998): 97–122.

Wolin, Richard. "The Banality of Evil: The Demise of a Legend." *Jewish Review of Books,* Fall 2014.

Womack, James P., Daniel T. Jones, and Daniel Roos. *The Machine That Changed the World.* New York: Free Press, 1990.

Wood, Daniel B. "Arizona Immigration Law Puts Police in 'Impossible Situation.'" *The Christian Science Monitor,* April 26, 2010.

Yanow, Dvora. *Conducting Interpretive Policy Analysis.* Thousand Oaks, CA: Sage Publications, 2000.

Zacka, Bernardo. "Adhocracy, Security and Responsibility: Revisiting Abu Ghraib a Decade Later." *Contemporary Political Theory* 15, no. 1 (2016): 38–57.

———. "The Two Bodies of the Bureaucrat." *Public Administration Review* 72, no. 2 (2012): 302–305.

Zimbardo, Philip. *The Lucifer Effect: Understanding How Good People Turn Evil.* New York: Random House, 2007.

Acknowledgments

I have incurred a long list of debts while writing this book. I would like to first thank the staff of the NCDI for welcoming me in their midst and introducing me to the intricacies of street-level work. Many of the stories I have told are theirs, and I hope that what I have written offers a faithful account of their experiences on the job.

I would also like to express my deep gratitude to the members of my dissertation committee in the Department of Government at Harvard—Nancy Rosenblum, Michael Rosen, Peter Hall, and Michael Frazer—for their patient and discerning advice, as well as for their constant support and confidence in my work. I am also grateful to Eric Beerbohm, Michael Piore, and Dennis Thompson, who generously read and commented on several chapters, and to Kathryn Edin, who helped me find my way into the field.

This project bears the mark of many conversations with friends and colleagues at Harvard, Cambridge, Stanford, and beyond. Of those who helped me develop my ideas at Harvard, I am especially grateful to Jonathan Bruno, Steven Caton, Josh Cherniss, Prithvi Datta, Bradley Holland, Sean Ingham, Matthew Landauer, Yascha Mounk, Oded Na'aman, Bhavin Patel, Sabeel Rahman, James Reich, Emma Saunders-Hastings, Lucas Stanczyk, Andrea Tivig, and Don Tontiplaphol. I also wish to thank Adriana Alfaro, Johann Frick, Tae-Yeoun Keum, Charles Lesch, Russell Muirhead, Eric Nelson, Jennifer Page, and Richard Tuck.

As a Junior Research Fellow at Christ's College at the University of Cambridge, I had the pleasure of regularly discussing my work with Duncan Bell, Joel Isaac, Sam James, and Paul Sagar. For making my time in Cambridge and England so enjoyable and stimulating, I am grateful to them as well as to Gábor Betegh, David Runciman, Waseem Yaqoob, the fellows of Christ's College, and especially Lene Shepherd.

I had the opportunity to revise the manuscript in depth, and in good company, as a postdoctoral fellow at the Center for Ethics in Society at Stanford University. Warm thanks to Joanie Berry, Juliana Bidadanure, Eamonn Callan, Lindsey Chambers, Emilee Chapman, Brian Coyne, Prithvi Datta,

Amit Goldenberg, Ulf Hlobil, Lily Lamboy, Ted Lechterman, Desiree Lim, Alison McQueen, Anne Newman, Katharina Nieswandt, Josh Ober, Rob Reich, Debra Satz, and especially Oded Na'aman, who on more than one occasion helped me think through key parts of the argument.

I am also grateful to the Center of Ethics for organizing a book manuscript workshop and to the Stanford political theory community for taking part in it. I am especially indebted to Arash Abizadeh, Joe Heath, and Andy Sabl, who kindly accepted my invitation to participate and traveled from afar to do so. Special thanks also to Alison McQueen and Oded Na'aman, who provided comments on individual chapters, and to Alex Gourevitch and Leif Wenar, who joined us for the day. They might not be fully satisfied with the final result, but the manuscript was much changed thanks to their detailed criticism and constructive suggestions.

Over the years, I had the opportunity to develop some of the arguments that make up this book at conferences, workshops, and colloquia. I had the good fortune to meet Evelyn Brodkin and Steven Maynard-Moody, who took an interest in the project and introduced me to the community of scholars working on street-level bureaucracy. For helpful feedback on individual chapters, I would also like to thank Loubna El-Amine, Carly Knight, Meira Levinson, Alisa Rosenthal, Celeste Watkins-Hayes, and Lena Zuckerwise.

For generous financial support at various stages in the completion of this project, I am beholden to the Edmond J. Safra Center for Ethics, the Center for American Political Studies at Harvard, the Mahindra Humanities Center, the American Academy of Arts and Sciences, the Center for Ethics and Society at Stanford, and Christ's College at Cambridge. Thanks also to Rachel Krebs and John Ennever from the Committee on the Use of Human Subjects at Harvard, who guided me through the IRB approval process.

I owe a special debt of gratitude to two anonymous reviewers for Harvard University Press for helpful and encouraging feedback, and to my editors—Michael Aronson, who first took the project on board, and John Kulka, who saw it to completion.

The years I spent in Boston were made immeasurably better by the presence of Michel Rbeiz and Ziad Sultan. The many memorable evenings we spent together, often in the company of Michel Dahan, made the city feel like home. In Beirut, for longer than I can remember, I have had the privilege of engaging in lively conversations with Samer Ghamroun, Ramzi Mab-sout, Rabih Daher, and Abdallah Daher. As friends, they have expanded my horizons in more ways than they can imagine.

I met Valentina Pugliano as I was revising this book for publication, and I have been extremely fortunate to have her in my life since. Besides helping me untangle countless difficulties with the argument and prose, she has kept me smiling, grounded, and hopeful in difficult personal times. I can only hope that I will one day be able to repay her kindness and generosity.

Completing this project would have been impossible without the love and unstinting support of my parents, Marc and Yolande, and my sister, Bruna. I owe them more than I can say.

My greatest thanks go to Melodie Chika Ogawa. She has taught me more about politics and how to study it than anyone else. Her sense of humor, intellectual integrity, and discerning irreverence not only kept me going as I was writing this book but also gave me something to look up to. For this, and for all the happy moments we shared, I am immensely grateful.

Index

Accountability: direct, 181, 272n44; electoral, 46; goal clarification and, 51; hierarchical, 179–180, 195; impossible situations and, 227, 229–230; informal moral taxonomies and, 178–182; market, 291n40; performance-based, 201–202, 204–205, 208, 210; plural regime of, 195; professional, 181–182; rational systems perspective and, 42; street-level discretion and, 14–15, 35. *See also* Peer-level accountability

Adaptive preference formation, 283n30

Administration and politics, 18–19, 37–38, 43–46. *See also* Public administration

Administrative constitutionalism, 264–265n30

Administrative rationality, 157, 247–250, 269n17. *See also* Instrumental conception of bureaucracy

Affective attunement, mode of, 85–86, 90, 99, 127. *See also* Dispositions

Agency, individual: conceptions of, 116–117; erosion of, 117–120. *See also* Moral agency

Alienation, 231–232

Ally principle, 264n27

Ambiguity: as characteristic of street-level work, 20, 22, 25, 38–39; in policy goals, 45–46; as source of street-level discretion, 49–51

Analogical reasoning, 168–170, 175, 178–179. *See also* Casuistry

Antigone (Sophocles), 225–227

Antipoverty agency. *See* Norville Community Development Initiative (NCDI)

Applbaum, Arthur, 101–102, 107

Arbitrariness: basic income as safeguard against, 269n10; concerns about, 14, 36, 42; informal taxonomies and, 172, 178, 194; insulation from at point of service provision, 279n51; peer-level accountability as safeguard against, 244; person-neutrality as safeguard against, 101; rules as safeguard against, 49; tradeoff between kinds of, 56. *See also* Accountability; Domination; Peer-level accountability

Arendt, Hannah, 115, 119, 129–132, 284n36, 284n42

Articulate consistency, requirement of, 157–158, 197–198

"Attitudes," clients with: category of, 164–167; disagreement about response to, 191–193; instance of, 153, 184–185

Automation, 24. *See also* Technology, in public service delivery

Autonomy: of bureaucratic agencies, 43; as incentive to bureaucrats, 62, 216; personal, development of, 129–133; as program of moral formation, 129–133, 284–285n45; regard for client's, 100, 105

Barnard, Chester, 155

Bartky, Sandra, 231–232, 235

Basic income, proponents of, 254, 269n10, 300n10

Bateson, Gregory, 230–231

Berlin, Isaiah, 51, 96, 223

Bias: confirmation, 127, 277n32; countering one's, 101, 140–144; in groups, 190, 292n49; identifying statistical, 180; implicit, 161, 180, 195; informal taxonomies as haven for, 161; in interactions with police, 108, 280–281n70; political, 252, 255; related to dispositions, 99, 127, 244, 256–257; in street-level decision-making, 14–15, 46, 106, 108